THE MUSIC POWERS THAT BE...

TO SUCCEED IN THE MUSIC INDUSTRY

By

C. CIROCCO JONES

Featured Advisors

Joel Katz (Greenberg Traurig) **DJ Toomp**
Vince Phillips, Esq. (BME) **Manuel Seal Jr.**
Mr. Collipark (formerly DJ Smurf) **Emperor Searcy** (Radio One)
Raaqim Knight, Esq. **Alvin Speights**
Uleses C. Henderson, Esq. **Jim Zumpano** (ZAC Recording)
Ben McLane, Esq. **Kevin Wales**
Dina Andrews Management **Debra Killings**
Future of Music Coalition **Big Oomp**
Harry Lyles (Lyles Media) **Sabrina Montgomery** (DCE)
Wallace Collins, Esq. **Mick Spence. Esq.**

THE MUSIC POWERS THAT BE...
TO SUCCEED IN THE MUSIC INDUSTRY
By Charles Cirocco Jones

ISBN: 0-9760331-0-0

Published by MusicPowers – I-Media Company (In association with WRM Productions, Inc.)

The Music Powers book contains copyrighted material from the following authors:

Raaqim Knight, Esq. & Uleses Henderson, Esq.
"Selling & Leasing Beats...To Slang Or Not To Slang" - © 2005 - all rights reserved
Written exclusively for and licensed to Music Powers – iMedia – MusicPowers.com

Additional copyrighted material used by permission from: Ben McLane, Esq., Wallace Collins, Esq., Future Music Coalition, Mick Spence, Esq., Harry Fox Agency, BMI, Chris Stranding, RIAA

To the best of the Author and Publisher's knowledge, the information contained in this book is accurate. However, because of the nature of the music business, and the fact that music industry people change jobs on a continuous basis, the Author and Publisher assume neither responsibility nor liability for errors or any consequences arising from the use of the information contained herein.

Music Powers is offered to you as a reference tool only. None of the information is intended to represent legal advice.

No guarantee is given with regard to the current accuracy of any listings or directory provided, and Cirocco, nor the Music Powers – iMedia Company shall not be liable for any damages or liability whatsoever arising from any of the information provided here. It is suggested that you consult with an attorney before entering into any agreement.

MUSIC POWERS – I-Media – WRM, Inc.
3529 Church Street, Suite A
Clarkston, GA 30021
www.MusicPowers.com

Front Cover Design by Sara Glover - Glover Graphics | www.glovergraphics.biz
Additional Graphic Design - Zack Vaz
Back Cover design – Sara Glover, Cirocco, and Michael Reid at Designsnprint.com
Additional Graphics – Sandy de la Bretoniere, Steve Miguel and Neo-Teo
Editing / Proofing – Dr. Tina Pipkin, Brandi Hunter, Natosha Kennedy, Vic Clark
Additional Research – Sabrina Montgomery, Eric "Ezy" Campbell, William Morrow
Directory Layout – Ed Blair, Brandi Hunter, Vanessa Rolle
Transcripts – Accentance.com
For more resources & industry contacts, updates, new articles, video and audio snips, and other industry information, visit us on-line at: www.MusicPowers.com | e-mail: info@musicpowers.com
Bulk Orders Available: (414) 803-2892 - Dante Chestnut | e-mail: cococaddy@musicpowers.com

Printed in Canada by Hignell Printing

DEDICATION

This book is dedicated to
The Power that is most important
in my life...

My Lord and Savior,
Jesus Christ

A wise man is mightier than a strong man.
And a man of knowledge increases and strengthens his power.

...Proverbs 24:5

Thank you Lord,
Cirocco

In Memory of my sister, Pamala Jones-Malave (1966-2006)

Music Powers

ACKNOWLEDGMENTS

Special thanks to the following
'HEAVEN-SENT HELPERS'

William R. Morrow & Family
The Speights Family
The Jones Family
The Malave' Family
Lois Butler
Allen Jones
Victor Clark
Courtney Holmes
Eric Butler
Brandon & Ebony Sams
Tassili, Khajit & Arata
Raaqim A. S. Knight, Esq.
Ben Mclane, Esq.
Uleses Henderson, Esq.
Wallace Collins, Esq.
Mick Spence, Esq.
BMI
Laurie Jakobsen
Harry Fox Agency
Jenny Toomet
Future of Music Coalition
Michael Mavrolas
Genuine Representation
Jim Zumpano
Zac Recording
Dianne Franks / Jacopo
Zack Vaz
Motown Records
Geffen Records
Artisan Pictures
Pinnacle Systems
Tony - Pro Music Outlet
Peter McCabe
Brad Buxer
Jheryl Busby
Manuel Seal Jr.
DJ Toomp
Vince Phillips, Esq.
Andrew Paul Helms
Crunk Energy Drink
Harry Lyles
Niko Simpson
ASCAP
Teresa F. Thomas

Joel Katz
Vel Carmona
Greenberg Traurig
Don Perry
Lisa Sanders
Madeline Zachery
Big Oomp
Kevin Wales
Al & Marion Ashworth
Sigidi
Dallas Austin / DARP
D-Roc & Kaine
Ying Yang Twins
TVT Records
Michael Crooms
Dina Andrews
Aaron Walton
BloodRed – 1.5
Sabrina Montgomery
Dreamcatchers
Chris Standring
RPM Direct
All Music Guide
Rolling Out Magazine
Ida Harris
Georgio Allen
Soundcastle Studios
Encore Recording Studios
Jeff Glixman
Creative Loafing – Atlanta
AJC Newspaper
Interland Web Hosting
Titanium Recording
Rebelvision.net
Tanya M. Graham, Esq.
Designsnprints.com
Sara Glover
Errol Norman
Emperor Searcy
Jonathan 'Lil' Jon' Smith
Debra Killings
Matt Gibbs
Dante T. Chestnut, Sr.
HipHopCanada.com

Bishop Eddie Long &
New Birth Missionary
Pastor Marion Croom
Charles Blake &
West Angeles COGIC
Tommy Tunes
Chuck Woo - Earwax
Wendy Powell -Tower
Jason Block
Guitar Center
Galaxy Music Store
Charlayne Hutchinson
Kinko's
Willie Hunter
Brian Bolden
Rev. Black & Beulah
Dr. Charles Stanley
Black Collar Entertainment
Brandi Hunter
Tina & Altrell Pipkin
Marzette Watts
Ken Wright
Hannah Smith
Kelly Woods
BME Recordings
Hot 107.9 - Atlanta
Ramona Debreaux
Soulversive (Cheryl)
SoundClick.com
Urban Insight
Billboard
RnB Mistress (Ruth)
Eric 'Ezy' Campbell
Mike Krakalovich
Hignell Book Printing
Natosha Kennedy
Sandy de la Bretoniere
Signature Graphics
Jawar
Lloyd Duhaime
Siccness.net
Jermaine Dupri / So So Def
One & Red
Vince & Shyhigh

Contents

Music Powers

FOREWORD

Music Powers Is A Powerful Resource For Learning The Music Business

By Willie Hunter
Entertainment Reporter / Music Publisher

I am pleased to see that one of the most talented and gifted artists/producers of our time – Cirocco, is now sharing his vast knowledge of the music industry with those who are beginning, and those who are already traveling down that 'Yellow brick road' to music success.

We know that many other professions in life such as medicine, dentistry, law, social work, and other professions require discipline, research, and numerous hours of study to prove one's worthiness to participate gainfully in the field. And so, the music industry is fast becoming an area requiring many of the same elements for participating in it, and making the most of what the business has to offer.

The Music Powers That Be… by Cirocco is certainly a major step in the direction of providing those who wish to engage in the music business with the information and the resources necessary to launch careers on both the business and the creative sides of the exciting world of music.

I have had the opportunity to work with Cirocco during a large portion of his career. He is without a doubt, one of the most talented, knowledgeable and articulate songwriters/producer/engineers I've ever met. He is well respected by gold and platinum selling producers in the industry, especially those who live in Atlanta (Dallas Austin, DJ Toomp, Manuel Seal Jr., Alvin Speights, John Croslan II, etc.) where Cirocco launched his career. Names on the receiving end of his creative gifts include many major companies like Motown, RCA, BET/Viacom, PepsiCo, Sega and Artisan pictures, and also artists like Johnny Gill, Howard Hewett, Georgio, The Boys, Michael Jackson, TLC, The Good Girls, The Temptations, and many others.

Now that this resource is available to the public, there should be no excuses in regards to artists, managers, producers, songwriters and others lack of knowledge about the music business. *The Music Powers That Be...* will certainly impact the business in such a way that it, more than likely will be in print for many years to come. The Music Powers book will be an ongoing resource for music people who come from all areas of life.

INTRODUCTION

F or the most part, I guess there are some, or at least a few in the industry that believe I know quite a bit about the many phases of the music business, and I humbly thank everyone for their support over the years... I try. It was many of these colleagues and clients who felt that I should make the Music Powers book a reality. See, the original idea and purpose for this book, basically was just a little *survival* guide - to help *my own circle* of artist, songwriter and producer friends who needed answers for their music business problems, or sometimes, just advice and strategies to make better career decisions. Also, what's so crazy to me is that there is all of this information available through books, magazines, DVD & video, seminars, and a mind-boggling amount of information accessible on the web. But, as many already know, some of this information is not always practical, nor is it easy to comprehend for new talent.

So, after many years of dealing with many different artists, producers, songwriters, engineers, and a few managers... who would call or write me asking for help or advice, I realized that although there *is all this information out there*, almost everyone was finding it a little difficult to truly *understand* most of these industry reference books they had bought, or articles they found on the internet. Many of these readings just seem to be made for other lawyers and *not* for creative folk, especially music people. And then there are also a lot of people putting information out there; writing books and web articles; doing workshops, and giving advice about the music business, but some of these people have never really been on the bigger side of the music industry. But maybe what's more frustrating than any of this, especially for urban talent... is that the information that *is* available, is many times not *applicable* or even relevant for how things really work in Hip Hop, Rap, and R&B music. Nor does it speak to the level of *where most new artists and producers are* in their career - 'up-and-coming'. And this is where I believe Music Powers will effectively make a difference for new urban talent.

The Music Powers book is what I propose to be a *better* book & resource guide for Rap, Hip-Hop and R&B artists, songwriters, and producers... we even have some priceless information for up-and-coming managers, djs, Indies, and engineers too. Information and knowledge to hopefully make it easier for you to understand more about the business of music, and become knowledgeable of many of the issues, trends and 'real-world' information that you will need to know.

Now I imagine that this is the part where I'm suppose to say, *"KNOWLEDGE IS POWER!"* and *POWER IS* ... blah, blah, blah, blah... *whatever*. Listen people, here's the deal: After 20+ years of being in the music industry, and a few deals gone good... and a few gone bad, I've come to the place of what I'd like to think of as, one in a position to help the next man through what I've learned, who I've come to know, and an honest effort to teach and share those resources.

And hopefully, you will be careful to avoid some of the tragic mistakes that so many new artists and up-and-coming producers are making everyday that causes millions of dollars to end up in someone else's pocket. And as an on the rise artist, producer, manager, or indie label, you must *plan* for success.

> Any enterprise is built by wise planning, becomes strong through common sense, and profits wonderfully by keeping abreast of the facts.

> ...Proverbs 24:3,4

Honestly, for your plan and your own journey to be successful, you will need some good direction, the right mindset, and then knowing the *powers that be...* which simply means becoming aware of the *knowledge that is, or the ways that exist* that will prepare you to play the music game.   And if you're going to play the game, you better have a clear understanding of the rules.

The Music Powers book has been written primarily for up-and-coming and unsigned talent who want to get in the music business, and it gives some very good examples of insider ways that others in the industry have done things to get them where they are.

When I finally agreed that I would take on this project, I decided that what *I know...* I felt, just wasn't good enough if Music Powers is to *be...* absolutely the best help you can get, especially if you're loaded with talent, and not cash. Why? Because even *with* what I do know about the music industry, there are people around me who know so much more; the ones that I myself respect, look up to, and rely on for help. Therefore, instead of relying solely on my opinion, or any one person's point of view, the chapters, articles, and advice that is offered is a breakthrough collaborative of *many* of the top music industry professionals in urban music.   It's like having an All-Star Team or Mix Tape of *established professionals* who have already had certified Gold & Platinum success in the industry, come together to share their insight, their wisdom, their answers, their advice, their counsel, and even their cautions ... to help *you* make better decisions, and have access to some of the information you *normally* could not get without having many thousands of dollars for consultations, or ... a whole lot of connections and many years in the music business, or, all of the above. Our goal is to help *you* get a better understanding about the industry, and hopefully help you make better choices to get in and *succeed* in the music business.

Overall, what I have done is to combine essential information on the fundamentals of music business, added some great 'insider advice' from a few of my colleagues, and then thrown in some extras like great resources and contacts of companies and industry people who may be able to help you further in your journey towards success ... and catered it for unsigned urban talent who are mainly focused on Hip Hop & R&B/Pop music. Music Powers is about winning; winning guidance from the experience and insight of people who have had both business *and* personal achievements in the music industry, and then were willing to contribute what they know, in hopes of helping you on your *own road* to success. Music Powers is also about giving you something *today*, that you will be able to use *today*, and tomorrow too ... knowledge and understanding. And that IS EMPOWERMENT! Knowledge of the industry through the latest business trends, knowledge with having the right attitude and mindset, and understanding a few proven techniques and approaches to help you create that 'buzz' you'll need. Included also is many of the industry contacts you may need. And just for the record, the Music Powers directories have been painstakingly put together, and checked over many times... in hopes that we could put out the latest accurate information for *you*. And although it's possible that a few numbers and contacts have changed, each and every management company was contacted by us, and they *do know* you may be soliciting to them... but, if you are ready for that, I highly suggest that you first complete this entire book, absorb the advice, articles, and knowledge we offer ... and then, apply what you have learned *before* reaching out to them.

Honestly, I absolutely challenge anyone out there who is ready for something more, to walk away *without* knowing and understanding a whole lot *more* than you knew before reading Music Powers. This book has some very powerful information, only it's explained very simple, and it's bundled with *other* resources like real-world advice from the insiders that *are* responsible for much of what's going on in today's industry.

Throughout my career, I have learned quite a bit... on all levels; the creative and business side of recording, publishing, and production deals; to the money and contacts that I've gained... and sometimes loss over the years. And as a result of the challenges that I've gone through, hopefully, you can use what I've come to know, to *your advantage*. And just to make sure I had something 'real'; something that could genuinely help you, I literally spent over 3½ years making Music Powers ... in hopes of giving you the very best book I could.

Music Powers is here to help you, and I propose that if you apply the information offered, not only will you be able to get some of the help *you* need, but you may also become helpful to the next man needing a little assistance.

So use the wisdom, the advice, and methods being presented by many of the music industry's most powerful people, who came together to share some of their knowledge and experience, as your own personal guide to advise you, direct you, and sometimes even warn you... to help you reach your goals of making it in the music business. So without further delay, I am very proud to finally present to you...

The Music Powers That Be... To Succeed In The Music Industry

Once you have completed Music Powers...

DEFINE YOUR GOALS & MAKE A PLAN

MAKE YOUR COMMITMENTS

LIST YOUR PROSPECTS & OUTLETS

MAKE CONTACT & SET UP YOUR MEETINGS

ALWAYS FOLLOW THROUGH ... WITH NO EXCUSES!

CHECK OVER YOUR GROWTH AND PROGRESS

STAY FOCUSED & BE PATIENT - KEEPING YOUR DESIRE TO SUCCEED A PRIORITY

GIVE BACK - TEACH OTHERS WHAT YOU HAVE LEARNED

Music Powers

PERSONAL MANAGEMENT

INTRODUCTION

T he personal management chapter is a look into the fundamental things an artist or producer will need to become familiar with when seeking and also hiring a personal manager. Finding and securing good management is very important in this sometimes-challenging music business, and is to be valued once you connect with the right candidate. Having a great personal manager in your corner can make the *difference* between you *having* a *successful career* in the music industry, and you just being one of the many frustrated artists and producers who are searching for ways to make something of their talent. Much of what you are about to discover about personal management can be useful in your music career at *any* artist or producer level; *unsigned or signed*. So read it, absorb it, and embrace this information, until you get a *genuine* understanding of these essential ABC's of seeking and *dealing with* the whole personal management relationship. Once you have read and thought about this chapter, you must then do what I feel is the most important step of all...*apply what you have learned.*

IT ALL STARTS WITH 'THE PLAN'
"If you fail to plan, you are planning to fail!"

Like building anything else in life -- a business, a home, a marriage, or even a bridge, you start the process (if you're smart) with a plan. And if you want your music endeavors as an artist to be successful, then you definitely *need* a plan. And one of the key people needed to help you get *that plan* together is a personal manager.

Personal managers play a vital role in helping you come up with a plan and also *a strategy to implement that plan*. This plan will involve the manager helping you get hold of the many other people needed on the your team; producers, an attorney, publishers, an accountant, talent agencies & promoters, a record company, and if need be, helping the act put together their own label or entertainment company. Your personal manager will be one of the most important people involved with each and every step it takes to assure the success of your career. And to assure this success, no matter *what* level you are on, you MUST create; formulate; devise...and then *march* your plan into action (you don't leisurely walk to a goal). So get this in your head; good management is *absolutely* necessary to help you execute 'The Plan'

EXPERIENCE + KNOWLEDGE = POWER!

One of the first priorities in seeking a qualified manager is making sure your candidate has experience in the music business. In most cases, it is best to sign with management who's knowledgeable of the latest music industry (*business and commerce*) trends. He will also need skills in negotiating contracts and doing business on a level that others in the music industry respect. If you don't *think* that this matters, then maybe you should *rethink* the whole idea of even *being in this business. Please*, it's best that you understand now, *before* you move on, your manager's experience, reputation, and knowledge of the music industry, will definitely *influence* the *other* players you need to come aboard your team, and *also* influence the *other* industry insiders you will need to help you succeed. So if you are planning to be successful *and great,* surround yourself with great and *successful* people...and this definitely includes connecting with good management.

CONNECTIONS

Your personal manager will also need to have connections within the music industry. This means he can get in touch with other important industry players, when needed. And if he leaves a message... *he actually gets a returned phone call!* Note to the new guys: *"If you hire your 'Uncle Junior' to manage you... just because he's got his little black book of music contacts, and hangs out at the club every night, this doesn't mean he can actually get key people in the music industry to take him or you serious."*

Now, I certainly am not saying that 'Uncle Junior' can't get *some things* done, but please, be smart; seek out the best management you can find! And use a little wisdom; if 'Uncle Junior' is "down-wit-ya"... and truly "got your back", then bring him onboard in a different way... *after you* get hooked up.

www.MusicPowers.com

THE CATCH-22

Trying to find good management can sometimes be a vicious circle; to get good management, you normally have to have a lot of great things *already* going for you… and to usually get a lot of great things working for your career, you need a good manager. The solution? Get as much going for yourself *on your own* (at first). Stay focused, determined, and don't just "settle" for the first guy who's interested, unless he's qualified and *genuinely* excited about you. If you keep these priorities in order, along with a strong desire for success, with the right mind-set and a little patience (and luck), you *will* eventually meet a *qualified* candidate for management. But *you* have to be ready and *qualified* to grab hold of the opportunity.   …Reality check: I guess now might be a good time to say, *"You don't need management, if you have nothing to manage!"*

DO YOUR HOMEWORK

It is best that you do a little homework when you're searching for management. Find out what acts the manager is currently representing, and/or has managed in the past. Ask questions about his past know-how when it comes to the particular deal *you are seeking*. Try getting a list of his current and/or past clients, then find out if these acts have had some success while they were with the management. If the management had some achievements with new artist in the past, then they probably have a good idea of what it takes to be successful regarding new artists they take on as clients.

SEEKING MR. RIGHT
By Ben McLane, Esq.

Probably the best way for you to find a manager is for a manager to find you. If you are an artist and are playing live dates and developing a following, it is just a matter of time before a manager *will* approach you. You can also contact potential managers through a variety of music directories.

Beware of any manager that wants you to sign a contract on the spot or who makes grandiose (extravagant) promises of success. You should seek out a *real professional* that honestly believes in you and likes what you are doing musically. Marks of a professional would be: (1) having a meeting to discuss your needs and any ideas he has for developing you as an artist; (2) letting you know that although he cannot *promise* success, that if all involved work together, your potential has a better chance of being recognized; (3) suggesting that you have an attorney review any contract *before you sign it*. The bottom line is to find a manager that you trust and with whom you can communicate.

BUILD IT – AND THEY WILL COME ...TO YOU

Now what many of you aspiring artist (and producers) who are seeking a reputable manager don't seem to know, is that if you are really good; and you have some way to get your music heard… either with a great live show, a good demo or video, and you have made yourself known to a few industry folk (either directly or through word of mouth), then you can bet… that *eventually*, both regional and established managers *will* find you. But as a new artist, you have to be ready when the opportunity presents itself… which could mean performing right on the spot, or having a demo that blows people away. Remember, anyone that is truly in a position to help you as a manager sees and hears new artists and demos all the time. So, make sure whatever you have to present is your *best* effort, so that you don't have to make any excuses. Believe me, I know from experience, many times over… if a reputable manager thinks you have the stuff, and then if he wants to represent you, he is thinking he can help *himself* by representing you. So look at it like this: If a potential manager thinks you are awesome, and can get your career really going, etc, he is actually saying that you are good enough to help him keep his own bills paid, feed his family, etc. So remember, if you really have something great to share with the rest of the world, and you make the effort to get your talent and music exposed to the public and industry people, reputable managers *will* start seeking you out, and try to persuade you, and also, probably 'court' you, so that you might consider having them handle your music career.

READY, AND... ACTION!

As mentioned earlier, your personal manager will be the *main* person to help you put your plan together. Once this is done, he'll turn "the plan" into actions that will help guide your career. Here's a few of the many duties your manager usually will assist you with: setting up prospective talent agents and outlets to get you booked for performances, helping you get your image, bio, and media package together, getting you in a studio, putting you with the right photographers, getting you prepared to record and select songs, finding featured vocalist and musicians for your project, helping you get the right producer or production situation to put together your music, getting potential labels (if you're not signed) to check out your finished demo package. And even though most books and resource guides might *tell you* that your manager isn't the one to get you gigs; that a talent or booking agent is used for that – I can tell you from my own personal knowledge and professional experience, *managers will go out there (whether they're suppose to or not) and book you gigs too*. Now yes, talent agents are the one's licensed and are actually monitored and regulated to do the whole booking thing, but I have never met a manager that didn't *also do some type of bookings* at some point for their artist(s).

Your manager will also play a role in securing your other interests, like publishing, endorsements, television, and also film work. And he's essentially "The Guy" that's going to be out there on the grind, planning and helping out to put together your marketing and publicity campaigns. This is why it's so important to have a manager who's on-point! After all, most times it will be your manager who will be *professionally* representing you to the rest of the music industry and the entertainment business world.

DECISIONS... DECISIONS

Once you've made up your mind in choosing who will be your manager, plan a meeting so that both of you have a clear understanding, and mutually agree on *where you are trying to go* in your career. You both should have a written outline of what the plan is, and what goals you both would like to see achieved. So *make the time* to sit down and openly discuss "exactly" where you want to go. The two of you can do more, working together, than one of you doing twice as much ...alone!

GET IT IN WRITING!

When you finally get offered a contract with the management you've chosen, you'll want to get what's called a "key person clause" provision in the agreement. This way, if the main person involved with handling your career loses his job at the management firm, moves to another company, or just retires and moves to some uncharted isle in the Pacific (with Mary-Anne & Ginger ☺), you should have the option to either *walk from the company,* or at least renegotiate your deal.

It may also be in your best interest to get a clause that states that the management must "perform" by generating a certain amount of *anticipated* income and/or closing a certain amount of deals within an agreed upon time. If the management *doesn't* perform, you should be able to get out of the deal or at least, as mentioned earlier, renegotiate your current deal with him.

...Key Person Clause?

* *A key person clause provision in your contract basically means if a manager leaves a* company, you can also leave the company with **no monetary** or **lawful** obligations.

YOUR MANAGERS CUT

Most managers should be compensated anywhere from 15% to 20% of your income. But there are a few managers out there who will want 25% to 30%. This really will depend on their reputation and status; like how much power they have in the music industry to get the deal you want, and so on. You may want to avoid the guy asking for 30%, but on the other hand, if you *clearly* see his track record with evidence of the ways in which he *can bring in more income for you*... go with it!   After all, it is *better* for you to receive 70% of $1,000,000.00+ that he helps to generate and makes happen for your own pocket, as opposed to you getting 85% of $100,000.00 a year through a *different* management firm. This is especially true if you find yourself having to work *twice as hard, twice as much, and with more drama than you prefer* – just to make a decent living doing music.

GROSS VS. NET

You should always try to avoid paying a manager his percentage based on your "gross" or over-all income *without expense deductions*. Most of the time there will *always* be expenses that "have to be paid" *...many times before you have gotten paid anything at all.* As an artist, many times you should *seek* to pay your manager his or her commissions based only on what you *actually collect* as income *...after any indispensable expenses* like tour costs, recording, etc.

For example: Say you signed a pretty big record deal with Sony to do your album, and the total deal was $1,000,000. After you paid recording costs, paid the producers, paid other featured artists and get all the samples cleared, you *might* have about $300,000 left. Your manager would be entitled to his 20% from *that*, or $60,000. So basically remember that your manager should get a percentage of the "net" income of whatever can be filed as your music industry *income*.

www.MusicPowers.com

KEEPING YOU IN THE MIX

The right manager will know to keep your music in circulation to other work opportunities. This includes labels, publishers, TV and Film. Every *good* manager that I've ever worked with knew this. I moved to LA in 1991 to simply do one song on a group at Motown. And after I found the *right* manager (who actually found me), I ended up doing everything; Pepsi commercials, Cues for BET's Comic View, songs for both major and indie labels & production companies, video game music, and even some silly music for parents who 'Hate Barney The Dinosaur.' Your management *shou*ld know that you have to have income in between the other projects that you *really* like doing. And *actually*, you end up learning how to apply the new things you learn from what I call "corporate" paying projects... to your desired projects. Managers, who know their stuff, *usually* know *to* – and know *how* - to keep you in the mix... so they *can* keep getting paid ($).

Quick Note: Now I don't know if this is the "standard", but every *single* manager that *I have ever had* over the years, *never* collected commissions for "side artist", musician or programmer session work ...or background vocal work I was doing, *unless* the session was as a "featured royalty artist" or producer, or re-mixer... or some "high-dollar" guest appearance on a project. But, for musician sessions or any of the live or taped TV performances...*as a musician*, I've never had a manager that asked for a commission on those types of gigs. So, that may be something worth bringing up with your manager, or candidate for management.

MORE ABOUT COMMISSION$

%   There are times when your management should not receive a commission. These are instances when you will receive advances for tour support or recording costs as an artist from the record company. It is not reasonable for the management to receive money from these advances because they are just *that*... Advances or loans from the record label... and must be paid back from royalties.

You should also be aware, that it is entirely fair for a manager to *continue* to receive commissions from income that he has generated for you; even *after* the management term has ended. But there should be some type of limit on his commission amount, and also a limit of how long to keep paying him. You better realize now, as an up-and-coming artist, producer or songwriter, potentially you may be obligated to pay *some* commission to your previous management for as long as five or maybe even ten years *after the termination* of your agreement. Please be conscious of this, to take the necessary steps with your attorney - so that this concern is addressed properly.

One of the things that you *can do* in your management agreement - *before you sign it* - is to have your attorney write in what is commonly called a "Sunset clause." If you are *not* wanting to get caught up in the whole circumstance of paying out the same commissions to a *former* manager *after* their management agreement has expired; *especially considering you are still going to have to also be paying your new manager too*, then this "Sunset" type of clause in your management contract can help you find a balance to have everyone treated and paid a little more reasonably. See, the Sunset clause in your contract primarily will say that if you decide to change management or when the "term" is up, you *agree* to pay the management you are leaving a *limited* commission *after* you make the switch to a new manager, but, at a *reduced* percentage than his *original* commission, and also with a cutoff date; a *limited* time of 3 to 5 years. And once those years are up, you stop paying. Tell him to sing along with Elton John… *"Don't Let The Sun (set clause) Go Down On Me."*…☺.

"SUNSET…?"

For example: If initially you were paying 20% to Uncle Junior Management, who originally got you gigging and making a few indie releases, but then later in your career, you didn't renew Uncle Junior's contract, and decided to move on to a 'big-time' New York management firm, then if there was a Sunset clause, Uncle Junior might be compensated 20% in the 1st year after termination; 15% in years 2 and 3; and 10% in the 4th and 5th year. But, once the 5 years are up, Uncle Junior will not be getting any more commission payments. But, for 5 years, Uncle Junior was still getting paid from *your* income.

INDECENT PROPOSAL?

Now, if you want to know what the *possible* 'chess-move' from the manager *whom you asked for this* "Sunset Clause" *might be*… he is *possibly* going to show just a *little more interest* in owning part of your publishing. JUST SAY NO! Unless the manager, *as a publisher*, is going to *do the things* a reputable music publisher is *expected* to do, like first of all, put some cash on the table for an advance as incentive, and then shop your catalog of songs to other music projects and film, TV, soundtracks, video games, background cues, commercials, advertising, and of course, all the other CD music projects, etc… then just say no to the co-publishing proposal, unless you and your attorney believe it's in your true best interest.

HOW LONG ON THE

EXCLUSIVE ROAD AHEAD?

You can expect most management contracts to be at least three years. And expect him to want as many years as five. Remember, it *will* be in your best interest to have the option to terminate the agreement if certain goals are not met. For example: If your agreement is for 3 years, and the plan that you both agreed to says that your goal was to secure a record deal within 2 years, then if you have not gotten signed in that time, you should have the option to get out of the management contract… or renegotiate it.

Also, most personal management agreements will be exclusive. This means that you shouldn't have someone else running around, taking on the duties of your manager, and you're signed to another management company "exclusively". Now on occasion, there are instances where a co-management agreement is set up between the artist, and two *different* managers. But just so you know, I once tried this… and it was *total* confusion.

Listen up; unless the two managers are covering *completely different territories*…i.e., one in North America and the other in say, The United Kingdom, you should avoid this. If both managers are handling your interest within the same area of the world, it *usually* becomes too confusing to the other prospective outlets in the entertainment industry; booking agents, promoters, radio, TV, A&R people, etc. Basically people within the entertainment field will probably not know exactly who IS the *main* contact person or spokesman for you. So I highly suggest having only one person representing you as your manager – if nothing else… just to avoid the confusion of a co-management situation.

LOAN$ AND LIMITS

You may possibly, *from time to time*, receive advances from your management. Many personal managers go out and spend *their own money* for things that an artist might need - at the time of need… *and this is a good thing!* But, your manager will need to be reimbursed for his expenses! So, in your contract with him, you should put a *limit* on how much he (your manager) can spend, *without authorization from you.*

Also, you must to limit your manager's access to your business account. And never give your management total "Power Of Attorney". This is an *absolute* "no-no!" Now on the other hand, you may choose to give your manager "Limited Power Of Attorney". This basically breaks down to meaning that you and your manager will mutually make a list of the things that "he *can* sign off on"...*in your behalf*. It is also very important that you get in writing what your manager's spending limit will be. Make sure your agreement clearly states that your manager will need *written approval* from you for any major expenses (in your behalf). "You don't want your manager going out and spending $20,000.00 into *anything* in your behalf without your knowledge of the expenditure(s) up front!"

...Power of Attorney?

*When you give someone the authority to act on your behalf, you are granting **power of attorney.***

* ***Limited powers of attorney*** *grants only narrow rights, like giving a friend your check-writing powers while you are on an extended vacation. Limited powers are revoked if you become mentally disabled.*

* ***Ordinary powers of attorney*** *give broader powers over your finances. They expire if you become mentally disabled.*

* ***Durable powers of attorney*** *usually grant the broadest powers of all. A durable power of attorney remains effective if you become incapacitated.*

PAY ATTENTION TO HIS MOVES

Last, but not least, your personal manager should never be allowed to sign over your management agreement to another party without your *expressed written approval*. If this matter comes up, you should call your attorney immediately. Not following this rule is going to mean that your former manager can just hand over all of his former duties and responsibilities to someone else...and this should be avoided!

If your manager *is trying to pass your contract to someone else*, you better *make the time* to truthfully analyze what's going on. There are a few deceptive managers out there that sometimes make "less than honorable" moves regarding *your music career...especially* if they think you're not looking or paying attention!"

So pay attention, stay focused, and "be about your business." And recognize that securing good management is one of the *key* ingredients for you, your music, and your career to have a real "shot" at achieving success in the music industry.

TYPICAL MANAGEMENT DUTIES

HELPING YOU GET A PLAN AND STRATEGY, AND THEN ✓
PUTTING THAT PLAN INTO ACTION

HELPING YOU GET INTO A RECORDING STUDIO FOR RECORDING ✓

HELPING YOU FIND AND SELECT SONGS ✓

HELPING YOU GET OTHER MUSICIANS AND FEATURED VOCALIST ✓

HELPING YOU GET WORK AS A FEATURED ARTIST

ASSISTING YOU TO FIND THE OTHER INDUSTRY PEOPLE YOU'LL NEED
ENTERTAINMENT ATTORNEYS
LABELS & A&R REPS
PRODUCERS
BUSINESS MANAGERS / ACCOUNTANTS
BOOKING AGENTS & PROMOTERS

HANDLING MOST OF THE DAY TO DAY ASPECTS OF YOUR MUSIC ✓
CAREER

COORDINATING YOUR MARKETING AND PROMOTIONAL CAMPAIGNS ✓

HELPING YOU TO SECURE VARIOUS CONTRACTS, WHEN NEEDED
RECORD DEAL
PUBLISHING DEAL OR SONGWRITER CONTRACT
PRODUCTION DEAL
ENDORSEMENT DEALS

COORDINATING SHOWS AND GIG SCHEDULES

HELPING YOU TO GET TELEVISION AND MOVIE WORK & EXPOSURE

GETTING YOU COMMERCIAL WORK

BEING THE MAIN CONTACT PERSON AND SPOKESMAN FOR YOU

GOOD LUCK!

For
more on
Personal Management

Please visit

www.MusicPowers.com/24

Personal Manager, Music Consultant & Administrator

Dina Ruth Andrews launched her professional career in the entertainment industry in 1978 with a five-year stint with Dick Griffey Productions/Solar Records and held various positions including Administrative A&R Director and the label's International Liaison. In 1982, Dina was introduced to musicians James Harris III and Terry Lewis who were then performing with Warner Bros. recording artist, The Time. Andrews took on the responsibility of Personal Manager and assisted the pair in building the foundation of Flyte Tyme Productions—now a multi-million dollar business for the song writing/producing duo known as Jimmy Jam and Terry Lewis.

After shopping the team to Dick Griffey, their demo landed Jam and Lewis their first production project on the group Klymaxx for Solar Records. Andrews went on to secure projects for Jam and Lewis with the likes of Cheryl Lynn, The S.O.S. Band, Cherelle, and Alexander O'Neal. Andrews also introduced the duo to music industry executive, John McClain, which later led to their phenomenal song success with Janet Jackson.

In 1992, recording artist, Pebbles approached Andrews to take on the role of General Manager of her production company, P.T. Entertainment, which managed and produced LaFace Records' recording artist, TLC. Andrews took on additional projects including working on the "Hammer" tour as the liaison between legal and business affairs.   After the completion of the P.T. Entertainment assignment, Andrews set up her management company in Atlanta. Under Dina Andrews Management, Inc., Andrews built a solid clientele that included songwriter/producers: Derek Bramble (David Bowie, Vanessa Williams), Alton "Wokie" Stewart (Bell Biv Devoe, Stephanie Mills, Keith Sweat), and 2x Grammy-winning mix engineer Alvin Speights (India.Arie, TLC, B5, Madonna, Dallas Austin, LaFace, Darryl Simmons, Toni Braxton, Outkast, and others). Andrews has also consulted songwriter/producer Dallas Austin (Boyz II Men, TLC, Toni Braxton and Madonna) on various projects.

Knew Beginnings Entertainment / Dina Andrews Management
1266 W. Paces Ferry Road, PMB #582
Atlanta, GA 30327
www.knewbeginningsent.com

Music Powers
SPOTLIGHT
Dina Ruth Andrews

Personal Manager, Music Consultant & Administrator

PRESENT CLIENTS

ALVIN SPEIGHTS

PAUL JACKSON, JR.

TWB

CHANDRA CURRELLEY

NANETTE MAXINE

GEORGE SELMAN

PAST CLIENTS

JIMMY JAM & TERRY LEWIS

HOWARD HEWETT

DEREK BRAMBLE

WOKIE STEWART

DALLAS AUSTIN

JOYCE IRBY

TONY HAYNES

VINCENT BRANTLEY

P.T. ENTERTAINMENT

MOTOWN PRODUCTIONS

AXIOM ENTERTAINMENT

DICK GRIFFEY PRODUCTIONS/SOLAR RECORDS

Music Powers

Exclusive Advice from Music Powers Advisor

Dina Ruth Andrews

Personal Manager, Music Consultant & Administrator

FOR NEW ARTISTS SEEKING RECORD DEALS

1 What advice can you give new artists who want a major recording contract?

Sometimes you only get one opportunity to sit before the *"Powers That Be"* to sell yourself. So make *sure* you have the best songs, producers, and representation that you can afford. Another important thing is to never become satisfied with your *own opinion* of how great your music is. **IMPORTANT:** Seek out the *unbiased* opinions of people *outside* of your organization or crew *to get feedback without them knowing you have anything to do with the music or project.*

➢ You must give your music strong consideration before presenting it to music industry professionals. These things are important if you want serious consideration for a record deal.

2 What is the present trend with A&R at the major labels, as far as signing new talent *directly* vs. signing deals with independent companies? *Summer 2005*

➢ It really depends on the record company and the person presenting the project. The industry has changed drastically in the past few years. There was a time when production deals, imprints, and joint ventures were unlimited. Today that's not so. These days, major record companies desire to either sign self-contained artists directly, or tap into the pool of artists that *established* producers have already signed and developed. Of course, if there is a hot artist, with a sales base that a production company or indie label has developed, the major label *is going to go after them*, because it's *all about the money.*

3 What are the biggest mistakes most artists make when negotiating to sign with a record label?

➢ I think there are two major mistakes that many artists make when negotiating, or renegotiating to sign a deal with a record label;

➤ **Problem #1: Negotiating your own deal.** Many artists are negotiating their own deals with managers that are not knowledgeable enough about the business, rather than seeking *sound* legal counsel to negotiate on their behalf. Or they're telling their counsel *what to do without the knowledge to suitably direct their attorney.*

➤ **Problem #2: Wrong Perceptions.** Many artists operate from *wrong perceptions.* Not having the correct understanding of how deals are structured and what the standard deal points are, many artist think their legal counsel made a bad deal for them when in actuality at *their level* it was actually cool because *"it is what it is"* ...at that level. If there is no proven sales base, securing a deal is the door opener to allow an artist to prove their ability; setting up an atmosphere for a more favorable deal to be renegotiated once the artist has been proven to

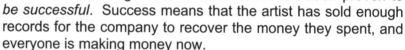

be successful. Success means that the artist has sold enough records for the company to recover the money they spent, and everyone is making money now.

"...Success is not the hype the record company creates to make people pay attention!"

BEING READY

4 How does an artist know if they are *"ready"* ... or *"all-that"*?

➤ **If you are all that** - you not only have the skills, talent and a look... but you already have music on CD for a professional to be able to take with them to listen to. It also means that you have a vision for where you want to *see yourself* in the future. And you're willing to work harder than you've ever worked before in your life when the door of opportunity opens.

➤ **When you are "ready"** - you *already* have a show put together and a location where someone can go see you perform whether it's in your garage, basement, rehearsal hall, church or club... when they ask to see you live

➤ **When *"you're all-that"*** - you'll stop and put on a performance right then and there, and *it will be all that!*

➤ **When you're *really* "ready" or "all-that"** - you will make a professional take a look at you, because you're confident, creative, and charismatic... and you'll have your act together when the door opens for you. *You gotta be ready. It's not about getting ready after the fact!* And if someone takes a chance on developing you further, please *don't* take the opportunity for granted by depending on him or her to develop you for a lifetime.

ADVICE FOR PRODUCERS

5   What's the number #1 rule a Producer must follow, in order to make sure he can get a decent size advance...*and also see back-end money?*

➤ I would say the #1 rule is to remember to say, *"You can call my manager!"* Producer advances are based on a number of different variables:

1.   The budget allotted for the particular project the producer is producing.
2.   The producer's past and present success.
3.   The ability to make a record that will sell through to produce income.

It is best to have someone who knows what is going on behind the scenes at record companies, and someone who understands your value... to negotiate on your behalf.

"...So don't try to negotiate your own deals!"

Having proper representation is very important when it comes to the fine print of a contract and it's interpretation. If you remember that an advance is just *that*, and whatever monies are advanced will be recouped *before* you see any royalties, you may be more inclined to think about how much of an advance that you seek. If the money is there because you're producing an *established* artist, then fine. But if the money is *not there,* and you have a passion for a project or want to do a friend a favor... don't worry about the advance; just make sure you have an agreement in writing for your future royalties.

CREATING A "BUZZ"

6   You took a new group and have successfully gotten them released independently, getting air-play, CDs in the stores, and promoted/marketed enough to create a buzz that will no doubt open up big opportunities for the next release or stage of getting a new act "out there". Give an outline on your strategy, and the steps that *worked* for you to accomplish this.

➤ As an independent privately funded company, we had to think of ways we could expose a new group with little money and get *maximum exposure* for our dollar. Consequently, we built our foundation on the *relationships* that we established over the years *in all aspects of the music industry*, and called on them in diverse ways. And even though we had these *industry* relationships, we still had to establish a consumer base because the group didn't have a following.

"...So we had to create a 'buzz'."

➤ To create a positive 'buzz' about your project, group, or company, you must take in consideration your overall conversation, presentation, and *what you leave your audience with.*

1.   HYPE. Always talk about your upcoming projects, and talk about them with excitement.

2.   EXPOSE YOUR ARTIST BEFORE THEIR RECORD IS RELEASED. Send your artist(s) to industry events just to mix and mingle *before their record is released.* If they are charismatic and stand out, this will leave a subtle lasting impression with people that they will remember when the project is released.

3.   HAVE SOMETHING VISUAL AS A REMINDER. Creatively design 4 color post cards or something that causes your group or company to stand out and do mass mailings to radio, retail and media a few months before you release your project. We designed 2 different types of postcards for mass mailings and stickers to go on everything we sent through the mail or put in someone's hands.

4.   SPEND YOUR MONEY WELL. Sponsor, co-sponsor, or book your artists at events where you will get a room full of national radio announcers in one room; an event where you can *get national retailers in one room;* and places where you can expose them to industry tastemakers. If you can sponsor an event, or get your group booked on an event/program where you can accomplish *all three goals at the same time*, that's even better.

5.   THE WORLDWIDE WEB. Make sure you create a website and do regular e-mail blasts and announcements to *keep the industry and consumers aware of what your group is doing.* Also, get as many positive Internet articles on your company and group as possible.

6.   GET A CONSUMER BASE. To build a consumer base we sponsored the group on a *national* television show that reached several million.

⇒ We booked them on local shows, cable shows, community programs, or *wherever* we could get exposure for them. **THIS IS KEY:** *Nothing is too big ...or too small.*

⇒ We booked them on promotional shows and several industry sponsored events and concerts in various markets that gave them consumer exposure and *favor with the radio stations.*

⇒ We also built a consumer base by having fans fill out post cards or forms with their addresses so we could *keep them informed.*

7.   PHONE CALLS

➢ In-house we had interns on the phone with radio announcers, retail clerks and managers and media daily for 6 months pumping up the project.

8.   PROMOTIONAL GOODS

➢ We allotted promotional material for radio, retailers, the media, and even a few fans that may *not have had money to buy our product.*

9.   ARTIST NEED TO BE PREPPED

New artist especially need to be prepped for interviewing and what to say when in public *no matter how intelligent* or seasoned they are in life.

➢ We teach our artists to always maintain a *positive attitude* whether they sell any CD's, or they do a bad performance, or people don't initially like them or *whatever the situation may turn out to be.* Note: It's easy for artists to be pleasant when people are telling them they're great, but it's *something else* when they are *not being well received.* The thing about music is depending on someone's mood they may not like what they see or hear one day, and they may love you the next!

➢ When our artists have great performances, we tell them to rejoice but don't take themselves *too seriously.*

➢ We teach our artists that to be a professional, this means whether the place you perform meets the *highest standards or the lowest standards*, you perform *for your fans.* And as Christians you perform as unto the Lord

ADVICE FOR EXECUTIVES & MANAGERS

7 What are some good policies new managers or new music entrepreneurs should follow to accomplish both success *and* respect in the music business?

➢ Maintain a *creative mind* as it pertains to *always being open to new ideas* you or your crew may come up with that may not have been tested, but could work if you give it a try.

❑ ADVICE FOR MANAGERS & EXECUTIVES

❑ Respect other people no matter where they are in their career.

❑ Never stop growing intellectually and seek the advice of mentors and peers

❑ Be as honest and open as you can... without hurting yourself ...or anyone else

❑ Be loyal to your clients, even when it hurts

❑ Remember that your job is a mediator to make everything work between your clients and the rest of the world

❑ Be strong, innovative, and aggressive

❑ Always have your creative thinking cap on because it takes creative business people to survive in the entertainment business

❑ Have fun!

❑ Don't take things personally, even though the business is Personal in nature

❑ Don't believe *your* hype ...And don't let your clients believe their hype

KNEW BEGINNINGS ENTERTAINMENT
DINA ANDREWS MANAGEMENT
1266 W. Paces Ferry Road, PMB #582
Atlanta, GA 30327
DinaAndrewsManagement@aol.com
www.KnewBeginningsEnt.com

Music Powers

PERSONAL MANAGEMENT DIRECTORY

The Music Powers Management directory is a listing of many of the most reputable personal managers that represent artists and/or producers in Hip Hop and R&B/Pop music. Each has been contacted beforehand, so they do know you're coming. But, *before you solicit to them, please have only your BEST songs ready.* Also, please pay attention to *their particular policy.* If you see "Solicited demos by referral only" this means that if you want to send them your demo, I suggest that you make contact with them through one of the Entertainment Attorneys listed in Chapter 2. If you see "No need to call first," this means you have the green light to send your music, but I suggest that you *still contact them* to follow up on the status of your submission.

…Good Luck

- Client Roster
- ➢ Demo policy
- ❑ Get referral

A

DINA ANDREWS

Dina Andrews Management, Inc.
1266 W. Paces Ferry Road, PMB #582
Atlanta, GA 30327
770-434-1316
DinaAndrewsMgmt@aol.com
www.KnewBeginningsEnt.com

- Undisclosed
- ➢ Consulting only: Record Producers
- ➢ Independent labels, Production Co.

THE ARTIST FACTORY

Hiram Hicks, Monica Ewing, Vernon Slaughter
1741 Commerce Dr.
Atlanta, GA 30318
404-352-0404 / Fax 404-352-0405
www.artistfactory.com
info@artistfactory.com

- Undisclosed Client Listing
- ➢ Send Unsolicited material to **John Kegler**
- ➢ Send 1 picture, a bio, contact information
- ➢ Send 3 – 4 songs or tracks
- ➢ Please *Call first*

ARTISTIC CONTROL

MAULDIN BRAND AGENCY
Michael Mauldin, Lucy Raoof
1350 Spring Street – Suite 700
Atlanta, GA 30309
404-733-5511 / Fax 404-733-5512
www.artisticcontrol.com

- *Bone Crusher, Bow Wow*
- *Kenny Latimore, Chante Moore*
- ❑ Solicited demos accepted only by referral

CARLINE BALAN

825 8th Avenue, 28th Floor
New York, NY 10019
212-333-1452
cibalan@balaninc.com

- Undisclosed / Credits: *Jay-Z*
- ➢ Send to **A&R**
- ➢ Send 1 picture, a bio, 3 songs or tracks
- ➢ No need to call first

BAR ENTERTAINMENT

1501 Broadway, Suite 1503
New York, NY 10036
212-765-5800

- Not disclosed
- ➢ Send unsolicited demos to **Uncle Ray**
- ➢ Send 1 picture, a bio, 2 songs for artists
- ➢ Send 3 tracks if you are a producer
- ➢ No need to call first

BE RICH MANAGEMENT

Bernard Parks
1612 Ezra Church
Atlanta, GA 30314
404-641-5685

- *DJ Toomp*
- ➢ Send demo package

SHANTE BROADUS

1142 S. Diamond Bar Blvd. #504
Diamond Bar, CA 91765
www.doggystylerecords.com

- *Snoop Dogg*
- ➢ Mail demo **attn: A&R**

C

JOHNNIE CABBELL
HITT AFTA HITT ENTERTAINMENT
3939 La Vista Road, Suite E #481
Tucker, GA 30084
404-798-0197
johnnie@hittaftahitt.com
www.hittaftahitt.com

- *Crime Mob, Mac Breezy*
- ➢ Send solicited demos only

COLLIPARK MUSIC
DJ SMURF (MR. COLLIPARK)
PO Box 387
Lovejoy, GA. 30250
678-545-1306

- *Ying Yang Twins, Kadalack Boyz*
- ➢ Send your demo attn: **DJ Smurf**
- ➢ Send 1 picture, your bio, 3-4 songs
- ➢ No need to call first

D

TONY DAVIS & COURTNEY BENSON
9648 Olive Blvd, Suite 232
St. Louis, MO 63132
314-533-1155

- *Nelly, Murphy Lee, St. Lunatics*
- ❑ Solicited demos through a referral

JEFF DIXON
EBONY SON MANAGEMENT
1867 7th Avenue - Suite 4C
New York, NY 10026
212-665-9634

- *Ludacris*
- ❑ Send solicited demos through a referral

CAROL DORSEY
PO Box 8887
Metairie, LA 70011
504-940-5793
www.choppercitymusic.com

- *Big Tymers, Lil Wayne, Gotti, Baby, Bo*
- ➢ Send demos to **A&R Dept**
- ➢ Send 1 picture, a bio, 4 songs or tracks
- ➢ No need to call first

DP MUSIC MANAGEMENT
Darian Pollard, Sean Michaels
2645 La Cienega Blvd. – Suite 1275
Los Angeles, CA 90211
310-927-6887
www.dpmusicmanagement.8k.com
dpmusicmanagement@hotmail.com

- **Carey Kelly, Demarie "Meech" Sheki**
- **Jason "Poohbear" Boyd**
- ➢ Send demo package to: **Sean Michaels**

DUCK DOWN
341 Lafayette Street – Suite 571
New York, NY 10012
212-475-0287
dduckdown@aol.com
teksteele@aol.com
www.duckdown.com

- *Buckshot, Cocoa Brovaz, OGC*
- ➢ Send in your Demo
- ➢ See website for more

E

JAMES ELLIS
900 South Ave - Suite 262
Staten Island, NY 10314
718-568-3655
ellisentertain@aol.com

- *Redman*
- ➢ Producers only
- ➢ Send tracks/snippets to: **James Ellis**
- ➢ Send 1 picture, a bio & 3-4 songs or tracks
- ➢ No need to call first

ERVING WONDER
A DIVISION OF SANCTUARY GROUP
Julius Erving, Troy Carter, Tamara Houston
1500 Sansom St
Philadelphia, PA 19102
212-599-2757
Emily@ervingwonder.com
www.ervingwonder.com
New York office: **212-599-2757**
Los Angeles office: **310-205-5000**

- *Mase, Eve, Floetry*
- *Jadakiss, Angie Stone*
- *Sleepy Brown, Freeway*
- ➢ Send unsolicited material to **Erving Wonder**
- ➢ Send 1 picture, a bio, contacts
- ➢ Send your best songs or tracks

F

ANDREA FAIR
DAS COMMUNICATIONS
83 Riverside Drive
New York, NY 10024
212-877-0400

- *Wyclef Jean, The Black Eyed Peas*
- ❑ Solicited demos by a referral

FAMILY TREE MANAGEMENT
581 ENTERTAINMENT, INC
2356 Park Central Blvd.
Decatur, GA 30035
678-418-9973

- Undisclosed / Credits: *Jagged Edge*
- ➢ Send 1 picture, a bio, 4 songs
- ➢ No need to call beforehand

THE FIRM
9465 Wilshire Blvd. Suite 600
Beverly Hills, CA 90212
310-860-8000

- Undisclosed
- ❑ Solicit your demo through a referral

DEBBIE FONTAINE
205 S. Beverly Drive - Suite 212
Beverly Hills, CA 90212
310-471-8631
www.fontainetalent.com
info@fontainetalent.com

- *Dream, Allison Paige, Natasha*
- *Jason Celaya, Ghostlight, Billie Jean*
- ➢ Send demo to **Fontaine Music**
- ➢ 1 photo, 1 bio, 3 songs/tracks
- ➢ Not required to call first

CRAIG FRUIN
HK MANAGEMENT
PO Box 151470
San Rafael, CA 94901
415-485-1444
suzana@hkmanagement.biz

- Undisclosed
- ❑ Solicited demos by referral only

G

GENUINE REPRESENTATION
Michael Mavrolas, Greg Johnson,
Trey Bellows
11271 Ventura Blvd., Suite 3225
Studio City, CA. 91604
818-505-6870
genuinerep@earthlink.net

- *Pro-Jay, Damon Sharpe, Brion James*
- *Gregg Pagani, Mark Feist pka Real MF*
- *Tone Capone, Sam Sneed, Greg Charley*
- *Tony Issac, Sean Blaze, Claudio Cueni*
- *Chuck Giscombe, Duane Covert*
- ➢ Send unsolicited demos to: **A&R Dept**
- ➢ Send 1 picture, 1 bio, 4 songs
- ➢ No need to call first

JASON GETER
GRAND HUSTLE ENTERTAINMENT
PMB 161541 10th Street
Atlanta, GA 30318
info@grandhustle.com
www.grandhustle.com
404-456-1778 / Fax 404-522-5114

- *T.I., Kuntry King*
- *XTACI, Mac Boney & AK*
- ➢ Send 1 picture, 1 bio, 3-4 songs
- ➢ Send to **Doug in A&R**

FERNANDO GIBSON
INDIA.ARIE MANAGEMENT
PO Box 101
North Bergen, NJ 07047
201-522-0688
coobaa@aol.com
mail@muzic365.com

- Undisclosed
- ➢ Send 1 picture, 1 bio, 4 songs/tracks
- ➢ Send unsolicited demos to **Erika Hill**

TRUDY GREEN
HK MANAGEMENT
9200 Sunset Blvd – Suite 1000
Los Angeles, CA 90069
310-550-5240
suzana@hkmanagement.biz

- Undisclosed / Credits: *Michael Jackson*
- ❑ Solicited demos by referral only

H

SHIBA HALEY
MAHOGANY ENTERTAINMENT
PO Box 4367
Mitchellville, MD 20775
301-390-8408
www.mahoganyinc.com
mahoganyinc@comcast.net

- *Yolanda Adams, Sheba Freeman, Tone*
- ❑ Solicit your demo through a referral

BARRY HANKERSON
BLACKGROUND ENTERTAINMENT
155 W 19th Street, 2nd Floor
New York, NY 10011
646-638-2585

- *Tank, Jojo, Yoni, Timbaland, Pink*
- Credits: *Aaliyah, R. Kelly, Toni Braxton*
- ➤ Send unsolicited demos to **Dawn Styles**
- ➤ Send 1 picture, 1 bio, 4 –5 songs
- ➤ No need to call first

LYNN HARLESS
JUST-IN-TIME ENTERTAINMENT
PO Box 1070
Windermere, FL 34786
407-909-8872

- Undisclosed / Credits: *Justin Timberlake*
- ❑ Solicited demos through referral

JEROME HIPPS & MICHAEL MCARTHUR
MAMA'S BOYS MANAGEMENT
1030 N. Delaware Avenue
Philadelphia, PA 19125
215-634-3456
Jamie@mamasboysmusic.com
www.mamasboysmusic.com

- *Musiq, Aaries, Skillz, Camui*
- ➤ Send unsolicited demos to **A&R**
- ➤ Send 1 picture, 1 bio, 4 songs or tracks
- ➤ No need to call first

J

JaEdD MUSIC GROUP
Jasmine Diaz, Eddie Diaz
2345 Rancho Del Oro Road - Suite 70
Oceanside, CA 92056
760-967-1237 / Fax 760-967-6774

JaEdD MUSIC GROUP continued

Info@jmusicgroup.com
www.jmusicgroup.com

- *Tika Rainn, Kevin Gray, Jenn Takahashi*
- *Juliana Frailoli, Kelly Marie, Soultry*
- *Jasmine Diaz, Christian Davis, Rachel*
- ➤ Only represents artists, *no producers*
- ➤ Send demo package

K

MICHAEL KNIGHT
67 Hanson Place
Brooklyn, NY 11217
917-603-2614
Mikesnavi2000@aol.com

- Past clients/credits: Undisclosed
- ➤ Send unsolicited demos to **Michael Knight**
- ➤ Send 1 picture, 1 bio, 4 songs/tracks
- ➤ No need to call first

MATHEW KNOWLES
MUSIC WORLD MANAGEMENT
Music World/Sanctuary Urban Management
1505 Hadley Street
Houston, TX 77002
713-772-5175
information@mwe-online.com

- *Beyoncé, Kelly Rowland, Michelle*
- *Mario, Play, Mason Rd*
- *Ray J, O'Jays, Kool & the Gang*
- ❑ Solicited demos through referral only

Package Contents:

For Artists:
- ➤ Send 3 or more *original* songs on CD
- ➤ Songs must be studio quality
- ➤ Send picture, bio and experience
- ➤ Include address, e-mail and phone contact

For Producers:
- ➤ Send studio quality *open tracks*
- ➤ Send CD - music in *song format*
- ➤ Send discography
- ➤ Include address, e-mail and phone contact

- ➤ Mail your package to:
  A&R Department
  Demo Submission
  1505 Hadley Street
  Houston, TX 77002

STEVEN KURTZ
MARQUEE MANAGEMENT
274 Madison Avenue
New York, NY 10016
212-889-0420
sekurtz@aol.com

- Credits: *Christina Aguilera*
- ❑ Solicited demos by referral only

L

CHRIS LIGHTY
VIOLATOR MANAGEMENT
36 West 25th Street - 11th Floor
New York, NY 10010
646-486-8900
www.violator.com

- *Lil Scrappy, G Unit, 50 Cents, Missy Elliot*
- *Busta Rhymes, Tweet, Lil Mo*
- ➢ Send unsolicited demos to **Andrea Neal**
- ➢ Send 1 picture, your bio & 3 songs
- ➢ No need to call first

M

MARVELOUS ENTERPRISES
Marvin McIntyre
2020 Howell Mill Rd, NW
Atlanta, GA 30318
404-367-9122

- Credits: *Keith Sweat*
- ❑ Send your solicited material via referral

MICHAEL MAULDIN
1350 Spring Street – Suite 700
Atlanta, GA 30309
404-733-5511 / Fax 404-733-5512
www.artisticcontrol.com

- *Bone Crusher, Bow Wow*
- *Kenny Latimore, Chante Moore*
- ❑ Solicited demos accepted only by referral

ORLANDO MCGHEE
SEVENTY-TWO MUSIC CONSULTANTS
PO Box 161786
Atlanta, GA 30321
404-524-1266
ormcghee@aol.com

- Undisclosed client list
- ➢ Solicited material only

ROB MCDOWELL
BME RECORDINGS
2144 Hills Avenue - Suite D2
Atlanta, GA 30318
404-367-8130 / Fax 404-367-8630
www.bmerecordings.com
bmeinc@bellsouth.net

- *Lil Jon & the Eastside Boyz, Trillville*
- *Oobie, Chyna White, Lil Scrappy*
- *Crime Mob, E 40, Bohagon*
- Producer: *Lil Jon*
- ➢ Send unsolicited demos in mp3 format to:
  bmeinc@bellsouth.net
- ➢ Send 1 picture, 1 bio
- ➢ Send 2 mp3 completed songs
- ➢ Send up to 10 mp3 tracks

BENNY MEDINA
HANDPRINT ENTERTAINMENT
1100 Glendon Ave. - Suite 1000
Los Angeles, CA 90024
310-481-4400

- *Mya, Brandy, Mariah Carey*
- ❑ Send solicited demos by referral only

MES ENTERTAINMENT
Mark Stewart, Judi Stewart
19200 Nordhoff St. - Suite #1601
Northridge, CA 91324
818-709-7701 or **310-925-0657**
judi.stewart@mesentertainment.net
www.mesentertainment.net

- *Laney Stewart, C. Tricky Stewart, J.Que*
- *Penelope Magnet, The Lovehammers*
- *Traci Hale, Todd Herfindal, Audia*
- *Kevin "KD" Davis, Chelo*
- ➢ Solicited material only

ROBERT MITCHELL
ROYAL FLUSH ENTERTAINMENT
PO Box 20084
Atlanta, GA 30325

- Credits: *Lil Jon & the Eastside Boyz*
- ➢ Send unsolicited material to **A&R Dept**
- ➢ Send 1 picture, 1 bio
- ➢ Send 4-5 songs (for artists)
- ➢ Send 5 songs (for producers)

SABRINA MONTGOMERY

DREAMCATCHERS ENTERTAINMENT
ILLNOISE ENTERTAINMENT
PO Box 262
Atlanta, GA 30086
404-454-4200
Sabrina@DreamCatchersEntertainment.com

- Undisclosed
- Send unsolicited demos to **Sabrina**
- Send 1 pic, 1 bio, contact information
- Send 4-5 songs for artists
- Send 5-10 tracks for producers

N

NOONTIME

SHONUFF RECORDINGS
237 Peter St. - Suite A
Atlanta, GA 30313
404-275-4332

- *Ciara*
- Send solicited demos only

P

TERESA PAGE

WRIGHT ENTERTAINMENT GROUP
7680 Universal Blvd. - Suite 500
Orlando, FL 32819
407-826-9100
www.wegmusic.com

- *Justin Timberlake, Janet Jackson*
- *Boys II Men, P.Diddy, NSYNC*
- *Backstreet Boyz, Christina Milian*
- Send solicited demos to **A&R Dept**
- Send 1 picture, 1 bio, 3 songs

JONNETTA PATTON

J PAT MANAGEMENT
3996 Pleasantdale Rd. - Suite 104A
Doraville, GA 30340
770-416-8616
www.jpatmgnt.com

- *Usher*
- Send unsolicited demos to **A&R Dept**
- Send 1 picture, 1 bio, 3 songs
- No need to call first

+
USH ENTERTAINMENT
400 Interstate N. PKY. #1220
Atlanta, GA 30339

DON PERRY

GREENBERG TRAURIG CONSULTING
The Forum
3290 Northside Pkwy
Suite 400
Atlanta, GA 30327
678-553-2215
perryd@gtconsulting.com
www.gtconsulting.com

- Undisclosed
- Send demos to **Don Perry or Joel Katz**
- Send 1 picture, 1 bio
- Send 2 songs

R

LUCI RAOFF

ARTISTIC CONTROL
1350 Spring St NW, Suite 700
Atlanta GA 30309
404-733-5511

- *Bone Crusher, Bow Wow*
- Solicited demos *accepted only by referral*

SIMON RENSHAW

THE FIRM
9465 Wilshire Blvd. - Suite 600
Beverly Hills, CA. 90212
310-246-9000

- Undisclosed roster
- Solicited demos accepted only by referral

JEFF ROBINSON

MBK ENTERTAINMENT
240 W. 35th Street, 18th Floor
New York, NY 10001
212-397-1307
mbk4keys@aol.com

- *Alicia Keys, Shawn King, Focus*
- *Mike Mills, Jessica Wilson*
- *Tre of Naughty by Nature*
- Send solicited demos to **Baloo**
- Send 1 picture, 1 bio, 5-6 songs or tracks
- No need to call first

PHIL ROBINSON
BAD BOY ENTERTAINMENT
1710 Broadway
New York, NY 10019
212-381-1540 / Fax 212-381-1599

- *Loon, Mase, Sean "P Diddy" Combs*
- *8 Ball & MJG, Carl Thomas, Mario Winans*
- ➢ Solicited material only

RON ROBINSON
440 9th Ave, 17th FL
New York, NY 10001
212-333-1330

- Credits: *Ja Rule*
- ➢ Send unsolicited demos to **Errol Vaughn**
- ➢ Send 1 picture, 1 bio, 3 songs

ROCKSTAR ENTERTAINMENT
126 Presidential Blvd
Bala Cynwyd, PA 19004
215-533-6080

- Undisclosed
- ➢ Send demos to **Sherman Byers**
- ➢ Send 1 picture, 1 bio, 3 songs

PAUL ROSENBERG
GOLIATH ARTISTS
151 Lafayette St.
New York, NY 10012-3327
212-324-2410 / Fax 212-324-2415

- *Eminem, Cypress Hill, DJ Muggs*
- ➢ Send unsolicited demos to **Riggs**
- ➢ Send 1 picture, 1 bio, 3-4 songs
- ➢ No need to call first

RUFF RYDERS ENTERTAINMENT
c/o **Spank or Duke Rich**
12 West 21st St, 7th fl
New York, NY 10010
212-359-3058
www.ruffryders.com

- Check roster at website
- ➢ Ruff Ryders is looking for up-and-coming Producers & Artists
- ➢ Call Spank or Duke Rich: **212-359-3058**

S

SERGE ENTERTAINMENT GROUP
Sandy Serge
6918 Heritage Place
Acworth, GA 30102
678-445-0006
SergeEnt@aol.com
www.serge.com

- See website for artists
- ➢ Send demo to: **Sandy Serge**

LINDSAY SCOTT
8899 Beverly Blvd - # 600
Los Angeles, CA 90048
310-860-1040
lsmgt@aol.com

- Credits: *Pink, Janet Jackson, Cher*
- ➢ *Call 1st – Normally does not accept!*

MONA SCOTT
VIOLATOR MANAGEMENT
36 West 25th Street - 11th Floor
New York, NY 10010
646-486-8900
www.violator.com

- *Lil Scrappy, G Unit, 50 Cents, Missy Elliot*
- *Busta Rhymes, Tweet, Lil Mo*
- ➢ Send unsolicited demos to **Andrea Neal**
- ➢ Send 1 picture, your bio & 3 songs
- ➢ No need to call first

DAVID SONENBERG
DAS COMMUNICATIONS
83 Riverside Drive
New York, NY 10024
212-877-0400

- *Wyclef Jean, The Black Eyed Peas*
- *Next, Bone Thugs and Harmony*
- ❑ Solicit your demos through a referral only

SQUEAKY
SHONUFF RECORDINGS
237 Peter St. - Suite A
Atlanta, GA 30313
678-772-2393

- *Jody Breeze*
- ➢ Solicited demos only

CHRIS STOKES

THE ULTIMATE GROUP
848 N. La Cienega Blvd, Suite 202
Los Angeles, CA 90069
310-289-3050
www.ultimategroup.com
www.tugentertainment.com

- *Omarion, Marques Houston,*
- *N2U, Grand Barry, Gina, O'Ryan*
- ➢ Send solicited demos to **A&R Dept**
- ➢ Send 1 picture, 1 bio, 3 songs

T

TRIPLE F UNLIMITED

Jamel "Mdot" Carter
244 Fifth Ave. – Suite 2798
New York, NY 10001
212-561-0519
info@triplefunlimited.com
www.triplefunlimited.com

- Check website for roster
- ➢ Accepts producer & artists demos

W

KEVIN WALES

WORLD WIDE ENTERTAINMENT GROUP
3150 Keenan Ct.
College Park, GA 30349
404-729-4070
Mrworldwide@comcast.net

- *B5*
- Credits: *112, Mario Winans, Monica*
- ➢ Send unsolicited demos to Kevin Wales
- ➢ Send 1 picture, a bio, contact information
- ➢ For artists - Send 3 songs
- ➢ For producers - Send 5-10 tracks

AARON WALTON ENTERTAINMENT

515 S. Flower St, 7th FL
Los Angeles, CA 90071
323-938-2233
www.awent.com

- Credits: *Dakota Moon, Andrew Logan*
- ➢ Send unsolicited demos to **Sean**
- ➢ Send 1 picture, 1 bio, 4 songs

HILLARY WESTON

424 W. 54th Street, 2nd FL
New York, NY 10019
212-974-7740
hillary.weston@queenbee-entertainment.com

- Undisclosed / Credits: *Lil Kim*
- ➢ Send unsolicited demos to **A&R Dept**
- ➢ Send 1 picture, 1 bio, 4 songs
- ➢ No need to call first

MICHAEL "BLUE" WILLIAMS

AQUEMINI - PURPLE RIBBON - FAMILY TREE
684 Antone Street, NW
Atlanta, GA 30318
404-350-3332 or 212-333-8241

- *Outkast*
- ➢ *Producers only!*
- ➢ Send material to **Mitch or Regina**
- ➢ Send 5-10 tracks, bio, and contact info

JOHNNY WRIGHT

WRIGHT ENTERTAINMENT GROUP
7680 Universal Blvd. - Suite 500
Orlando, FL 32819
407-826-9100 / Fax 407-826-9107
www.wegmusic.com
requests@wegmusic.com

- *Justin Timberlake, Janet Jackson*
- *Boys II Men, P.Diddy, NSYNC*
- *Backstreet Boyz, Christina Milian*
- *Nicholas Jonas, Stevie Brock*
- *Brooks Bufurd*
- ➢ Check website for new talent auditions!
- ➢ Mail your demo to:
    Wright Entertainment Group c/o
    Demo Submission
    PO Box 590009
    Orlando, FL 32859

Z

CHAKA ZULU

EBONY SON MANAGEMENT
1867 7th Avenue - Suite 4C
New York NY 10026
212-665-9634
www.dtprecords.com

- *Ludacris*
- ➢ Send unsolicited demos to **A&R Dept**
- ➢ Send 1 picture, 1 bio, 4 songs

For more listings of Personal Managers – log in at: www.Musicpowers.com/24

SECTION TWO

ENTERTAINMENT ATTORNEYS

by Cirocco - Collins - McLane

INTRODUCTION

One of the first people you will also need to explore for your lineup is a reputable and knowledgeable entertainment attorney. This member of your team can be your dealmaker and deal breaker. See, it's like this; the entertainment industry is mainly built on relationships and contracts, meaning that many lawyers have very powerful connections, and some know to use those connections, together with their experience and skills - to *make or break* contracts or deals. And just for the record, you better know that you *never* sign any contract in the music business without *first* consulting your attorney.

WHEN ASKED TO SIGN

If you are asked to sign anything other than an autograph, you absolutely do need an attorney…period! Too many aspiring creative artists want to get a deal so badly they will sign almost *anything* that promises them a chance to have a deal. Even successful careers have a relatively short life span, especially in the music and entertainment business. For this reason, it is important for you to get **maximum** returns in the good years and *not* sign away your rights to valuable income.

As previously stated, never sign anything without having your own lawyer review it first. Do not rely on anyone else (or even their lawyer) to tell you what your contract says. Your lawyer will "translate" the deal for you and explain to you *exactly* what you are getting into. Do not let anyone rush you or pressure you into signing any agreement for any reason.

DO YOUR RESEARCH!

Your entertainment attorney must have a very thorough knowledge of today's industry and deal making trends. Along with this, he needs to be well connected throughout the entertainment industry. This means that he not only has plenty of industry contacts, but also, and more importantly, *makes use* of his many industry connections and resources. If the attorney you plan on hiring has been in the music game for a while, he more than likely will be able to show you *how* to make the best deal (more money), and maintain control of your music at the same time.

Seek to find out what types of deals the particular attorney has made… not only in the past, but what type(s) of deals they might *presently* be negotiating. Also, *if possible*, find out what others in the industry have to say about them.

SEEKING COUNSEL

Collins

When looking for a lawyer, you should *not* be afraid to interview a few candidates before retaining one. Some lawyers are with large firms but many are solo practitioners. Attorneys have a range of personalities and legal skills and you should seek out a situation where the "vibe" is right. Although your first contact may be on the telephone, you most likely will have an initial interview for which, if you so request in advance, there is *usually* no charge. Remember, your lawyer's time is money, so be prepared and be on time for your appointment.

It is not necessary that your lawyer likes or even *understands* your music. It is more important that you feel he or she is a trustworthy and competent advisor. The lawyer/client relationship is known as a "fiduciary" relationship which means that a lawyer must *always* act in your best interest and not his own …or that of anyone else. Your lawyer is also under a duty to keep your conversations with him confidential. It is often in your best interest that it stays that way.

McLane

To find an interested attorney, you should locate a list of music attorneys, call them, and ask if they will are willing to listen to new material for possible representation. Most attorneys will probably suggest that you send in a demo. If the attorney hears potential, and wants to represent you to labels and publishers (i.e., submit the demo), the lawyer will expect to be compensated. And there are several different ways to structure a lawyer's fees.

ATTORNEY FEE$

There are some attorneys that charge a flat fee for their service. But in most cases you can expect to pay an hourly rate which can range anywhere from $100 to $400+ per hour. In "all" cases… low or high, be sure that you get an outline of what duties is expected from your lawyer. You should also request an itemized list of charges or an invoice from him, regarding services done on your behalf. If you have *any* questions about what your charges are, then don't be afraid to ask about them. Also, make sure that there are no HIDDEN charges that were not discussed up front. Try to limit your attorney's contract negotiations to 3 or 4 months at most. Otherwise, it may become too expensive on your wallet. Ok crew, this is important… "It is not a good idea to use an attorney who is also working for the opposite group or company you are in negotiations with." This is called a "conflict of interest".   You don't want the same guy negotiating your contract, who is also getting a retainer fee from the opposing side.

ATTORNEY'S DUTIES

A g o o d attorney will be able to navigate you safely through the minefield that is

Collins

the entertainment industry. Record contracts, publishing agreements, and licensing arrangements can be extremely complicated. Proper negotiating and drafting requires advanced legal skills, as well as knowledge of entertainment business and intellectual property practice. Your lawyer can explain the concepts of copyrights, trademark and patents to you and assist you in securing proper protection for your work. In addition to structuring and documenting a deal to maximize the benefits to you, some attorneys also actively solicit deals for their clients. Additionally, if you are not properly paid in agreement with your contract, you will look to your lawyer to put a lawsuit in motion.

…Intellectual Property?

- *Intellectual property is an idea, invention, creation, conception, etc., which can be protected by law from being copied by someone else (Provided courtesy of Dictionary.Cambridge.org)*

MORE PIE… PLEASE?

There are times when an attorney is paid by getting a *percentage* of your income. But in many cases it really may be in your *best* interest to avoid this…*if feasible*. If your attorney is getting paid by receiving a "cut of the pie", and *especially when he's not paid anything up front*… who's interest do you think he will *really* be looking out for? More than likely he will be looking for options so that somehow, he *can* get paid? (Yeah!) Because of this concern, many lawyers will not do any work without getting paid *something* up front. So essentially, it is wiser to retain an attorney, by fee. This way, when you do have a legal or contract situation, you can call them up for advice… and their efforts to counsel you will apply towards your retainer.

…What exactly is a retainer?

- *A retainer is a contract between a lawyer and his client, in which the attorney agrees to represent and give legal advice to the client… in exchange for money. The signed retainer begins the client-lawyer relationship from which flow many responsibilities and duties, primarily on the lawyer, including to provide accurate legal advice, to monitor limitation dates **and to not allow any "conflict of interest" between himself and his client**. (Courtesy of Duhaime & Company)*

HOW MUCH RETAINER?

Primarily, the main thing a lawyer has to sell …is his time. And with the odds of success in this business being what they are, *very few lawyers* will agree to work for you and wait for payment until you are successful and can pay your bills. This is why most lawyers will require a payment of money in advance or "retainer", which can range anywhere from $1,000 to $10,000. Even those who take a percentage of the deal as a fee may require that you pay a retainer. In addition to the hourly fee or percentage, you are usually required to reimburse your lawyer for his out-of-pocket costs, including long distance telephone calls, photocopies, postage, fax, etc.

You should realize that in retaining a lawyer you are making a contract even if your agreement is *not* written. In return for a fee, the lawyer promises to render legal services on your behalf. On the other hand, some lawyers may want a fee arrangement in writing (specifically in connection with a percentage deal) and/or a payment direction letter (a cautious lawyer will advise you that you have the right to seek the advice of another lawyer as to the propriety of a percentage fee arrangement).

DEAL $HOPPING

If you're an aspiring artists, you have probably already discovered, while trying *unsuccessfully* to submit material to record companies and publishers, that many companies' policy is that submissions are *only accepted* from an attorney or manager. So, outside of some *creative* approaches to having material heard by the industry, your attorney or manager will at some point become a necessary member of your inner circle. This section will discuss the people that are often considered to be the most powerful players in the music industry of today: Attorneys.

McLane

With the recording industry becoming more corporate, the importance of industry attorneys has also increased dramatically. Today, many deals come about as a direct result of the artist's attorney's connections, reputation and experience. Essentially, labels *and publishers* are so flooded with new material, that they simply do not have the time to review it all. By limiting who they accept submissions from (i.e., attorneys), they can *generally* be more certain that the product has some artistic merit or value, because they are assuming (sometimes illogically) that the attorney has already weeded out the wheat from the chaff. So, because of the harsh reality that labels and publishers now seem to favor receiving demos from attorneys, you should attempt to find an interested attorney to help the cause. Not only can your attorney help find you a deal, but your attorney also has the ability to understand and negotiate complex and sophisticated contracts, which can have massive financial and professional ramifications for you, the artist.

SO, HOW MUCH PIE...?

Now, if your attorney is shopping you a deal, you can expect to pay about 5 percent (but as much as 20 percent) of the deal. And by the way, try to avoid paying from the gross amount of the deal (*unless you're getting "all" the money*). There are many times that "you may not be the recipient" of the entire amount of funds involved with the deal. In other words, you should only seek to pay your attorney a percentage on what was negotiated for your "net" income... as related to the deal.

WHAT IF I HAVE NO MONEY?

If you have been presented with a contract or some agreement that needs the attention of an attorney, and you are low on funds, there is an organization that can help you. It's called the **Volunteer Lawyers For The Arts**. Get in contact with this organization, and tell them "your" particular situation. The cost to you may NOT be free... but the price will be something you "can" afford depending on your finances.

Here is a select list of agreements that you should *always* seek the guidance and counsel of an entertainment attorney

Artist Agreements
Producer Contracts
Selling & Leasing Beats
Live Stage Productions
Branded Media
Endorsements
Deal Shopping
Sponsorship
Talent Employment
Internet-based Entertainment Ventures
Investment and Financing
Joint venture
Merchandising Contracts

P&D and Distribution
Music Publishing Contracts
Music Publishing Administration
Partnership Agreements
Producer Agreements
Production Company Agreements
Recording Agreements
Royalty and Participation Audits
Talent Contracts
Trademark and Copyright
Touring Agreements
Management Agreements
Live Engagements

THE BIG PICTURE

In most cases, an experienced attorney in the music business will see (and has seen) where and what you want to be. But, be alert to know, sometimes you'll need to find a way to get them to *clearly* see a bigger picture regarding your career.

I have *personally* experienced hiring a "more than qualified" entertainment attorney to handle a deal with one of the largest major record labels in the world. And although he had a reputation as being one of the *best* contract lawyers in the business, if I had not stepped in, to increase his focus on what *I really wanted* (and needed) out of the deal, I would have cheated *myself* out of $300,000.00 *ouch...yeah!* And so you know, just because my attorney had not *expected* a new artist/producer to get *that* kind of deal, *does not mean* that he wasn't *qualified* to handle my contract. It just meant that he really didn't *see* The BIG Picture, as I did.

So *stay focused*, be of strength, and courage, and have *a lot of faith*. And *most of all*...use some wisdom and discernment in your decision-making! The bottom line is that you need a great attorney; one who is competent and knowledgeable of this business. Contracts should NOT *ever* be taken lightly, and a great entertainment attorney will make sure that your agreement is thorough enough for your best interest. A detailed contract forces *both parties* to ask questions, and in the process – think a lot more *clearly* about the whole deal.

"Thank you India.Arie for your song "Strength, Courage & Wisdom" ...You are truly incredible!"

GOOD LUCK!

Wallace Collins, Esq. *is an attorney in private practice in New York who is currently "of counsel" with the firm of Serling, Rooks & Ferrara, LLP specializing in Entertainment Law & Intellectual Property. www.wallacecollins.com*

Ben McLane, Esq. *of McLane & Wong, is a full service global entertainment law firm specializing in music law www.benmclane.com*

McLane & Wong

Biography

Joel Katz is one of the most prominent entertainment lawyers in America. A

graduate of the University of Tennessee and Hunter College, Katz expertise in the areas of entertainment and corporate law are second to none. A co-managing shareholder at Greenberg Traurig, LLP-Atlanta, Katz is also the Chair of the National Entertainment Practice-Atlanta and the Music Industry Representative, State of Georgia, Film, Video and Music Advisory Commission, Appointed by Governor Sonny Perdue. He is also the former chairman of The Recording Academy (NARAS).

Joel Katz represents more than fifty recording artists, as well as record producers, star athletes and Fortune 500 companies. His clientele ranges from entertainers like Christina Aguilera and Sheryl Crow, to major corporations like Coca-Cola and Sony. Over the years he has received accolades and recognition from the NARAS and been listed in all editions of the Best Lawyers of America, in the Who's Who in Entertainment, Who's Who in America, Who's Who in Georgia and the Who's Who of Executives and Professionals. In 1999, Katz prestige and achievements earned him the honor of the University of Tennessee rededicating its Law Library to Katz as the Joel Katz Law Library. In addition to practicing law, Katz has written and published countless articles for different law publications and conducted several lectures across the country.

Joel A. Katz

GREENBERG TRAURIG, LLP
THE FORUM – 3290 NORTHSIDE PARKWAY, NW   SUITE 400
ATLANTA, GA 30327
678-553-2222
www.gtlaw.com

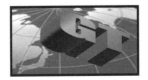

Music Powers
SPOTLIGHT

Greenberg Traurig, LLP

Joel A. Katz
Entertainment Law

IMMEDIATE PAST CHAIRMAN OF THE AMERICAN BAR ASSOCIATION'S ENTERTAINMENT & SPORTS LAW SECTION

Select Clientele

Christina Aguilera	The Recording Academy	The Convex Group, LLC
Collective Soul	Anschutz Entertainment	Kenny Chesney
Sheryl Crow	Sammy Hagar	Nokia Corporation
Sony Corp of America	Brooks & Dunn	IMG
Clear Channel	B.B. King	Convex
Entertainment	Jimmy Buffett	Wurlitzer
Universal-Vivendi	George Jones	Country Music Association
Time Warner Telecom	Gibson Guitar	Baldwin Piano Company
The Coca Cola Company	Alan Jackson	

Select Awards

BEST LAWYERS IN AMERICA (ALL EDITIONS)

WHO'S WHO IN ENTERTAINMENT

HEROES AWARD - ATLANTA CHAPTER OF THE RECORDING ACADEMY

WHO'S WHO IN AMERICA

WHO'S WHO AMONG OUTSTANDING AMERICANS

GEORGIA MUSIC HALL OF FAME INDUCTEE

WHO'S WHO IN EXECUTIVES AND PROFESSIONALS

Joel A. Katz
GREENBERG TRAURIG, LLP
THE FORUM – 3290 NORTHSIDE PARKWAY, NW   SUITE 400
ATLANTA, GA 30327
678-553-2222
www.gtlaw.com

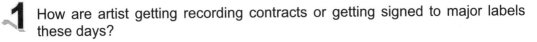

Exclusive Advice from Music Powers Advisor

Joel Katz

ADVICE FOR ARTISTS SEEKING RECORD DEALS

1 How are artist getting recording contracts or getting signed to major labels these days?

Artists are still getting signed by being viewed by A&R personnel from the various record companies. A "buzz" will start in a particular city and an A&R representative of a record company will hear about the "buzz." A meeting will be set up for the A&R to hear the act, as well as a demo tape. Hopefully, the artist will then get signed.

2 What advice can you give a new urban music artist to accomplish the idea of getting signed to a major or very strong independent label?

➤ The best advice one can give a new urban music artist is to have great regional material. Record companies seek a sense of *originality* with which to become involved.

3 What is the present trend with A&R as far as signing new talent directly vs. signing deals with independent companies?

➤ Companies are still signing artists directly and through production companies. The reason for production companies is that the A&R representatives know the individuals who own the production companies.

4 Is it better to have management in place *before* shopping a demo … or *after* getting the attention of someone in A&R … and then going with a manager already in the network of the industry players involved?

➤ It is better to have management in place before shopping a demo. The reason for management is to coordinate and deal specifically with record companies so that the artist is not placed in the middle of a compromising situation.

ADVICE FOR PRODUCERS

5 What's the biggest factor or rule a producer must follow, in order to make sure he can get a decent size advance… and actually see some royalties down the line… if the project is successful?

➤ The biggest fact or rule a producer should follow is to have a signed agreement. Without a signed agreement, a producer or any party to a new artist's development situation cannot feel safe or that they will continue after the artist is signed to a record company.

6 A lot of new or young producers want to sell their beats or tracks outright - *with no license needed.* Is this trend "good business"? …As opposed to producing a song or just getting paid to program or arrange on the song, but keeping the ownership privileges.

➤ I think new or young producers who want to get into the business will do just about anything necessary to make themselves known. I understand this on a short-term basis, but on a long-term basis once you are known, obviously this is *not* "good business."

7 A thorough contract forces both parties to ask questions, and in the process think more clearly about the agreement …please explain in your own words why it's so important for an artist or producer to *always* have legal counsel to draft and negotiate contracts beyond a simple proposal?

➤ It is always important to have legal counsel representing an artist, a producer or any member of a creative team. You can be certain that the other side has had a lawyer draft the contract and probably negotiated the contract long before it ever gets to the artist. The artist must be represented to be on an equal or safe footing. I say the same for a production company or for a producer.

8 A new artist/producer writes: "What's the best way to get my music to record labels so they would listen to it? …Should I leave a bio of myself and contact info along with my CD? …What's been known to really work?"

"…The best way to have your music listened to by record labels is to have a manager or lawyer submit the music to the individuals he or she knows in A&R at the record companies."

Joel Katz represents many of the world's best-known artists, producers, record labels & Fortune 500 companies

Music Powers
SPOTLIGHT

BME RECORDINGS   # Vincent Phillips, Esq.

Entertainment Law

Biography

Photo courtesy of David Ellis

For Vince Phillips, work in the music industry did not begin with a law degree. He began his endeavors in the music industry by handling marketing and promotions with three childhood friends, Jonathan "Lil' Jon" Smith, Emperor Searcy, and Rob McDowell. Using what he had learned in those areas to establish contacts and learn the ropes of the industry, he and his friends turned a common love for music and concert promotion into a successful partnership, and Phillips turned his love for business into his trademark.

As a result, Vince Phillips is by far one of the best entertainment attorneys in today's music industry. Known by his colleagues and fellow entertainment attorneys as a "Young Shark", Mr. Phillips is definitely no stranger to attaining & negotiating major label record deals …and making opportunity turn in to RIAA Certified Gold & Platinum.

Phillips is general counsel to, and a partner of Black Market Entertainment (BME) along with Smith, Searcy & McDowell, who are also among his clients. His clientele also includes: Big Oomp Camp, Lil' Scrappy, Trillville, Pastor Troy, KP & Enyvi, Chyna White, Lyrical Giants, Oobie, Don Vito Productions, and quite a few other independent labels.

A distinguished graduate of Georgia State University & John Marshall School of Law in Atlanta, Vince has served as an associate with well-established attorney Kendall Minter (Goodie Mob & Shabba Ranks), and also attorney Monica Ewing (Outkast & 112). From those two successful relationships, along with the conception, partnership and building of BME, Vincent Phillips, Esq. has become one of the most important 'key' music industry insiders and dealmakers in today's Urban Music scene.

VINCENT P. PHILLIPS, ESQ.
Entertainment Law

BME Recordings
2144 Hills Avenue - D2
Atlanta, GA 30318 USA

Music Powers
SPOTLIGHT
VINCENT PHILLIPS

SELECT PAST & PRESENT CLIENTELE LIST

BME Recordings
Lil Jon
The Eastside Boyz
The Youngbloodz
Atticrew
DJ Toomp
Cooly C
Pastor Troy
Big Oomp Camp
Kenny Flav
Don Vito
Bloodraw
Rob McDowell
Emperor Searcy
The Superfriends
The Aphilliates
DJ Mars
DJ Trauma
Bonecrusher
Lyrical Giants
Break em off Records
Royal Flush Management
Seventy-two Consulting

Exclusive Advice from Music Powers Advisor

VINCENT PHILLIPS

THE KEYS TO SUCCESS

1 In 2003, Billboard Magazine acknowledged BME as "The #1 Indie Label of The Year" …what's the secret of your success?

➤ Part of our thing is that we try to create new sounds. There are a couple of different ways of going at creating and *being* creative. Sometimes, it's largely

what they call market trends where whatever the market is doing, you kind of do the same thing and try to sell it again, which there is *absolutely nothing wrong with… but everybody cannot do that*. You might look at some labels or producers, who have a history of repackaging what the people are buying, reproducing it in a different way, and then reselling it to you, as opposed to what we do, *which actually takes longer* and is a little bit more difficult in some ways.

If you look back at the earlier days when we were doing *Rhythm and Quad* with "My Boo" and "Shorty Swing My Way", it was just a different sound; the "R&B Bass Sound." And nowadays, over the past few years, we are pushing the Crunk thing. The beauty of it is when I think the industry

decides, or the buyer and public decide they are looking for something new like us, and we happen to be at the right place with something new. So even though we have been pushing the Crunk thing for several years, I think there was a time that the people were just looking for something else, *and there we were*, and there was *Lil' Jon and The Eastside Boyz* pushing something new, something different.

2 What do music entrepreneurs, managers, entertainment attorneys, and/or heads of production companies *need to know* to achieve the type of success that your record company is having?

➤ Watch your reputation, and be protective of your reputation. Do your best to do *good* business, and be someone that people will find a pleasure to do business with… *as much as possible*. I guess the way we came through it as an independent; when you are coming up against major labels and even attorneys, and people who have been around for some time, the question would be, *"How can we get air-play on the radio stations when there are only 40 slots on Top 40 Radio?"* or, *"How can you get your video on BET and MTV when you have got major labels that will spend amazing amounts of money to get on?"* The only way you can compete is for the people to genuinely like you, and want to work with you. **Honestly, someone genuinely liking you often can go further than the money you spend.** I watched a guy that came into a great opportunity with us (BME) *and with the music industry in general*, and he basically *blew it* because he had a really bad attitude, and people quickly learned not to like him.

GETTING THE HOOK-UP

3 How can new artists accomplish the idea of getting hooked up with a major record label or strong indie label and what is a proven technique that works?

➤ **The best way do it right now, is to build a buzz.** This requires you getting out there being a part of the scene for whatever your market is. Being a part of the scene requires you to go out there and figure out *who are the important starters of a record.* Who are the starters *for you*? It is probably a DJ; it is probably going to the local club DJs, the local scene, as well as the guys who break records at radio.

"You have got to get into the circle with them and make relationships and be liked so that the next time you come around with a record in your hand that you've produced…they may give it a chance!"

➤ If you can do *that*, and put a little money into yourself; get some flyers, and make people aware who the record is when they hear it, then you can build a buzz. Also… *BME has signed every artist that it's signed so far, from a* **demo.** So, we have not ever signed someone that was like a friend, or a friend of a friend. Interestingly enough, everybody we signed, we had no idea who they were when we signed them.

Crime Mob got signed off of a buzz. *Trillville* sent me a demo… *I didn't know who they were.* I *saw Scrappy when I went to see Trillville, but ultimately, it was the* **demo**.

*Pictured left to right right, CD releases by
BME Artists:* **Crime Mob, Trillville & Lil Scrappy**

Additional artists signed to BME's roster include Chyna White, who sent a demo to Lil' Jon, Bohagon was a part of a group and the demo was sent to Lil' Jon, and Oobie sent in a demo

4 What is your connection with Break Em Off Record's Bone Crusher?

Bone Crusher used to be signed to BME *...for many years*. Even when we were doing the marketing and the promotion stuff, he was always a part of what we were doing. Sometimes things don't happen the way you plan for them to happen, but you're glad to see things happen *regardless*. I introduced Bone Crusher to the people at

Break Em Off, which was a new client of mine… an independent label. At that time, they went to work and just by luck of the draw at that point, Bone Crusher came out with that hit record, "Never Scared". That was a great opportunity for Bone Crusher and a great opportunity for Break Em Off.

ADVICE FOR FUTURE PRODUCERS

5 What's the *best* advice you can give for up-and-coming or future record producers who want to get hooked up on major projects?

➢ My best advice is really just recounting how things happened for us (BME). The way we got in was to find tracks that we thought were hot, find the acappella from the wax, and just remix it and send it in; so we made relationships the best we could at the labels. Use e-mails… you can pretty much get responses from e-mail. If you call, get to know assistants. If you cannot get to know the A&R *themselves*, get to know the assistants. Do some research, and actually be strategic so that you can know who is working on what projects in A&R, and who is the point person on what projects… so you can know which ones you are interested in. You'll always be able to get the assistants, because that is who answers the phone. Then make a bit of a relationship; it is about being liked. The first track that was sold through any of us was the "Cableton Tour Remix" which turned into a huge classic record for Lil' Jon, and then, it was big for Cableton as well. And Jon didn't know who Cableton was. Jon just did the record for him, got it out there, and then he actually started pushing it around and started getting some DJs to play it in Atlanta - to the extent that people wanted it …and more and more people wanted it.

Then, Searcy (Emperor Searcy) and Rob (Rob McDowell*), the first thing they

did (as producers) was when Ginuwine's first album came out, which had a song called "Pony" on it. They did like a booty-shake bass-remix to it. They sent it out to Epic. Epic heard it, they liked it, gave them a check, *a pretty small check*, but still… gave them a check that gave them an *opportunity* to

be able to say, *"Yeah, we did a Ginuwine Remix,"* and that turned into more and more work.

* Rob McDowell is one of the co-founding partners of BME. He is also a seasoned record producer and manager.

"...BE PROACTIVE AND JUST GO OUT THERE AND DO IT! Just act like you are already there. Pick something you like and just remix it. Get the acappella, and be aggressive about it!"

ADVICE FOR PRODUCERS SELLING BEATS

6 What's your best advice to be successful at selling or leasing beats?

➢ **It's about reputation.** You've got to get a reputation for having the right loops. And if you're a sample producer, "*are they looking for samples or are they looking for somebody with a good ear for samples*"...then you've got to get known for that particular thin*g*; whatever it is that you should have a reputation for. So if you've got the hot drum patterns, then you've got to get out there and build a reputation and let people know that *that's what you do*; You've got hot drum patterns or you've got a good ear for picking a little sample off of an obscure jazz record... then, *make that known* and really do it. It's difficult because everybody obviously thinks that they have the right talent, but you generally know it when you get the right response from a certain number of people.

7 What if you are part of a production crew or production company, and the "main" producer is going to use the beat that you make?

➢ If you get signed to a production company as an on-staff producer based on your agreement, it depends on what you want for yourself. You may just want to be a creative person and get a check and you don't mind if somebody else's name is on it as the producer. But I would say that if you are writing the music, try to maintain control of the writing - because that is the publishing ($). **Keep your writers credit, then that turns into your publishing check.** If you are not actually *producing* the record... but you are *writing the music*, then that is what it will (or should) be. Trillville has a song "Never Eva" which when we first came to the record, it *was* the same music that it is today, *but*, it didn't sound like it sounds. We couldn't put it out the way it *sounded*. It was produced by one of the members of Trillville, and he was just getting started as a producer, so his growth was not where it is now. So Lil' Jon actually came in and reproduced the song. If you look at the credit, you'll see *Produced by Lil' Jon*, but it says *written by Don P.* Jon didn't change the actual notes in the music; he just went in with a better ear - for what it *should've* sounded like.

VINCENT P. PHILLIPS, ESQ.
General Counsel of, and a partner of BME - Black Market Entertainment.
His Clients include Lil' Jon & The Eastside Boyz, Lil' Scrappy, Trillville, Pastor Troy, Bone Crusher & more.

ATLANTA ATTORNEYS

Select Entertainment Attorneys in Atlanta, GA

A

ALSTON & BIRD LLP

One Atlantic Center
1201 West Peachtree Street
Atlanta, GA 30309
404-881-7000 / Fax 404-881-7777
bjohnson@alston.com
www.alston.com

MARVIN ARRINGTON, JR.

775 Houston Mill Rd - Suite #4
Atlanta, Georgia 30329
404-633-3396 / Fax 404-633-4650
Mobile: 404-402-4361
Marvin@ArringtonLawFirm.com
www.ArringtonLawFirm.com

B - C

JOSEPH M. BECK

Kilpatrick, Stockton LLP
1100 Peachtree Street - Suite 2800
Atlanta, GA 30309
404-815-6406 / FAX 404-541-3126
www.kilpatrickstockton.com
JBeck@KilpatrickStockton.com

BEITCHMAN & HUDSON

215 14th St. NW
Atlanta, GA 30318
404-897-5252 / Fax 404-897-5677
www.arts-entertainmentlaw.com
hudson@arts-entertainmentlaw.com

MICHAEL BENNET

Swift Currie McGhee & Hiers LLP
1355 Peachtree Street, NE
Suite 300
Atlanta, GA 30309
404-888-6161 / Fax 404-888-6199
mike.bennett@swiftcurrie.com
www.scmhlaw.com

IVORY T. BROWN

Tower Place Center - Suite 1800
3340 Peachtree Road, NE
Atlanta, GA 30326
404-816-0244 / Fax 404-816-0744

SANDRA BROWN

Greenberg Traurig
3290 Northside Parkway, Suite 400
Atlanta, GA 30327
678-553-2100 / Fax 678-553-2212
browns@gtlaw.com
www.gtlaw.com

LISA BURNETT

999 Peachtree Street, NE
Atlanta, GA 30309-3996
404-853-8130 / Fax 404-853-8806
lsburnett@sablaw.com
www.sablaw.com

BURR & FORMAN LLP

171 Seventeenth Street, NW
Suite 1100
Atlanta, GA 30363
404-815-3000 / Fax 404-817-3244
www.burr.com

CARTER & ANSLEY

Suite 2300 – Atlantic Center Plaza
1180 W. Peachtree Street
Atlanta, GA 30303
404-658-9200 / Fax 404-658-9726
www.carteransley.com

RUSSELL CARTER, ESQ.

315 W. Ponce De Leon Ave.
Decatur, GA 30030
404-377-9900 / Fax 404-377-5131

UWONDA S. CARTER

The Carter Law Firm, LLC
83 Walton Street, Suite 203
Atlanta, GA 30303
404-954-6625 / Fax 404-954-6626
ucarter2@yahoo.com

JOHN CHRISTMAS

P.O. Box 615
Union City, GA 30291
770-374-8294 / Fax 770-306-0664
jochristm@aol.com

ALAN S. CLARKE

Clarke & Anderson, P.C.
3355 Lenox Rd Suite 750
Atlanta, GA 30326-1332
404-816-9800 / Fax 404-816-0555
jsalegal@aol.com
clarke.anderson@mindspring.com

LAWRENCE A. COOPER

Riverwood 100 - Suite 2220
3350 Riverwood Parkway
Atlanta, GA 30339
404-814-4054 / Fax 404-816-8900
lacooperatty@mindspring.com

ERIC CROONE

775 Houston Mill Rd - Suite #4
Atlanta, GA 30329
404-313-2015 / Fax 404-633-4650
Eric@musicandfilmlaw.com

REBECCA A. CULPEPPER

999 Peachtree Street, NE
Atlanta, GA 30309
404-853-8257 / Fax 404-853-8806
raculpepper@sablaw.com
www.sablaw.com

E

MONICA EWING, ESQ.

1741 Commerce Drive
Atlanta, GA 30318
404-352-0404 / Fax 404-352-0405
monicaewingesq@mindspring.com

F

JASON M. FREIER

Bondurant, Mixson & Elmore, L.L.P.
3900 One Atlantic Center,
1201 W. Peachtree St., N.W.
Atlanta, GA 30309
404-881-4100 / Fax 404-881-4111
www.bmelaw.com

G - H

TANYA M. GRAHAM, ESQ.

5295 Hwy. 78, Suite D-359
Stone Mountain, GA 30087
770-469-0802 / Fax 770-469-9868
tmgraham@mindspring.com

SHULI L. GREEN

127 Peachtree Street, N.E. Suite 300
Atlanta, GA 30303
404-222-8411 / Fax 404-222-8412
slgreen@dandrpc.com
shuligreen@yahoo.com

GREENBERG TRAURIG, LLP

The Forum
3290 Northside Parkway Suite 400
Atlanta, GA 30327
678-553-2100 / Fax 678-553-2212
www.gtlaw.com

ERIC J. HADE
999 Peachtree Street, NE
Atlanta, GA 30309
404-853-8108 / Fax 404-853-8806
ejhade@sablaw.com

HARVEY E. HALES JR.
999 Peachtree Street, NE
Atlanta, GA 30309
404-853-8077 / Fax 404-853-8806
hehales@sablaw.com

VICTOR P. HALEY
999 Peachtree Street, NE
Atlanta, GA 30309
404-853-8302 / Fax 404-853-8806
vphaley@sablaw.com
www.sablaw.com

HAWKINS & PARNELL
4000 SunTrust Plaza
303 Peachtree Street, N.E.
Atlanta, GA 30308-3243
404-614-7400 / Fax 404-614-7500
www.hawkinsparnell.com

A. KENNETH HEWITT, ESQ.
Hewitt, Katz and Stepp
945 E. Paces Ferry Road, Suite 2610
Atlanta, GA 30326
404-240-0400 / Fax 404-240-0401
khewitt@atlantalawofc.com

HIGGINS & DUBNER
3333 Peachtree Rd. NE, Suite 230
Atlanta, GA 30326
404-264-1011 / Fax 404-264-1044

HOLLAND & KNIGHT LLP
1201 West Peachtree Street, N.E.
One Atlantic Center, Suite 2000
Atlanta, GA 30309
404-817-8500 / Fax 404-881-0470
www.hklaw.com

HUNTON & WILLIAMS
Bank of America Plaza
600 Peachtree Street, N.E., Suite 4100
Atlanta, GA 30308

404-888-4000
kpowell@hunton.com
www.hunton.com

K – L - M

JOEL A. KATZ
Greenberg Traurig, LLP
The Forum
3290 Northside Parkway, NW
Suite 400
Atlanta, GA 30327
678-553-2222 / Fax 678-553-2212
katzj@gtlaw.com
www.gtlaw.com

JUSTIN KERENYI
Hall, Booth, Smith & Slover
1180 West Peachtree NW
Atlantic Center Plaza -Suite 900
Atlanta, GA 30309-3479
404-404-954-6961 / Fax 404-954-5020
jkerenyi@hbss.net
www.hbss.net

KILPATRICK STOCKTON LLP
Suite 2800, 1100 Peachtree Street
Atlanta, GA 30309
404-815-6500 / Fax 404-815-6555
www.kilpatrickstockton.com

JANNE' MCKAMEY-LOPES
44 Broad Street NW, Suite 501
Atlanta, GA 30303-0060
404-589-9000 / Fax 404-832-4120
firm@lopesmckameylopes.com
www.lopesmckameylopes.com

CLIFF LOVETTE
1800 Peachtree St. NW
Atlanta, GA 30309-2517
404-355-9000 / Fax 404-475-0680
cliff.lovette@lovettegroup.com

DANTE A. MARSHALL
D. Marshall Entertainment Group, LLC
Atlanta, Georgia
404-794-4582 / 614-893-5618
www.dmentertainmentgroup.com

JONATHAN MASON
One Atlantic Center, Suite 3500
1201 West Peachtree Street
Atlanta, GA 30309
404-888-7466 / Fax 404-870-4856
jmason@wcsr.com
www.wcsr.com

EPHRAIM MICHAEL
Michael Law Firm
2233 Lake Park Drive, Suite 220
Smyrna, GA 30080
770-433-1666 / Fax 770-433-0599
ephraimm@yahoo.com

CARMEN SUAREZ MILLS
2100 Riveredge Pkwy, Suite 700
Atlanta, GA 30328
770-956-1984 / Fax 770-956-1381
csmills@mindspring.com
www.dwslaw.com

KENDALL MINTER, ESQ.
Minter & Associates, LLC
5398 E. Mountain St.
Stone Mountain, GA 30083
770-879-7400 / Fax 770-879-5695
BESLA Co-founder
kamlaw@aol.com
www.kendallminteresq.com

C. R. MCQUEEN
2970 Clairmont Road, Suite 1010
Atlanta, GA 30329
404-522-3541
404-420-5913 / Fax 404-522-3677
crmcqueen@gbjm.com
www.gbjmlaw.com

P

VINCENT PHILLIPS, ESQ.
BME Recordings
2144 Hills Avenue - D2
Atlanta, GA 30318 USA
404-367-8130 / Fax 404-367-8630

LAW OFFICES OF VINCE PHILLIPS
PO Box 20084
Atlanta, GA 30325
404-522-8000 / Fax 404-522-7643
VphilEsq@aol.com
www.bmerecordings.com

POWELL, GOLDSTEIN, FRAZER & MURPHY LLP
191 Peachtree Street, N.E., 16th Floor
Atlanta, GA 30303
404-572-6600 / Fax 404-572-6999
www.pgfm.com

R - S - T

PHIL RANSOM, ESQ.
P. O. Box 42346
Atlanta, GA 30311
404-472-9960 / Fax 404-472-9994
ransom11@bellsouth.net

JESS ROSEN
Suite 400, The Forum
3290 Northside Parkway
Atlanta, GA 30327
678-553-2230 / Fax 678-553-2231
RosenJ@gtlaw.com
www.gtlaw.com

ROBERT ROSENBLOUM
Greenberg Traurig, LLP
Suite 400, The Forum
3290 Northside Parkway
Atlanta, GA 30327
678-553-2100 / Fax 678-553-2212
www.gtlaw.com

SCOTT D. SANDERS
Peachtree 25th Building, S. Tower
1718 Peachtree St NW
Atlanta, GA 30309
404-873-4422 / Fax 404-873-4480
scott@entlaw.com

JAMIE SHIPP
3290 Northside Parkway
Suite 400
Atlanta, GA 30327
678-553-2100 / Fax 678-553-2212
shippj@gtlaw.com
www.gtlaw.com

STEVEN SIDMAN
Greenberg Traurig
3290 Northside Parkway
The Forum - Suite 400
Atlanta, GA 30327
678-553-2100 / Fax 678-553-2212
www.gtlaw.com

JEFFREY SLADKUS
One Atlantic Center, Suite 3500
1201 West Peachtree Street
Atlanta, GA 30309
404-962-7538 / Fax 404-879-2995
jsladkus@wcsr.com

VERNON SLAUGHTER
1741 Commerce Drive
Atlanta, GA 30318
404-355-2755 / Fax 404-355-2720
slaughterv@bellsouth.net

ELLEN SMITH
999 Peachtree Street, NE
Atlanta, GA 30309-3996
404-853-8583 / Fax 404-853-8806
www.sablaw.com

SMITH, GAMBRELL & RUSSELL
Suite 3100, Promenade II
1230 Peachtree St, N.E.
Atlanta, GA 30309
404-815-3500 / Fax 404-815-3509
www.sgrlaw.com

NONI ELLISON SOUTHALL
Counsel - Turner Entertainment Group
Atlanta, GA
404-885-4552
BESLA Member
noni.ellison@turner.com

H CRAIG STAFFORD
3575 Piedmont Road NE
15 Piedmont Center, Suite 1560
Atlanta, GA 30305
404-264-1292 / Fax 404-264-0161
craigstafford@matthewssteellaw.com

SUTHERLAND ASBILL & BRENNAN LLP
999 Peachtree Street, N.E.
Atlanta, GA 30309-3996
404-853-8000 / Fax 404-853-8806
www.sablaw.com

SWIFT, CURRIE, MCGHEE & HIERS
1355 Peachtree Street, N.E., Suite 300
Atlanta, GA 30309-3238
404-874-8800
www.swiftcurrie.com

W

KARL M. WASHINGTON
The Washington Law Firm
2818 East Point Street, Suite 2B
East Point, GA 30344
404-768-3963 / Fax 404-768-3966
karlwashington@att.net

WILLIAM K. WHITNER
600 Peachtree St., N.E.
Twenty-Fourth Floor
Atlanta, GA 30308
404-815-2228 / Fax 404-815-2424
kwhitner@cswebmail.com

DONALD M. WOODARD
Greenberg Traurig
Suite 400, The Forum
3290 Northside Parkway
Atlanta, GA 30327
678-553-2270 / Fax 678-553-2212
woodardd@gtlaw.com
www.gtlaw.com

For additional listings please visit us on-line at: www.MusicPowers.com

LOS ANGELES ATTORNEYS

Select Entertainment Attorneys in Los Angeles, CA

A - B

AKIN GUMP STRAUSS HAUER & FELD
2029 Century Park East - Suite 2400
Los Angeles, CA 90067
310-229-1000 / Fax 310-229-1001
www.akingump.com

ALPERIN & GOLLAND, LLP
11355 W. Olympic Boulevard, Suite 200
Los Angeles, CA 90064
310-444-7505 / Fax 310-444-7885
MHGolland@aol.com

ALSCHULER, GROSSMAN, SUITEIN & KAHAN
1620 26th Street – 4th Floor- N. Tower
Santa Monica, CA 90404
310-907-1000 / Fax 310-907-2000
www.agsk.com

LARKIN ARNOLD, JR.
280 S Beverly Dr - Suite 206
Beverly Hills, CA 90212
310-858-8330

BAKER & HOSTETLER
333 South Grand Avenue, Suite 1800
Los Angeles, CA 90071
213-975-1600 / Fax 213-975-1740
www.bakerlaw.com

STEPHEN D. BARNES
Barnes Morris Klein Mark & Yorn
1424 Second Street, Third Floor
Santa Monica, CA 90401
310-319-3900 / Fax 310-319-3999
www.bmkylaw.com

BERGER KAHN
4215 Glencoe Ave., Second Floor
Marina Del Rey, CA 90292
310-821-9000 / Fax 310-578-6178
www.bergerkahn.com

ARTHUR BERGGREN
169 Pier Ave.
Santa Monica, CA 90405
310-392-3088 / Fax 310-392-0931
aberggren@aol.com

BERGER KAHN
4215 Glencoe Ave., Second Floor
Marina Del Rey, CA 90292
310-821-9000 / Fax 310-578-6178
www.bergerkahn.com

JACOB BLOOM
150 S Rodeo Dr – 3rd Floor
Beverly Hills, CA 90212
310-859-6800 / Fax 310-659-2788

LEROY BOBBITT
Bobbitt & Roberts
1620 26th St. - Suite 150 S.
Santa Monica, CA 90404
310-315-7150 / Fax 310-315-7159
Contact: dfrazier@bobroblaw.com

AL BOELTER
330 Washington Blvd., # 400
Marina Del Rey, CA 90292
310-822-5037 / Fax 310-823-4325
boltperr@comcast.net

BRYAN CAVE LLP
120 Broadway, Suite 300
Santa Monica, CA 90401-2386
310-576-2100 / Fax 310-576-2200
www.bryancave.com

KENNETH BURRY
Greenberg Traurig
2450 Colorado Avenue -Suite 400E
Santa Monica, CA 90404
310-586-7810 / Fax 310-586-7800
www.gtlaw.com

C

CARROLL, GUIDO & GROFFMAN, LLP
9111 Sunset Boulevard
Los Angeles, CA 90069
310-271-0241 / Fax 310-271-0775
www.ccgglaw.com

JIM CHARNE
425 Idaho Avenue, Unit 9
Santa Monica, CA 90403
310-458-9345
www.charnelaw.com
charne@usa.net

CHRISTENSEN, MILLER, FINK, JACOBS, GLASER, WEIL & SHAPIRO, LLP
10250 Constellation Blvd., 19th Floor
Los Angeles, CA 90067
310-553-3000 / Fax 310-556-2920
www.chrismill.com

JAY COOPER
Greenberg Traurig
2450 Colorado Avenue - Suite 400 East
Santa Monica, CA 90404
310-586-7888 / Fax 310-586-7800
www.gtlaw.com

CROWE & ROGAN LLP
100 Wilshire Blvd. – 200
Santa Monica, CA 90401
310-917-4500 / Fax 310-917-5677
www.croweday.com

D - E - F

DAVIS, DIXON & KIRBY LLP
9200 W. Sunset Blvd., Penthouse 25
Los Angeles, CA 90069
310-278-5703 / Fax 310-278-7306
www.davisdixon.com

BRENDA FEIGEN
KENOFF & MACHTINGER, LLP
1901 Avenue of the Stars - Suite 1775
Los Angeles, CA 90067
310-552-0808 / Fax 310-277-0653
bfeigen@feigenlaw.com
www.feigenlaw.com

BERTRAM FIELDS
Greenberg Glusker
1900 Avenue of the Stars
21st Floor
310-553-3610 / Fax 310-553-0687
bfields@ggfirm.com
www.ggfirm.com

FOLEY & LARDNER LLP
2029 Century Park East, Suite 3500
Los Angeles, CA 90067
310-277-2223 / Fax 310-557-8475
www.foley.com

SANDY FOX
Fox Law Group
14724 Ventura Blvd - Penthouse Suite
Sherman Oaks, CA 91403
818-461-1740 / Fax 818-461-1744
www.foxlawgroup.com

G

MARIO GONZALEZ
2450 Colorado Avenue - Suite 400 East
Santa Monica, CA 90404
310-586-7815 / Fax 310-586-7800
www.gtlaw.com

GORRY MEYER & RUDD LLP
2049 Century Park East, Suite 2100
Los Angeles, CA 90067
310-277-5967 / Fax 310-277-5968
thefirm@gorrymeyer.com
www.gorrymeyer.com

GREENBERG TRAURIG LLP
2450 Colorado Avenue
Suite 400 East
Santa Monica, CA 90404
310-586-7700 / Fax 310-586-7800
www.gtlaw.com

H - I - J

HAHN & BOLSON, LLP
1000 Wilshire Boulevard, Suite 1600
Los Angeles, CA   90017-5704
213-630-2600 / Fax 213-622-6670
www.hahnbolsonllp.com

AKIN GUMP STRAUSS HAUER & FELD
2029 Century Park East - Suite 2400
Los Angeles, CA 90067
310-229-1034 / Fax 310-229-1001
phaviland@akingump.com
www.akingump.com

ULESES C. HENDERSON, JR.
Foley & Lardner LLP
2029 Century Park East, Suite 3500
Los Angeles, CA 90067
310-975-7961 / Fax 310-557-8475
uhenderson@foley.com

ISAACMAN, KAUFMAN & PAINTER
8484 Wilshire Blvd., Suite 850
Beverly Hills, CA 90211
323-782-7700 / Fax 323-782-7744
www.ikplaw.com

CHANNING JOHNSON
Akin Gump Strauss Hauer & Feld
2029 Century Park East
Suite 2400
Los Angeles, CA 90067-3012
310-229-1075 / Fax 310-229-1001
cjohnson@akingump.com

JOHNSON & RISHWAIN
12121Wilshire Blvd., Suite 1201
Los Angeles, CA 90025
310-826-2410 / Fax 310-826-5450
www.jrllp.com

K

KATTEN MUCHIN ZAVIS ROSENMAN
2029 Century Park East - Suite 2600
Los Angeles, CA 90067-3012
310-788-4400 / Fax 310-788-4471
www.kmz.com

KAYE SCHOLER, LLP
1999 Ave. of the Stars, Suite 1600
Los Angeles, CA 90067-6048
310-788-1000 / Fax 310-788-1200
www.kayscholer.com

KEATS MCFARLAND & WILSON LLP
9720 Wilshire Blvd - Penthouse Suite
Beverly Hills, CA 90212
310-248-3830 / Fax 310-860-0363
www.kmwlaw.com

KIRKPATRICK & LOCKHART, LLP
10100 Santa Monica Blvd.- 7th Fl
Los Angeles, CA 90067
310-552-5000 / Fax 310-552-5001
www.kl.com

KLEINBERG & LERNER, LLP
2049 Century Park East, Suite 1080
Los Angeles, Ca 90067
310-557-1511 / Fax 310-557-1540
www.kleinberglerner.com

KMZ ROSENMAN
2029 Century Park East, Suite 2600
Los Angeles, CA 90067
310-788-4400 / Fax 310-788-4471
www.kmzr.com

RAAQIM A. S. KNIGHT
Manatt, Phelps & Phillips
11355 W. Olympic Blvd
Los Angeles, CA 90064
310-312-4323 / Fax 310-312-4224
rknight@manatt.com
www.manatt.com

L - M

DINA LAPOLT
9000 Sunset Blvd., Suite 800
West Hollywood, CA 90069
310-858-0922 Fax 310-858-0933
www.lapoltlaw.com

LATHAM & WATKINS
633 W. 5th St. Suite 4000
Los Angeles, CA 90071-2007
213-485-1234 / Fax 213-891-8763

LAVELY & SINGER
2049 Century Park East, Suite 2400
Los Angeles, CA 90067
310- 556-3501 / Fax 310-556-3615
www.lavelysinger.com

RONALD LEBOW
12400 Wilshire Blvd, Suite 400
Los Angeles, CA 90025
310-571-9141 / Fax 310-455-2407

RICHARD LEHER
2450 Colorado Avenue - Suite 400E
Santa Monica, CA 90404
310-586-6501 / Fax 310-586-0501
www.gtlaw.com

LENARD, BRISBIN & KLOTZ
1100 Glendon Ave., Suite 1650
Los Angeles, CA 90024
310-806-4190 / Fax 310-806-4159
alenard@lbkmusic.com

LEE & KAUFMAN, LLP
633 West Fifth St. – 51st Fl.
Los Angeles, CA 90071
213-239-9400 / Fax 213-239-9409
www.lklaw.net

LOEB & LOEB LLP
10100 Santa Monica Boulevard, #2200
Los Angeles, CA 90067
310-282-2000 / Fax 310-282-2200
www.loeb.com

JAY W. MACINTOSH
1925 Century Park East - Suite 500
Los Angeles, CA   90067
310-789-2034 / Fax 310-471-8802
www.jaywmacintoshlaw.com

MANATT, PHELPS & PHILLIPS, LLP
11355 W. Olympic Blvd
Los Angeles, CA 90064
310-312-4000 / Fax 310-312-4224
www.manatt.com

MAYER, GLASSMAN & GAINES
11726 San Vincente Blvd., Suite 400
Los Angeles, CA 90049
310-207-0007 / Fax 310-207-3578

BEN MCLANE, ESQ.
McLane & Wong
20501 Ventura Blvd., Suite 217
Woodland Hills, CA 91364
818-587-6801 / Fax 818-587-6802
bcmclane@aol.com
www.benmclane.com

MITCHELL, SILBERBERG & KNUPP
11377 W. Olympic Blvd.
Los Angeles, CA 90064
310-312-2000 / Fax 310-312-3100
www.msk.com

MORRISON & FOERSUITER, LLP
555 West Fifth Street, Suite 3500
Los Angeles, CA 90013-1024
213-892-5200 / Fax 213-892-5454
www.mofo.com

O - P - R

O'DONNELL & SHAEFFER, LLP
550 South Hope Street - Suite 2000
Los Angeles, CA 90071
213-532-2000 / Fax 213-532-2020
www.oslaw.com

DONALD PASSMAN
Gang, Tyre, Ramer & Brown
132 South Rodeo Drive
Beverly Hills, CA 90212
310-777-4800 / Fax 310-777-4801

**PAUL, HASTINGS, JANOFSKY
& WALKER LLP**
515 South Flower Street – 25th Floor
Los Angeles, CA 90071
213-683-6000 / Fax 213-627-0705

L. LEE PHILLIPS
Manatt, Phelps & Phillips
11355 West Olympic Boulevard
Los Angeles, CA, 90064
310-312-4111 / Fax 310-312-4224
lphillips@manatt.com
www.manatt.com

PIERCE GORMAN, LLP
9100 Wilshire Blvd, Suite 225 E. Tower
Los Angeles, CA 90212
310-274-9191 / Fax 310-274-9151
www.piercegorman.com

BRUCE M. RAMER
Gang, Tyre, Ramer & Brown
132 South Rodeo Drive
Beverly Hills, CA 90212
310-777-4800 / Fax 310-777-4801

VIRGIL ROBERTS, ESQ.
Bobbitt & Roberts
1620 26th St. - Suite 150 S.
Santa Monica, CA 90404
310-315-7150 / Fax 310-315-7159
Contact: dfrazier@bobroblaw.com

S – Thru - Z

SCHLEIMER & FRUENDLICH
9100 Wilshire Blvd Suite 700W
Beverly Hills, CA 90212
310-273-9807 / Fax 310-273-9809
www.schleimerlaw.com

NINA L. SHAW
2120 Colorado Avenue, Suite 200
Santa Monica, California 90404
310-979-7920 / Fax 310-979-7999

STANTON L. STEIN
Alschuler Grossman Stein & Kahan LLP
The Water Garden - 1620 26th Street
Fourth Floor, North Tower
Santa Monica, CA 90404
310-907-1000 / Fax 310-907-2000
www.agsk.com

GARY STIFFELMAN
1801 Century Park West
Los Angeles, CA 90067
310-552-3388 / Fax 310-553-7068

TISDALE & NICHOLSON, LLP
2029 Century Park East, Suite 900
Los Angeles, CA 90067
310-286-1260 / Fax 310-286-2351
www.t-nlaw.com

VALENSI ROSE & MAGARAM PLC
2029 Century Park East - Suite 2050
Los Angeles, CA 90067
310-277-8011 / Fax 310-277-1706
www.vrmlaw.com

GARY A. WATSON, ESQ.
1875 Century Park East, Suite 1000
Los Angeles, CA 90067-2533
310-284-3400 ext. 269
gwatson@huronlaw.com

VENICE A. WONG, ESQ.
McLane & Wong
20501 Ventura Blvd., Suite 217
Woodland Hills, CA 91364
818-587-6801 / Fax 818-587-6802
www.benmclane.com

LEE YOUNG, JR.
5900 Wilshire Blvd. – Suite 2750
Los Angeles, CA 90036
323-933-4100 / Fax 323-933-4157

KENNETH ZIFFREN
Ziffren, Brittenham, Branca, Fischer,
Gilbert-Lurie, Stiffelman & Cook, LLP
1801 Century Park West
Los Angeles, CA 90067
310-552-3388 / Fax 310-553-7068

**ZIMMERMAN, ROSENFELD,
GERSH & LEEDS**
9107 Wilshire Blvd., Suite 400
Beverly Hills, CA 90210
310-278-7560 / Fax 310-273-5602
www.beverlyhillslaw.com

For additional listings please visit us
on-line at: www.MusicPowers.com

NEW YORK ATTORNEYS

Music Powers

Select Entertainment Attorneys in New York

A

DANIEL AARON, PC
New York, NY 10022
437 Madison Avenue, 4th Floor
212-684-4466 / Fax 212-684-5566
daaron@earthlink.net
www.djaaronlaw.com

ABRAMS, GARFINKEL & ROSEN LLP
237 W. 35th St., 4th Floor
New York, NY 10001
212-201-1170 / Fax 212-201-1171
jmisher@agmblaw.com
www.agmblaw.com

CHARLOTTE ANDERSON-BEDFORD
305 Madison Ave., Suite 449
New York, NY 10165
212-886-9024 / Fax 212-957-1912
charjurisdoc@aol.com

CHRIS ANDERSON
11th St. - Suite 6A
New York, NY 10009
917-287-8112 / Fax 212-614-8855
cgandersonlaw@nyc.rr.com

B

SCOTT L. BAKER, LLC
200 Park Avenue South, Suite 1614
New York, NY 10003-7760
212-758-2020 / Fax 212-758-2025
www.scottbakerlaw.com

STEVEN C. BEER
Greenberg Traurig
200 Park Avenue
New York, NY 10166
212-801-9294 / Fax 212-801-6400
www.gtlaw.com

BELDOCK LEVINE & HOFFMAN LLP
99 Park Avenue
New York, NY 10016-1503
212-490-0400 or 800-275-4977
www.blhny.com

BEINSTOCK & MICHAEL, PC
250 W. 57th St., Suite 1917
New York, NY 10107
212-399-0099 / Fax 212-399-1278
rsbesq@aol.com

BLANK ROME LLP
The Chrysler Building
405 Lexington Avenue
New York, New York 10174
212- 885-5000 / Fax 212-885-5001
www.BlankRome.com

BOMSER & STUCKNICKY, LLP
853 Broadway, Room 1001
New York, NY 10003
212-254-0500 / Fax 212-254-0003
abomser@pipeline.com

LARRY BRAY
1001 Ave. of the Americas, 4th Floor
New York, NY 10018
212-244-8060 / Fax 212-244-8070
www.braylawoffices.com

JOEL BROOKS & ASSOCIATES
1500 Broadway
New York, NY 10036
212-730-8015

SUSAN P. BUTLER
295 Greenwich St., Ste 350
New York, NY 10007
212-786-9425
www.susanbutler.com

C

ROBERT A. CELESTIN
250 West 57th Street, Suite 2331
New York, NY 10107
212-262-1103 / 212-262-1173
www.intelligentmusic.com

WALLACE COLLINS, ESQ.
254 West 54th St. - 14th Floor
New York, NY 10019
212-245-7300 Ext. 125 / Fax 212-586-5175
wallace@wallacecollins.com
www.wallacecollins.com

COUDERT BROS, LLP
1114 Ave of the Americas
New York, NY 10036
212-626-4400 / Fax 212-626-4120
www.coudert.com

**COWAN, DEBAETS,
ABRAHAMS & SHEPPARD**
41 Madison Avenue, 34th Floor
New York, NY 10010
212-790-9200 / Fax 212-575-0671
www.cdas.com

EDWARD CRAMER
110 E. 59th - Suite 3201
New York, NY 10022
212-421-3350 / Fax 212-826-9315

CUTLER & SEDLMAYR
200 Park Ave S., 1408
New York, NY 10003
212-925-3456 / Fax 212-925-0554
www.csentlaw.com

D

DEDRA S. DAVIS
26 Broadway, Suite 400
New York, NY 10004
877-MUSIC LW
DedraDavis@musiclw.com

F

**FRANKLIN, WEINRIB
RUDELL & VASSALLO P.C.**
488 Madison Avenue, 18th Floor
New York, NY 10022
212-935-5500 / Fax 212-308-0642

FRANKFURT, KURNIT, KLEIN, & SELZ
488 Madison Ave
NY, NY 10022
212-980-0120 / Fax 212-593-9175
www.fkkslaw.com

G

GALLET DREYER & BERKEY
845 Third Avenue - 8th Floor
New York, NY 10022-6601
212-935-3131
www.gdblaw.com

GREENBERG TRAURIG, LLP
885 Third Avenue - 21st Floor
New York, NY 10022
212-801-2100 / Fax 212-688-2449
www.gtlaw.com

GREENBERG TRAURIG, LLP
MetLife Building
200 Park Avenue
New York, NY 10166
212-801-9200 / Fax 212-801-6400
www.gtlaw.com

ALLEN J. GRUBMAN
Grubman Indursky & Schindler, P.C.
Carnegie Hall Tower, 152 West 57th Street
New York, NY 10019
212-554-0400 / Fax 212-554-0444

J

MARC JACOBSON
Greenberg Traurig
200 Park Avenue
New York, NY 10166
212-801-9200 / Fax 212-801-6400
www.gtlaw.com

K

KATTEN MUCHIN ZAVIS ROSENMAN
KMZ Rosenman
575 Madison Avenue
New York, NY 10022
212-940-8800 / Fax 212-940-8776
www.kmzr.com

KAUFF, MCLAIN & MCGUIRE
950 3rd St., 14th Floor
New York, NY 10022
212-644-1010 / Fax 212-644-1936
www.kmm.com

HENRY KAUFMAN
11 East 44th Street, Suite 900
New York, NY 10017
212-880-0842 / Fax 212-983-0415
hrkaufman@aol.com

EDWARD KELMAN
100 Park Ave., 20th Floor
New York, NY 10017
212-371-9490 / Fax 212-750-1356

KENYON & KENYON
One Broadway
New York, NY 10004-1050
212-425-7200 / Fax 212-425-5288
www.kenyon.com

MATTHEW L. KLETTER
183 Madison Ave
New York, NY 10016
212-726-0090 / Fax 212-447-6677
mkletter@msn.com

ALAN H. KRESS
36 West 44th Street, Suite 1111
New York, NY 10036-8102
212-944-6622 / Fax 212-944-0487
ahkress@aol.com

STEPHEN KOPITKO
1780 Broadway, Ste 805
New York NY 10019
212-245-6720 / Fax 212-245-2918
vibelaw@aol.com

L

LOEB & LOEB LLP
345 Park Avenue
New York, NY 10154-0037
212-407-4000 / Fax 212-407-4990
www.loeb.com

M

MASUR & ASSOCIATES
101 E. 15th St.
New York NY 10003
212-931-8220 / Fax 212-931-8221

MANATT, PHELPS & PHILLIPS, LLP
7 Times Square
New York, NY 10036
212-790-4500 / Fax 212-790-4545
www.manatt.com

MCGUIRE WOODS LLP
9 West 57th Street Suite 1620
New York, NY 10019-2602
212-548-2100
www.mcguirewoods.com

MCGUIRE WOODS LLP
Park Avenue Tower, 65 East 55th Street
New York, NY 10022-3219
212-421-5555
www.mcguirewoods.com

MCLAUGHLIN & STERN LLP
260 Madison Ave
New York, NY 10016
212-448-1100 / Fax 212-448-0066

MORRISON & FOERSTER
1290 Avenue of the Americas
New York, NY 10104-0050
212-468-8000 / Fax 212-468-7900
www.mofo.com

L. LONDELL MCMILLAN
156 w. 56th St., 10th Floor
New York, NY 10019
212-399-8900 / Fax 212-399-0337

MATTHEW J. MIDDLETON, ESQ.
475 Fifth Avenue, Suite 1516
New York, NY 10017
212- 573-8100 / Fax 212-573-6113
BESLA Member
m.middleton@middletonlawgroup.com

ANTHONY MULRAIN
Greenberg Traurig
200 Park Avenue
New York, NY 10166
212-801-9200 / Fax 212-801-6400
www.gtlaw.com

THE MUSIC GROUP LLC
250 W. 57th St Suite 917
New York, NY 10107
212-245-4125 / Fax 212-245-6293
www.themusiclawgroup.com

O

CHARLES B. ORTNER
1585 Broadway
New York, NY, 10036-8299
212-969-3000 / Fax 212-969-2900
www.proskauer.com
P

PADDELL, NADDELL, FINE, WEINBERGER
156 W. 57th St. 4th Floor
New York, NY 10019
212-957-0900

**PAUL, HASTINGS,
JANOFSKY & WALKER LLP**
75 E. 55th Street - First Floor
New York, NY 10022
212-318-6000 / Fax 212-319-4090
www.paulhastings.com

**PAUL, WEISS, RUFKIND,
WHARTON & GARRISON**
1285 Ave of the Americas
New York, NY 10019
212-373-3000 / Fax 212-757-3990
www.paulweiss.com

R

ALEX T. ROSHUK
325 Eighth Street
Brooklyn, NY 11215-3313
718-788-6696
www.roshuklaw.com

**RUBIN, BAILIN, ORTOLI,
MAYER & BAKER, LLP**
405 Park Ave., 15th Floor
NY, NY 10022
212-935-0900 / Fax 212-826-9307

S

JENNIFER SCHWARTZ, ESQ.
121 St. Mark's Pl., Ste 14
New York, NY 10009
917-622-6606 / Fax 212-268-9686

SEDLMAYR & ASSOCIATES
200 Park Ave. S. - Suite1408
New York, NY 10003
212-925-3456 / Fax 212-925-0554

**SELVERNE, MANDELBAUM
& MINTZ, LLP**
1775 Broadway, Suite 2300
New York, NY 10019-1903
212-259-3900

SERLING, ROOKS & FERRERA LLP
254 W. 54th W. 54th St., 14th Floor
New York, NY 10019
212-245-7300 / Fax 212-586-5175

STUART SILFEN, P.C
488 Madison Ave., 17th Floor
New York, NY 10022
212-826-5548 / Fax 212-688-1292
ssilfen@fkkslaw.com

NOEL L. SILVERMAN
200 Park Avenue South, Suite 1614
New York, NY 10003-7760
212-758-2020 / Fax 212-758-2025
www.nls-law.com

**STROOCK & STROOCK
& LAVAN LLP**
180 Maiden Lane
NY, NY 10038-4982
212-806-5400
www.stroock.com

T

ANDREW TAVEL
Greenberg Traurig
200 Park Avenue
New York, NY 10166
212-801-9200 / Fax 212-801-6400
www.gtlaw.com

PETER M. THALL
1740 Broadway. 2nd fl
New York, NY 10019
212-245-6221 / Fax 212-245-6406
www.thallentlaw.com

W

JON M. WAXMAN, ESQ.
302 W. 12th St.
New York, NY 10014
212-929-2562 / Fax 212-229-1625
jonwaxman@compuserve.com

WEIL, GOTSHAL & MANGES
767 Fifth Ave
New York, NY 10153
212-310-8000 / Fax 212-310-8700
www.weil.com

WHITE, FLEISHNER & FINO
140 Broadway, 36th Floor
New York, NY 10005
212-487-9700 / Fax 212-487-9777
www.wfflaw.com

WLODINGUER, ERK & CHANZIS
15 E. 26th St., Suite 1803
New York, NY 10010
212-683-4200 / Fax 212-683-4329
www.wecnyc.com

For more listings in other cities – visit
us on-line at: www.MusicPowers.com

Music Powers

VOLUNTEER LAWYERS FOR THE ARTS

Never make the excuse that you cannot afford an attorney. In reality, you can't afford NOT to have an attorney... especially when making crucial career decisions and/or contract(s) needing the attention of a professional counselor. If you are thinking you can't pay for some type of legal services, *think again*. Volunteer Lawyers provide starving artists with workshops, arbitration services, nonprofit incorporation, copyright information, contract negotiation(s), tax information, educational resources and more.

GEORGIA

SOUTHEAST VOLUNTEER LAWYERS FOR THE ARTS
Bureau of Cultural Affairs
675 Ponce De Leon Ave. NE, #550
Atlanta, GA 30308
404-873-3911
www.glarts.org

CALIFORNIA

1212 Broadway St., Ste. 834
Oakland, CA 94612
510-444-6351

Fort Mason Center, Building C, Room 255
San Francisco, CA 94123
415-775-7200

1641 18th St.
Santa Monica, CA 90404
310-998-5590
www.calawyersforthearts.org

NEW YORK

19 Clinton Ave.
Albany NY 12207
518-449-5380

1 E. 53rd St., 6th Fl.
New York, NY 10022
212-319-2787
www.vlany.org

Music Powers

HIRING A PRODUCER

Possibly the most important, and sometimes most challenging step in getting your music done *right*, will be securing the help of a good producer

INTRODUCTION

The Producers section you are about to explore has been put together to help artists that *do not* produce themselves. This chapter, although helpful to anyone in the music business, is primarily an informative guideline for those who are *in need of a produce*r. Later on, in the Producer's Forum, we will go over some great advice and key information that artists/producers or stand-alone producers may want to know more about in relation to *"record production."* For now, we will discuss the importance, the role, and also some of the practical things to consider for getting a Hip Hop or R&B/Pop music producer on your team.

...By Definition: What is a Producer?

• *A producer is... 1. One that produces, especially a person or organization that produces goods or services for sale. 2. One who supervises and controls the creation and public presentation of a project, or similar work. (Courtesy of Dictionary.com)*

DO YOU REALLY NEED A PRODUCER?

Usually you are going to need the help of a good producer, just like most major label artists need help when making a record. Very seldom will you see *any* successful records made on *any* major record labels or even a strong independent, without the help of a *qualified* producer. I say qualified, because having someone who knows what they are doing to guide and help you make your music come together should not be left into the hands of someone without skills in record *production*. And don't just think I'm trying to say that you need a producer simply because that's the way other artists do it. I'm saying that you need a producer; *a good producer,* because you want to make sure that you maximize your chances of getting your music to "sound" it's best. Also, beyond the skills required to produce a record *effectively*, a producer is also there to be objective, which is incredibly hard to do all by *yourself*. And there are some *new artist* trying to skip the idea of hiring a producer for help, but if you *honestly* look at what has to happen musically (and sometimes politically too) to insure the success of a project, an artist might be asking for self-inflicted failure by trying to do *too much*, and being "too close" to their own music to be impartial. In other words, most guys that are great producers can usually look at the concept of what has to happen from a discerning musical, creative, *and marketing approach*. And this is a skill and an art in itself. Artists need producers as much as most actors need good directing. You will most times *need* that "heads-up" professional to be on the project to assure it having a *better* chance of success anyway. And plus, producers many times deal with everything from writing and creating the idea for the song, to dealing with the human variables of *attitudes, emotion* and the *atmosphere of working with all the many different people attached to the project*; Managers, A&R, Radio and Club DJs, Musicians, and of course, the actual artist themselves. And just so you know, there is an *art* to producing, just like there is an art to sampling, dj scratching, singing, rapping and playing an instrument. And even though technology does allow many artists (and non-artists) who never thought that they could make music productions "sound" pretty good...*without* having a producer... in truth, most of it is far from being *"well-produced"*, or good enough to release, or give a contract where a Company's *revenue* is at stake. So if you are an artist, I believe you should *highly* consider taking the most *sensible* approach to getting your record or demo project completed; meaning that you'll need to find either a reputable and *experienced* producer, or a hot new, *up-and-coming* producer that has "*reel*" evidence of developed skills to make a song sound *finished*. Or at least find a producer who will sell or license you some great tracks to use.

..."Reel Evidence?"

- *A Producer's "Reel" is a compilation of snippets or completed songs that is used as "evidence" of what the producer has done to let potential clients; artists and different music companies hear for work opportunities. This reel is basically a producer's demo reel, and will usually be accompanied by his discography (record & project credentials). This "reel" will usually contain the best of his present and past music projects, all to show a demonstration of his ability, his particular sound and his production credits. Of course, if he's got some great credibility and also has songs currently available on the market, then he might just tell you to drop by your local record store to pick a copy of whatever he has out.*

THE RIGHT PRODUCER

Whenever you start putting your songs together, and you plan for these songs to be heard by the *rest of the world*, whatever your music "sounds like", will ultimately need to be the best way of representing yourself...*as far as records go*. And the main person responsible for *how* your music turns out or sounds like - will be your producer. Having a great producer on your team *will make the difference* in "what" your music is going to end up as a finished musical representation of your talent and songs. And for that reason, if you are an artist, and you are *serious* about making the best record or demo you can, know that getting the *right* producer working with you, can many times *make or break the outcome of your whole project*. So at some point, it will be very important that you get a producer *with some skills …and a pretty good track record doesn't hurt either*.

CREDIBILITY

You also need to recognize *that* your producer's past and present music credentials and successes may increase your *own opportunity* to get your finished production(s) into the right hands. His credibility may also get other industry insiders to take *you* a little more serious about what you're doing as an artist. For example: Imagine if you are able to put on your demo or your independent CD release, "Produced by Trackmasters". If nothing else, just the whole idea of you having that "piggybacked" credibility, will open up doors to you that were probably not there before. So do not take the idea of having the right producer(s) working with you lightly. Commit this to memory; *much of the music business is built around both business and personal relationships…and also associations*. At the *end of the day*, the music industry circle in Rap, Hip Hop and R&B is actually *not as big* as you might *think*.

DIFFERENT TYPES FOR DIFFERENT HYPE

Ok, first of all, there *are* different types of producers. So if you're going to hire a producer, you'll first have to figure out what *your* particular needs are and then go from there. One of the things to consider when deciding on *who to work with* will greatly depend on your *own style* as an artist. Also, your own skill level as an artist and your budget will also be things to think about, but we'll deal with the money and talent thing a little later. For now, let's just talk about the style you are doing. It will be important for you as an artist to feel confident in your producer's ability and know-how in the style of music you are doing. His knowledge of *your* particular style will help in determining his production chores and how well he can "create" the best music tone for the performances needed. I mean, you may be asking for a *headache* if you are going for the Usher or India.Arie *market*, but you go out and get with a producer who primarily has his only experience in the Underground Rap market…*especially* when it comes down to doing vocal *overdubs* and *comps*. This is mainly because - this is not *his normal* area of expertise *in production*. Now on the flip side of that idea, every now and then when you make productions that go *away from the normal combination* of producer and talent, and the whole "*process*" involved in the

creation…it is possible to come up with a *whole "new" unique sound or style*. For example: Just look at what producer Lil' Jon, known for his "Crunk" & "Dirty South" style productions did with the smooth, soulful vocal style of Usher. The mixture of these normally *different* sounds; Lil' Jon's music and Usher's vocal style, created a whole *new* sound; "Crunk & B". Also check out the work of producer Jazze Pha and his artist Ciara, "The First Lady of Crunk & B".

...Overdubs?

- An **overdub** is a recording technique used in the studio that allows artists and musicians to record parts "over" previously recorded parts or takes (attempts). This technique allows artists and musicians to create different recorded performances...without affecting any *earlier* recorded parts or performances in the recording.

...Comps?

- The term **comp** is short for **compilation**. When you make multiple **overdubs** or takes of the same part, **but on different tracks** in the studio, a compilation track of the **best of these overdub tracks** is sometimes needed. This new single edited performance track is called a "comp". This will usually require the producer and his engineer to have a great ear and technical ability to assemble these "best of" parts, all so that the finished comp is not only the best overdubs, but it is also a **consistent "sounding" track** of the performance. For example: A producer may have you go into the studio and record your performance three different times, on 3 "different" tracks. Later on, he and his engineer will sit and make a new "best of" track, from the best sections of the first three tracks. If this new "comp" track was done correctly, the sound & performance on tape will be consistent in tone, performance, quality and feel.

PRODUCER - DIRECTOR OF SONG CONSTRUCTION

Ok, now back to the different types of producers. You need to know that there are very different types of production guys (or gals like Missy or Beyoncé) who know *how* to make the artist and song (*even if it's them*), stand out through record "*production*", which many of you need to start thinking of as record *construction* or record *direction.* When you look at it as constructing or directing a record; from *the creative, the technical, and the whole building and directing process that goes into making a record*, maybe *then* you will see (and hear) that you can build different styles, with different approaches, with different types of construction specialist or directors (producers).   And whoever is the right producer that works best for the type of building or music *image* that you *need* (your style) – make sure that the candidate you choose has the skills at *whatever they do*... all to deliver a great – *finished* - product. The producer's main job is to deliver great product, *that's why he's called a producer. (See Introduction)*

KNOW HIS M.O.*

*Modus Operandi means:
- A technique of operating
- A person's way of working

So what are the different producer types? In the many urban music trends of today, you will find *traditional* musician-type producers like Scott Storch, Babyface, Pharrell, or Manuel Seal, Jr. Then there are those who are *basically* stand-alone beat-maker type producers like Swizz Beatz. There are producers who mainly sample from other productions, and then *creatively* use their *own cleverness* to make "new" productions like Kanye West. Next there is the combination of DJ and musician producers like DJ Toomp and Lil Jon; who use a mixture of great synthesizer hook riffs *combined* with the actual energy *"the sound itself makes"*. The DJ-Musician-producer will also know how to use samples and *sound placement, along with a touch of musician skills to get the job done right*. And basically, all the types mentioned – *if they have already done a few successful records*, are all *credible* types of producers. Credible meaning, they have a method to make the project c o m p l e t e through *whatever* method or approach that they use. These are the producers that know *how* to get the job done, and done right...with proof. He's that guy that "knows" and oversees *whatever* has to happen - to make a *finished record ready for the market*. The complete producer also usually u n d e r s t a n d s at least a little something about *all of the above* methods or approaches to making a recording come together. He's the "supervisor" or *builder-developer and director* of song *construction*. And he *regularly* knows how to use his experience *and* knowledge to deliver...*regardless* of *who* actually does some of the work involved too.

FOR EXAMPLE: Jermaine Dupri, Dallas Austin, P. Diddy, Lil Jon and a few other great producers, have all had very successful productions on very *different types of recording artists*; from rappers to soul-singers to pop artists. And a large part of their successes comes from *understanding* the "how" process of getting the job done. This *understanding* normally comes from years of know-how and also *years of surrounding themselves with great people in the studio*. These are the producers that are *skilled* at incorporating what "they do" and what *"to do"*, and with *"who"* to do it with. For reference, go and research LA & Babyface productions...and then look for names like producers Darryl Simmons and Kayo. See getting the job done is like this; *from time to time* when a seasoned producer needs a better arrangement, sample loop or maybe a hot new beat or keyboard added...or maybe some great DJ scratching, or "ghosted" vocal adds, etc... they recognize this: Whether or not *they actually go in and do the "hands-on"*, or physically do beats or sampling or arrangements themselves, is *not as important* as just finding the *right people* to come in and enhance *their sound*. But whatever happens during the *whole music construction* process...happens under *their direction*.

...Ghosted Vocals?

• *Ok kids – Here's the deal. Ghosted vocals are usually vocals that are put into or left in a recording to support the vocal performance of the featured artist. Sometimes a vocalist is hired to come in - as a guide or as "icing" to lay down vocal parts that are basically the same as the featured vocalists parts. In the decision process of picking which vocals make the record, these "hired vocals" if they are great, are left in the track "underneath" the featured vocalist performance to enhance things… and as a result, is called a "ghosted" part. Ghosted vocals are not out front, but below the featured vocalist parts.*

DECISIONS

Finding the right producer may be very challenging, and is *probably* going to come down to you either having money…or resources, or in the best situation; money *and* resources. This means that you either have enough money *and talent* to get the producer that you *want*, or you have made some type of relationship with an established or up-and-coming producer who is willing to help you get your music done right for little, or maybe even *nothing* up front. In some cases, established guys have been known to take on a new artist project entirely on a "spec" or speculative basis… with the idea being that the talent is so hot, the finished product will surely get some attention or a deal. So the established producer is willing to risk working without any advance money at all; to be paid when the artists gets some type of distribution deal in place. Recording studios have also been known to do "spec" deals with new artists.

…Spec Deal?

- *A **"Spec" Deal** is an agreement that some artists who are in need of studio time or production services will enter into with producers and/or recording studios - to get their demo recorded. The **"spec" deal** is short for **speculative**. Spec Deals can be ok, as long as you make sure to get everything done in writing and also get a grip on "who" actually will own the masters.*

Now please don't assume that if you have plenty of money, that you can just go out and easily obtain a music license for a hot beat or track, or simply hire "your producer of choice". You need to know now; just because you *have money*, and you approach someone who is "in the loop" and has songs out on the market (national *or regional*), *this does not mean that they will stop their production schedule and jump on your project*, *especially* if you aren't quite developed as an singer or rapper. I personally know of a multi-millionaire who saw this kid on "Showtime At The Apollo", and decided to get behind the kid's career as an investor. Since Janet Jackson was the hot item at the time, He "thought" because of his money, he could just go and hire her producers - Jimmy Jam & Terry Lewis to do production. He soon found out, even with his money, and even though the kid was talented, *Jam & Lewis didn't say no, but…* they still could not even *consider* doing any work with this kid for *at least* 18 months. This was because of their heavy production schedule with artists who already had their deals in place. And in general, a producer will have *more interest in talent that already has a deal* or some type of distribution in place. So even though you may have the cash, you may only get to add your name to the waiting list - if the producer has a demanding work calendar.

…Music License?

- *A **Music License** is an agreement that gives someone permission to use music that is owned by the copyright holder. There are different "types" of music licenses; Mechanical Licenses, Performance licenses, Sync Licenses, Print Licenses, etc. All of these licenses will be covered in the Songwriting and Publishing section.*

STILL RAW!

Another reality is that you may not be *developed enough as an artis*t, especially for a great producer to take you on. For instance, if you go to some producer who is constantly doing a lot of major or independent work in your area, and you have a couple of thousand dollars to spend - to hire him, even if you can "get *in* his schedule", if you're not coming with something that's really hot, to help him in the long range of things, a few thousand dollars is actually not a whole lot of money because *that may be all the money that he'll see!* So basically, you are a higher than *normal* risk to make any big money from royalties or publishing income. To him, as an artist, you just aren't developed enough to either *get a deal* or get any substantial sales independently. So when he makes an evaluation of "you" and a projection of *working with you*, it might be a waste of time until *you develop yourself* more. Trust me, he wants the money, but he also wants to invest his time wisely too. And I guess I should say this, since it is very real, producers, including myself, from time to time, have been known to take the money of an artist that actually *isn't ready*. So, whomever you are looking into - to hire as a producer, you should also seek out some evaluation of *where you stand* as an artist (as far as talent). *No one really knows* who is the next star or next hit...*but*, when people who have evaluated your rapping or singing or songs *agree about your development - good or bad*, you should have a pretty good idea of *where you are*. So please take all of this into consideration, "before" putting out your hard-earned money. I can name some very big and successful producers who have done this; charging big money for a demo on an unsigned artist, that they know isn't ready for much of anything other than a great CD coaster.

EXPERIENCE AND REP

Experience and reputation, in most cases, *is* a very big deal in this industry.

Cirocco at Stonehenge Recording   Alvin Speights at Titanium Studios

When I say "experience", this means the producer has finished recordings put out into the marketplace for sale. So, if you decide to hook-up with the producer who has great experience and a track record, especially if the producer has great relationships with other industry people (attorneys, A&R, etc.) then you are talking about having a connection and also being *linked* with a producer *in the industry* that may be able to do more for you than just make a great song. This means that because of *their* personal and business relationships *and credibility with other key industry people*, they may seek to get *your project* in *their* network of music people. And the beauty of this is that all you had to do is get them as your producer or get a track and deliver. Since he will have his name attached to *your* project, *and if it's hot*, he just may decide to get the project into the right hands *without you asking.* Of course, this sometimes may mean you as the artist - possibly signing into other things like being a part of the producer's production company or possibly giving him a little more of the publishing percentage than you might normally. But all of this will depend on the weight of who he is, who he knows, how genuinely excited he is about you as an artist, and what *you* as an artist brings to *his own agenda.* But let's be clear, if you have great skills, great management in place, a great entertainment attorney, *and you also have his producer's fee in-hand*, then most times he should not be asking for *anything* extra. He should be more than happy to work with you for a negotiated fee, depending on his production schedule.

THE UP-AND-COMING PRODUCER

Up-and-coming Producer "Sun" at Titanium Recording

Now a different option you may want to consider, is trying to find a producer that has the quality you seek, but just hasn't gotten the big reputation yet. You may be able to take as little as a few hundred dollars, *or maybe even free*, and work with someone who hasn't had a record out. B u t, he has some *really hot tracks* and finished productions that you've heard on other artists. And even though he may be an unknown, his productions just speak for themselves. This is why I said earlier that you could possibly find a new guy to produce you, or get tracks from - but *only* if you have *some "reel evidence" of his finished work.*

In most cases, I would say you would be better off with choosing a producer who has a lot of experience, but sometimes it's the new up-and-coming rookie producer that has the better stuff.   Think about the 2004-2005 NFL Football Season, when Ben Roethlisberger of the Pittsburgh Steelers was *only a rookie Quarterback*, but was *still* talented enough to get his team into the playoffs. Not only did he get his team there, but he also won all 13 of his starts ...*as a rookie*. See, it's kinda like this...every now and then; you *can find people around you* who can *do great things*, and do them *without* a great deal of experience.   So, even though they don't have the years behind them, they are still just as good, *and sometimes even better* than many of the veteran guys doing the same thing. I say all of this to present to you a very different option to finding a good producer for *your* team; consider getting an up-and-coming guy that really has the skills beyond his experience.

BEING RESOURCEFUL

If you are out there searching for a producer for your team, and you find a new up-and-coming producer whose like the *next* Pharrell, and he's coming with the hottest beats like Lil Jon ...or maybe he's got the R&B/Pop thang down like Manuel Seal, Jr. or Scott Storch... *hook up with them!* In other words, you use *that* resource; the resource that *you can get to - if you don't have the money* to go with experience. Sometimes these up-and-coming producers may be willing and *able* to spend more time and be more dedicated to you because they are still very hungry...*just like you*. If you approach him right, and your talent is tight, you may find a new partner that can make your music shine and your project come out very good...but without the normal price tag. Sometimes it is just getting a beat from them, sometimes its getting complete tracks from them, sometimes it is you and him just sitting and cranking it out, 24/7, *until you get something right*. And even though you may spend months helping each other develop more, in the end, that collaboration with getting with an up-and-coming producer can also prove to be priceless - if you're able to still get a great finished project. But let's not get too carried away, it will be that "if factor", that you will have to concern yourself with the most...*using the new guy*. So make sure you *"hear"* what he can do, not "talk about" what he can *potentially* do. Once you like what you *hear*, then you can make an intelligent decision on what to do as far as your production needs and working in the recording studio.

 PRODUCER PAYMENT$

If you are ready *as an artist*, and you've got a little money to hire a producer that is *credible*, then it will be a matter of you making yourself prepared to let him do his thing... to make *you* shine. It will probably cost into the *thousands of dollars*, so don't go into shock when he starts giving you quotes for his fees. A good producer will *usually* charge just like *any other specialist* in any given field; their price will be according to their skills, credibility and experience.

Most producers will always have to be paid an advance before they perform any services. And the form of this payment can come in different ways and different amounts. This all will depend on *your* particular situation, finances, and how willing the producer is to possibly compromise and deal with *your* specific situation. These payments can come by way of, but are *surely not limited to* the following ways:

➢ An advance payment from you, or the record label, or whatever company that may be representing you. Along with this advance will also come an agreement to pay the producer a percentage (points) of the record sales (*usually* 3 points or more of the retail price)

➢ If you are not signed to a company, the producer may charge you a flat fee to do production work. It is very unlikely to get a working producer to stop and take the risk of doing any tracks for you for free, unless he is possibly planning on signing you or you have some type of great friendship, *which is sometimes better than money*. But in almost every producer situation, you should still expect to pay the producer points, once you get a deal or some type of distribution.

➢ One alternative practice that a few producers have been known to do, is to charge you 10% of whatever their "normal" production fee might be, and then once you get a record deal or advance in place, you pay up the balance due...*the other 90%*. For example: You may approach a producer that has credibility on some records, and offer to pay him 10 % of his normal advance fee. If he normally charges $5,000, then you pay him a non-refundable $500 up front, you pay the recording costs, and then you have a written agreement with him to pay $4,500 *when you (the artist or company) get your deal in place*. And the producer will keep the masters for collateral. Please note: *This is only an example, and every producer and situation will be different.*

...*Producer Points?*

• ***Producer points*** *means the producer's royalty percent. In other words, 3 points would mean a 3 percent royalty payment. The producer is usually paid a percentage of record sales based on either suggested retail list price or wholesale, depending on what is in his agreement.*

...*Royalty?*

• ***Royalties*** *is money that is to be paid to an artist, producer, songwriter or publisher from the sale or performance of their music, normally to be paid "after" deductions of expenses and advances.*

...Advance?

- An **Advance** is just what it sounds like; advance money or "up-front" money. Basically an advance is money paid "in advance" of royalties paid that hopefully you (or the producer in this case) would earn in the future. The majority of advances are non-refundable, and whatever is advanced to you or paid up front - is recovered by balancing the "future-earned royalties" against the original money that had already been paid...in the "advance".

SO, HOW MUCH?

Producers, like everyone, want as much as they can get! Realistically, you should prepare to pay most producers anywhere from $2,000 - $17,500+ per song, *especially if you're making a record*. But "sticky" this: There are many "Hot" producers getting $25,000 to $50,000 a song. And for "Superstar" producers... well, if you must ask...*you can't afford them!* ($60,000 – $100,000+) And these fees may or may *not* include recording costs or be "all-in" production fee. That will depend on your negotiation of what *you need*, what you have to spend, and their own schedule and willingness to help you. Of course if you are no more than making a demo, then you can start realistically searching for help, once you get anywhere from $500 to $1,500 in your hands (per song). Anything lower than that, then you may be asking for *unrealistic* results. For the most part, if the producer is *really good*, there probably isn't any *real (reel) difference* between his demo and what he basically turns in for a finished record. Of course, many artists are purchasing and leasing beats or tracks to work on their music, which is another alternative - to the "typical" way to get produced...but we'll go *over and through* the whole "Beats For Sale" subject later... and will tell you the *right* way to do it.

...VERY IMPORTANT NOTE!

- If you start asking the producer for too much of a discounted price to produce your song or project, you may also be asking for the producer to compromise the quality of the work involved. So, please be very careful when negotiating. Most producers want to do their very best to deliver a great product, but if you put them into a compromising position financially - to get "you" together, you may ultimately be putting yourself in a compromising position to "be together". And that's usually not good. Even the best "low-budget" producer will still need supplies, recording costs and at least a little incentive to do the job.

..."All In?"

- "All in" is a term used that is short for all-inclusive. There are different types of all-in deals, but the basic meaning **when referring to a producer's "all-in"** fee, means that all of the costs for making the production; Producer fee, Engineer, Studio, tape, hard drive back-ups, etc... will all be included in a budget which includes all the expenses to make the song. The producer instead of the company will manage this "all-in" budget. In other words, everything to produce the song is included in the Producer's fee. Once the producer has an "all-in" fee in place, It will then be the responsibility of the producer to budget and manage the expenses himself...all to deliver a finished product. If by chance the producer goes over budget, then normally he has to "eat" the costs. If by chance he falls under budget, then he gets to keep the extra for himself. Normally The Company or the Artist (these days) will direct the Producer payments in 1/3s or ½'s.

❏ *We will go over more Producer details in the Record Deals Chapter.*

YOUR PRODUCER'S "EQ"
"Experience Quota"

➢ If the producer you hire has a good track record, then you can be assured that he's probably more than qualified to oversee and make sure your songs will turn out presentable and professional. This means your songs will be ready for broadcast and pressing.

➢ Most producers in Urban Music are also songwriters or at least create tracks. This can be a great asset to you when it comes to helping you pick out material and also combining your lyrics with music. This collaboration can also make the difference in what kind of deal(s) you are seeking...*as in a Publishing.*

➢ You'll usually know when you have an experienced producer working with you, because he will have some of the same skills that a movie director has... in that most producers will be "directing" you in the studio, offering feedback and constructive criticism to find a way to get the *best from your performance.* He will then use his expertise to decide on the best vocal takes and compile it all through editing, to showcase your best efforts.

...Quick Note:

•   *As an artist, you must focus on the specifics, without becoming defensive to your producer's direction. You have to trust him every single time he says, "try it again" or "one more time". Know this: No one wants you to complete whatever phrase and/or phase of your song performance quicker (in the studio), than your producer. To give you guidance from "His point of view" is exactly what you're hiring him for to begin with.*

➢ Proven and experienced producers will no doubt have relationships from past and/or present projects with record labels, film producers, managers, attorneys and sometimes radio people. And if the producer you hire has had some pretty good success in the past... or is currently doing well on the charts, "*his* influence" and buzz throughout the music industry "from other projects" may prove to be a "priceless" commodity that can help skyrocket your *own* career. Imagine if you're a hot new rap group, and your CD says...

PRODUCED BY LIL JON

TRILLVILLE & LIL SCRAPPY
WITH THE HIT SINGLES
"NEVA EVA" AND "HEAD BUSSA"
PRODUCED BY LIL JON

➤ Because the producer you hire should have the expertise and experience to deliver quality, "finished" product, you should be able to more freely concentrate on being creative and performing your best for your project.

➤ Because most experienced producers are able to see the "big picture" of things - concerning your music and image, he will be able to help you choose the right songs that work to represent *you* correctly. This is extremely important! How you are presented and represented *musically* should work hand in hand with your visual image style too. In other words, if you were going to serve a very "nice" *elegant* dinner, you wouldn't *normally* place the finished meal in a brown paper bag to serve it.

➤ Because as an artist, you really don't need the added stress and concerns that come with picking out the best recording facility, the right engineer, mixing, finding and arranging sessions for background vocalist and musicians, etc., you should ultimately be able to count on your producer to take charge and *handle these responsibilities* (with of course, *your* approval).

PROSPECTING

So, now it's time to take whatever *you* do, and believe in yourself enough to approach the producers that you really like ...*and can also get access to* for your project. So start paying attention to the hottest new demos floating around, and try to find out who are the different producers behind the artists and *their* music. Get out to the showcases in your region, and then start networking with other artists and producers, so you know who's who, and who's doing what. Get in the clubs (if you are old enough) and make connections with the DJs, who usually know what's hot.   Also, many of these DJs are producers themselves. You should also get out to the club talent showcases, and you see *and hear* who's doing what; you hear *who's got the hottest stuff,* and *who's got the 'bomb' tracks.* And when you hear something that you find yourself saying, "Oh man, that was *hot!* That was *tight*! Who did *that* track?" Well, you go and find out... *you do your research.* And of course, you also listen to what's going on, on records and CDs that you hear, and then find out *who* is responsible for what you are hearing. After that, it's a mater of you being prepared through your own development, representation, finances, and what many don't get, but is maybe *more important that anything else*; your *attitude* and *heart* to not be denied... and succeed. You must know that most can't be Whitney Houston, but some still get in the door. And everyone will not flip rhymes like "Twista", *but they still find a way to get in.* And let's just keep it real; some of these artists that are getting deals and actually doing well, really can't sing or rap... but guess what? So. They got the right attitude, desire, and heart to win... and they just *find a way* to *not be denied.* But, the one common thing, to just about all talent making records, whether good or mediocre, successful artists normally will have some pretty good producers working on their music.

So basically in the end, whether you have money, whether you have untapped resources, whether you have both, you will ultimately have to sell "you" to get a good producer *really interested* in being part of your team or project. You will have to be who you say you are. If you are the next Usher... *then show it*! And it definitely will not hurt if you are doing shows *all of the time*, getting exposure. Because, before they sometimes agree to working with you... seeing you *live* may *very much* help persuade both the veteran and the rookie producer to get excited about working with you.

MORE RESEARCH

Inclosing out this section, take to mind that whatever producer is right for your particular needs will come down to you researching and reviewing the producer's past and present projects. If you think his style will compliment the sound you are trying to achieve, and you like his vibe, plus he is excited about working with you... go with it! As you begin working together, after a song or two, it will be sensible for you as an artist to *evaluate* what has actually gotten accomplished... in other words, check your progress. Your Producer should be able to bring out the "potentially great" in *you* and also your best performances - locked into what *he gets recorded*! Always know, that at the end of day (the project), he gets to move on to the next gig...but you may have to live with your recorded project for a minute. So if you are a singer, a rapper or maybe even a great up-and-coming songwriter who needs a producer, please do not take the idea of getting the best you can find for granted. The bottom line is, producers are *very important* to have on your team and in your corner - to ensure that you give yourself the *best shot* of having a professional *sounding* demo or a well-produced presentation to potential music opportunities. Whatever skills, experience and talent that your producer brings to the table should be complimentary of *your style* and sound...all to make "you, and *what* you do"... *ready* for the m a r k e t p l a c e .

TYPICAL PRODUCER RESPONSIBILITIES

- ❑ **Overseeing the recording sessions & pre-production of a project**
- ❑ **Delivering a *quality* broadcast master or a demo-master recording**
- ❑ **Hiring the right musicians, djs, vocalists, engineers, etc.**
- ❑ **Handling (or hiring someone for) administrative paperwork**
- ❑ **Helping in the song selection and many times, in it's creation too**
- ❑ **Making the recording "complete" and ready for mixing**
- ❑ **Getting the best performance from the artists and side artists**

GOOD LUCK!

Music Powers
SPOTLIGHT
MANUEL SEAL JR.

Producer - Songwriter - Artist

Biography

If you've enjoyed listening to songs by superstar artists like Mariah Carey, Usher, Mary J. Blige, Jagged Edge, Da Brat or Destiny's Child, then most likely, you've already experienced the songwriting artistry and production magic of Manuel Seal, Jr.

Manuel Seal, Jr., is currently signed with publishing giant BMG Songs, and is a long-time collaborator with producer Jermaine Dupri. Manuel is recognized worldwide as an "A-list" hit-maker, which makes him one of the most sought after record producers in the music industry. His musical background is broad, with a strong musical ancestry rooted in gospel, classical and jazz. His musical presence can be heard and felt on some of the most successful recordings of modern-day music history.

Manuel Seal's hit list includes the Dianne Warren penned Hit, "Give Me You" by Mary J. Blige, Mariah Carey's #1 Hit single "Always Be My Baby", and 4 different #1 Hit singles for Usher; "You Make Me Wanna", "Nice n' Slow", "My Way", and most recently, "My Boo", performed by Usher and Alicia Keys. "My Boo," which is one of Manuel's several collaborations with producer Jermaine Dupri has been nominated for "Best R&B Song" of the year for the 47th Grammy Awards. "My Boo" also held down the Number #1 spot in Billboard for 4 weeks in a row.

Adding to his notable arsenal of skills, Manuel is also an exceptional singer, and will soon be adding more songs to his hit list for his latest project… "Himself", Manuel Seal, *the artist.* Manuel humbly adds, "I'm now in that zone again." "When you're able to be passionate about what you love, and what you are doing, you can sometimes do unbelievable things."

Unbelievable? Yes, without question. Manuel's ability to consistently create hit after hit after hit, is proof enough that his *amazing* success as a producer and the ability to create #1 Hit records is something magical, and is easily measured as a thing that most of us can only dream about.

Music Powers
SPOTLIGHT
MANUEL SEAL JR.

Producer · Songwriter · Artist

A Select Discography

Confessions
Usher
Producer

U Don't Have to Call
Usher
Producer

Destiny's Child
Destiny's Child
Producer

Nice & Slow
Usher
Producer

Daydream
Mariah Carey
Producer, Vocals

Now & Forever The Hits
TLC
Producer

My Way
Usher
Vocals, Producer

Tamia
Tamia
Vocals, Producer

I Gotta Be
Jagged Edge

Funkdafied
Da Brat
Keys, Producer

BeBe Winans
BeBe Winans
Producer

Mary
Mary J. Blige
Keys, Produce

Mariah Carey's Greatest Hits
Producer

Jermaine Dupri Presents - 12 Soulful Nights Christmas
Producer

Baby-Sitters Club
Original Soundtrack
Producer

Ballads
Mary J. Blige
Piano, Producer

Soul Food
Original Soundtrack
Producer

Number One's
Mariah Carey
Producer

Off the Hook
Xscape
Keyboards

Greatest Hits
TLC
Producer

Anuthafunkdafiedt antrum
Da Brat
Keyboards, Producer

I'll Be Right There
Jagged Edge

With Me
Destiny's Child
Producer

With Me, Pt. 2
Destiny's Child
Producer

Let's Get the Mood Right
Johnny Gill
Vocals, Producer

Best of Love
Michael Bolton
Remixing

Levert.Sweat.Gill
LSG

Sabelle
Guitar, Keyboards,
Producer

Here We Go Again
Aretha Franklin
Producer

Inside of You
Aaron Hall
Producer

Love & Consequences
Gerald LeVert
Guitar, Producer,
Keyboards

My Little Secret
Xscape

Heart Mind & Soul
El DeBarge

A Jagged Era
Jagged Edge

I Wanna Go There
Tyrese
Producer

Oxygen
Wild Orchid
Producer

Rose Is Still a Rose
Aretha Franklin
Producer

Greatest Hits
Ruff Endz
Producer

Live
Usher
Vocals, Producer

Love Crimes
Ruff Endz
Producer

No More
Ruff Endz
Producer

Ambushed
Da Bush Babees

All I Got
Al Jarreau
Keyboards

21...Ways to Grow
Shanice
Producer

Anuthatantrum
Da Brat

Music Powers

Exclusive Advice from Music Powers Advisor

MANUEL SEAL JR.

"THE ZONE"

1 You have consistently made hit, after hit, after hit…do you *hear* your songs being hit records *before they get released*? …And what is your approach?

Well, on *"You Make Me Wanna"* …yes, I heard that one. *"Nice and Slow"*. Yes, I heard that one *too*.   But on *"My Way"*…I didn't hear it. So when it went #1, I was surprised.

As far as the approach goes, it all starts with the song…and that *is my approach* or point of view. Mentally my thing comes from the melodies. I hear melodies first. I hear them; they wake me up out of my sleep. Basically you have to develop your writing skills, always working on your songwriting ability, getting it to a place where you can get into that "zone." Maybe a lot of people don't really understand this, but getting in that zone is essential. Like the first things I ever did in the music industry, I wrote two #1 Platinum records, and they went to the top of the charts. And then there were three Platinum singles on Usher. You see, I call that a zone. When you get in a zone where you're able to have a certain *consistency* to doing your work… that's the zone. *(On October 1, 2004, "My Boo" (Usher & Alicia Keys) was also certified as a Platinum* Single)*

* The RIAA Platinum award means 1,000,000 copies sold

> Usher CD releases:
> My Way & Confessions

➢ As far as the production approach, it's about catching the dream and the vision, and then you go to defining *how you are going to work*. You also figure out who you are going to work with… *then you bring it all together!* The music should be the easy part if you just let it flow…and as long as you're *not fighting yourself* or fighting somebody else inside the project. You can't put a bunch of people in a room and expect something good unless they gel… *or have a natural gel*. And you don't want to be in a situation where you are calling each other names, or where there is some dissension or something like that. You want to be able to see yourself working with that person because you're on a common bond and have a common goal to make the song and production come together.

ATMOSPHERE AND ATTITUDE

2 Are there other examples that you can give that can help artists to get a clearer picture of what *getting into "the zone"*… or *that* "state of mind" is all about?

> See, the hidden element on a lot of these records is the "atmosphere" that surrounds *the making of the records*. Getting into that zone has a lot to do with the atmosphere or *environment and your attitude*. There is no limit to the thing I call "atmosphere and attitude". See, we are in this information age, and you should *forever* be learning. And as a musician or artist or whatever you are *defining yourself as*, you should take *that* state of mind or *attitude*, and then you build from there. See, the only person that can stop us from doing anything is our *self.* Or, it's a failure to come into the knowledge that you're *supposed to have;* or the failure to *implement what it is* and *what you're supposed to do*. In life, you have two "ugly" brothers that can *stop us* from doing whatever we must do to succeed. *1) "Doing-nothing-at-all", and 2) "Procrastination".* And that is not only in music, but also in everything that we want to do!

"…Doing nothing and procrastination will put you right out the game!"

With Usher's projects, it was always a joyous atmosphere. We had fun. We played video games, we laughed, *and we also did a lot of work!* It was *that kind of energy* that was a common thread to a lot of the stuff that happened over at So So Def Recordings. We would get in there and knock the work out in that kind of atmosphere. For example: Working with Usher is a pleasure. *I think Usher is the epitome of what an artist is.* The way he works hard; his mindset is that "do-or-die" mindset or *attitude*, and he continues to have this to this day. Usher would be in the studio doin' his sit-ups, and push-ups (laughing), but he was inputting on the project too. Usher was *really learning a lot also*… like with all the production stuff, and he was *hungry to learn it!* So basically, the So So Def work environment; atmosphere, and Usher's mindset; attitude, is an example of what I call *"Atmosphere and Attitude."*

So So Def Recordings

• Producer Jermaine Dupri formed So So Def Recordings in 1992. The Atlanta based label is the home to recording artists J-Kwon, 3LW, Youngbloodz, Bone Crusher, Anthony Hamilton and Da Brat. So So Def has also played a major role in the success of Usher and some of the most successful record producers in the Hip Hop and R&B music industry like Bryan Michael Cox, LaMarquis Jefferson, L Roc and Manuel Seal.

TAKING USHER TO THE TOP

3 What was the concept in planning the music production for Usher'?

With Usher, we didn't want him to be too "goody-two-shoes", but we didn't want his thing to be a *bad thing* either, so we decided to just put him right smack dab in the middle. We said, "Let's take a little bit of Michael Jackson, and then take a little bit of Bobby Brown, and *then put it together*, and let's give him some nice songs. For me, I was already hearing some Latin influences because I was listening to Latin music, and said, "*I knew that Latin music and Black music could make a nice blend*", then we incorporated that for *"You Make Me Wanna"*. And by the way, that guitar riff on "You Make Me Wanna"...*that's keyboards, not guitar*. A lot of people don't know that.

RELATIONSHIPS IN THE MUSIC BIZ
More Atmosphere & Attitude

4 Does the "Atmosphere & Attitude" concept carry over into the business side?

 Yes, relationships politically dominate the music business. In other words, business with *one person* will mean more than business with *another person*. Let's just tell it like it is; If you're doing a deal with somebody, and you're first stating out, your key guy or whatever may value their relationship with the person they have already been doing business with, *before you; the new guy.* This is because they've already been doing business longstanding with the other guy...*and a whole lot longer too.* For example: When I first started out, it was like, "*Well, who are you Manuel?*" That's because, if you are the new man, you *may* do something, but then, you *may not*...do something. So that allegiance may be with the person that's *already* "in". And you will have to keep all of this in mind, and you keep all of that in focus when you are going after what you must get! So what's the thing to do? *"Atmosphere and Attitude."* Like the saying goes, *"Being forewarned is to know."* So it's good to get all of this knowledge, and all of the things that are being mentioned...and then some, so that we're forever learning. And you also have to think about the economics in the music business. And most of us don't understand this, but it is, "Music... *Business*!" So you have to find out "how" everything works. If you look at rebates; most companies are banking on you to "*not*" fill that rebate out... to get your money back!" They are banking on you "not to know" what's going on or how it works. You always pay for what you don't know!

TESTING YOUR MUSIC

5 What is the best way to test your songs to determine what you *really* have?

 When you're doing your music, its got to be relatable, which means that you must test it. People come to me all the time and ask, "What's a hit record?" And I say, "Hey, I don't know!" The *people* decide. So what you should do with your music is form a relationship with the DJs and people like that, and try to get your music played by them to see what the people say about what you have going on. That will be your indicator of if you are going in the right direction with what you're doing…cause you're basically doing research and development.

THE BREAK

6 How did you get your first break and link up with Jermaine Dupri?

I've known Jermaine since he was 19 years old, and I know his father Michael Mauldin too. The "hook-up" happened when I was over at the Hotel Lennox and I had just come freshly from Illinois. I had that one person that believed in me, and had brought me to Atlanta. They put me in a hotel, and got me doing a lot of meetings and so forth… in hopes to see LA Reid, and possibly get on the Toni Braxton project. And as I was getting ready to leave out to go to one of the meetings, the phone rang, and it was Michael Mauldin saying, *"Yo, my son Jermaine Dupri wants to meet you, and I heard that you were a bad boy."* He said that Jermaine wanted to come by the hotel and pick me up, so I said ok. And I really remember that day. Jermaine showed up while I was downstairs, down in the lobby of the hotel playing the piano, and there was this *huge* crowd of people. And me being from this small town… I'm feeling this right (smiling). And there were people telling me, "Hey, play it my way, and I'll pay you $2,000 or $2,500 or whatever, and I'm like, *"Oh man, wow, there's money up in here!"* (laughing). So Jermaine saw this, and he always had *that knack* of seeing what would draw or what gets attention…even from as far back as Kriss Kross. So after that, we went to his house. And then once I got in his studio, I think I must have crafted 2 or 3 songs right there - right on the spot! And then He just *offered me a deal*…right there at the studio. He said, "I know, *I know* that if LA Reid hears you, he will sign you!" *That's what he told me.* So at the time, because I was green to all of this, I'm thinking to myself, *"Shoot, this is just another way to get paid! …And I'm getting my production papers fast as lightning!"* (laughing) And actually in reality, that was the goal *anyway.* And I also knew that I would get my production shot *faster* in Atlanta than I would out in Los Angeles. The LA thing is kinda rough. (laughing). But I was aware of everything that was going on. I also knew that if I was, who I *said I was…* then I would survive with whatever I had to survive *with.*

THE WILL TO SUCCEED

7 Getting your break sounds like a your determination to survive and succeed, is this true for most new talent - hang in there and pay some dues dues?

➢ You have to pay some dues. You have to get in. I paid my dues, and that's how got on then, *and that's how I get on now!* We all are going to pay dues. But the human spirit is amazing. You *can do anything* you set your mind to. For me, to get where I am, it was basically, "Do or die... I'm walking this tightrope, *and I cannot fail!*" So my actions had to be coinciding with my thinking. Like the Bible says, "As a man thinketh, that's how he is." Your thoughts will dictate who you are. That's why it's so important for you to get that knowledge in you; not just in your head, but when you get passionate, you get it in your heart.

➤ When I first came to Atlanta, I was like a pit bull... *with blinders on*. There were no parties, or this...or that. Just focus! And then you may be working with someone else, who has already achieved some things already, and they may be a little comfortable...and that's another enemy; "comfortable ability." If you get comfortable, you're not operating at your peak. The best time for me was when I was hungry! Those are the best times because you are "sharp." "When you're hungry and sharp, you will get up; you're gonna do what you gotta do!" Survival!

> *"...One of the worse things you can do, is for someone to come in and put a whole bunch of money in your hand...and you start thinking, "Oh man, I'm set now...I'm all right"*

WORKING WITH JERMAINE DUPRI

8 What's it like working with Jermaine Dupri in the recording studio?

➤ Jermaine Dupri is a great guy and is mad cool in the studio. We have a relationship where *he does what he does, and I do what I do.* I'm more musical and idea generating, with *that* input and *that whole thing.* And Jermaine does the beats, and keeps it "Black"; He keeps it "Urban." In the studio, I'll do something, and then I'll get out of his way. Or he'll do something, and then... he will get out of *my way.* And then we just put it all together. That seems to work for us. We never have arguments, and I consider Jermaine like a little brother. So Jermaine and I have a great relationship.

...And what about the business relationship with Jermaine Dupri?

➤ Well as a businessman, I look at it like, we have a *Hit-making history together*, and no one can deny that. And it's also been a very *lucrative* situation for me as well. So I look forward to entertaining that situation even more, especially now that I understand the game a lot better, I will be able to profit even more. So, a lot of mistakes that I made before, I can correct those mistakes and enhance the future opportunities.

Manuel Seal with So So Def
Producer Jermaine Dupri

THE AGE FACTOR

9 Has age been an issue to get in and also succeed in the music business?

➢ Well, for all of you who *think* it's too late for you to get into the music business, *I didn't start my career until I was 31 years old.* I was the *adult* person who came into Jermaine Dupri's camp. So I've proven that *it can be done.* Once you set your heart and your mind, then there's nothing that you can't do! Some might be saying, "Well, he's too this, and he's too that!" But your talent will always make a way for you. That's the way I was taught. You can be whatever age, but if you're writing hit records, then do you think they won't hear you or listen to you? See, *that's why you take the time to develop your craft...so you can follow your dream!* If that's what God gave you to do, you follow it and just "be real with yourself"... because you're going to get better. I don't shoot pool, but if shoot pool everyday for the next 5 years, then I will be able to shoot some great pool!

THE TRIPLE THREAT

10 Songwriter, Producer, Musician...what do you see yourself as first?

➢ I don't consider myself as the technical definition of a musician because most musicians have a repertoire; he's able to play all these songs he has to memory. I *do consider myself a composer and a theorist.* And I consider myself a singer *before all of that.* That's the relationship of how I hear my stuff. Now, I do have the *knowledge* of a musician, so I can communicate with musicians.

➢ As far as a producer… *actually*, I never wanted to produce. All I wanted to do is be an artist. See, I knew if I just came to Atlanta; got some producer credits, it wouldn't be a problem, and labels could say, "Hey, he can produce himself…because he's done all this other stuff, so naturally, he *should* be able to produce himself!" So, how I came about, it was songwriter first, and then a producer, and I was always a musician as far as knowing "how" to play. I really wanted to be a guitar player originally, but when I grew up, the piano was the only thing in the house. So the keyboard playing is my *technical* stuff; it's the jazz; it's the "I know where I'm going"; it's the frame work; it's the building of whatever I have to do… for understanding, like on string arrangements.   And I *do play* guitar, but I only know enough so that it's not overly done. The guitar is my rhythmic instrument that I basically use to feel the beat and rhythms while I'm playing.

11 So would you advise others to take the approach of being "multi-skilled," and be *without the limitations* we put on ourselves as songwriters & producers?

➢ You don't limit yourself. Sometimes people will say, "I can only do *this*, or I can only do *that*, and I can only do…*whatever!*" Those are limitations, and you have to try to eliminate those limitations. The more you're able to do, the more valuable you make yourself. The more valuable you make yourself, the more valuable you are to others. Like Cirocco for example, he can jump to another genre of music if he chooses to, that's because he doesn't have those limitations. Or, he can go to a whole different situation, which many producers may need to adapt to, and do television and movie work.

12 Do you work in the studio alone or with a crew?

➢ I work it a bunch of different ways, but to answer your question truthfully, when I got into running this *as a business* and stuff, I kinda took my hands off of a lot of things, and got a crew. I have an engineer, and I also have other producers that I have signed. It really depends on the nature of the project. I may go in the studio and be totally hands-on and set the pace for everything. Like, I might sit down and put the guitar parts down for them to follow that to have that exact pulse-beat from the guitar that I want to have. I put down enough for him or her to be able to sing the song, because the song has already been written. Then once I get a performance on the vocals, even though I usually do vocals myself…. but I'm also in evaluation; I'm trying to see how *well* my people can cut vocals. I want them to be "finishers". I'm trying to develop finishers for the production. That way, if I want to go work with Dianne Warren or someone else in another *physical place*, work is still getting done, and work is still getting finished.

THE FINISHER – THE PRODUCER

13 There are many out there who just started who may not know what a "finisher" is in production, please enlighten them.

A finisher means, "being a *complete* producer." A finisher or a complete producer makes sure that the process from the in-start of the song, from whatever ideas there might be in the beginning, to the song being prepared to get ready to go to mix. A producer should not only be able to lay down beats, but he should be able to cut the vocals too. He's got to be able to handle the *whole* process and also *keep track of the process* of the song. Like with vocals, you have to make sure those vocals are "woke up!", so that the singer is delivering emotionally and then delivering what they are supposed to be delivering. It's a "big difference" singing out at a live performance and singing in the lab. When you're in the lab, you have that "microscope" on you. So you cant just use emotionalism or sensationalism to deliver. In the studio you have to make people *feel your words.* You must wake certain words up. *There are certain words that you have to psychologically make that connection to people.* As a producer, it's your job to make the singer "sound" good or at least take them to the next level. There are many different things that have to be addressed to make the vocal thing successful. Some important concerns include diction, pitch, tone, pronunciation, timing, and flow. You know you can't have different vocal tones throughout the song, and if you haven't developed your ear to a point, to recognize this, then the track will not be consistent. You can't have one vocal tone on the one part of the record, and a different tone on another section of the record. You have to have a consistency over that 3:20 or 3:45 time frame. There has to be a consistent flow both musically and vocally. And that's when a finisher producer will make sure all of that is done, and then on to the next project.

SKILLS & DEVELOPMENT

14 How important is it for songwriters & producers to educate themselves?

➤ It's about skill and proficiency. Also, you can't be afraid to collaborate and find out new ideas, because that's *how you learn.* Artists have to be educated. I'm trying to do my part by *developing* talent. I know how to take talent from raw, and then take it to what it *supposed to be.* And that's what the industry is lacking… "Artist development". People are not developing their skills. Maybe you *can't* depict a hit record, but anybody that develops their skills *can* be like a "sharp shooter" who has gotten proficient with their skill, and then learn how to hit that bull's eye. So what I'm talking about is being proficient at a skill-level to do that. And when you look at the track record I have, that's basically what you are seeing; you're seeing a skill level *lyrically, melodically, musically and just being able to adapt.* For example, when I sign a writer, I help them to *develop as a writer.* Most publishing companies can sign you, but they *can't teach you* and develop you on "how" to write. So in my company or situation, what I try to do, you'll have benefit, *if I sign you*, that I'm going to put you in an situation or I'm gonna put you in an atmosphere where you can learn the *craft* of songwriting. *It's about atmosphere & attitude...*the ingredient to any good recipe. There is a certain skill that you develop. This is what a lot of people are missing out on now. When you sit down and then say, "Hey, I wanna write a hit song." Everybody thinks that they are a writer now because of the greed factor... but there aren't *that many* good songs out there. Not a lot of clever lyrics, the songs aren't fashioned and formed, there isn't consistency; they don't even do a change in the music anymore.

> *"...A lot of people just edit a loop and call it a day!"*

➤ There are so many sounds that have been abandoned...that can be revamped and rehashed, and brought back to make it happening now. This is especially true on the R&B tip. We only have one sound out there right now. I'm listening and hearing the same sound and same production ...almost. But back in the day, you had artists like Earth, Wind & Fire, where there was brass, and all these different sounds, and *they did what "they did"*. And that's what we need to get back to – doing what "you do" as opposed to A&R coming in and saying, "Yo, I need a record like *this record here* or "Hey, I need a record like *that record there!*" When I look at that, production wise, I say that there is another focus that can be addressed. Remember that hot sound that Devonte Swing had? I mean there are sounds that were just really, really dope that have just been abandoned, that you can go back, revamp it, and then make it happening for *now*...instead of just dealing with the same old things out there.

WORKING WITH VOCALS

15 What is the approach you take when working with a great singer in the studio, someone like Aretha Franklin, Mariah, or even a Whitney Houston?

➤ I think you can't remake something that's already beautiful; that's already solid. You can enhance it, or you can maybe put it in a different setting...like a precious ring, but you *let that jewel be that jewel*. I think some people come in, and then try to give greats like Aretha Franklin a production where they say, "Well, if you do this, and sing this like that..." or whatever. But to me, that's not going to to work for her. What works for Aretha is giving her a great song. You get a song and then a good production; something that is believable so that when they look at it and listen, *which is very important*, they say, "Oh, wow... did you hear the newest Aretha record? Did you hear *what she was saying*? Did you hear *how she was saying it*? Did you *feel it*? And I think that's what a lot of the artists are... jewels. I didn't think producers should try to remake them. And then there is Whitney Houston, who is another jewel. All Whitney needs is great songs, and great productions.... neither of which I think she probably gets with an unskilled producer because how many people out there right now can *really* actually work with a vocalist that really truly sings at Whitney's level?"

➢ Producers have to have developed *that* skill of producing to be able to do it like that. So that they are proficient enough to say, "Oh, I *hear* that you're flat", or, "I *hear* that you're sharp"... or, "Hey, you need to go here" or "Here goes the chord passages to the song." I believe in song playing; so that if you're going to give her the track, *then give her the track!* You have to learn what key... *"She sings in".* I believe in song playing so that you know, "Oh, she sings in *this key."* So many have it all wrong. You are supposed to conform to the singer, *not the singer conforms to the track!* I tell my singers in the studio, "We're gonna build this sound around you." And that's what I do in sound architecture. It's like, "Yo, "Let me feel your energy, let feel where you coming from!" Then you can say, "Ok, I got it now!" Then you develop the music and the songs, around the artist, so that the whole thing is believable.

16 Manuel, you have worked on rappers like Da Brat and also singers like Mariah Carey, how do you make the transition from Hip Hop to R&B?

➢ It's being aware of all your tools that you are using in a given composition; or track or song. See, there are certain things or certain elements that are in Hip Hop, and then there are certain elements that are *musical...* that's in R&B or whatever. So, for me... it's a "state of mind"... or I get into a "state of mind". If I'm ready to do some Hip Hop stuff, then, that's what I'll listen to...and I'll absorb *that*, before I start dealing with it! The other stuff is easy because that's what I was raised on – the R&B stuff. So that's just a "state of mind". I go in the studio, close the door... and *'Bam!' I'm there!* These tools or mind set are ready for me.

So it's just definition – it's defining *what it is* ...and *how* you're going to be working it.

THE MANUEL SEAL MUSIC SEMINARS

17 Tell us about your Seminars for Artists, Songwriters and Producers.

➤ The seminars are for educating talent...to let them know, *"Yo, this is how you gotta do it!"* I run into these situations where people are paying money through these various outlets to get their stuff heard, and *that* hurts our industry too. *Man,* that's about the d u m b e s t thing I've ever heard; they charge a $1,000 fee, *but you can put your $250 down!* People are getting cheated like that, and *that* doesn't have *anything to do with the music industry!* Either you have something going on, *or you don't!* It's like one of the first things you learn, *"You don't pay the publisher, the publisher is suppose to pay you!"* So are you going to go *pay* somebody else to "hear" your song... to get your song placed or whatever? It doesn't work like that! There are just a lot of problems plaguing our industry right now, and there are a lot of people that are feeding off of it too. And they make a living off of that kind of thing. But to me though, that just further says that the ones who "do know," are not doing their job. Or, we all got to come together and start saying, "These problems are plaguing us." Because that's what part of business is *too*, "solving problems." So first we have to identify and define the problems, so we can deal with them. If we never identify and define the problems, then become responsible, we won't have anything to pass down.

➤ My point in doing the music seminars is to also raise the "art" factor in production and songwriting. Whatever you're doing musically is an art... like sampling. "Sampling is an art!" And learning h o w to put all of those things together *is an art form. "That"* process of creativity is a beautiful thing. But a lot of people don't understand that...if they don't develop that process. For example, when you can understand the *process*, you can do things like take someone else's humming, and then know *"how" to make it work.* Or just take someone else's guitar idea, and then "you" understand how to make *that* work.

➢ When you *understand* the creative process, you will know *how to hear it*, and know how to put what you hear into perspective and *how to use it.* That's the skill and ear training that I learned from Church. In the Church, someone might be singing, and then holler at the musicians, "Catch me!" ...And that developed my ear. And then once you get it to a point where you start hearing melodies in your head, and you start learning the "how to" in the creative process; putting the harmonics with the melodic, you then put those two things together, and it all becomes easy. So once you learn *this*, when you do the music production, you can "build" from any piece; a drumbeat, a guitar line, a vocal part, a bass line, or even a string line. We can then put together the "whole song," from just one little thing. And that's what the seminars are all about, learning.

"...We should forever be learning!"

MANUEL SEAL JR.

Multi-Platinum - Award Winning Producer & Songwriter
Manuel's credits include Jermaine Dupri, Usher, Alicia Keys, Destiny's Child, Jagged Edge, Da Brat, Mary J., Gerald Levert, Johnny Gill, Mariah Carey, and many others

www.ManuelSeal.com

Music Powers
SPOTLIGHT
DJ TOOMP

Producer – Executive Producer - Songwriter
Biography

At the age when most teenage boys are interested in fashion, sports, and girls, DJ Toomp was handling his business and cut his first record/hit song with Raheem the Dream in 1985. This began a dynasty of his credits to date. A prodigy of his father the lead singer for the group The MVP's who taught him how to harmonize at the age of six; its no wonder that music is in his genes. "I always knew about music, but I never thought I'd be creating it," he says.

Right out of high school DJ Toomp hit the music scene spinning the sounds that resonated in his soul. It was only a matter of time that this young and energetic mastermind of a musician would come full circle of his first love—creating music and making stars.

"I like producing artists," Toomp says. "I like for them to come to my studio and just vibe, more than just take a track and put something to it... I'd rather work with an artist so that things don't go wrong along the way."

His latest has resulted in TI's debut album; I'm Serious, which was released in 2001 on Arista Records. As Associate Producer, Toomp was responsible for a good majority of the album including "Dope Boyz," "Do It" and "Heavy Chevys." As Executive Producer for TI's sophomore effort - Trap Muzik - Toomp strung together a succession of hits that catapulted the young star into the limelight and deemed him worthy of the "King of the South" proclamation that he so often likes to claim. Among Toomp's own were "Trap Muzik," "Be Easy" and "24's."

Through Zone Boy Productions, Toomp Stone Publishing and his independent record label, Nzone Entertainment, DJ Toomp is currently grooming a host of artist that the world will soon come to know and love.

"I've done good in the industry, but I still don't think I've won," says an optimistic yet humble DJ Toomp. "I have these eyes and ears, and I know what it takes to be successful in this business. I want to discover a star... I want to win." And if the past starts are any indication of the future, the world is in for a treat from this multifaceted musical genius.

Music Powers SPOTLIGHT

DJ TOOMP

Producer – Executive Producer – Songwriter

A Select Discography

T.I.
Ludacris
Lil Jon & The Eastside Boyz
Boyz In Da Hood
DSGB
Pastor Troy
Luke
Ken Fluid
Kavious
Raheem the Dream

Movie Soundtrack Credits:

"Dick In the Dust," (New Jack City)
"Push 'Em Up" (Dr. Doolittle)

Music Powers

Exclusive Advice from Music Powers Advisor

DJ TOOMP

PRODUCER – EXECUTIVE PRODUCER – SONGWRITER

"SHOWTIME" VS. BEHIND THE SCENES

1 More and more producers today seem to be getting very famous by producing, and they are in the spotlight like artists... What are your thoughts?

For me, I play a little part in music videos; I don't really try to do "all-that" though. But there are producers like Pharrell, Jazzy Pha, Lil' Jon, Kanye, Puffy... but these are producers who are also being artists. But most people who strictly "produce" and kind of want to play "the back", stay out of most videos; like Rodney Jerkins, Jam & Lewis, you know... and every now and then you might see a producer like Just Blaze, who might pop-up every once-in-a-while, but he's not like "all-in-the-camera". All of that is cool, but for me, I just want to be that guy who can just be rich; a multi-millionaire... and still pull-up on the scene and "kick-it"... you know what I'm sayin'. I want to still be able to go to the video shoots, or go out of town; enjoy myself... and still go into a grocery store or a mall.

➤ Look at Darryl Simmons, who use to be with Babyface & L.A. – he was real "low-key" ... and calls his thing "Silent Partner". He was getting paid just like Babyface and L.A.; producing too... and behind a lot of their success, and a lot of those hit records... but behind the scenes.

"...Look at Smurf (Mr. Collipark),
He's "killin' them on that executive level.
He's that silent-executive-rich producer,
And everybody (the public) doesn't have to
Know all about it".

PRODUCTION TOOLS - WEAPONS IN THE LAB

2 So what tools are you using in production in the studio to contribute to your particular sound?

DJ Toomp

One thing is the ASR-10 Sampling Keyboard (Ensoniq), which plays a part, as far as everything, because I got that when it first came out. The ASR is set up like; whatever sound that you have, if it needs to be fattened up, you can just take the outputs and sample it back into itself (looped from the outputs – back to the sample inputs). I have a few joints that I use that technique. Like on T.I.'s first album, I use it like that. I will sometimes just sample *my own music* and trigger the samples on different keys. I will hit different notes of – in my loop.

Ensoniq ASR - 10

➤ That ASR-10 is the one. And I'm learning the Phantom by Roland right now too. But as far as a sampling keyboard, to me… the ASR is like the king. See the thing about it is if you have an ASR, you *have to be creative*. With most samplers, it will have all these internal sounds waiting for you to use, but the ASR, there is *nothing* in there… and it's waiting on you to do your *own* thang. There is no library or banks that come up loaded or whatever. That keyboard comes up empty, so it just forces you to be creative.

➤ There are a lot of other producers who use it too. Producers like The Neptunes, Buggs; Kanye uses it; Brian Kidd who's down with Timbaland uses it. Actually, there are a lot of songs that Timbaland did, and it was *just with the ASR-10… by itself!* Everybody uses it. So to me, it's just awesome.

> ➤ *The ASR-10 has put people in houses (laughing). It has really made people's bank accounts grow too… you feel me.*
> *…So yeah man, it's dope.*

Remember - Log on to: www.Musicpowers.com/24 to see videos.

3 Do you think that to become a good producer, people need to keep their creativity and skills in tact, and also developed with learning their gear?

➤ Yes, because they are making it so easy nowadays. Now, you have Reasons, and programs like Fruity Loops… man, you don't have to do anything now. Honestly, as far as becoming a producer goes… I think they need to make it a *requirement* that you learn the Akai MPC. And right now, it's almost a requirement that every producer needs to learn how to use Pro Tools. You need to learn at least some of it. I might know about 40% of it, but I really just track with Pro Tools so I wouldn't have to haul my equipment back and fourth to the recording studio.

➤ At first I had the Roland 1680, and that was cool, but how many studios can you go to and they have a 1680 set up? But 90% of recording studios will have Pro Tools. So, I had to invest; I went and bought my little "joints". I have this little G4 (Apple Macintosh Computer) over here.

Pro Tools 002

"…And just like Pro Tools is required,
No matter what comes out next year,
Or the year after on a computer,
Producers still need to
Learn the MPC."

Akai MPC 2000

➤ The MPC and those drum pads give you that feel of playing. So, whoever was in school playing their beats on their school desk needs the MPC.

ADVICE FOR INDIES PUTTING OUT RECORDS

4 What is your best advice as far as putting out a new artist or new songs as an independent company?

➤ See, I play it safe; I "drop" some singles. It's almost like fishing; don't go and record a *whole album* and release it *right away*, because the vibe can get old. If you record a whole album in here right now, and then it's just "bubbling" under on the charts; not really getting what it's suppose to get, then you'll be in trouble. Let 6 months go by, and then you're thinking you might need a re-mix or whatever. So you just got to go grab it right then; you got to put that music out when it's hot (as a single)!

RECOGNIZING TALENT & THE GENIUS OF T.I.

5 How did you discover T.I. and recognize he had the talent, along with what "you do" …all to become a success?

➢ Well, there was this guy named 'Toot" (TOOT, not Toomp). You know that part on the song "Rubber Band Man", where it says, "Rest in peace to my cousin Toot." That's him, but I got phone calls because people thought it was saying, "Toomp" (me), and they thought something had happened to me. Toot was a guy from the neighborhood that I'd known since I was in the 5th Grade, and also throughout my music career. But anyway, what happened was that Toot called me and told me that he had a cousin that *"Ain't no joke! ...And I know you've been lookin' for a rapper for a while."* So Toot brought T.I. to my house, and when I heard him it was "hot" … bangin'. So, I gave T.I. like 5 tracks, and that week I think he wrote to 4 of those tracks. The thing about it that is crazy… you know like everybody is buggin' about Biggie Smalls and Jay-Z can go in the studio without paper; they don't write anything… well, T.I. was doing that in 1997 or '98. Everything that you hear from him, he doesn't write anything… period! He just goes in there (the studio) and just "spit-it". "He doesn't write nothing!" It's like genius. Pharrell was on V-103 radio this morning saying that T.I. is one of the "dopest" rappers that he had ever dealt with outside of Jay-Z. And man, when you're a producer, and you're use to a guy having to learn his raps and whatnot. But when you run into this one guy out of ten that can just go in there

and just "hit it"… you're like "damn!!"   For example, what T.I. will do is walk around the room for a minute, and his manager might say, "Hey man, we got this song with a title called 'Heavy Chevys' … and he'll just listen to the beat'; he'll look at everybody; case out the mood and vibe, and then he'll just say, "Cut the microphone on!" And then he'll just go in the vocal booth and just "nail-it"! I mean it's crazy… he's "sick" man, he's "sick" dude! He's actually the best artist that I've ever worked with so far.

"…When you have an artist that can bring almost anything to life; and you can dig through your stack of tracks and pull up whatever the way T.I. does; you just know you have something special."

6 So was the song 24s a custom thing for T.I., or did you already have it?

➢ It was not custom yet. I already had the beat, but it still didn't have the breakdown and all that. But all of the song came together when T.I. started writing to it. That is an example of a beat that has been programmed… but isn't a song yet.

➢ **For example:** You might have a guy that can just program a beat; well that's a beat programmer… you made the beat. But I "produce" artist; I don't just sell tracks, I produce artists, I don't "sell" tracks. When you're selling tracks you're not even there to tell them anything or "Hey man, this is what type of "flow" this needs", you're just giving it to them. But at that time, with this track, that's what I had at the time, a programmed track.

➢ Anyway, I was cutting T.I.'s hair, and the track was playing real low in the background, and he couldn't keep his head still. So I'm like, "You like that?" He said, "I got something' for that!" Then he started singing, "Money H*@'s, cars and clothes, that's what all my ni*#@% know." And I was like, "*man*, that's cool, I think young cats will like that!"

SIMPLICITY - THE KEY TO A HIT RECORD

➢ It was like that "bouncing-ball" in the cartoons that follows the words and man, just so you know, simplicity will always work. Sometimes when people have too many words in the hook, it doesn't work.

"…You have to make it simple for the people. That's one of the ingredients for a hit record."

7 How important would you say it is for a producer to concentrate on having hit records and making big money?

➢ Well it's not "all-about-the-money" to me. This whole thing is fun to me, and I just like making good product. I'd put the same energy into something that the check might not be as big as another project… but my name will be on it. So, I still know I have to put that same energy behind the project.

GRINDING, TIMING ...AND GETTING THE DEAL

8 Tell us your strategy, your steps - how you finally were able to get that major record deal for T.I.?

➢ **1ST:** It was perfect man, I must say. I guess the stars were lined up right, and the moon or whatever; everything fell right in place.

➢ **2ND:** See, with the song 24s... we had a plan to the point to where we said, "alright, cool, lets do this!"... Because we had already recorded about 12 songs, but what we did was choose the best song(s) to pull out as a single release and just work the streets ourselves. So on that "strength" we got everything rolling.

➢ **3RD:** We also knew that the NBA Basketball All-star Game weekend was coming, and this was going to be the first one in Atlanta... and big. And we also knew that this; this type of event would bring *every type of executive you could think of into the city at one time*. At that time we had gotten all our relationships with the stations in good standing too. So we were able to let them know that we had this new single we were getting ready to come with...24s. Honestly man, as soon as we left the mastering lab with 24s, and we got through all that Atlanta traffic from the big All-star weekend, we had the song playing on the radio, and right between that 6 and 10 spot; DJ CoCo Brotha from HOT-107.9 played the song. CoCo played the song like 3 times in a 4-hour block. See, people heard it once, and then people just kept on calling in, "Let me hear that new T.I. again!" See, all it takes is that phone call... man it got crazy!

➢ **4TH:** We just kept getting that push behind the song; we hit all the clubs. That way, the clubs will have an influence on the radio. Whatever people hear about from the clubs, they will end up calling the radio stations... like, "Hey, we heard this new song by T.I., do ya'll got it?" And CoCo would be like, *"Yeah, I got it right here"*... and he will put it on, sometimes right on the spot! DJs like CoCo Brotha will tell you, *"Whether I like it or not... it ain't up to me, but if I put it on these airwaves... we'll see what you got."* And for us, people were calling in like crazy.

COCO BROTHA
DJ - HOT 107.9

➢ **5TH:** We also had a buzz going on from "Never Scared" with our own underground Mix-CD release.

➢ **6TH:** Over that whole All-star weekend we got all of the Mix-show DJs playing and mixing the song. Every time you would look around you would be hearing a mix of 24s.

➢ **7TH:** After that we went to A&R guys Kevin Lyles, Mike Caren, etc., and everybody was like, "We need to talk, we need to talk!" Every executive was hearing about us. Man, when these guys were down here in Atlanta, they would be in these Limos or whatever... with the driver taking them around town, and they kept hearing about T.I. and 24s. So all of this was happening on the strength of 24s, and "boom", after meetings with everybody; Columbia, Universal, Def Jam, Bad Boy, and Atlantic, it ended up being a first single when we got the deal with Atlantic.

 What influenced you all to do the deal with Atlantic Records?

Atlantic was the only label that was willing to really "jump" behind that single (24s) and continue to push it. They were like, "Hey, you can sign the contract, and within a week we're gonna be ready to do the music video!" So they were ready to get on-it!! Where everyone else was like, "You may not be able to come out until first quarter of 2005." And when we came back to Atlanta, everybody was like telling us, "Ya'll should have went with Def Jam or Bad Boy and Puffy... or whatever." But, unless you're in this situation, don't tell me what I should have done. Because what happens with a lot of label deals ... you end up putting something out independently, and it ends up being a hot-hot single... but by the time you got with a major label, you have *some* who may want to "jump on it", but *some* don't. Next thing you know, the momentum has faded away. The song or project might have played out. So, Atlantic were the ones willing to jump on things. And I ended up having the first "joint" on there, and I got to be the Executive Producer too... and it was a pretty good deal too; everything was good.

BE ORIGINAL – STAY ORIGINAL!

10 How important is it for artists and producers to be, and stay original?

➢ You know, it's only a few that can rap like Eminem, that boy is *AWESOME!* All the most *successful* rappers out here... like Ludacris, you can *identify*. Nobody sounds like him. Ludacris throws *words* at you; that's *his* style; *"Cadillac grill... Check out the oil my Cadillac spills."* He *throws* words, that is *Ludacris'* style... and nobody else needs to try that. Also, look at the flippin' rap-style, let Twista have that. Nobody needs to touch that style right now Let Twista *have that*. And look at T.I. now ... some people are kind of jumping on his style a little bit. Sometimes I'll be busting my brains to stay original… like, man, I got to stop that beat, it sounds too much like Lil' Jon. And then, sometimes I might hear something on the radio with *my* little snare sound; and *my* little drum roll, and people trying to play with the horns and strings, just like in my productions. But luckily, thank God I can just come up with something else. I'll just start playing with other instruments in my songs that a lot of other people use to cross over on. So you have to be creative man and just keep coming with it. Whenever somebody tells me that they hear something of mine and it reminds them of something else out there… then I just switch it up. I like to surprise people.

11 So is having an original sound *and* image one of the "keys" to being successful?

➢ Yes. Like back a few years ago, you had young groups like ABC (from Dallas Austin), and they had an image. You were able to identify young new acts like Kriss Kross… that Jermaine Dupri took time to develop and be original. They were like, "Hey man, we're going to wear our clothes backwards! …That's going to be our thing." And Xcape, they had their own thing, even though Jodeci was wearing the boots too. If I had all my records right here, right now, we could go through some album covers, and I could tell you which ones *really* sold some units. Like Freddy Jackson, he wasn't a muscle-bound man, that man just had good songs; and he's just smooth. And to this day, you can still listen to some song by the Spinners, and then say, "Oh, that's the Spinners!" Or, you might hear a song and say, "That's The Whispers … that's one of the 'twins' *on that part.*" Even like The Neptunes, those boys… they make a lot of songs that don't sound alike. It's the people who they produce, who keep saying, "Hey man, give me one like you gave Jay-Z." Man, The Neptunes have (different) beats. I've heard some stuff from them where you really wouldn't know that it's The Neptunes until somebody says it.   You also have A&R saying things like, "Why don't you give me something on that Lil John feel?" But, if I "walk" something in, which I really believe in… from my experience and my ears, and how I *feel* music more than listen to it, I want to make sure that the company is going to get behind it being original.

"…When I walk in a new artist, I want A&R saying,
"This is something special;
This doesn't sound like T.I.
This doesn't sound like Lil' Jon,
This doesn't sound like Jay-Z.
This doesn't sound like Ludacris …or anybody.
This is something brand new!"

DJ TOOMP

PRODUCER – EXECUTIVE PRODUCER – SONGWRITER

For more - visit www.Musicpowers.com/24

Music Powers SPOTLIGHT
MR. COLLIPARK

...Formerly DJ Smurf, aka Beat-In-Azz, aka Michael Crooms...
CEO of Collipark Records – Multi-Platinum Producer - Songwriter

Biography

Mr. Collipark is the CEO of Collipark Records; he's a multi-platinum producer and songwriter; and he's also one of the brightest young entrepreneurs in the music industry. Originally one of Atlanta's hottest DJs, and also a solo recording artist under the name 'DJ Smurf', Mr. Collipark who's real name is Michael Crooms, is now winning in the music game by turning his vision and business savvy into Collipark Music, a multi-million dollar, hit-making record and production company. Mr. Crooms' productions and trance-like beats, along with the original genius of D-Roc and Kaine of the Ying Yang Twins, have made a new place in Hip-Hop music history. Ying Yang,

along with Collipark, have taken *what they do* to that *next level* of success.

The Atlanta based company Collipark, and Ying Yang have been on the grind over the years... staying focused and patiently working their gift – all to become superstars. They've taken it from the 'street'... to the penthouse 'sweet'! And maybe in the beginning, Ying Yang and Smurf may have been famous as a "party act" ("Whistle While You Twurk"), but now they've *also* emerged as one of the hottest and most original Hip-Hop performing, production & writing teams in the music industry. Their "history-making" #1 collaboration with Lil' Jon & The Eastside Boyz ("Get Low"), along with their recent innovative hit record "Wait" (The Whisper Song"), makes it clear that "Ying Yang and Mr. Collipark ain't no joke!"

Look for the Ying Yang Twins & Crooms (Mr. Collipark) to be around for a long, long, long (loop that) time... *"Shoot... they're just getting' started!"* And for all of you, who *thought* that Ying Yang Twins were just a "One-hit-wonder", stop the hate! For one and all... Michael Crooms and the Ying Yang Twins are indisputably here to stay!

SPOTLIGHT
MR. COLLIPARK

...Formerly DJ Smurf, aka Beat-In-Azz, aka Michael Crooms...
CEO of Collipark Records – Multi-Platinum Producer – Songwriter

Select Discography

DJ SMURF

ColliPark Music

Mr. Collipark

YING YANG TWINS
LIL JON & THE EASTSIDE BOYZ
YOUNG JEEZY
DAVID BANNER
TWISTA
LUKE
B.G.
SO SO DEF BASS ALL-STARS
RHYTHM & QUAD 166, VOL. 1
KADALACK BOYZ
HOMEBWOI
BUCK POWER
CRUNK'D
DA BLOCK PARTY
THRILL DA PLAYA
281 BOYZ

Music Powers
Exclusive Advice from Music Powers Advisor

MR. COLLIPARK

Formerly DJ Smurf, aka Beat-In-Azz, aka Michael Crooms
CEO of Collipark Records – Multi-Platinum Producer – Songwriter – DJ

RECOGNIZING TALENT – DISCOVERING YING YANG

1 How did the Ying Yang Twins come about as artists for Collipark Records?

Really, when I first saw D-Roc and Kaine, I was not even into being a record label or anything like that. The way I first heard them rap was when D-Roc came into the studio to do a feature rap on my own album. He was supposed to bring in a completely different "cat" to rap with him, but they "fell out" right before the recording session. So he brought Kaine in the studio instead. And when I heard them together, I was like, *"Damn!"* I think I told them right then, before I was even trying to get them together as a group, *"Yall need to do some songs together!"* So that's how the whole *Ying Yang thing and me* started.

2 What was it that you heard or felt that made you *know* D-Roc and Kaine was it? Was it their rapping skills, their writing, …what?

➤ It was "MAGIC!" It was intangible; it was "that *thang!*" You know, it's like when there's a record you might love. See, you might be able to say that someone can really rap well, but it's still really something that you can't even say what it is. Or explain it. That was the first time "for real" man… I was checking out *that* type of magic in an act; it's rare (like the artist Kilo) …only certain *type* of people "got *that*" thang… that I personally know.

"…D-Roc and Kaine just had this thang going on that I hadn't heard before.

Especially from some guys younger than me!"

3 What was the next move that happened to get things going for you and Ying Yang?

➤ The next thing that came up was the So So Def All-stars thing. I was on the phone with Searcy (Emperor Searcy of BME) and he was telling me they had this great track and what kind of song they needed. And this was after The Organization came out. So when I called D-Roc in to do the record, D-Roc came with what I expected. And comin' clean; D-Roc has *always* been one of the

most "Crunkest" guys I've ever know in my life; even before Lil' Jon. He has always had that energy. And Kaine, who had never rapped to the type of record we were making, he actually wrote his rap to one of the gangster raps that were out at the time. And when they came together on that track, it was like something new.

D-Roc (above) – *Courtesy of TVT*.
Kaine (right), writing in the studio.

➤ So I told Searcy, "I got the perfect 2 guys for yall!" So I hooked them up with Searcy, and they did this record called "True City Thugs," and to me it was the hottest record on that album, but it was ahead of its time.

At that point, Ichiban, the label I was signed to, was going out of business, and my contract got sold to the company that was coming in to buy them out. And through me putting that project together, this is when I first realized that I had what it took to put records together. I went and got people like Luke, Kid Money, etc... all the people I wanted to work with. I went and actually recorded the album and had it done before I even had a budget. I shot a little video and then got the "buzz" going on my record. And I'm thinking when everything kicks in; things would be "on". But overall nothing happened. So I said forget this, and that was the last record I did as an artist. And at that point, "No Limit" had kicked in, and the whole music scene in Atlanta had changed. And I was like, "I can't compete with all this as an artist." And at that time Raheem The Dream had put Drama out. And every interview that I do, I try to give Raheem his props. To me, Raheem was always the ideal businessman. So I figured if I apply a business plan to the whole thing with Ying Yang, along with my music, we could do this. And that's when we cut "Whistle While You Twurk." And it blew up, and we did the original deal with Universal. But the whole lawsuit thing came out, and Universal didn't wanna be a part of the lawsuit, so at that time they stepped back from the project and just threw it out there because they didn't wanna be a part of the whole sample issue.

 After that, it came to a point where we were still signed to Universal, but being the major that they were at that time, they were sitting on our project. And we still had other stuff on the album, and nobody knew that Ying Yang is for real... but us. They didn't believe in anything else on the album. So I told them, either put another single out, or put me in the studio to put *another* album out, or let me go. So Universal said, "send us some more records for the next album, and we'll go from there.' So we cut "Iy Yi Yi," and I sent it up to them, and when they heard it, they were like, "*Naaaa*, we will let you go!" And then that's when we went to Koch.

➤ See, in the process of me going to all these labels, I had sent out some test CDs to the DJs I dealt with, and the record that they picked was "Iy Yi Yi." And see, everybody (the labels) thought Ying Yang was done. But after I found out on the street-level what "Iy Yi Yi" was, I didn't care what label I did the deal with because I knew I had another hit. And that's how we ended up at Koch. So I made a little production / distribution deal with them. But Koch only signed a one-year deal with us... with NO options! Which is how we were able to move on from Koch to TVT.

ONE YEAR DEALS

4 Why would Koch only sign you to a one-year deal?

➤ Because the label was so use to signing acts that were basically on there way out. Koch thought Ying Yang; "The Whistle While You Twurk" group was only good for those last 20 or 30,000 records to be sold. And I didn't accept a big advance from Koch because I had seen this whole thing happen before. So once I saw those same signs on "Iy Yi Yi" ...that I saw on "Whistle While You Twurk" I was like, "I can take a smaller deal" because I was seeing the signs of a true hit record in the making.

5 For the next Indie Label on the come-up, tell us the kind of numbers (sales) that were involved in the whole process of getting from your original indie release on your own, all the way to the Koch single album deal?

➤ We sold 100,000 units through SMD (Southern Music Distribution), and it was still an undetermined amount of singles sold of "Whistle While You Twurk", which was the first single of the first label that we put out. Then, we re-released the album on Universal, and I don't know the exact sales numbers up until the date of the Koch album.   But, it let people know; the ones who bought the first album… that Ying Yang makes solid records.   So our fan-base from that first release was for-real; it wasn't just a *fluke*-thing.

➢ What we did was to really take it to the street; the clubs and club DJs. At that time, I had built up relationships with DJs as an artist, not as a record company. And I had brothers who were the top DJs in their market… who I would send my music to. And if they test it, and they come back and say, "Dogg, this record is out the roof!" And I'm getting calls back to back. And if I get that from about 4 different markets, I know I have something - a hit. So that's what I saw with the "Iy Yi Yi" record. I had about 400 to 500 radio-spins before Koch even opened up the radio budget.

TIMING – BEING IN SYNC WITH THE UNIVERSE

God was on our side too. A lot of great things happened for us; the radio spins

kicked off; we shot a great video for $35,000; and I was learning how to get my "biz thang" on, like learning how to work with nothing… as a company; to shoot a good video in one day and one location, and getting the most you can out of that, etc. And that "Iy Yi Yi" video came out better than anyone expected.   And then there was the blessing that came out of nowhere; Denzel Washington and Halle Barry won those Oscars. See, because of that, the TV broadcast of B.E.T.'s 106th & Park Show decided to go "live", and they decided to debut the Ying Yang video – one day before the album came out. At that time only "big" artists were on 106th & Park. And then A.J., the host of the show had the CD in his hand, and he was saying, *"This album comes out tomorrow and go buy it!"* And I remember sitting at home being blown away, and knowing that God was working for us. And from all the "B.S." it was all finally coming together and paying off. We came out bustin' 20 to 30,000 units in the first week, and back then in 2002, and on a small label like Koch, that was unheard of. In addition to all of that, Ying Yang Twins are complete artists. It's just that no one else seemed to know it… except us.

➢ So after the first week with releasing "Iy Yi Yi," we didn't drop our sales like most records do… we stayed up there. If the first week we sold 20,000 units, then the second week we might have sold 16,000… and we kept hangin' around those numbers… all the way into the single "By Myself." And at this point I don't think Koch realized they only had a 1 album deal with us, with no options. And I think by the time we had shot the "By Myself" video, Koch might have looked back at the contract and finally realized that whole one-year thing. So then they started panicking big-time (laughing).

DON'T TRY TO PLAY ME

6 So since Koch only had a one-year deal set up, was there a chance for them to renegotiate the whole thing to further the success with Ying Yang?

➢ Well, when we went to renegotiate the album situation, they made all these promises at first... *and I actually believed the hype.* But, then they made the mistake of sending me a statement showing us in the negative... off of the most  successful rap record they had ever had. How in the world do you send me a statement showing me in the negative, and you're trying to get me to sign again? So, they played themselves in the renegotiation! But then, the *"real"* renegotiations started after that. And this was the point where I *knew there was no future with Koch;* they tried to renegotiate money that they *already owed me,* as a *part of the advance* for the *next* album.

...And I'm thinking, "Do I look that stupid?"

7 So was Koch not willing to get the renegotiating and come to the table correct, and give us your philosophy in dealing with labels in general?

➢ My thing to Koch was like; the ball is in your court to both do the right thing, and let's make some money *together*... because you're not going to "pimp" me. It's not going to be a one-way situation, or I'll just shut it all down. See, I let companies know that *they are not* the only place I'm getting a check. So, I let them know that I can go without their check and still eat. See, when you take that away from them, if messes up their whole thing. I made it clear with Koch that you either do the right thing, or I'm "bouncing"! And I guess they didn't believe what I was saying. So we were free agents and in the best possible position.

GOING WITH TVT RECORDS & "ON-POINT" A&R

8 So why the decision to go with TVT Records?

➢ Well, there were only a few companies who I was willing to entertain the idea of being with; I didn't even want to meet with everybody. *I wanted to win!*

➢ TVT was on my radar simply because the fact that Jon (Lil' Jon & The Eastside Boyz) wasn't selling a whole shipload of records, but they stuck with his album big-time! And what seemed like... for *no reason!* So I'm analyzing it like,

"Why is he still putting videos out… and singles too, and they are working his releases *into his next album?*" And that was some unheard of stuff. I watch stuff like that. And I watched everybody else with these major deals, and they were not serious with this stuff. So it came down to TVT, and a few others as choices.

9 What was the edge TVT had over your other choices to sign with?

The main difference between TVT and the other companies was the A&R over at TVT - Brian Leach. He's a young guy, with the mentality of the whole rap game on that New York "tip"; you know, because they're on another level up in New York… because that's where it started. We aren't even on that level yet down here in the South. Our thing down here in the South is on some real primitive stuff as opposed to how the "New York-game" is.

Along with this, he was the first person that I actually talked to in a position to do anything that actually understood what we were doing… musically! It's like; this 'cat' "got it!" He got the whole thing. And the fact that he was doing what he was doing with Lil' Jon let me know Brian Leach knew what to do with it… before "The Kings of Crunk".

➢ See, an independent label has to "do what they got to do"… no matter what. They don't care what's popular or what's not popular; they just do what they got to do! And when I see moves like what Brian Leach and TVT were doing, I have to recognize, "Man, these folk TVT doing some "gangsta-moves" for a record label".

KEYS TO GETTING PAID

10 So what's is key to up-and-coming artists and producers who may be in a situation where negotiations for money or a deal is at hand?

➢ To me, this is one of the "key" things: Anytime your check is limited to only that "one" company or person, you are screwed out here! These folk will make you want to kill them... you know what I'm saying. And I'm not a gangster, but I'm human. So, I never want to let anybody; "not-one" company or person think that they are my only means of getting "bread" out here... because that's when everything can get cut off.

    ❏   *...Let's repeat this for those of you who were not paying attention!!!*

11 So what's is key to up-and-coming artists and producers who may be in a situation where negotiations for money or a deal is at hand?

To me, this is one of the "key" things: *Anytime your check is limited to only that "one" company or person, you are screwed out here!* These folk will make you want to kill them... you know what I'm saying. And I'm not a gangster, but I'm human.

So, I never want to let *anybody*; "not one" company or any person think that they are my *only* means of getting "bread" out here... because *that's when everything can get cut off!*

12 Give us your best advice for new artists and producers who are trying to "get on" or who are trying to get A&R at labels interested enough to sign them to a deal?

It begins when you can *make a record*... that's *good enough* to take somewhere ... to get a response from your peers, or the area where you live, and it warrants someone having some interest in you. For instance, I can go to some nightclub when they have their little talent night, and I might hear 30 groups singing the same record. All of these people are making the same type of songs. And it's to the point where I can't even tell the difference. But out of those 30, it's 1 or 2 songs that people pick out of those 30 that really jam. The "Knuck If You Buck" record was one of those type songs.

You gotta try to make some music that will compete with what's going on out here. You're competing against Ying Yang, you're competing against Lil' Jon, you're competing against Ludacris. *Everything that's out here is your competition!*

> Just tryin' to "get on" is the wrong way to look at it. It's a "Dog-eat-dog" competition, so you got to go bust these established people butts who are already "on".

13   So where would you test the potency of your song?

> With everything I just said in mind, maybe I'll have take my music over to a hot club, and break the DJ off … if that's the route I gotta take, so then I may need to give the DJ $20 or whatever as a tip. But the point is, when he plays my stuff, I have to (and you must too) *take notice*. Because for every hit record I ever had… you might have a couple of people who will keep dancing, but look around at the people who are *sitting down…* to see if people are groovin' in their seats; noddin' and boppin' their heads, etc.   *You have to have hot product, because outside of that … it's the "who you know".*

14   And what is the trend at the labels as far as what labels are looking for?

> These labels want to give deals to people who got some kind of get-up-and-go about them, because they don't really want to do A&R development anymore. That "Step Daddy" record was an example of that. I had just put my name on the BDS, and a week later we had the deal on the table.

"…So, if you're gonna be out here, it's a competition; you're running against the best.

And if you can't get out here (and really compete), you ain't ready …you just ain't ready!"

For more, visit us on-line at: **www.Musicpowers.com/24**

Formerly DJ Smurf, aka Beat-In-Azz, aka Michael Crooms

CEO of Collipark Records – Multi-Platinum Producer – Songwriter – DJ

Music Powers
HIP-HOP - RAP - R&B/POP MUSIC INDUSTRY
PRODUCER CONTACT DIRECTORY

The Music Powers Producer's Contact Directory is a list of many of the most established, seasoned, and successful Hip Hop, Rap and R&B/Pop Record Producers in the US. If you are a musician, a background vocalist, a programmer, engineer, DJ, or possibly a "new" producer looking to be part of a team, then you should know that getting your package with the producers who are making records and already have relationships with A&R and managers is a *must*. So we have supplied you with this contact information so that you, *whenever your music or presentation is ready*, can send them your best material. The contact information is also a must for any artist, label, or manager that is *ready* to "hire" a seasoned p r o f e s s i o n a l to help get their project to the *next* level. The company has been called to have their info verified, but please NOTE: These "professionals" are *e x t r e m e l y* busy, so remember to be very professional and courteous for *any* solicitations that you may be considering.

...GOOD LUCK

A - B - C

DALLAS AUSTIN
FREEWORLD / DARP
576 A Trabert Ave. NW
Atlanta, GA 30309
404-351-6680
www.cyptron.com

* *TLC, Madonna, Pink, Sammy*
* *Boys II Men, Michael Jackson*
* *JT Money, India.Arie*

BABYFACE
HERVEY ENTERTAINMENT COMPANY
PO Box 877
Chaptaqua, NY 10514
914-238-8947

* *Madonna, Toni Braxton, Mary J.*
* *Boyz II Men, Mariah, Johnny Gill*
* *Whitney Houston, Outkast, Nsync*
* *EnVogue, Goodie Mob, Pink*

DAVID BANNER
BANNER BEATS, LLC
c/o Wendy Day
99 South 2nd Street, Suite 274
Memphis, TN 38103
917-501-6100
wdayrapco@aol.com

* *Nelly, DSGB, Bone Crusher*
* *Lil' Flip, Chingy*

BEAT-IN-AZZ
'MR. COLLIPARK' (DJ SMURF)
COLLIPARK MUSIC, INC.
PO Box 387
LoveJoy, GA 30250
678-545-1306 / 678-545-1365

* *Ying Yang Twins, Young Jeezy*
* *Lil Jon & The Eastside Boyz*
* *Mike Jones, Sammy Sam, Luke*

SWIZZ BEATZ
SWIZZ BEATZ PRODUCTIONS, INC.
3519 Lakewind Way
Alpharetta, GA 30005
678-624-9317

* *Busta Rhymes, DMX, Eve*
* *Jay-Z, Limp Bizkit, Ludacris*
* *Mary J, Mya, Nas*

JOE "DA BINGO" BING
Atlanta, GA
404-425-8794

* *Lil Scrappy, Trillville, Crime Mob*

JUST BLAZE
BASELINE STUDIO
127 West 26th Street - Room 801
New York, NY 10001
212-741-7400

* *Busta Rhymes DMX Jay-Z*
* *Mariah Carey, Nelly, Snoop*

SEAN BLAZE
GENUINE REPRESENTATION
11271 Ventura Blvd. - Suite 225
Studio City, CA 91604
818-505-6870

- *50 Cent*

DARRELL BRANCH
SIX-FIGGA ENTERTAINMENT
P.O Box 43861
Atlanta, GA 30336
info@sixfigga.com
www.sixfigga.com

- *Jay-Z, Jennifer Lopez, Cam'ron*

CARLOS BROADY
CAZZYDOG MANAGEMENT
919 Westminster Dr.
New Jersey, NJ 08753
732-270-6971

- *India Arie, Mary J., Notorious B.I.G.*
- *Nas, P. Diddy, Lil Kim, 112*

TONE CAPONE
GENUINE REPRESENTATION
11271 Ventura Blvd. - Suite 225
Studio City, CA 91604
818-505-6870
genuinerep@earthlink.net

- *Jay-Z, Scarface, SWV*

GREG CHARLEY
GENUINE REPRESENTATION
11271 Ventura Blvd. - Suite 225
Studio City, CA 91604
818-505-6870
genuinerep@earthlink.net

- *B2K, Whitney Houston, Gerald LeVert*

CIROCCO
MUSIC POWERS – BLAIR VIZZION
c/o Titanium Recording Studios
3529 Church Street, Suite A
Clarkston, GA 30021
678-508-7259
musicpowers@aol.com

- *Johnny Gill, Good Girls, Howard Hewett*

- *Quincy Jones, Michael Jackson*
- *TLC, La La, Dymond, Georgio, Sega*
- *Artisan Pictures, BET, Viacom, PepsiCo*

DUANE COVERT
GENUINE REPRESENTATION
11271 Ventura Blvd. - Suite 225
Studio City, CA 91604
818-505-6870
genuinerep@earthlink.net

- *India.Arie, Blackstreet, Keith Sweat*

BRIAN MICHAEL COX
SO SO DEF PRODUCTIONS, INC.
PO Box 491048
Atlanta, GA 30349
+
So So Def
1350 Spring St., # 750
Atlanta, GA 30309
404-733-5511 / 404-888-9900
Fax: 404-888-8901
www.sosodef.com

- *Toni Braxton, Faith Evans, 112*
- *Usher, Destiny's Child, Fantasia*
- *Christina Milian, J-Kwon, Aaliyah*
- *Jagged Edge, Dave Hollister, Mariah*
- *Ginuwine, Monica, Nivea*
- *Lil' Mo, Tyrese, Dru Hill, Corey*
- *Jessica Simpson, B2K, Bow Wow*
- *Nate Dogg, Jermaine Dupri, Da Brat*
- *Janet Jackson, Tamia*

CLAUDIO CUENI
GENUINE REPRESENTATION
11271 Ventura Blvd. - Suite 225
Studio City, CA 91604
818-505-6870
genuinerep@earthlink.net

- *2Pac, Nas, Jordan Knight*

D

DR. DRE
AFTERMATH
2220 Colorado Blvd.
Santa Monica, CA 90404
310-865-7642

- *Eminem, Snoop Dogg, 50 CENT*
- *Eazy-E, Tupac, The Game, Nas*

JERRY DUPLESSIS
DAS COMMUNICATIONS
83 Riverside Drive
New York, NY 10024
212-877-0400

- *Black Eyed Peas, Destiny's Child*
- *Wyclef Jean, Fugees, Mya*
- *Whitney Houston, City High*

JERMAINE DUPRI
SO SO DEF PRODUCTIONS, INC.
PO Box 491048
Atlanta, GA 30349
+
SO SO DEF
1350 Spring St., # 750
Atlanta, GA 30309
404-733-5511
404-888-9900
www.sosodef.com
+
c/o **RUSSELL CARTER**
315 W. Ponce De Leon Ave.
Decatur, GA 30030
404-377-9900

- *Da Brat, B2K, Destiny's Child*
- *Mariah, Bone Crusher, TLC*
- *Jagged Edge, Ludacris*
- *Usher, Alicia Keys*

E

MISSY ELLIOTT
GOLD MIND
2528 Calumet Drive
Virginia Beach, VA 23456
757-426-8994
www.missy-elliott.com
- *Tweet, Aaliyah, Christina Aguilera*
- *Mary J., Beyoncé, Destiny's Child*
- *Whitney Houston, TLC, Monica*
- *Pink, Mya, Tamia, Madonna*

EMINEM
SHADY RECORDS
151 Lafayette Street
New York, NY 10013
212-324-2410
www.eminem.com

- *50 Cent, Jay Z, D-12*
- *2 Pac, Nas, Obie Trice*

JASON EPPERSON
4246 Forest Park Ave. - Suite 2C
ST. Louis, MO 63108
314-533-1155

- *Nelly, Murphy Lee*
- *Brian McKnight, Justin Timberlake*

EDDIE F.
UNTOUCHABLES
100 Piermont Road
Closter, NJ 07624
201-767-6924

- *Usher, Donell Jones*
- *Luther Vandross, Queen Latifah*
- *Tyrese, Next*

F

MARK FEIST (REAL MF)
GENUINE REPRESENTATION
11271 Ventura Blvd. - Suite 225
Studio City, CA 91604
818-505-6870
genuinerep@earthlink.net

- *Kelly Rowland, Destiny's Child*
- *Babyface, Donnell Jones*

MANNIE FRESH
CASH MONEY RECORDS
PO Box 547
Saint Rose, LA 70087
504-466-5115 / 504-466-7575
www.cashmoney-records.com

- *Juvenile, Hot Boys, Lil Wayne*
- *Big Tymers, Murphy Lee*
- *Toni Braxton, Notorious B.I.G.*

G

TONY GALVIN & FOXX
BLACK MOB GROUP
1093 West Avenue SW, Suite - 241
Atlanta, GA 30315
blackmobgroup@aol.com

- *Trick Daddy, Mystical, Trina*
- *No Good, C-Lo, PSC, T.I.*

CARLOS GLOVER
GLOVER PRODUCTIONS
Atlanta, GA
770-477-8764
- *Goodie Mob, TLC, Curtis Mayfield*
- *Outkast, Monica*

DAME GREASE
BAR MANAGEMENT
1501 Broadway, Suite 1914
New York, NY 10046
212-765-5800

- *Eve, DMX, Mary J, Nas*

H

CHAD HUGO
THE NEPTUNES
6 W 57th Street
New York, NY 10019
212-830-0776
www.startrakmusic.com
+
STAR TRAK ENTERTAINMENT
1755 Broadway, 3rd floor
New York, NY 10019
212-841-8040 / Fax: 212-841-8099
www.startrakmusic.com

- *Britney Spears, P. Diddy*
- *Justin Timberlake, Usher*
- *Mystikal, Busta Rhymes*

I

TONY ISSAC
GENUINE REPRESENTATION
11271 Ventura Blvd. - Suite 225
Studio City, CA 91604
818-505-6870
genuinerep@earthlink.net

- *Busta Rhymes, Bone Thugs & Harmony*

J

JAM & LEWIS
FLYTE TYME PRODUCTIONS
1809 W. Olympic Blvd.
Santa Monica, CA 90404
310-401-5180 / Fax 310-401-5199
www.flytetyme.com
sueowens@flytetyme.com

+
8750 Wilshire Blvd.
Beverly Hills, CA 90211
310-358-4292
www.flytetyme.com
+
4100 West 76th Street
St. Edina, MN 55435
612-897 3901
www.flytetyme.com

- *Janet Jackson, Usher, Mariah*
- *Mary J., Yolanda Adams, Boys II Men*

BRION JAMES
GENUINE REPRESENTATION
11271 Ventura Blvd. - Suite 225
Studio City, CA 91604
818-505-6870
genuinerep@earthlink.net

- *Justin Timberlake, Babyface*
- *Brian McNight, EnVogue*

WYCLEF JEAN
DAS COMMUNICATIONS
83 Riverside Drive
New York, NY 10024
212-877-0400

- *Destiny's Child, The Fugees*
- *Black Eyed Peas, Mya*
- *Whitney Houston, O.D.B.*
- *R. Kelly, Cypress Hill*
- *Santana, Michael Jackson*

LAMARQUIS JEFFERSON
1946 Briarwood Ct.
Atlanta, GA 30329
404-271-8166

- *Lil Jon, Lil J, Run DMC*

RODNEY JERKINS
RODNEY JERKINS PRODUCTIONS
810 7th Ave
New York, NY 10019
212-830-2000
+
DARKCHILD ENTERTAINMENT
503 Doughty Road
Pleasantville NJ-08232
609-652-7906

RODNEY JERKINS - continued

- *Jennifer Lopez, Brandy*
- *Mya, Nsync, Britney Spears*
- *Aaliyah, Backstreet Boys*
- *Mary J., Big Punisher*
- *Toni Braxton, Destiny's Child*
- *Whitney Houston, Michael Jackson*
- *Spice Girls, TLC, Tyrese*

LIL JON

BME RECORDINGS
2144 Hills Ave, Ste D2
Atlanta, GA 30318
404-367-8130
www.bmerecordings.com

- *Lil Jon & ESB, Usher, Outkast*
- *David banner, Ying Yang Twins,*
- *Luke, Ciara, Murphy Lee, Trillville, T.I.*
- *Lil Scrappy, Twista, Young Jeezy*
- *Brooke Valentine Nappy Roots,*
- *Trick Daddy, Scarface, Young Buck ,*
- *Mobb Deep, Master P , Barbershop 2*
- *Raheem, Too Short , So So Def B.A.S.*
- *Rhythm & Quad 166, Luke*

LIL J

BME RECORDINGS
2144 Hills Ave, Ste D2
Atlanta, GA 30318
404-367-8130
www.bmerecordings.com

- *Lil Jon & ESB, Crime Mob*

STEVEN " J " JORDAN

17328 Ventura Blvd.
Encino, CA 91316
818-776-0565

- *Kelly Price, LL Cool J, Mariah*

K - L

R. KELLY

BLACKGROUND ENTERTAINMENT
155 W 19th Street
New York, NY 10011
646-638-2585

- *Aaliyah, Britney Spears, B2K, Mary J*
- *Toni Braxton, Johnny Gill, Big Tymers*
- *Janet Jackson, J. Lo, 112*

- *Marques Houston, The Isley Brothers*
- *Kelly Price, Changing Faces*

L-ROC

SO SO DEF PRODUCTIONS, INC.
PO Box 491048
Atlanta, GA 30349
+
SO SO DEF
1350 Spring Street, # 750
Atlanta, GA 30309
404-733-5511
404-888-9900 Fax: 404-888-8901
www.sosodef.com

- *Murphy Lee, YoungBloodZ, Lil Jon*
- *David Banner, Young Jeezy*
- *Too Short, Immature*

DARREN LIGHTY

100 Piermont Rd.
Closter, NJ 07624
201-767-6924

- *Aaliyah, Queen Latifah, Next*
- *TLC, Tyrese, Luther Vandross*

MARK LOMAX

GENUINE REPRESENTATION
11271 Ventura Blvd. - Suite 225
Studio City, CA 91604
818-505-6870
genuinerep@earthlink.net

- *Brandy, En Vogue, Adina Howard*

RICCIANO J LUMPKINS

PLATINUM WORLD PROJECTS
PO Box 44923
Atlanta, GA 30336
404-787-8910

- *TLC, 3LW, Sammie, JT Money*
- *Monica, OutKast,Ciara, Mya*

IRV LORENZO

THE INC
825 8th Ave – 29th Floor
New York, NY 10019
212-333-1330
www.murderincrecords.com

- *Ashanti, DMX, Ja Rule*

M - N

MARLEY MARL
183 N. Martel Ave., Suite 217
Los Angeles CA 90036
323-965-1540
www.worldsend.com

- Rakim, LL Cool J, TLC, Roxanne
- Biz Markie, KRS One, Pete Rock

CHRIS "BC" McCORD
554 Lynhaven Drive.
Atlanta, GA 30310
404-210-8196
castle1fambc2002@yahoo.com

- JT Money, Kilo, Castle Family

NITTI
SO SO DEF PRODUCTIONS, INC.
PO Box 491048
Atlanta, GA 30349
+
1350 Spring St., # 750
Atlanta, GA 30309
404-733-5511
404-888-9900 Fax: 404-888-8901
www.sosodef.com

- Gangsta Boo, Eightball

O - P

BIG OOMP CAMP
DJ JELLY, BIG OOMP, MC ASSAULT
1079 MLK Drive, NW – Suite 2
Atlanta, GA 30314
404-758-4210
www.BigOompRecords.com

- YoungBloodz, Pastor Troy, 112
- Rasheeda, DSGB, Baby D
- Crime Mob, Lil Flip, Eightball
- Young Jeezy, Sammy Sam

ORGANIZED NOIZE
c/o **DEE DEE MURRAY**
PO Box 360291
Decatur, GA 30036
404-241-5523 / Fax 404 241 9559
mmmc2000@bellsouth.net

- Xscape, Goodie Mob, En Vogue

- TLC, Outkast, Ludacris, Org. Noize
- Sleepy Brown, Pebbles, Dungeon

DON P
DON P PRODUCTIONS
3519 Lakewind Way
Alpharetta, GA 30005
678-624-9317

- Trillville, Lil Scrappy

GREGG PAGANI
GENUINE REPRESENTATION
11271 Ventura Blvd. - Suite 225
Studio City, CA 91604
818-505-6870
genuinerep@earthlink.net

- Will Smith, 3LW, Leann Rimes

JAZZE PHA
SHONUFF RECORDINGS
237 Peter Street, Suite A
Atlanta, GA 30313
404-523-0434

- Ciara, Fantasia Barrino
- T.I., Twista, Nelly, Houston, Trick Daddy
- Ruben Studdard, Big Tymers, Bow Wow
- YoungBloodZ, Too Short, ATL
- Murphy Lee, Angie Stone
- Monica, Keith Murray, Cee-Lo
- 2Pac, Tank, Field Mob
- Pastor Troy, Lil Wayne, Greg Street
- Ludacris, Eightball & MJG, Rasheeda
- Jim Crow, DJ Jelly Too Short, E-40
- Changing Faces, Dave Hollister, LSG

PHARRELL
THE NEPTUNES
ROCKSOUL ENTERTAINMENT
6 W 57th Street
New York, NY 10019
212-830-0776
+
NEPTUNES
STAR TRAK ENTERTAINMENT
1755 Broadway, 3rd floor
New York, NY 10019
212-841-8040 Fax: 212-841-8099.
www.startrakmusic.com

- Jay-Z, Mariah Carey, Usher
- Kelis, Busta Rhymes, The Neptunes

- *Justin Timberlake, Snoop Dogg*
- *Toni Braxton, TLC, Britney Spears*
- *Austin Powers (Soundtrack), T.I.*
- *Funkmaster Flex, Mystikal, SWV*
- *Beenie Man, MC Lyte, Mase*

PRO-JAY
GENUINE REPRESENTATION
11271 Ventura Blvd. - Suite 225
Studio City, CA 91604
818-505-6870
genuinerep@earthlink.net

- *Christina Aguilera, Mya*
- *Mark Antony, En Vogue, 2Pac*

R

GUY ROCHE
4007 West Magnolia Blvd.
Burbank, CA 91505
818-843-2628

- *Brandy, Christina Aguilera, NSYNC,*
- *Michael Bolton, Celine Dion, Rod Stewart*

ROCKWILDER
c/o **ELLIS ENTERTAINMENT**
900 South Ave, Suite 300
Staten Island NY 10314
718-568-3655
ellisentertain@aol.com

- *Big Punisher, Lil'Kim*
- *Jay-Z, Beanie Siegel*

S - T

MANUEL SEAL JR
SEAL MUSIC PRODUCTIONS
www.manuelseal.com

- *Usher, Mariah, Jagged Edge*
- *Jermaine Dupri, Da Brat, Xscape*
- *Gerald Levert, Mary J. Blige, Johnny Gill*
- *Destiny's Child, LSG, Tyrese*

DAMON SHARPE
GENUINE REPRESENTATION
11271 Ventura Blvd. - Suite 225
Studio City, CA 91604
818-505-6870
genuinerep@earthlink.net

- *Jennifer Lopez, Kelly Rowland*
- *Monica, Ginuwine*

SAM SNEED
GENUINE REPRESENTATION
11271 Ventura Blvd. - Suite 225
Studio City, CA 91604
818-505-6870
genuinerep@earthlink.net

- *Scarface, JT Money, Jay-Z*
- *Snoop Dogg, G Unit*

DARYL SIMMONS
SILENT PARTNER PRODUCTIONS
588 Trabert Ave. NW
Atlanta, GA 30309
404-355-3530

- *Aaliyah, TLC, T. Braxton, Lionel Richie*
- *BeBe Winans, Whitney, Pink, Elton*
- *Destiny's Child, Monica, Dru Hill,*
- *Deborah Cox, Xscape, Mya, Tamia*
- *Boyz II Men, Babyface, Usher, Mariah*
- *Johnny Gill, After 7, The Boys*

SNIPE
BME RECORDINGS
2144 Hills Ave, Suite D2
Atlanta, Ga 30318
404-367-8130

- *Lil Jon & East Side Boyz*

ALVIN SPEIGHTS
ALVIN SPEIGHTS ENGINEERING
c/o **Dina Andrews Management**
1266 W. Paces Ferry Road, PMB #582
Atlanta, GA 30327
770-774-2585 / 770-434-1316
www.alvinspeights.com
dinaandrewsmgmt@aol.com

- *India Arie, TLC, Madonna, JT Money*
- *Outkast, Michael Jackson, Boys II Men*
- *Jermaine Dupri, Arrested Development*
- *Trina, Jagged Edge, Monica, Jon B*

CHRIS "TRICKY" STEWART
1410 Hills Place NW
Atlanta, GA 30318
404-351-3270

- *B2K, Mya, Brittany Spears*

- *JT Money, Blu Cantrell, Madonna*
- *Tyrese, Mya, Tamia, Charlie Wilson*

LANEY STEWART
1410 Hills Place, NW
Atlanta, GA 30318
404-351-3270

- *Blu Cantrell, Charlie Wilson*
- *B2K, Chante Moore, KC & Jo Jo*
- *Go West, Shanice, The Whispers*

DANA STINSON
c/o **James Ellis**
900 South Ave - Suite 262
Staten Island, NY 10314
718-568-3655
ellisentertain@aol.com

- *Busta Rhymes, Christina Aguilera*
- *Jay-Z, Lil Kim, Nas, Redman*
- *Mya, Janet Jackson*

CHRIS STOKES
848 N. La Cienega Blvd, Suite 202
Los Angeles, CA 90069
310-289-3050
www.ultimategroup.com
www.tugentertainment.com

- *Marques Houston, Omarion, B2K*
- *Destiny's Child, Immature*

SCOTT STORCH
c/o **ARTHOUSE ENTERTAINMENT**
2324 El Contento Drive
Los Angeles, CA 90068
323-461-3400 / Fax: 323 375 0490
Stephen@ArtHouseEnt.com

- *Ricky Martin, Twista, T. Braxton*
- *50 Cent, Lil Kim, Missy, Mario*
- *The Game, T.I., TuPac, Beyonce*
- *JadaKiss, Jay-Z, Sean Paul, Justin*

TIMBALAND
BEAT CLUB
2220 Colorado Blvd.
Santa Monica, CA 90404
310-865-8007
757-435-3910 (Eric Spence)
www.timbalandheaven.com

BLACKGROUND ENTERTAINMENT

49 West 27th Street
New York NY 10001
212-684-1975

- *Bubba Sparxxx, Missy, Ludacris*
- *Aaliyah, Destiny's Child, Nas*
- *Eminem, Ginuwine, Jay-Z*
- *Pastor Troy, Snoop Dogg, TLC*
- *Justin Timberlake, Nelly Furtado*
- *Jadakiss, Alicia Keys, Lil Kim, Mya*

DJ TOOMP
ZONE BOY PRODUCTIONS
Atlanta, GA.
678-698-4333

- *T.I., Ludacris, Lil' Jon*
- *DSGB, Luke, Boyz In Da Hood*

TRACKMASTERS
550 Madison Ave.
New York, NY 10022
212-833-7962

- *Jay-Z, LL Cool J, Nas, Big Pun*

TRACK STARZ
EBONY SON MANAGEMENT
c/o **Chaka Zulu**
66 11th Street
Atlanta, GA 30309
404-875-7323 / Fax 404-873-4187

- *Chingy, Houston, Vanilla Ice*

U - Z

DON VITO
DON VITO PRODUCTIONS
2020 Howell Mill Rd, Suite 255
Atlanta, GA 30318
donvito@bellsouth.net

- *Mya, Blu Cantrell, Gangsta Boo*

RICO WADE
DUNGEON
684 Antone St, Suite 100
Atlanta, GA 30318
404-629-9643 / **404-350-3332**

- *Bubba Sparxxx, OutKast, Dungeo*

Music Powers

RECORDING STUDIOS
'THE LAB'

The popularity of digital recording and making music from the comfort of a home computer or workstation has undeniably become the current movement in today's recording world. However, although this trend is rather convenient, it's also caused a lot of headache for some new artists and their management and "real" studio engineers having to take on the onslaught of poorly recorded tracks (especially vocals), and less than professional recordings when it gets to the mix.

While sales of home studio software may be up, the professional *quality* standards that it normally takes to make a record ready for broadcast, or for having a product to sell through a record label or distributor has gone down somewhat as far as what's being brought into the mixing stage from new producers. And recently, this problem effected my own investments and business.

In late May of 2005, while still working on Music Powers, I decided to take on the role of an Executive Producer; investing my *own* money into an up-and-coming rap artist that had been grinding; performing and recording his own music with different up-and-coming or "future" producers in Atlanta. After working out the studio payments and a spec deal for a great mix engineer, I soon found out that even though the producer and artist had a good song and a great performance recorded, the actual *recording* itself left a lot to be desired. It was pretty "low tech" and distorted, and eventually my high-priced, hi-profile mix engineer said that it really needed re-recording… meaning *more* money and more time put into something that should have been done right… the *first* time.

Ok crew, check it: If you are going in the studio; planning on recording a project to release, or getting a finished CD to a label for some type of real deal opportunity… your recording, whether done at a "real" studio, your basement, your laptop, or your granny's bathroom… it should be approached with some knowledge, proficiency and also a little detail. *Why?* Because poor recordings create poor pockets, when it's time to mix and master. So for any of you who are at this stage, I am going to briefly make a quick list of things that I believe new talent and producer/engineers doing their *own* tracking, should at least come into some awareness about *before* taking their project to the pro mixing stage. Also, I am going to provide a few other helpful hints about recording and studios in general, for those of you who want to be more prepared for your next session.

MEASURE TWICE - CUT ONCE

Sometimes, I think it's good if an engineer or producer/engineer take the approach of a surgeon or good carpenter when it comes to recording or "cutting" a part. I'm sure many of you have heard the old saying, "measure twice, and cut once." This is what any good woodworker, construction crew, or surgeon lives by. And I believe that when tracking parts for a production or music project, it should be the same concept. Taking the time to make sure that levels and the overall sound quality is adequate, saves yourself a lot of potential grief and aggravation (and money) in the long run.

Also, everything cannot be fixed in the mix, and this is especially true when it comes to vocals. You can't undo the clipping of a microphone or mic pre-amp, or the distortion that's been recorded when you're sitting in the mixing studio, no matter how much fancy gear and technique is used. So, when you are preparing to record or track your vocals, it's very important to have everything set like you want, checked a *few* times, and then *checked again*; ensuring that the vocal performance will get recorded as good as you possibly can capture it.

If you are the audio engineer recording everything, then it's your job to make sure that your input (and outputs) are *not* distorting, humming, or buzzing, especially if it's being recorded along with the performance or instrument. See, if any of these things are present, then the recording may possibly be useless when it's time to do a "real" mix. Too many times, new producers or new engineers just do not take enough time to make sure that the level is correct or not too hot. And something as simple as checking your levels a few times *before* you start recording can save you a whole lot of heartache.

So whether you are going into a big professional studio, or you're doing it at home with a workstation, or home recording software, there are a few things that you can do to make sure that you're "on-point", so that you can *keep* that great vocal performance, and use it for the "real" mix. Also, if you get that big recording contract, you may not have to go back in to a studio and attempt to re-create the vocal performances because of a bad recording that was made.

CUTTING VOCALS

Try to make sure you take enough time and care into "cutting" your vocals clean. You want to start off by using a decent microphone. Now you don't have to go out and buy the most expensive microphone on the market, nor do you have to get the *best* mic-pre to go along with it, unless, you have the budget for it. Of course, it would be great if you can invest in both a good mic and a mic pre, but, if you can't get both, definitely get a decent vocal mic to do vocals. And there are many, many decent, low budget mics available on the market. One of my favorite manufacturers that make great quality, low-to-mid budget condenser mics is from Rode.

Also, when you get your mic, make sure you get a pop filter to go along with it. This will keep all those nasty "p" and "popping" sounds that sometimes happen that can ruin great vocal performances. This is especially needed in rap because of the sometimes-aggressive vocal performance artists do. Words like *paper*, *player*, *pimpin'*, *poppin'*, and *peeps* will come across *pretty* distorted *without* a *pop* filter or *pop* screen in front of the microphone. And if you can't get to a professional pop filter, just run down to your local convenience store and buy a package of panty hose or stockings, and make your own with the help of a coat hanger and tape.

Pop Filter

⇒ **Quick Note 1:** If you *can* afford a good mic pre-amp, by all means get it. Most times, there is a definite audible difference in the sound quality.

⇒ **Quick Note 2:** Have the singer or rapper put his or her fists together; right pinky to left first finger, in front of the mic. Then, tell them to never get closer to the microphone than the length of those 2 fists together (about 6 or 7 inches). This is a technique that *I was taught* when I was in audio engineering school that I'm now passing on to you. (Thank you Ken Wright, ESP & DBII Studios).

VOCAL COMPRESSING

Now, another thing to be concerned with is compression. If you find yourself frustrated by trying to record an aggressive vocalist that "hits" the mic pretty hard, then you may need to use a little compression. And with that reality, I think it will be in your *best* interest, to go out and invest in some type of decent compressor. Even something economical that fits into your budget may be better than using nothing at all. See, without a compressor, it can be just too difficult to find a suitable recording level that works *through* a vocal performance, especially one with a lot of dynamics; loud in one spot, soft in another.

COMPRESSOR SETTINGS

Of course, every piece of gear will have it's own characteristics, and there is NO absolutes with the "*art* of recording" and using gear, but, I do suggest starting with a compression *ratio* of 2:1. And, as far as the *attack* and *release* settings; fast as you can get away with, and a release setting that does not modify the sound of things on the vocal too much… and then work it from there. Now, this will all take some experimentation for you, but it is very much worth the time it takes to understand how to use your compressor, at least a *little*… if you are going to be doing the tracking yourself.

TRACKING LEVELS

One of the main things that many of you as up-and-coming engineer/producers should remember is that if you are tracking *digital*, you do NOT have to "hit" zero; you *stay under* zero! Actually, when I'm *tracking*, I firmly believe that -2 dB in most digital recorders is *plenty* for a *peak* level. And even at the −1 DB level, you're still ok, buy why even risk the *chance* of clipping.

EQ & EFFECTS PROCESSING

Ok crew, let's all repeat this together, you DO NOT patch the reverb or delays or sound effects *with* the vocals, *in the recording chain* going to the recorder. If you want to hear some effects on the vocals when you are tracking, set up your effects so that you are only hearing the desired effect in the monitors and the headphones, but not in the signal path to the recorder. If you add the effects while going into the recorder, you may end up with an effect that that needs to come off in the mix, and replaced with a better or more desirable processor. Plus, in general, you can easily add effects to a vocal performance later on, without *affecting* the original vocal that was performed. You can't remove reverb and delays later on if the vocal performance already has effects "printed" along with the performance on the track. So *always* cut your vocals "dry"

EQ.? ...If you *need* to EQ the vocals you are preparing to record, then by all means, do it. But, try not to *over do it.* If you find that you are "boosting" any frequency *over* 10db when adjusting the EQ for vocals, you *may* want to re-examine the mic and your overall settings on everything associated with the path from the mic to the recorder. Personally, I think you should EQ the vocals as little as possible. This will also help if you have to come back in the studio to finish a vocal, and then not have the task of matching the tone of your last vocal session. Then of course, if you have made EQ adjustments in the first session, you should write them down on a track sheet, or add it to the notes section of the file you are saving.

ELECTRONIC INSTRUMENTS

One of the things that can make a tremendous difference in the overall fatness and quality that I've found out over the years is to use passive (or active) direct boxes or transformers hooked up *between* my keyboards, drum machines, etc....going to the mixer, with the *shortest* possible cable. (See below)

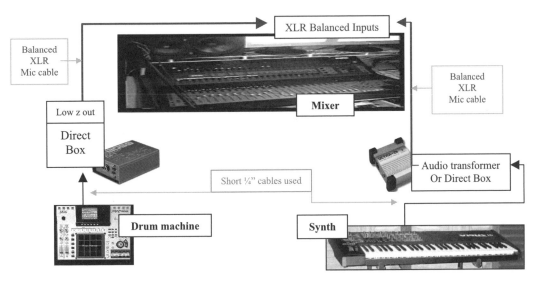

Now, according to many "experts", synthesizers and drum machines have enough line energy to just hook them straight into a patch bay or the line input, but I, along with a many other engineer friends of mine have always used this as our little weapon to keep the signal quiet and "super-fat". The passive transformer or direct box will take your ¼" hi-impedance cord and signal, and then convert it to a lo-z (low impedance) *balanced* output to plug into the balanced XLR inputs on your mixer.

QUALITY TOOLS

Important: A recording studio does not have to have all the latest toys for you to have success in the facility (this is more determined by you talent, patience and heart). So don't panic if the studio "you can afford" doesn't have the latest "Pro Tools Version – Super XT-RA." As long as the studio has the capability to take an accurate "picture" of your recording (if you are tracking), and develop that recorded image into a beautiful representation of your finished performance (mixing), then you'll be just fine. Now, I am not necessarily trying to say that *Pro Tools* should or should not be regarded as the way to record your project, but, I will say this, "*Pro Tools* has become the industry standard to pro recording and mixing." So what this means to you is that if you are planning on working in *Cubase, Logic, Nuendo, Fruity Loops, Reasons…* whatever, then if you plan on mixing your music with an engineer that *prefers* Pro Tools, then make sure that you have the tracks imported into Pro Tools *before* you take it to him. See, you're going to pay big for everything that you don't have ready at mix time, and it's a lot cheaper to do this in a pre-mixing stage, so it doesn't cost so much.

Another thing is to make sure that the studio you choose has a sufficient mixer and automation system (digital, analog or digital virtual). Also, if you are tracking vocals, a "good" microphone, microphone pre-amp and compressor will be necessary. And if you are mixing, you will need a few outboard pieces like delays, de-essers, gates, compressors, reverbs, etc. (digital, analog or virtual plug-ins). Again, a producer and/or engineer should be able to help you make this determination.

MORE TO THINK ABOUT

BEFORE MIXING

Make sure you have your tracks organized; know which tracks are *actually* going to be needed and used for the mix. Good organizational skills in the studio are the engineer and producer's responsibility, so everything should be labeled; track sheet notes or digital text notes made.

FOR PRODUCERS RECORDING VOCALS

Even if you do the entire recording of instrument tracks at your own home studio or private studio, if you *do not* own or have access to a good microphone, a good compressor, or a decent mic pre, then please consider taking your artist or project to a recording facility that does. And if the artist is paying money, then you should just include that cost in your budget. Even on a low budget, you can find studios with the tools you need for under $50 an hour.

For your artist, especially if the artist is a good, *paying* client, you end up putting them in a better atmosphere to work, and they will appreciate you more for that. And, for you, the producer, you have made the smartest move to get the vocals done well, and also, you are doing what is stylishly correct in the music industry; treating your *paying* client with a lot more importance. See, it's ok for "you" to sit at home a grind; working on the instrumentation and so forth, in *any* kind of environment you want, if you choose to. But, you better "sticky" this to your forehead: Artists who are *paying clients*, would rather you take them into a "real" studio. So, when it's time to cut vocals, and if you *don't* have a great place to record vocals at the house, then take that client to a nice place to do their vocal parts. And as you grow, and *really* get further in the music industry, you will find out and begin to understand that this is one of the number one rules for producing, especially as you get better and better clientele. Believe me, all of the producers I know, understand the importance of this.

THINGS TO ASK WHEN PICKING OUT A STUDIO

• What's the studio's "bottom line" best rate, and are they willing to work within your budget?

• Does the control room come with a competent engineer, and what outboard gear is included in the price?

• Does the studio have a successful track record, and who are some past clients?

• Is the staff and studio manager courteous and concerned about having *and keeping you* as a client?

• Is the room technically sound to deliver Broadcast quality recordings? (Hums, buzzes, distortion, and crackles should not be tolerated.

• Do you have to "jump through hoops – doing back flips" to get relatively simple chores done when recording, editing or mixing?

• Are you aware and knowledgeable of what format (digital hard disk, digital tape, analog, virtual, etc.) you are using to record?   Also, if you are recording in a software-based environment, are you aware and knowledgeable of *which software* (and version number) is being used, along with any other computer related information that may be essential if you ever need to take your project to a different studio.

• Does the studio have a good microphone?

IT'S GOOD TO HAVE FUN, BUT STAY FOCUSED

There are many studios that have all the bells and whistles to accommodate your project, dependant on your budget. But, more important than the catering some provide and the game room upstairs, try to focus on the tools that you require, so that you feel confident in the studio's ability to get you to your destination... a great sounding record. A competent producer or engineer can also help you find a great place to record and mix your project. Believe it or not... you may "think" that the game room is there for you to maybe relax and "chill." And actually, that's true. But, you best know now, *before* you heat up the *PlayStation* or *X-Box*... the studio owner knows that it helps you waste a lot of time too! So with that reality, stay focused, and remember the *reason* that you're in the studio is to get your music project complete.

QUICK "EQ-TIPS"

Before I closed this section, I do want to touch on something that I have found to be very helpful when approaching the mix stage.

1. Try listening to some good sounding reference material *right before* mixing and/or applying EQ to anything.

2. Instead of always looking to *boost* certain frequencies in your EQ settings, try "cutting" the frequencies you don't like, and then *lightly* boosting the frequencies on a particular sound that you *do* like.   Too many new engineers and producers only turn their knobs to the *right*, but that's not always the "right" way.

Ok, in closing this section out, I can't stress enough, how important it is to stay focused and on top of things in the studio. Recording facilities normally charge by the hour, ranging from $25/ hr to $2,500 (or more) for a day block. So as an artist or producer, don't misuse or waste your budget playing around or getting "too stoned" to make sound decisions. The only people who profit this way are the engineers and studio owner. And speaking of studio owners, if it seems I've been a little rough on them by saying earlier they like you wasting time... then you should ask them, "why are there no clocks *anywhere* in the facility? (Ahem... yeah!) So anyway crew, please keep your focus and priorities in order. Now, go and make some great recordings!

GOOD LUCK!

AN AUDIO COMMUNITY
WORLD-CLASS RECORDING & MIXING FACILITY

STONEHENGE RECORDING   ZAC DIGITAL

Zac's Stonehenge recording studio houses the largest SSL 4000 series G+ mixing console in Atlanta; an 88 channel, 4080 G+ mixing console, which was custom-built from the ground up in Rockland, MA. Those crazy techs at PAD, Boston did a complete refurbish on each module, rewired the entire desk and bays with Mogami cable, stocked it with 48 "E" series dual line channels, 24 "G" series channels, and 8 Stereo channels. This desk has the cool phase meter, VU's, and the fattest specs. On the 2Mix busses', it's got all the stuff you know and love about SSL's G+ software, Ultimation, Total Recall, and that trusty Stereo compressor.

The facility's ProTools' suites have hosted both tracking and mixing dates for artists that include Dre 3000, 112 and Primal Screen Productions. Both ZAC Digital rooms offer ProTools, tons of plug-ins, and a great analog front end. The studios professional, comfortable, *acoustically tailored* control rooms are a cost effective alternative to hanging out at the house, struggling to get it to sound 'right'!

www.zacrecording.com
404-603-8040

WORLD-CLASS RECORDING & MIXING FACILITY – ATLANTA

STONEHENGE

EQUIPMENT & AMENTIES

SSL Custom 4088 G+, Ultimation, Total Recall, (2) Studer A827 24tk's / (3) Lynx, Syncronizers, ProTools HD3, 192 interfaces 32 in / 48 out / Mac G5, Flat Screen, Live Room 23" W x 25" D x 21" ceiling, Augspurger Mains, loaded with TAD components, Powered by Bryston, tuned by "Coco", 3 Gtr Iso booths, Lounge

OUTBOARD FX

AMS RMX reverb, AMS 15-80s DDL
Eventide H3000/sampler,Eventide 2016
MXR blue phaser, Sony R7 reverb
Sony D7 modulator fx, Lexicon 480L
Lexicon PCM 42 (2) DDL, Roland SDE 3000
DDL, TC 2290 DDL
TC M3000 reverb, Yamaha SPX 990

PROCESSORS

dbx 902 (2) deessr's.
Drawmer 1969- fletcher-ized stereo comp
EL Labs - Fatso stereo comp, EL Labs - (2)
Distressor, mono comp/brit. Mod, Kenetec la-2 type mono tube comp., Millinia media stereo eq., Millinia media stereo comp., Neve 33609 stereo comp., Pultec EQP-1As eq.Urei La-3a stereo comp., Urei LA-4 stereo comp., Urei 1176 Mono Comp. (2), TubeTech Cl-1b

ZAC DIGITAL A ROOM

THE RIG

ProTools HD3, 96i interfaces
Digidesign 16ch. ProControl Samsung 17"
Flatscreen, (2) 18 Gig drives, Sample Cell
Lucid Gen X WordClock, Two iso rooms

Mains - Custom Augspurger / Bryston amps, Nearfield - Yamaha NS-10m or choice

UPSTAIRS STUDIO

THE RIG

ProTools 5.1 MixPlus24, 3 Farm Cards, Mac G4/800, DDA DMR12 56 input console
(2) Digidesign 888/24 i/os, (1) Digidesign 1622 16ch. i/o, Masterlink CD player / burner
Monitors: Dynaudio M3 mains, Yamaha NS10, Hafler Transnova, Mackie HR824

Outboard gear includes Neve, API, TubeTech, Emperical Labs, Keyboards and Machines from Korg, Akai, Roland, EMU

Iso Booths / Private Studio and lounges

www.zacrecording.com

Music Powers
Exclusive Advice from Music Powers Advisor:

Jim Zumpano
ZAC RECORDING STUDIOS

Recording & Mix Engineer – World-Class Studio Owner

MICROPHONES & PRE-AMPS

1 There are many new up-and-coming producers and future engineers who don't realize that many of the vocals they hear are recorded with a *combination of* great microphones *and mic pre-amps.* (a) Can you tell us the importance of having a good mic pre, and also, (b). what's the deal with engineers *NOT* using the pre-amps that are built in the recording console to do vocal recordings, etc.

The mic pre is absolutely of *utmost importance* and will effect the entire characteristic of the microphone itself. Some very good mics can be seriously impaired by using a low quality mic pre - like lack of headroom or detail, along with various frequency anomalies (irregularities) not usually produced. The concept about the built-in mic pre-amps is that more time and money (ie...quality) can go into a stand alone pre-amp with one or two channels than will go into a console pre-amp trying to allow you 56 channels or more. We have many geniuses in the industry who strive daily to build the best path, with the highest quality components. So, by this logic, we *prefer* to use the outboard pre-amp for that signal integrity. Yet, many console pre-amps are still quite adequate for the job and should not be feared.

2 Which vocal microphone and mic pre-amp combinations seems to be used more than any other combo in your recording sessions at *your* studio?

➤ The Nuemann microphones - like the U-87, U-67 and U-47, going into a Neve Mic pre-amp, preferably the 1073 and 1084. Every engineer will provide a different answer, but typically, we pick the stuff to match a *particular* feeling for a song. But, this combo is often the safest bet with good results… across a wide variety of singers and acoustic instruments.

3 What are the most requested rental pieces as far as outboard gear; eq, compressors and mic pre-amps, etc.?

➤ Plug-ins have killed a lot of the rental outboard gear business, but Empical Labs Distressors and Fatso, Urei 1176 compressors, API pre-amps, Neve pre-amps, Neve compressors; basically the good, old stuff.

4 What mic(s) and pre-amp(s) do you consider the best bang-for-the "buck"?

➤ In *dollars* - Shure SM57, with Avalon 737

➤ In *quality* - An old used U-87, with a vintage Neve strip

VOCALS & COMPRESSORS

5 What about compressors and limiters when cutting vocals...are today's modern digital recordings still being made using older tube and vintage compressors like the Urei 1176s, etc.. or what?

➤ The 1176... *I gotta have it!* And of course, we do use the older stuff. it just sounds *right!* You will only know this when you try to strap on a plug-in digital compression thingy during your *own* session. They're horrible sounding and they are very finicky while trying to adjust them *"on-the-fly"*. Use of the analog compressor is art and is the secret weapon the old guys have. So, knowing that, we tend to use the compressor that will add the extra color depending on the material.

➤ It could be an 1176 or an LA2A, or maybe, *that DBX 160!* But, if you had an Emperical Labs *distressor*, you can emulate just about *any* type of compression you'd need - yet you'd still want to have a LA-2A or TubeTech CL-1b on hand for the fatness of real tubes.

Jim Zumpano – Owner of ZAC

"...Your setup and mileage may vary."

WHY ANALOG IS STILL GREAT, AND STILL USED

6 With all of the digital mixers and surface controllers working software based recorders, plug-ins, etc, how often are the "big boys" using any of the analog stuff... like the SSL Eq, etc, in the chain of the signal flow? And *why*, considering all of the technology out there?

➤ **FIRST:** Technology doesn't make sound, people do. And, the "big boys" have always chosen the SSL.

Why? Glad you asked. Jamming all your individual sound streams (up to 128 or more) down a *single* bit stream (stereo, eh?) tends to cramp up the stereo spectrum, technically referred to as *"audio constipation."* The mix summing bus in an *analog* desk provides considerably *more* useable headroom and signal integrity. Comparatively, the "in the box" mixing method is most commonly described as degrading the stereo image and depth of the soundfield.

➤ Also, using the SSL (or other mixers) also allows *easy* integration with the analog world, since you can insert your cool EQs and compressors *without* the inherent *delay* and *phase shift* that is the by-product of plug-ins and the digital process itself.

➤ *Why do engineers mix "in the box?"* This trend is due to the complete lack of production being put into the recording *process* and further lack of vision for the final product. Mixing "in the box" allows that engineer to have instant and complete recall of the last attempt and provides a fairly painless approach to those future production changes, like replacing the kick sound, singing replacement words for the clean version, or completely re-arranging the song. This is *technology in action.*

STUDIO MONITORS & AMPLIFIERS

7 **A new producer/engineer writes:** *"I am looking to buy a decent pair of monitors for my home studio. Can you recommend a few good choices that I should consider, so that when I go into a larger studio to mix, I will not be shocked by what I hear?"*

➤ Believe me, you'll still be shocked! The best monitors you can buy are the ones that make your mixes sound good EVERYWHERE you play them. *Where* you are listening is *more* critical than the speakers you're listening to; poorly designed rooms can make the *best* speakers *stink!* So, to *know* your room is to *know* your speakers... and vice versa.

⇒   *...and can you recommend a few good monitor amplifiers for the studio?*

➤ Bryston ...or Bryston, or *Bryston!*

TWEAKING IN THE LAB

8 **A new producer/engineer writes:** "When I'm at home, I put EQ and compression on, and do a lot of "tweaking" on my drums, keys, bass, etc., while I'm working up my songs. But, when I get to a *professional* studio to record, the engineers say, "we'll record it all flat, and "tweak-it" later, and it sounds terrible to me while I'm working. Is there something I can do to make my sessions be more "monitor-friendly" when I go in the big studio to record?

➤ First, you have to decide who's making the decisions (that's the guy who has the most to lose here). Then, get the sound...if you wreck it, then re-do it... *while* you are recording, *not* after. If it sounds right, then it *is* right. So why lose that? On the other hand, if you have no idea about the *final* sound, you could sonically wreck tracks that are performed the way you want them and, believe me, that sucks too! So, I say, if you're unsure, get extremely close to the 'right' thing, and go easy on the processing... and *know this: Wrong EQ is easier to fix than wrong compression!!!*

PRO FORMATS - RECORDING & MIXING

9 What is the *standard* when recording digital tracks...what format? And, what sample rate? *(Summer 2005)*

➤ *Professionally*, the standard file format at present is .wav, with most productions using the 24bit / 48K recording format.

10 What is the standard or most used *mixing* format these days for professionals? And, what are engineers mixing down to these days?

➤ My Studer A820 1/2" analog deck gets the most use (but, can you still buy tape?) The rest are satisfied bouncing back or printing stems into Protools.

Jimmy "Z" Zumpano is an award winning recording and mix engineer, and also the owner of ZAC Digital and Stonehenge Studios in Atlanta. His clients include Whitney Houston, She'kspere, Jermaine Dupri, Babyface, Toni Braxton, LA Reid, Tony Rich, Mariah Carey, Jazzy Pha, and many others

www.zacrecording.com

Music Powers
SPOTLIGHT
ALVIN SPEIGHTS

Mix Engineer - Producer - Musician

Alvin Speights has mixed hit records for an almost endless register of A-list producers and multi-platinum recording artists. Even as far back as Arrested Development's first album, *3 Years, 5 Months, 2 Days In The Life Of...* and the number one Hit single "Jump" by Kriss Kross, Alvin has been one of the premiere mix engineers in the Hip Hop, R&B, Pop music industry. His astonishing sense of creativity and drive for sonic excellence has won him two Grammy Awards; TLC's *Fanmail* and for the *Acoustic Soul* project by India Arie.

Alvin Speights - 2x Grammy Winning Mix Engineer / Producer for India.Arie, OutKast, Madonna, JT Money, 112, TLC

His mix production magic can also be heard on releases by Outkast, Madonna, Michael Jackson, Goodie Mob, B-5, Boyz II Men, BeBe Winans, Yolanda Adams, Jagged Edge, Monica and many others. Alvin has also mixed numerous motion picture soundtracks as well.

Encompassing his who's who list of industry credits, Alvin has recorded, mixed and/or remixed for just about every major label in the music business, and over twenty-five of the music industry's top producers, including Dallas Austin, Jermaine Dupri, Outkast & Goodie Mob, Daryl Simmons, Shannon Sanders as well as many others who are his recurring clientele. And regardless of how demanding the project, through his own exceptional and distinctive approach, Alvin has time after time been able to shape the sound of music productions for his clients to create the polished, "in-your-face" sound design he's grown to be so illustrious for. When recently asked about his success and what *he does* that makes his mixing stand out with the intensity it does, He teasingly remarked, "I try to refine the music to another level, and usually by the time I've finished, my clients either love it...or they hate it." Well let's just look at the "love"; Mr. Speights has won two Grammys, along with awards that most engineers can only daydream about, including honors from Ampex, Scotch and TEC for technical excellence, as well as a stockade of Gold & Multi-Platinum RIAA plaques as further testimonials of his incredible successes. And to add icing to his mixing skills, he is also a first class musician. So when you sum it all up, Alvin's "Midas touch" on hit singles and multi-million-selling recordings is proof enough that he is indisputably going to continue being one of the greatest mix engineers and most in-demand audio engineering specialist in the world.

Music Powers SPOTLIGHT
ALVIN SPEIGHTS

Mix Engineer - Producer - Musician

A Select Discography

112
Pleasure and Pain

Aretha Franklin

Arrested Development
3 Years, 5 Months, 2 Days
In the Life Of...*

B5 (2005)

BeBe Winans
Love & Freedom

Bobby Brown
Forever

Boyz II Men
Remix Collection

Brand New Heavies
Brother Sister

Craig Mack
Street Fighter

Curtis Mayfield
New World Order

D'Angelo
Brown Sugar

Deborah Cox
Deborah Cox

Debra Killings
Surrender

J. Jeff & Fresh Prince
Code Red

The Gap Band
Live and Well

George Clinton
500,000 K Of P-funk

Goodie Mob
Standing Still
World Party

India Arie
Acoustic Soul
Voyage To India

Jagged Edge
Hard

Jon B
Cool Relax
Are You Still Down

JT Money
Pimpin' On Wax
Blood, Sweat and Years

Keith Sweat
Keep It Comin'

Madonna
Bedtime Stories

Michael Jackson
HIStory

Monica
Miss Thang

Outkast
Southernplayalisticadillac
ATLiens

Sammie
From the Bottom To the
Top

Silk
Tonight

Tamia
Nu Day

TLC
Oooh On the TLC Tip
CrazySexy Cool
Fanmail

Toni Braxton
Toni Braxton

Trina
Da Baddest Bit..
Diamond Princess

Yolanda Adams
Songs From the Heart

SOUNDTRACKS
Original Film
Soundtracks
& Film Scores

Malcolm X
Hoodlum
Fled
Panther
Any Given Sunday
Cb4
Booty Call

ALVIN SPEIGHTS

2X GRAMMY WINNING MIX ENGINEER
PRODUCER –MUSICIAN

MIXING IT- TO THE *NEXT* LEVEL

1 When you approach mixing, do the mixes have all the polish in the producers work or what is it that you do when you come into the picture?

Usually the song is finished, as far as how far the producer can take it, but when I

Alvin Speights - 2x Grammy Winning Mix Engineer / Producer for India.Arie, OutKast, Madonna, JT Money, 112, TLC

get to them (the mix) I take everything somewhere else. Once I come in, I put the hi EQ where it is supposed to go; the lo EQ where it's supposed to go… and the mid EQ; clean up the tracks; and then make everything "in-your-face" where you cam understand everything, and listen beyond that "in-your-face" too. Usually by the time I'm finished with the mix, the producer will either love it… or hate it, and then they will give me opinion(s) of their direction.

2 Explain to new producers and engineers out there, what is "cleaning up the tracks"?

➢ Cleaning up the tracks is simply taking out all of the talking in the background and weird room sounds that come from bad tracking and sometimes-poor production.

ROOM TO MASTER

3 A lot of pro mix engineers leave a lot of room for the mastering process… but, you have a different approach that actually makes your *finished* mixes sound like they are already mastered, what is your philosophy on this approach?

➢ OK – this is the whole philosophy of how it goes: The Rock-and-rollers, see, they basically "mix-to-tape". So whenever you push up the faders, it sounds like

it is supposed to sound. So when you turn up the levels on the mixer, everything sounds good; everything is recorded where all the sounds sound good together.
➤ You make the sounds sound good when recording. But in the R&B field, there is a (raw) tracking process... and it's just the generic sound of everything, and in the mix you polish everything. And where I take it is... by the end of the mix, there is very little room or need for any mastering.

FREQUENCIES & PHASE

4 How do you approach mixing a song that is being prepared for radio play?

See when I'm mixing, especially for urban radio songs, I consider that when the song plays on radio, only certain frequencies (the frequency response) will play; the full frequency scope is not the same as a CD. The frequency response will not be the full 20 Hz to 20,000 Hz (20Khz) frequency range. So this means that for the mix to have a strong impact, you can't stack up your instruments and sounds in all of the same frequencies... you have to move things around like a pyramid... so everything can be "in-your-face", and *everything can be heard*.

5 Explain to us what you mean by this "like a pyramid"?

➤ What I'm saying is that, it's like a picture of a pyramid, and everything has its place *on that pyramid* - Panning, frequencies, processing, and phase. See, everything can't occupy the same "space"; frequency-wise; color-wise, etc. This means that where some sound is dominating one frequency... another sound can't. So either you have to move the sound colorization (frequency) above another sound or below it

6 You mentioned phase, tell our readers how to go about checking phase... and when listening, how to know if something is "out-of-phase"?

➤ Well, there are phase meters in just about all formats you use. And you will know what's "in-phase" or what's out of phase by just "hearing it". You will know if things are out of phase; if you lose things in mono you know it's phased-out.

STARTING THE SONG – PREPARING TO MIX

7 What instrument or sound is best to start with, when you set up the mix... kick drum, bass... what sound or instrument?

➤ Everyone will start differently... sometimes it depends on the song. If it's a vocal based song, then I will start from the vocals. But if it's a rhythm driven song, then I will start from the drums. If the song is real melodic, I'll start from the music. It will depend on the nature of the song.

8 What is the best starting process, when tracking a new song… where do you start?

First thing, when you cut everything on, you would start off by making sure that

there is NO noise in any of your lines. No buzzing; no humming; no glitches, etc. And you need to have your AC power "to-code"; making sure that there is no "trash" in the lines. There should be NO noise from the mixer, not even a low volume "shhhshhh".

Normally these days, people will do a lot of sampling… and some of that is dirty and noisy, but that's a characteristic of the sound, so you work with these sounds to where it is enhanced *in the music*.

Alvin Speights - 2x Grammy Winning Mix Engineer / Producer
for India.Arie, OutKast, Madonna, JT Money, 112, TLC

RECORDING LEVELS

9 Does it matter what levels you record at?

➤ Yes, it matters. It will depend on whether or not you are on analog tape and what alignment is being used for the machine and tape… and how hard you "hit" the tape. And for digital, you want to keep your levels up, but not past the threshold of where the sound is irritable. As long as you keep the sound under peaking in the digital recording process you should be fine.

10 With all of that said about record levels, would you say it is then better to keep the recording level softer, rather than trying to record things louder?

➤ Well, see if you end up working where you come back to an analog mixer softer, you will end up increasing noise. But if you are totally in digital mode, you should be safe by using a "normal" to nice level.

SEPERATION

11 Now getting back to mixing, and that process of separating sounds and frequencies, tell us how to approach this.

➤ It's like, if there were a bunch of people in this room and you decided to dress us up in the same clothes; and you gave us the same complexion; and you made

Alvin Speights - 2x Grammy Winning Mix Engineer / Producer
for India Arie, ClutKast, Madonna, JT Money, 112, TLC

us all look the *exact same way*... would someone be able to come in and *identify* any of us? .... NO!   So you want to make each individual – an *individual*, and sounds are no different. *So you use your EQ to color sounds as an individual.*

➤ See, these sounds (samples) sometimes come from a lot of other different songs from other projects, and they were intended for different reasons and different "musical" set-ups. So, within the song *you are working with*, you have a different spectrum of sounds and melodies, so you want some things to be more (or less) important than what *they were* in those original songs (the sound was sampled from).

➤ Now if you only had 2 instruments, they could be "full-frequency" all day long, and not get in the way of each other because there are just 2 sounds. But if you have 10 to 20 sounds, and you want all of them heard and felt, then they have to be "working" *different* frequency ranges... not drastic ranges, but subtle ranges.

❖ **Example1:** You have your Sub EQ – You have your Bass EQ – You have your Lo Mid EQ; then you have your Mid EQ – You have your Hi Mid – You have your Hi Frequencies, and then you have your extra Hi Frequencies.

❖ **Example 2:**   Let's say you have a Hi-Hat, a Triangle (which is higher in frequency or above the hat), and a Shaker going on in your mix at the same time. These all are hi frequency instruments, but they still have to occupy their own "space" in the mix to be significant. If you don't give these instruments their own space in the mix, the Hi-end in the mix will be over-bearing; when these instruments all hit together, there will possibly be distortion, or you really can't hear one or the other like you want to hear it. So when a person may turn their Hi-end EQ up on their personal system... the vocals may sound nice and bright, but the Hi-Hat, Triangle and Shaker will be clipping; distorted to where it will make the speakers sound torn up or maybe tear them up.

"...Everything needs to have its own frequency prominence & 'space' in the mix."

❑   *Log in to www.musicpowers.com/24 for video & audio*

FREQUENCY ANALYZERS

12 How important are frequency analyzers to a mix or recording engineer?

➢ The analyzers help you when you understand them. But if you rely on them, like as a main source to tailor your sound, then it will hurt you. Mixing is about a feel and your ears, and how the music feels to you. If you look at a piece of paper for emotion and passion you'll never get it. It has to come off of that sheet of paper and somebody has to say it; and present it; and someone has to present it... with feeling. So music is someone playing with feeling, and you have to make that come across. And analyzers are not going to do that. Analyzers will help you see what you are doing; you knowing a sound is in a certain realm, but you still have to use your ears to make things coax, and make it "move" colorfully.

GREAT MIXING "TO DO'S" & TALENT

13 Can you explain to us what the *feeling* thing is like when mixing... how would you know you are their in the zone of a great mix... what does if "feel" like?

It feels good... real good. It's like a "high". See, when you're at the end of your mix, and it "moves" you... even after listening to it all day; or 2 days to 3 days; or even 4 days - back-to-back, and the mix still moves you emotionally, that's when you know you have a (good) mix. It will "vibe" you, and moves you emotionally. And then you hope that the world feels what you feel... but you can't give them what *you* don't feel yourself.

14 How does a person or producer recognize great engineering *talent*?

➢ Part of the talent of this trade is to know what the problem is; like a mechanic. A (talented) mechanic, once you bring him your car, he can sometimes instantly know from the "sound" of your car... what's wrong. But, the ones who are not as good *have to* put it on a machine.

15 Can you give some advice on some of the most important things to do, to finish a mix?

➢ Well, I will basically try to make the vocals very clear and polished, or ruff and rugged... depending on the nature of the song. For a lot of rap songs it will be a little more rugged than in a "Pop" mix. In Rap, I would use different shallow reverbs and give the mix more "dimension", along with delays too – to give the mix more "image" dimension.   With mixing for radio, you want things more dimensional because there are different dimensions to the listener (especially in their car); back speakers; front speakers, etc.

➤ By the end of the mix, I would have made things more of a constant level by adding compression and EQ - to kind of touch on some *more* of the frequencies and elements that I look forward to hearing when I listen on full-range speakers.

MORE ABOUT MASTERING

16 Can you end up doing too much before going to mastering?

Yes, you can end up doing too much compression and ... too much EQ-ing before you *go to mastering*. And you can also have too hot of levels. Also, you may have emphasized the wrong frequencies overall too ... because they will be doing EQ-ing and compression too.

➤ Mastering is basically another set of ears on your mix. It's like after you wash your car, and then having your boss-man look over your car after you've finished.

It's another set of *experienced* ears; using reputable ears or people that will make changes based upon their experience in the music industry.

"...If you get a sorry mix engineer, then a great mastering engineer will not be able to help you. And if you get a sorry mastering engineer, but have a great mix engineer... it's the same."

REFERENCES – BASS - EDITS

17 So what is the key to a mixing a song that will be radio-ready, but does not need so much mastering?

➤ You have to use references of other songs that you like, and listen to them before mixing. You don't use anything, you use things that you consider great and you like for your song mix to sound. You listen to other artist like OutKast, Madonna or whatever.   Like for me, Michael Jackson recordings with Bruce Swedien, always sound great to me. I like Jimmy Jam and Terry Lewis mixes... Steve Hodge I love. So if you are an up-and-coming mix engineer, I think you should find a great reference point (other great mixes) of where *you want to go*. If you like what someone else is doing, most will follow their lead.

"For me, I will not ever mix a song without having a Michael Jackson record around, or a Janet Jackson around. These references get my ears "tuned" by just hearing something great! "

I do this because I think that these are great engineers working on these projects. And there are other people out that I'm listening to, but *Bruce Swedien and Steve Hodge are the tried-and-true*.

18 In today's music there's not a lot of bass-lines going on. What's the deal with that type of production?

➢ Well, It (these bass frequencies) just takes the place of the bass-line. Today, you have a category of music that *has* bass-lines in it, and then you have a category of music that uses bass *frequencies (sub tones, etc)*.

19 Now, back to you and getting "that feeling", are there things an engineer can do to create more feeling in the song mix?

➢ Yes. If the song doesn't climax at a certain point, and it gets dull or dry at a certain point, then you need to pay attention to *how the song flows*. You should try different "cuts" or "mutes" in the arrangement of the song. And that's to keep it interesting all the way to the fade-out of the song.

20 How important is mix pre-production? …Editing, etc? Before you're doing the mix?

➢ It saves you a lot of time in the mix session. It's important! The editing part of it, having everything edited and cleaned-up, and exactly the tracks you want, the tracks you're using... that will cut down half of your studio time right off the bat. I recommend that you do your editing at a lower rate… in your tracking situation or at home. To do your editing and cleaning up in the mix is where it's going to cost you the most time and the most money. But, sometimes, it's necessary to do it in the mix because maybe you or the producer can't hear it unless it's mixed... how you want to edit it. I've dealt with producers... they didn't really want to add any more to a song *until* the mixing session.

"…That's why it's important to track things how you want to hear them."

THE GEAR & ADVICE FOR ASPIRING TALENT

21 Tell us the equipment you like to use?

➤ I think Pro Tools is the format that makes everything easy, compared to the analog days. I like the Renaissance plug-ins as far as EQ goes. And Enigma. I like all the plug-ins because I can use them all for something... like with analog stuff, they have a lot of built-in things and you kind of go in and shape them, but I do the same thing when I get to Pro Tools. I've got to touch everything. I like Avalon, Neve, and Focusrite EQ. It depends on the character of the vocalist to what works well with the microphone. I still like the old Nuemann U-87. It just depends on the nature of the vocalist... what they sing, how they're singing. And basically just listen to a lot of mics, and then it's easier to pick a mic for a certain kind of vocalist. But you've got to have a working knowledge of what they sound like.

22 Can you give some words of advice and encouragement to the next up-and-coming engineers and producers who want to get in this business?

❖ **For Engineers**... First, you've got to figure out what kind of engineer you want to be. You've got to do a lot of everything to get a better handle on your plug-ins, your outboard gear, your microphone placement techniques, your pre-amps, etc... because all those are very *important to each other*. And Engineering School is great because it gives you a general working knowledge of some of the things you're going to have to deal with, because it's harder for somebody to sit down and just tell you everything you're going to need to learn... unless they're into the business of teaching you. *It's good to go to school to get general knowledge ... so when you get to those people with the industry experience knowledge; it's not as hard for you to get there too.*

❖ **For Producers**... Producers need to always keep their ears to the streets and know what's going on... and try to figure out the next thing. They need to be ahead of the game, and have a good idea of where things are going...or not. Don't jump on the "band-wagon" of each song that's ever being recorded and re-record it again. Producers need to be innovative... to take it to another level because those are the ones who are going to reach their market. The other ones are just going to follow suit... they *might* stumble on a hit.

"You have to pay attention to what's going on out there in the streets, the clubs, and what's hyping the people. If you don't, you'll lose touch with what you need to do... and that's how you stay fresh!"

For more, visit www.Musicpowers.com/24

2X GRAMMY-WINNING MIX ENGINEER – PRODUCER – MUSICIAN

ATLANTA RECORDING STUDIOS

SELECT RECORDING & MIXING FACILITIES IN ATLANTA, GA

A - B

ALLGOOD PROD.
770-956-9698

ARCADIA STUDIOS
770-448-9992

ATLANTA RECORDING
770-591-2221

BERT ELLIOTT SOUND
404-351-9061

BGN PROD.
404-761-7047

BIG BABY
770-994-9505

BLACK DOG
678-235-9035

BLACK JACKET
404-699-5870

BLUE FUNK STUDIO
678-556-3792

BRANNON PROD.
404-249-9418

C - D

CAPTIVE SOUND
404-325-4860

CATSPAW PROD.
678-624-7660

CHASE STUDIO
404-351-4990

COME CLEAN ENT.
404-763-8003

COS MASTERING
404-524-7757

CREATIVE SOUND
404-873-6628

CROSSOVER ENT.
404-352-3716 / 404-806-6920

DARP STUDIOS
404-351-3736

DE MIC PROD.
404-305-0160

DOGWOOD RECORDING
770-929-0102

DOPPLER
404-873-6941

DOWN 4 LIFE
404-761-2259

DREAM HOUSE STUDIOS
770-444-0350

E THRU H

ECLIPSE AUDIO
404-351-3589

ELITE SOUND PROD.
404-292-3386

EXOCET PROD.
770-455-7256

FAM CON ENT.
404-222-0464

G PRODUCTIONS
404-761-5005

GLOW IN THE DARK
404-584-2345

HAYWOOD'S RECORDING
404-523-0699

HEADLINE RECORDINGS
770-438-0305

HIT-CITY MUSIC
404-767-8887

J - THRU - M

JEWEL ENT.
404-255-6700

JOI RECORDING STUDIOS
678-418-9973

KNOCK HARD PROD.
404-321-4999

KNOTCH STUDIO
404-299-5302

LEVEL 5 RECORDING
404-346-7566

LOYALTY RECORDS
404-297-0222

MADD HOUSE
404-699-6056

MADD SOUNDZ
404-297-4654

MISSION RECORDING
404-297-0933

N - THRU - P

NICKEL & DIME STUDIO
404-249-7166

OASIS RECORDING
404-525-4440

OMP GROUP
770-416-2200

ON-LINE PROD.
404-634-5572

ORPHAN STUDIO
404-352-0666

OUT-DA-CUTT STUDIOS
404-241-6299

OUT FRONT MUSIC
404-810-9061

PARADISE STUDIOS
404-351-0086

PATCHWERK RECORDING
404-874-9880

PLATNUMSLANG
RECORDS
404-349-6453

PRO SOUTH RECORDING
678-479-0689

PROJECT 70 DIGITAL
404-875-7000

R – THRU – S

REX RECORDING
770-277-3448

RIOT ATLANTA
404-237-9977

RKM SOUND STUDIOS
404-874-3667

STR RECORDING STUDIO
770-384-1834

SAVEOIRFAIR ENT.
404-589-8223

GLEN SCHICK MASTERING
404-806-6920 / 770-451-1314

SILENT PARTNER PROD.
404-355-3530

SLATER RECORDS
404-244-4711

SOAPBOX STUDIOS
404-815-7557

SONICA RECORDING
404-350-9540

SONY MUSIC
770-392-1844

SOUL SMUGGLER
404-627-2270

SOUND LAB
770-803-0014

SOUND LEVEL STUDIO
770-469-2021

SOUND VIDEO
770-451-0210

SOUNDRIGHT MUSIC
404-209-0558

SOUNDSATLANTA
404-329-9438

SOUTHERN EXPRESS
770-499-7950

SOUTHERN SLANG
770-414-5961

SOUTHERN TRACKS
404-329-0147

SPIN SOUTH
770-486-7746

STA BIZZI
678-999-0116

STANKONIA STUDIOS
404-355-2121

STAR TREK
404-699-0383

STARGATE
404-534-0022

T - THRU - Z

TCR STUDIOS INC
770-222-0478

T J ENT.
404-794-7942

TANDI ENT.
404-352-0522

TITANIUM RECORDING
678-904-5590

TOTAL RECORDING
404-929-6770

TREE SOUND STUDIOS
770-242-8944

TWELVE OAKS
RECORDING
770-435-2220

VIDEO 3-V
404-753-6677

VISION MUSIC GROUP
770-754-4543

WARFARE RECORDZ
404-373-1370

WHIPPOORWILL SOUND
770-333-9372

WISH RECORDING STUDIO
678-205-0248

WRITESIDE PROD.
770-928-1955

ZAC RECORDING
404-603-8040

For more Atlanta Studio listings, including details of
address and studio rates, please log in to
www.Musicpowers.com/24

LOS ANGELES RECORDING

SELECT RECORDING & MIXING FACILITIES IN LOS ANGELES, CA

A - THRU - C

ART OF NOISE
323-874-2447

ATLANTIS RECORDING
323-462-7761

B-SHARP RECORDING
323-291-6513

BLUE ROOM
310-575-6671

CAPITOL RECORDING
323-462-6252

CHALICE RECORDING
323-957-7100

CHEROKEE
323-653-3412

CONWAY RECORDING
323-463-2175

CRITERION MUSIC
323-469-2296

D - THRU - G

DIGIPREP MASTERING
323-469-3575

DIGITAL SOUND
323-258-6741

ECHO SOUND
323-662-5291

EXECUTIVE SOUNDS
323-463-0056

FUTURE DISC
323-876-8733

GRAND MASTER
323-462-6136

BERNIE GRUNDMAN
323-465-6264

H - THRU - L

HITCLUB STUDIOS
323-954-8724

HOLLYWOOD SOUND
323-467-1411

ICON RECORDING
323-469-4444

IMAGE RECORDING
323-850-1030

LARRABEE 1
323-851-1244

LARRABEE 2
310-657-6750

M - THRU - P

MAD HATTER
323-664-5766

MASTERING LAB
323-466-8589

METROPOLIS
323-464-0630

MIX MAGIC
323-466-2442

MUSIC GRINDER
323-957-2996

OASIS DIGITAL
323-464-6858

OCEAN WAY
323-467-9375

ONE ON ONE
323-655-9200

PARAMOUNT
323-465-4000

R - THRU - W

RECORD PLANT
323-993-9300

SIGNET SOUND
323-850-1515

SKIP SAYLOR
323-467-3515

SOUNDCASTLE
323-665-5201

STANKFISH
310-273-4699

STUDIO 56
323-978-0522

SUNSET SOUND
323-469-1186

VILLAGE RECORDING
310-478-8227

WESTBEACH
323-461-6959

WESTLAKE STUDIOS 1
213-654-2155

WESTLAKE STUDIOS 2
323-851-9800

NEW YORK RECORDING STUDIOS

SELECT RECORDING & MIXING FACILITIES IN THE NEW YORK AREA

A – THRU - Z

320 STUDIOS
212-675-9537

440 STUDIOS
212-869-2666

ABC SOUND
212-456-5621

ABSOLUTE AUDIO
212-730-2044

ALLEN FLYERS
212-239-9797

ATLANTIC
212-275-1000

AVALON
212-684-7222

AVATAR STUDIOS
212-765-7500

AXIS STUDIOS
212-262-3120

BABY MONSTER
212-627-5410

**BACK POCKET
RECORDING**
212-633-1175

**BASS HIT
RECORDING**
212-627-9570

BATTERY
212-627-8200

**BEARSVILLE
STUDIOS**
845-679-8900

BEARTRACKS
845-362-1620

BENNETT STUDIOS
201-227-0200

BIG HOUSE
212-944-8790

BMG RECORDING
212-930-4800

**CHA-CHA
RECORDING**
212-714-2422

CITY SOUND PROD
212-477-3250

COUNTDOWN
212-691-9279

CUTTING ROOM
212-260-0905

D & D RECORDING
212-736-7774

EDISON
212-921-0505

ELECTRIC LADY
212-677-4700

**FIREHOUSE
STUDIOS**
212-645-0666

FUNHOUSE STUDIO
212-979-0366

GIANT SOUND
212-247-1160

GREENE STREET
212-226-4278

HOT SOUND MUSIC
212-243-0098

**HOWARD
SCHWARTZ**
212-687-4180

LAUGHING DOG
718-720-9497

LOOKING GLASS
212-353-2000

LRP STUDIOS
212-807-9363

**MANHATTAN
CENTER**
212-279-7740

MERCER STREET
212-219-3776

MERLIN STUDIOS
212-575-2744

MILESTONE
718-941-4005

MIRROR IMAGE
212-582-7280

MIX PLACE
212-759-8311

MIXED NUTS
212-972-6887

NETWORK STUDIOS
212-255-2160

NEW YORK SOUND
212-929-5719

NIGHT OWL
212-714-1122

PILOT RECORDING
212-255-5544

PLANET SOUND
212-594-7554

PLATINUM ISLAND
212-473-9497

PRO-JAM
212-281-1010

PROMIX STUDIOS
212-242-7300

PYRAMID
212-686-868

QUAD RECORDING
212-730-1035

RIGHT TRACK
212-944-5770

ROOM WITH A VIEW
212-545-9258

RPM SOUND
212-242-2100

SADLER
212-684-0960

SEAR SOUND
212-582-5380

SONAR STUDIOS
212-832-8127

SONY MUSIC
212-833-7480

SORCERER SOUND
212-226-0480

SOUND ON SOUND
212-757-5300

SOUNDTRACK
212-420-6010

SPIKE RECORDING
212-353-8181

STARK TRAKS
212-267-8858

STERLING SOUND
212-757-8519

TRITON SOUND
212-575-8055

**UNIQUE
RECORDING**
212-921-1711

UNITED RECORDING
212-751-4660

UNITY GAIN
212-477-4893

**WESTRAX
RECORDING**
212-947-0533

Music Powers SPOTLIGHT DEBRA KILLINGS

Professional Vocalist – Artist/Producer - Musician

Debra Killings is one of the most admired and gifted vocalists in the music industry. Her singing has been featured on releases by OutKast, TLC, Aretha Franklin, Madonna, Toni Braxton, Monica, Da Brat, and many other artists' recordings. Her musical skills and flexibility to work on diverse recording projects has *also* made her one of the music industry's most in-demand *musicians*. Musician? Yes, in addition to lending her vocal talents to many hit records, Debra is also an extraordinary bass player, and shows this on recordings by Jay-Z, Nelly, OutKast, TLC and also on her own CD release, Surrender (Verity Records). Debra also works with super-producer Dallas Austin, and is an essential part of his production sound and production company - D.A.R.P (Dallas Austin Recording Projects).

In addition to being a seasoned studio vocalist and musician, Debra is also a songwriter, with credits on recordings by Pebbles, Paula Abdul, Corey, Sammie, and Monica. She also co-wrote the song "Take Our Time" that appears on the #1 selling album *CrazySexyCool* by TLC.

After years of contributing her musical skills to other artists, now Ms. Killings has moved into the performer spotlight herself. On her debut CD, *Surrender*, Debra showcases her soulful vocals and heart-felt melodies all in the name of, and for her love of God. She wants everyone to recognize that her solo artist endeavor is not only for entertainment, but is also part of her personal walk to change the way people *see and hear* Inspirational/Gospel music. Debra adds, *"I want people who may have never gone to church or those who don't listen to gospel music, to know that you can come to Him however you are... wherever you are."*

With all of her credentials and musical experience on multi-platinum hit projects, it's pretty effortless to recognize that Debra Killings *is* one of the most gifted and skilled vocalist and musicians in the music biz. And on top of that, if you speak with her, you would quickly realize that she is also exceptionally humble, honest and grateful for her accomplishments and success. So what's next? Be on the lookout for Debra's vocals to be featured on many more hit recordings, and there will definitely be more and more solo releases. Her love and passion for singing, writing, and performing, combined with her love and worship of Christ, suggests a spirit of her coming into completeness. And with that truth, you can expect that she's about to take wing even higher.

www.debrakillings.com

Music Powers
SPOTLIGHT
DEBRA KILLINGS

Artist/Vocalist – Producer – Songwriter – Musician

A Select Discography

Debra Killings
Surrender

Toni Braxton
Toni Braxton
Vocals

Corey
I'm Just Corey

Deborah Cox
Deborah Cox

Da Brat
Unrestricted

Dungeon Family
Even in Darkness

Aretha Franklin
Rose Is Still A Rose

Goodie Mob
Still Standing
World Party

Hi Five
Faithful

Jay-Z
Blueprint^2: The Gift
Bass, Vocals

Killer Mike
Monster
Vocals

Monica
Miss Thang
Boy Is Mine
Vocals

Nelly
Suit
Bass

OutKast
Speakerboxxx/The Love
Below
Bass, Vocals

OutKast
Southernplayalisticad-
illacmuzik
ATLiens
Jazzy Belle
Aquemini
Vocals

Erick Sermon
No Pressure
Vocals

TLC
Fanmail
Bass, Vocals, Producer

TLC
Unpretty
3D
Bass, Vocals

TLC
...On the TLC Tip
No Scrubs, Pt. 2
Girl Talk
Vocals

Tamia
Nu Day
Vocals

Other Select Credits
Akon
Shanice
George Clinton
Sammie
George Howard
Jazzy Jeff-Fresh Prince
Another Bad Creation

Soundtracks
Diary Of A Mad Black Woman
Boomerang
Drumline
Nutty Professor
Waiting to Exhale

Various Artists
Yo! MTV Raps
Grammy 2004
Wow Gospel 2003 & 2004
Verity – The First Decade

Exclusive Advice from Music Powers Advisor:

DEBRA KILLINGS

Professional Vocalist – Artist/Producer - Musician

WHAT PRODUCERS LOOK FOR

1 When you are looking for work as a background or studio vocalist, what are the main things that producers look for, when hiring for vocal work?

Producers will want to know: **1.** Have you been on anything else, **2.** How *good* are you... are you well versed (skilled), **3.** How fast are you, *and*... **4.** Do you have a *good memory?* That's what a lot of new singers don't realize; Memory is important also.

2 Can you tell us more about the importance of working quickly and memory?

➢ Memory and working quickly is *very* important because if a producer is sitting back there, and you have to sing that note 50 times over, and it's the *same note*, and he's saying, *"No, you're still a little flat!"* ...It just *wears him out*! But, if you're able to work quickly, it makes things go easier for the producer in the studio. As far as memory goes, you being able to memorize things fast and *to get it...* the same as they tell you to *do it,* and on the *first or second take* is really *very* important because it's less work for *them*.

➢ Basically what you want to do, as a background vocalist, is to actually learn how to be an instrument. For example, if a producer wants to take the high frequencies out of his keyboard, or tweak his keyboard, he aught to be able to turn a knob, and it be able to do that. And it's the same as you standing back there behind that microphone. If the producer tells you he wants more air, or to sing it airier, but if it takes you 50 tries to *sing it* airier, and you *don't remember to do that*, it *really* works the producer. But, if you're able to do your vocal parts quickly, and you remember everything, it just makes the producer's life a lot easier.

"...If you make their work easier, they are going to call you back!"

THE GOOD SESSION VOCALIST

3 Are there other essential things that new singers need to keep in mind when working with clients, so that they are considered "good" session workers?

➢ I would say one of the main things to being a good session worker is that you go in and *you feel the producer out first.* What's more, you can't go in there pressing *your thing* on *the producer or client...* when it's *their record!* What *really works* is when the producer doesn't have to sit up in the studio with you *all night.* It's also works great when they can *give you a part*, and he or she can *leave,* and go eat for thirty or forty minutes, and then come back to the studio, and *everything is completely done!*

Also, producers like it when they don't have to *hassle* or *haggle with you* about any *percentages*, or *writer's credit*, or *arrangement credit*, or a n y *mess!* See, that's what a lot of people don't realize. The attitude to take is, "You are going to get *yours*, I'm going to get *mine*, and I'm not trying to take a *bite out of yours*. I'm here to get paid... and I want my money. I'm here to make the *your life easier...* so that I *can be called back* for another session!"

PAYING DUES & DOING EXTRAS

4 What is the best advice you can give background vocalist just starting out, who *are really* good, but feel like when they do a lot extra things like arranging and coming up with "new" vocal parts, they should get a lot more?

➢ I've had a lot of people call me asking that question, trying to get into this business so quick...*so quick!* But in essence, if a producer calls them on a session, and they're hired to do background vocals, and they *do a little bit more*, that's fine. But many new vocalists want their percentage right then or right now, *at that new stage* of their career. And they want a piece of *this*; they want a piece of *that*, but it *doesn't work like that!* These producers or people aren't going to give that up *you...* just that easy. You just have to learn how to let some things sleep. There are a lot of "green" people, and what I mean by green, is that they are just getting into doing session work, but they want to be in the industry, and they want to be in this music business *bad* ...and they'll do *whatever it takes to make the session go great*, but *then*, they feel like they have to get theirs *now*, or whatever. But, in reality...

"...You have to just work that thang and pay some dues first!" "

CHARGING FOR SESSION VOCALS

5 What is a fair price to charge for session vocals if you are just starting out?

Well, it matters whether or not if the session is for demos, small releases, independents, or majors… to me. I think if you're just starting out, for small and demo projects, between $150 to $200 is a fair price if you're good …$250 at the most, because you're trying to get up in there and you don't want to close any doors before you get going. And if you *are just starting out*, and you are too high and *not* seasoned, they will be saying, "Okay, well *no*, she costs too much! And she really doesn't know what she's doing!" And if you're dealing with somebody's own small personal label, most of those people are normally paying out of their own pockets, like *personal* money, so they are not going to have much money to deal with in the first place.

➢ I think if you're dealing with an independent record *label*, I think $200 to $500 a song is good. But, some of these Indies don't *really know* what it's supposed to cost, especially if you're in the union. They don't know that you're supposed to charge per track, or for every three hours or so… And then, if it's Sunday or a holiday, it's going to be *double scale* (laughing).

➢ Now if you're trying to *get somewhere*, and if you're *just starting out*, even $100 to $200 per track isn't bad… *to me.* That's just something you do so you *can get somewhere.* You can't just go in there saying; "Well, I want $500 dollars a track!" Five hundred dollars is a lot of money for somebody's "out-of-pocket" to pay for a background vocalist who is just doing this for his or her first time. And I'd say that this is true even when dealing with someone as big as Dallas Austin, especially if you're just starting out.

➢ A lot of times, many of these producers don't want to be up in the studio all night *anyway.* And they don't want to have to burn up their studio time with somebody who doesn't really know, or doesn't maybe have experience stacking vocals or whatever. A lot of times a producer may just give you a note and then give you the basic format of the part, and then he'll walk out. Producers don't want to *have to be up in the studio with you* in the first place.

➢ For major projects, if you are good, and in a situation where you "know" what you are doing, producers or companies will pay whatever you're charging basically. When I first started out, I was blessed enough to be able to work on the group ABC, and the TLC stuff, right off the bat. So I started out making $1,000 per song, *blessedly!* But I was dealing with *major* record labels and producers too…who I guess knew the value. And $1,000 per song, going back 10 or 12 years ago was a *lot of money* …*and a blessing to me too.*

6 Do you also handle doing the vocal *arrangements* in the studio too?

A lot of times, or at least in the past 5 years, clients have wanted *my* arrangements. They just say, "Do your do." For example: They may give me a note, like the first note or part, then they say, "Okay, now do what you do" ...which is fine, if that's called arranging. I would say 80% of the time I do the vocal arrangements, *if arranging is giving me the first note*, and then I put all the other stacks on, and the flavoring on top of it. But you should also know, arranging will mean different things to different producers or clients too. And maybe 30% to 40% of the time, I will actually come up with something different other than what was originally thought of, like a completely new background part. But that doesn't happen too often because most of the time when you walk in the studio, producers basically *know what they want from the get go.* So as far as coming up with the other notes to add in a phrase; harmonies, stacks, etc... yes, I will come up with more parts and do that.

7 Should a vocalist charge extra for the arranging, if that's needed on the session?

➢ Well to me, if they hired you for background vocals, they're also hiring you for your vocal *opinion ...if they've asked.* For instance, if the producer asked you, "Well, what note would be good here?" You sing a note. But, I wouldn't go in the studio and *write any lyrics*, and not expect to get *writer's credit* on the record or something like that. The main thing is that I'm there to help. I'm like an instrument. So if they've asked me to put a vocal arrangement on the song, I would. I would just do it (without charging extra).

8 Do you also do lead vocals as a guide for the feature artist?

➢ I've had plenty of circumstances like that. I'll go in, and do the demo for the song. And I'll do it *exactly* like the producer tells me to do it, unless they tell me otherwise.

9 What kind of time or work limitations do you think you should put into the session... do you do the job until it's finished or what?

Basically yes. That's with any job ...to me. To me, you do it until it's *finished*. Otherwise, if you walked out with it half mast, and didn't come back, you wouldn't be called again.

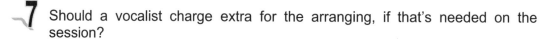

WORKING THROUGH THE UNION

10 What is your opinion about being in unions like AFTRA, and is that something that's good for singers?

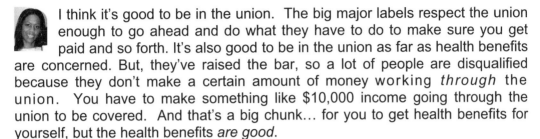

I think it's good to be in the union. The big major labels respect the union enough to go ahead and do what they have to do to make sure you get paid and so forth. It's also good to be in the union as far as health benefits are concerned. But, they've raised the bar, so a lot of people are disqualified because they don't make a certain amount of money working *through* the union. You have to make something like $10,000 income going through the union to be covered. And that's a big chunk... for you to get health benefits for yourself, but the health benefits *are good*.

11 AFTRA seems to really do a great job making sure singers and voice artist have a little muscle, as far as making sure singers get paid... has this been true in your own experience?

➢ Basically yes, but you know, I've done sessions in New York and LA, and when I was in Los Angeles on the TLC projects, by the time I got back to Atlanta, they ran the paperwork through or whatever, and they were like, "Okay, well, you have to join the union... it's time for you to join AFTRA." But, when I called the union here in Georgia, they were like; "No, Georgia is a *Free Labor State*... you don't really have to join the union if you don't want to." They told me, "No, you do not have to join the union." So, I know down here in Georgia, we're kind of relaxed.

➢ Also, *I haven't gotten paid in certain situations*, and the union wasn't able to do *anything*. I don't know if they, the AFTRA union here in Georgia didn't know what to do, or what. I was thinking that the union was supposed to protect me; to get me my money, or I get them the contact to the label and tell them, *"This record or project is not paying me my money over here!"* And then, AFTRA could go and get the money. But it wasn't like that. So I'm like, why am I here if they *can't* get me my money when I need it, when I have to be paid? And not even necessarily when I *have to be paid*, but if it's been several months, can I get you to call these people and get my money?

THE FIRST BIG BREAK

12 What was *your* first big break... how did you "get in" as a session vocalist?

➢ Well, I knew Dallas Austin from a couple of years back, even before he got started doing his major label stuff. Dallas needed somebody to sing background on his records, and at that time he was producing a group called ABC. And back then; they were just little boys that had never been in a recording studio before. I had worked in the studio... but I was still green too, *really*. But me being in the industry for years doing the Chitlin' Circuit clubs... singing, helped a lot. So, he was like, "Who can I call? Well, I'll call Debra, she's been singing for years, so she can help me out!" So, I went in the recording studio and it was like... ok. And I guess it just made things easier for him.

"THE CLICKS" – HOW CLIENTS VIEW YOU

 In the music business some of us know that there are certain clicks and circles. Does having experience as a background vocalist help you to "get in" and on projects as a songwriter and producer?

➢   You know, a lot of people ask me, "Well you know all these people, why aren't you writing on this, and producing on that? Or, why aren't you...?" And I tell them, when these people call me in, *to be professional about it,* they call me in to do *background vocals*. And every "thing" is a separate entity within itself. Of course, you know you have to be *"in the click"* in order to even get in to do some background vocals for all these sessions. So, *you are in the click!* But, you're in this click over *there (motioning to her right).* So you belong over there in the *background vocal click*. As a result, you're not *in as a writer or a producer.*

➢   For a long time, most of these people that I've done vocal work for didn't even know *I played bass.* So I mean, you're in as a *vocalist*, you're not *in as a bass player*. It's a trip. And that's what a lot of people standing on the outside doesn't realize. It takes a different click to get in as a *producer,* it takes a different click to get in as a *writer too*. And it's all the same people, but they just have to mentally *view you* different. So, for all of you new folk... it just doesn't work like that! Also, you don't want to go in the studio or into the project and press that side of your talent; to go in with your writer's hat saying, "This is what I wrote!" ...*That is not being professional.* What's more, they may not call you in for the *next session* because you've already been hounding them about *that song that you wrote.* So it's touchy.

STUDIO SKILLS

How important is it being a musician, when it comes to being a producer and songwriter?

➢   It's important. When I first started producing and writing, I really didn't know how to play keys or guitar that well. But, I think it's *really* important because of the fact that now when I want to write a song, I don't really have to *wait on anybody.* And me being a vocalist, singing melodies and things like that is easy, but it was hard to get keyboard players in. And you don't want to call players in on recording sessions and then *not be able to pay them.* So, I'm like, I'll just do this *myself.* So I had to press it out. It took a lot; I struggled to become fluent at keyboards. Guitar was a little easier because I was coming off of bass, but *keyboards*, I just had to struggle through it until I got fluent. And being that I don't play that often, I get kind of rusty in between, but I'm okay. I can hold it down.

 You are featured as the bass player on some pretty big projects; Nelly, Jay-Z, OutKast and of course with the TLC projects... what is your approach to playing bass, and how long did it take for you to get so good?

You know, I tell people this all the time, "If you're going to play bass, you've got to play *bold*, you've got to play *aggressive*, and you've *got to play loud!*" And I

 have to tell *everybody*, guitar players can *hide*, keyboard players can *hide*, but a bass player... *cannot* hide, and neither can a drummer.

As far as how long? I've been playing a l o n g time, and it really took some practicing...let me tell you. And most people say, "*Whoa*, she's good...she's good on that bass, *she's good to be a girl!*" And I'm like, you *know what?* That is *so wrong*; that is like a smack in the face... (laughing)

 How technical are you as far as getting around in the recording studio?

 I do what I have to do. Just like the musician thing, I had to learn how to play keys; I had to do this, and had to do that... so, I'm well vested on Pro Tools. I can take and break it down, hook it up, whatever. Whatever it takes; editing, moving parts, whatever...I can do it. And if somebody sat me in the studio and said, "You have to engineer for whomever," ...I'll be able. But when I first got the Pro Tools system, I was basically thrown into it and I had to do it *by myself!* I couldn't pay an engineer to come out to my own studio every day, so it was either *sink or swim.* So, that's how I learned. And also from calling people who knew about the system. I have never taken any official classes or anything like that, but some of that stuff is just common sense. And if you've ever seen anybody else work, or been involved with any engineer in the studio, you can basically figure out what to do.

17 What is the most important production tool for you in the studio?

The 4000, it's my preferred or favorite production tool. The Akai MPC 4000, 3000, 2000… an MP *period!* I think it's the most necessary tool. It's just what everybody's using, and I think to be compatible and up to date… *to hang in there with the big boys or whatever, you need an MP.*

18 A lot singers get nervous in the studio, especially when they are first starting out, do you ever get nervous, and are you still able to work and do a great job?

You work through it. I can remember a situation with Madonna, where Dallas Austin had called me in for her session. First of all, you're not intimidated, but you have that total respect thing happening, so you *actually are intimidated…* you know this lady is *"Madonna!"* Anyway, so I get in the booth, and I'm singing flat. And it seems like it takes me a *million years* to sing one part, to get… "One line!" And I'm like, "God, this is not me, what is up?" Plus, on top of that, 5 to 10 minutes into the thing, (the studio talkback button was still pushed in), so in my headphones, I hear her say, *"Her voice does not match mine! …This is not going to work; …this is not going to work!"* And I'm standing in there…and I'm like, *"Oh my God!"* I started sweating *instantly!* And Dallas was like, "But, this is *background* vocals, her voice is not *supposed* to match yours…this is how *I do things."* Then he said, "You said you wanted my sound, and this *is my sound, and I put her on everything I do!"* But she was still like, *"No, I don't like it, her voice doesn't match mine!"* But you know what, I *finished* the session, and I think I did two or three songs.  So, you just work through it. But I was… totally, mentally *intimidated.* That thing broke me down *so bad.* It was like if you had any kind (laughter) of ego before, you were tore up after that one…(laughter)!

GOD'S TIMING & GETTING SIGNED

19 How did you get your record deal …for you solo project?

➢ You know what? I had given up; I had totally given up as far as music, *period!* I had let it all go. I was like, you know what, I know God didn't call me for any confusion, so I had basically quit. I had been doing session work every now and then… still working a little. And then I was like; "You know what, I'm just going to write from my *heart."* So, I went and I wrote a couple of songs, as a matter of fact, *three songs.* The songs were "Oh I", "A Change", and I can't think of the third one. And then my Mom was like, well you know what Debra, I'm going to call Ian Burke and get him to hear these songs. So she called Ian and he was getting ready to go out of town, but something was in his spirit that had him like, "I've got to come out there and hear these songs before I leave to go to LA." So he came out to my place and heard the songs, and I guess he was blown away by the message...and just the whole vibe and avenue of it. So Ian sent the songs to this guy named Max Siegel, who was about to be signed in A&R over there at Verity Records, but he wasn't quite in the mix of things over there yet. But he was like saying, "Well, I love it!" But we didn't hear anything back from him for a couple of weeks. So I guess he was finalizing his whole deal with Verity. And when he finally settled in at the label, I was the first act that he laid on the table. And that's how it all came about.

"...I guess it was just God's timing."

DEBRA KILLINGS

Multi-Platinum – Award Winning Vocalist, Artist, Musician, Producer, Songwriter
Debra Killings' credits include TLC, OutKast, Nelly, Madonna, Toni Braxton, Jay-Z, Monica, Tamia, Aretha Franklin, Da Brat, and many others

www.DebraKillings.com

GETTING RADIO PLAY

Getting radio play is one of the hardest things to accomplish, especially for a new act. Also, it's hard for the majors to get radio spinning songs on *established acts*. So, if you're an Independent or "Indie" label, all I can say is determination and *creative* marketing will definitely help. O*f course, having a truckload of money won't hurt either, but that's a different book!* ☺

Outside of making sure radio stations have your song and promo material, *before you start trippin' by hassling' radio staff*, you should actually seek to get as much feedback as you can in the clubs. Clubs are a way to get an instant response of *how* receptive your song is to the public. If your song can keep people "*doing their thang*" on the dance floor, it may have a good chance of being able to compete with the hottest songs being played on radio as well. In addition, this is one of the best "accessible" ways of finding out which of your songs you want to push. It's very easy to be in love with your own song, not only since you wrote it, but also because you've heard it over and over again! But when you take the chance of bumping your track in public, against the best songs that are already getting play, you will *definitely* get a chance to "see" what others think (by their reactions). So just know - whether good or bad, you will get some type of feedback. Most people *hate* to get a whack track mixed in when they are dancing. And on the positive side, it may end up being your song that floods the floor. So just know that either way, you *will* get a response.

Now please don't think it's going to be all easy getting' the *hot* club DJ to play your record, just because he's a little more accessible than the DJ at the *big* radio stations. Keep in mind: Club DJs get paid to keep the dance floor *full*. For that reason, they're not going to like the idea of giving your song a spin, if you step to them with some whack song or song *production*. So make sure first, that the song is 'club friendly,' mixed, and mastered (if needed) properly. What your track *sounds like* is definitely a big deal. I have personally experienced testing songs in clubs, and have gotten a less than a desirable response, due to the song's mixing and mastering *not* being "DJ-mix friendly" with the other songs that the DJ was spinning. And of course, the timing of *when* a DJ plays your song will also come into play. For example, if the DJ is mixing "In Da Club" by 50 Cent, and you've got a Ruben Studdard sounding" track, you might be asking for trouble. So, once you get the 'green light,' and you *clearly* see the DJ bouncing the head with excitement, make the *next* 'appropriate' move – offer to buy him whatever he's drinking, *and make sure* you give him a healthy tip ($) for helping you out. So what's your next step? Take it to the street. Do freebies and promo handouts. Actually, just do whatever it '*creatively*' takes to expose your songs to the public, the potential fans and the market you are trying to reach -- *especially the ones who listen and request songs to radio stations.*

Basically, this means that you have to get out with your team to pass out and promote with postcards, flyers, posters, stickers, signs, local ads, etc. Also, don't be afraid to "piggy back" some of your advertising with other events, and with other artists who are doing the same things that you are doing. And since the goal is to spark a buzz to get some attention and create some hype ...*and some hopeful great fan reaction, make sure* some of your promo materials read: CALL & REQUEST IT TODAY!

Next step: If you don't have some type of following from doing live performances, you should *consider* doing free promo shows in your area. This includes opening up for larger acts that are sponsored by your local radio stations & club promoters. During your shows, you should not only sell your CD, but you'd better give them away too - with instructions to your 'Street Team' (who need to also be wearing your T-shirts) to be persistent in reminding everyone to call the radio stations to request your song. If enough people like your song, and the word gets out about your song being hot, radio stations *will* start getting calls about it. Once the station gets enough calls, the DJ may then go to the station's Music Director about either breaking the song or including the song in one of his mixes.

...Quick note:

•   *If you are putting out records "independently" or "on your own,"* **Do NOT approach the Program Director before approaching the Music Director and the DJs first!**" *There is normally a chain of command in almost all network soliciting. So* **start with the DJ, then the Music Director**. *They can then deal with the Program Director when it's time.*

BASIC, BUT VERY IMPORTANT GUIDELINES

YOUR PACKAGE

• Just in case people start calling in to request your song, make sure that the radio station's DJ and the Music Director have a copy of your song to play. I would actually suggest including a Professional Promo Kit, press releases and positive reviews that have been made in the local newspapers or trade magazines.

LYRIC FRIENDLY

ADVISORY
EXPLICIT CONTENT

• Make sure you have a *radio friendly* version of your song available to the station. This means that if the original song has language that is considered offensive to broadcast over the air, you need to get the station a remix or edited version of your song… *without* the profanity.

RADIO READY?

• Make sure your Production and Mix is Broadcast Quality. If the Radio station thinks it sounds bad, they probably will not air your song.

SMALL MARKETS

• You may want to work all of the smaller surrounding markets of the larger cities. Eventually and hopefully, if people are calling in the smaller radio stations, it will spread to at least one or two big stations. Then once a big station breaks your song, other stations across the country may also give it a shot. *Everyone loves a winner!*

TIMING

Timing can play a major role in breaking a record to other markets. If you are able to time a mass media campaign while other events are happening within the same market you are targeting, you stand a very strong chance of getting people from other markets to not only hear your song and see your promo items, but you also give yourself a great opportunity for those from out-of-town to take whatever you have distributed - back to their *own markets* and start a buzz. Imagine if you have your song playing at one of the small or major sporting events, or getting the clubs spinning your song and/or ads in print or on radio – ALL while some "other" big event or whatever is going on in the same town …*at the same time*. This means that the visitors from out of town now become potential fans of your music… without you having to be "in *their* town!"…☺ This means that you or your manager or marketing people should be keeping up with whatever is going on as far as other related and sometimes *not-related* events in the area you are seeking to get attention in.

OK – now that you have a basic understanding of what's ahead... let's move on & give you some other realities that you will come across.

RADIO PAY-FOR-PLAY

At some point you should be aware that payola does exist. Now, whether or not the radio industry now wants to call it payola *or* creative consulting... *well*, it still breaks down to being the same thing... ($ - Money)!

...PAYOLA?

• *Encarta describes payola as a bribe for promoting a product. – A payment given in exchange for promoting a commercial product, or the system of making such payments, especially to Disc Jockeys.*

...RADIO CREATIVE CONSULTING?

• *Basically it's a way to pay for radio play by way of a consultant. Since it's illegal for the radio station to be paid directly from the labels, the record companies use these consultants as middlemen.*

The whole issue of paying to have your song played is a *complete* book in itself. But you should be aware that if you have an Indie label going, you might be *expected* (at some point) to play along with the pay-for-play game like some others have done. Do you have to? NO. Should you? Hey, it's illegal... so *you* figure that out for yourself. Now, there are majors and indies spending stupid big money to keep records playing over & over again. So, I guess it may really boil down to your own promotional budget & principles. But to some, what use to be frowned on because it's illegal, is now deemed as just being the way some radio stations openly work ...behind *closed* doors.

For more research on paying to have your record played, I would suggest the following resources: *"The Record Game Can Be A Dirty Game"* - by Raheem & *"Payola City"* - In the Wild World of Urban Radio, Money Buys Hits ...and Nobody asks Questions - By Eric Boehlert (On the web), There is also a great article for you to research further from 20/20 at www.abcnews.com called: *"Pay for Play? Investigation: Independent Promoters in the Music Industry"*.

INDEPENDENT PROMOTION
By Ben McLane

Support from radio is *key* in order to make the masses aware of a new record. Unfortunately, obtaining radio play is very difficult *and* very competitive. Because of this, you may want to budget for the services of an independent promoter.

In order to compete with the majors, you must be able to take the steps that a major label would take - in order to promote a record. Since most independent artists don't have a promotion staff to service the hundreds of appropriate radio stations across the country necessary for an effective radio promotion campaign, a promoter is the vehicle to generate airplay. The promoter can gain the necessary radio "adds" for several reasons that the artist cannot, because they: (1) have years of experience, (2) have established relationships with program and music directors, (3) know how to *properly* pitch a record, and (4) know *who* to approach with the pitch.

Because a promoter is not cheap to employ, smaller labels and artists will generally just hire the promoter to work the record in a particular region. If airplay becomes significant in that region, often the record will then take on a life of its own and other regions will want to play the record. The hard part is developing those first important radio adds.

Promoters can be found in most large cities in the yellow pages under record promotion. Because a genuine promoter will not work a record unless they believe in it, you should call and make an appointment to play the record for the promoter. You should check references and the track record of the promoter also. Once you have located the right promoter, a contract should be entered into. The two most important points to cover are the fee and the duties of the promoter. Although the fees vary depending on the type of music and scale of the campaign, a good promotion person would require around $500+ per week; a proven hit-maker may charge a lot more. The promoter will want bonuses built into the contract to be triggered by certain happenings, such as having the record chart, entering the top ten, and hitting number one. Also, the promoter's expenses (i.e., phone, mail, travel) will have to be paid. You should require that the promoter specify the number and type of stations he or she will be contacting.

Finally, the you should not forget that it is meaningless to hire a promoter if the record is *not going to be distributed* in some way; otherwise, the listening audience cannot *buy* the record ...and this would *defeat* the entire purpose of *generating airplay*.

Used by permission of By Ben Mclane, Esq.

Music Powers SPOTLIGHT
EMPEROR SEARCY

Dewayne Searcy, a.k.a. Emperor Searcy, hails from Atlanta, GA, and is an On-Air Radio Personality / DJ on Atlanta's WHTA-FM HOT 107.9. Searcy is also The National Mix-Show Coordinator for the Radio One Networks, and has a syndicated radio show with Lil' Jon called "Crunk Radio", that targets Hip Hop, R&B & CHR (Contemporary Hit Radio) stations. American Urban Radio Networks CrunkRadio With Lil' Jon & Emperor Searcy opens on forty-two stations - with additional stations being added weekly.

As a Record Producer Emperor Searcy has created cutting edge Production & Beats for successful projects that include: Ginuwine's "Pony" Bass Remix, "Swing My Way" by KP & Envy, "Holiday" by Witchdoctor, So So Def Bass All-stars Compilation, and Nationwide Compilation with Too Short. And most recently Searcy signed a deal with Warner Brothers Records for Trillville and Lil' Scrappy.

On the Music Business side, you'll find Emperor "The Entrepreneur" Searcy handling his business at the headquarters of BME Recordings in Atlanta. This is where 'Mr.' Searcy is an Executive and Co-founding Partner of Black Market Entertainment - along with his other savvy business partners; Robert McDowell, Jonathan 'Lil' Jon' Smith and Vince Phillips. Billboard Magazine has recognized BME Recordings as: "The #1 Indie Label of The Year for 2003". This recognition was achieved after many weeks of holding down the #1 Chart Position on Billboard's Independent Album Charts.

With several Gold & Multi-Platinum RIAA Awards, a highly successful Record Company (BME), and one of the HOTTEST radio shows in the Atlanta Market, Emperor Searcy has many times been featured in music industry and entertainment publications such as "Holla!" and "Rollin' Out".

Emperor Searcy's further achievements include:

"The AIR Radio Award"
"Atlanta's Best DJ Award"
"Best DJ of 2003"

Recently, Source Magazine named Emperor Searcy as...
"One of Hip Hop's Most Influential DJs!"

EMPEROR SEARCY
A Select Discography

Crunk Juice - Lil Jon & The Eastside Boyz
Executive Producer

Against Da Grain - YoungBloodz
Producer

King of Crunk & BME Recordings Present: Trillville - Trillville & Lil Scrappy
Producer, Executive Producer

I Don't Give a @#&% - Lil Jon & The Eastside Boyz
Executive Producer

Get Crunk, Who U Wit: Da Album - Lil Jon & The Eastside Boyz
Performer

So So Def Bass All-Stars, Vol. 2 - Various Artists
Producer, Engineer

Rhythm & Quad 166, Vol. 1 - Various Artists
Programming, Producer, Performer

Next Stop the Ghetto - Black Dave
Remixing

So So Def Bass All-Stars, Vol. 3 - Various Artists
Scratching, Producer

Crow's Nest - Jim Crow
Producer

Kings of Crunk - Lil Jon & The Eastside Boyz
Executive Producer

Music Powers

Exclusive Advice from Music Powers Advisor

EMPEROR SEARCY

VISION, FOCUS & OPPORTUNITY

1 The original BME idea was a seed planted as far back as high school. Did all of the partners recognize that your vision could turn into what is now known as the company BME Recordings?

Our company, BME Recordings was an idea of Vince Phillips, Robert McDowell, Lil' Jon and me. We all grew up with dreams of being in the music industry, and there was something in all of us that said we could make this happen. We knew if we stayed at it, all of the hard work and dedication would manifest into something powerful.

2 You are a successful Producer & Executive Producer with major credentials, along with being one of the hottest "on-air" Radio Personalities. How do you keep focused and driven ...to be so successful with all 3 careers?

➢ The method to staying successful and focused is to *not forget the formula that allowed you to get where you are.* If it was the grind, hard work and dedication that helped to get you there - then you can't *stop* that grind. You have to continue to have the *same hunger* that you had from day one. I think that is what allows me to stay so focused and continue to be successful.

...And what about having all 3 careers?

➢ Juggling the jobs is a learned behavior that just comes with the desire to be in the music industry. I say that - *because in the beginning*, you may be doing *one job*, and then *realize* - you can also do this *other job* and make more contacts or money. You do another job over here - for someone that can *get you on*, and you may also have school or "that" job - that is there to actually pay the bills...or make sure you eat until it (get you on) happens. So in the beginning, you juggle a lot *anyways*. Some gigs *paid*, and some *unpaid*.

"...You either hop on ...or get left behind!"

3 What was the turning point or big break that happened for BME Recordings - to get so large?

➢ The success of BME was *years* of hitting the scenes, and the clubs... *saturating the streets*, and over-flowing the radio waves with the hottest new music in the ATL, *and* the region. Over time, we kept making continuous noise in the *streets*, in the *clubs*, and everyone continued to hear us, *and so did the labels*. We all know the rest...here we are!

➢ *"Get Low"* (Lil' Jon & The Eastside Boys w/ Ying Yang Twins) *definitely* put us *further* on the map, while *"Yeah"* (Usher w/ Lil Jon) followed with the hottest collaboration of Crunk and R&B.

4 How did you become one of the Hottest Djs in America?

Emperor Searcy @ Radio Station: WHTA-FM - HOT 107.9 in Atlanta

➢ My own success as a dj came with a plan. There *always* needs to be a plan. In that plan, *there needs to be an outline of hard work, dedication, determination, drive, devotion, commitment, and goals*. My own break as a dj came from that type of plan. The same desire to dj when I started is still there, too. *I still continue to dj clubs several nights a week* ...as I did when I began.

"...The grind never stops!"

DJS - PRODUCERS...SUCCESS & SKILLS

5 Since you are a successful Producer / DJ, what advice can you give new talent that want to "get in" the music biz as a Producer / DJ?

 For those that want to get into the biz as a producer or dj, they need to continue to study and work on there craft as does everyone else in any other field. For a producer / dj, this industry is *always* changing, so it's important to continue to make music and collaborations with other artist. Unless you know someone in the music industry that really loves your style & beats, and that will then help get you *on* (a project), the best thing to do is to collaborate with others that are *also* on the come-up; get on a few Mix CDs to get the *extra* buzz, and hit the underground scenes to check out other artist. An artist needs a producer as a producer needs an artist. As a dj, the key is to *continue* to hit the scene with the newest, hottest music mixed with a lil' technique until "you *are* the scene." Then continue to do whatever it is that gave you the following, once you get it...*all while continuing to work on your craft.*

6 How important has it been, being a DJ - to enhance your *own* production skills and also have an ear for hot talent?

➤ Being a dj allows you to keep up with what's hot and what's not! It also allows you to hear the track *behind the song*, which allows a better blend of mixes from one song to the next song. Being able to *hear* different tracks, and the *extra bells and whistles* that are added - enables a dj to put together tracks that are *just as hot*. Not to say that only Djs have an ear, but Djs spin and get a chance to hear and "*see* reactions" to different songs and beats first - *whether it's their own material or someone else's.* Djs can then take that knowledge and put together some pretty hot material. It may not happen *at first*, and it may not be the right formula in the beginning, but if he stays at it - he can be successful in the two.

...Eventually, you'll ace the test, if you study long enough!

GETTING AIRPLAY

7 What's the best advice you can give new acts who are trying to get their songs played on radio by stations like Atlanta's Hot 107.9 or any of the Hip Hop / R&B stations that are big?

➤ The *best thing to do* is to stay in the clubs testing your songs *before* going straight to a radio station. Make sure it's a hit *before* taking it into the station for review. If the fans start to vibe it, then it just may be time to take it to the station. Be sure to get those same fans or followers of your music to call and request your joint (song). Most cities have djs in clubs that are *also the same djs at the stations*. Now this *doesn't* mean that they control what's being played *at the station*, but if they're spinning in the clubs, then they may be able to assist with the review process - during new music meetings, or for play during the mix show.

FOR FUTURE PRODUCERS

8 What's the best advice you can give to future or up-and-coming producers who want to get hooked up on major projects?

➤ The best thing for producers is - to continue to make hot tracks that will make and create a name for themselves as hot producers. Your tracks will *eventually* start talking for you. Everyone says and *thinks* that their material is what's next - to hit all the airwaves, and they *should* (think & say that). No one else can have faith in your work *if you don't*. *However, you have to have that track that says it for you 'before" being able to just get on anyone's project that's major or underground!*

...And what is your view on selling beats & tracks by new producers?

➤ If new producers can sell their tracks, *then great*! They should be paid for their service as anyone else. However, if it's a hot project, then you may want to consider a small amount up front and a *bigger fee* on the back end, or even *all of it* on the back end - *if* someone's *willing* to put you on a major project.

9 How much testing do you do in the clubs with material?

➤ I'll test a song a number of times before the party really gets started to see if people are actually "vibing-it", or to see if there are positive reactions, heads bobbing, people not leaving the dance floor, etc.

➤ If people stay on the dance floor or actually seem to vibe it, then I'll chance spinning it later in the night - once it's been tried a few times. After so many attempts (if no response), it just makes it obvious that it may *not* be the right song for an artist to push at the time or maybe *never*. They may just need to try a new song or stay in the studio 'til they think they have another hit.

10 What advice can you give to *"get in the music biz"* and actually *"be successful"* like yourself and your company.

"...Study your craft, learn the business, and look to books such as Music Powers to help guide you in the right direction."

➤ There may not be just *one right way* to get into this biz, but whatever your journey may be, stay focused and driven, and if you don't already have a plan or strategy, *then devise one and attack it!* And don't let *anyone* tell you that you can't make it happen. Follow your dreams as Vince Phillips, Lil Jon, Robert McDowell, and myself have when we started BME Recordings.

 Billboard Magazine voted BME as The #1 Indie Label of 2003. BME Recordings is home to Lil Jon and the Eastside Boyz, Lil Scrappy, Trillville, Crime Mob, Oobie, Chyna White, Bohagon, and E40.

Emperor Searcy at: WHTA-FM - HOT 107.9 in Atlanta with The Music Powers book

Emperor Searcy is an On-Air Radio Personality & DJ on Atlanta's HOT 107.9 FM & The National Mix-Show Coordinator for Radio One, Inc. He is an award winning Producer & Executive with BME Recordings. Searcy also has a syndicated radio show: Crunk-Radio with Lil Jon on American Urban Radio Networks.

Harry Lyles - President of Lyles Media Group

The Lyles Media Group creates customized Programming, Marketing, and Sales for leading broadcast groups, radio networks and Internet media companies across the U.S. and Canada.

Harry Lyles has successfully demonstrated his Programming and Marketing expertise by working with some of the top broadcast companies in America and Canada. Companies like Clear Channel, Emmis, Apex Charleston, Miller Of The Carolinas, Radio People, Citadel and Barnstable have used his programming strategies, and plans.

Established in 1990, Lyles Media Strategies is the premiere programming specialist. Originally launched as Lyles Consultancy, the company has since broadened its focus into Marketing and Sales. Harry's background also includes knowledge and success in other formats like Adult Contemporary, CHR and Classic Rock

In 2003, The International Black Broadcasters Association honored Harry Lyles as Consultant of the Year. Mr. Lyles has also been a frequent speaker at national conventions such as the National Association of Broadcasters, National Radio Advertising Bureau and The Arbitron PD Clinic.

THE LYLES MEDIA GROUP, LLC
770-594-7171
hlyles@urbanradio.com
www.urbanradio.com

HARRY LYLES ▲ LYLES MEDIA GROUP

S E L E C T   C L I E N T E L E

CLEAR CHANNEL

EMMIS

APEX CHARLESTON

MILLER OF THE CAROLINAS

RADIO PEOPLE

CITADEL

BARNSTABLE

Exclusive Advice from Music Powers Advisor

PRESIDENT OF LYLES MEDIA GROUP

THE TRUTH ABOUT MAJOR RADIO PLAY

1 What's the best advice you can give new artists who are trying to get their songs played on major radio stations...*on their own*?

The truth is that *most* major radio stations will not play any (None...Zero!) songs *unless a label presents them.* For those of us in the business we know there are all sorts of "charting" conditions that must be met. My best advice is to present their music to a label.... either a major label or a good independent and follow their lead.

2 How important are other channels & media (TV, Internet, Print, etc) ...to aid in getting an artist more spins or play on Major Radio stations?

➢ **All that matters to radio is radio.** While there have been a few odd cases where radio has picked up a song from a video channel etc. 99% of the time all that matters is how a song is doing on radio (reference Q #1).

3 Many Indie artists & labels complain about the same 30-35 songs played in rotation...over & over... any comments?

➢ You must remember that radio has little to no interest in the success of any given song. Radio is a business dedicated to making money. Radio makes money through selling advertising. The rate that stations can charge for commercials is determined by ratings. History has proven over and over that the stations that play the Top 30 or 40 songs over and over again have the *highest* ratings. That's why Radio does this. It's not about the art of music; it's about *making money*.

THE SUCCESSFUL PATH

4 What is your best advice to new talent & artists, to help them get a leg up getting *in* the music biz ... and actually being successful?

➢ My advice is to hire someone who knows how to design and *create a plan* that will take you where you want to be. There are a lot of great singers who go unheard because they refuse to follow the path to success designed and implemented by the music industry.

Harry Lyles (on right) with Errol Norman - Owner of Titanium Recording Studios in Atlanta, GA

➢ Finding and hiring a *good* manager who has established himself or herself in the industry is *paramount* to the success of the artist. I know a zillion great singers who have tried to buck the system and failed. You've got to remember this is a business and like any other business there is a right way and a wrong to attack the project. Take the easier road... go out and hire a professional who *does this for a living* and do what they say. It may not be exactly what you *want to do* - but after you become wildly successful, you can direct your career to wherever you want to go.

Harry Lyles is President of Lyles Media Group.
Email your comments, thoughts or suggestions to Harry at **hlyles@urbanradio.com** or visit his website at
www.urbanradio.com

Music Powers

RADIO STATION DIRECTORY

Select list of Urban & CHR / Rhythmic Radio Stations in the United States

NEW YORK

WBLS - 107.5 FM
3 Park Avenue
New York, NY 10016
212-447-1000 / Fax 212-447-5211
PD - Vinny Brown
MD - Deneen Womack
www.wbls.com

WWPR - 105.1 FM
1120 Sixth Ave.
New York, NY 10036
212-704-1051
PD - Michael Saunders
MD - Mara Melendez
www.power1051fm.com

WKTU - 103.5 FM
525 Washington Blvd -16th Floor
Jersey City, NJ 07310
201-420-3700 / Fax 201-420-3787
PD - Jeff Zuchowski
MD - Skyy Walker
www.ktu.com

WQHT - 97.1 FM
395 Hudson St.
New York, NY 10014
212-229-9797 / Fax 212-929-8559
PD - Tracy Cloherty
MD – Ebro
www.hot97.com

WRKS – 98.7 FM
395 Hudson Street
New York, New York 10014
212-242-9870
PD - Toya Beasley
MD - Julie Gustines
www.987kissfm.com

CHICAGO

WVAZ - 102.7 FM
233 N. Michigan Ave., 28th floor
Chicago, IL 60601
312-360-9000 / 312-540-2000
Fax 312-360-9070
PD - Cliff Winston
MD - Armando Riviera
www.v103.com

WPWX - 92.3 FM
6336 Calumet Avenue
Hammond, IN 46324
219-933-4455 / Fax 219-933-0323
PD – J. Alan
MD - Barbara McDowell
www.power92chicago.com

WGCI - 107.5 FM
233 North Michigan Ave, Suite 2700
Chicago, IL 60601
312-540-2000
PD - Elroy Smith
MD - Tiffany Green
www.wgci.com

WBBM - 96.3 FM
630 N. McClurg Court
Chicago, IL 60611
312-202-3497
MD - Erik Bradley
www.b96.com

WASHINGTON, DC

WKYS - 93.9 FM
5900 Princess Garden Parkway
8th Floor
Lanham, MD 20706
301-306-1111 / Fax 301-306-9540
PD: Daryl Huckaby
MD: Paul 'P-Stew' Stewart
www.939wkys.com

WPGC - 95.5 FM
4200 Parliament Place, Suite 300
Lanham, MD 20706
301-918-0955
PD: Jay Stevens
MD: Boogie D
www.wpgc955.com

ATLANTA

WHTA - 107.9 FM
75 Piedmont Avenue - 10th Floor
Atlanta, GA 30303
404-765-9750
PD - Jerry Smokin' B
MD - Ramona Debreaux
www.hot1079atl.com

WVEE - 103.3 FM
1201 Peachtree Street, Suite 800
400 Colony Square
Atlanta, GA 30361
404-898-8900
PD - Reggie Rouse
MD - Tosha Love
www.v-103.com

WBTS - 95.5 FM
1601 W. Peachtree Street, NE
Atlanta, GA 30309
404-897-7500 / Fax 404-817-0955
MD - Jonathan Maverick
www.955thebeat.com

LOS ANGELES

KDAY - 93.5 FM
5055 Wilshire Blvd. #720
Los Angeles, CA 90048
323-337-1600 / Fax 323-337-1633
PD - Anthony Acampora
MD - Chris Loos
programming@935kday.com
www.935kday.com

KKBT - 100.3 FM
5900 Wilshire Blvd. 19th Floor
Los Angeles, CA 90036
323-634-1800
PD -Tom Halacochie
MD - T. Sharp
www.thebeatla.com

KPWR - 105.9 FM
2600 West Olive Ave. - 8th Floor
Burbank, CA 91505
818-953-4200 / Fax: 818-848-0961
PD - Jimmy Steal
MD - E Man
www.power106.fm

PHILADELPHIA

WUSL - 98.9 FM
440 Domino Lane
Philadelphia, PA 19128
215- 508-1200 / 215-263-6699
Fax 215-483-5930
PD: Thea Mitchem
MD: Kashon Powell
www.power99.com

WPHI - 100.3 FM
1000 River Road - 4th Floor
Conshohocken, PA 19428
610-276-1100
PD: Colby Tyner
MD: Sarah O'Conner
soconnor@radio-one.com
www.1003thebeatphilly.com

WRDW – 96.5 FM
555 City Ave. – Suite 330
Bala Cynwyd, PA 19004
610-667-9000 / Fax 610-667-5978
PD: Chuck Tisa
MD: Kannon
www.wired965.com

HOUSTON

KPTY - 104.9 FM
1415 North Loop West
Houston, TX 77008
713-407-1415
PD: Pete Enriquez
MD: Homie Marco
www.party1049.com

KBXX - 97.9 FM
24 Greenway Plaza, Suite 900
Houston, Texas 77046
713-623-2108 / Fax 713-300-5751
PD: Terri Thomas
www.kbxx.com

DALLAS

KKDA - 104.5 FM
621 NW 6th Street
Grand Prairie, TX 75050
972-263-9911
PD/MD: Skip Cheatham
www.k104fm.com

KBFB - 97.9 FM
13331 Preston Rd. - Suite 1180
Dallas, TX 75240
972-331-5400
PD: John Candelaria
MD: Big Bink
www.979thebeat.com

KZZA - 106.7 FM
5307 E. Mockingbird Lane - Suite 500
Dallas, TX 75206
214-887-9107 / Fax 214-841-4215
PD: Dean James
MD: Dean James
www.casa1067.com

SAN FRANCISCO

KYLD - 94.9 FM
340 Townsend Ave. Suite 4-949
San Francisco, CA 94107
415-538-9494
PD: Dennis Martinez
MD: Travis Loughran
www.wild949.com

KMEL - 106.1 FM
340 Townsend St – Suite 5106
San Francisco, CA 94107
415-538-1061
PD: Stacy Cunningham
MD: Big Von Johnson
vonjohnson@clearchannel.com
www.kmel.com

MIAMI

WEDR - 99.1 FM
2741 N. 29th Ave.
Hollywood, FL 33020
305-444-4404
PD: Cedric Hollywood
MD: Shelby Rushin
www.wedr.com

WMIB - 103.5 FM
7601 Riviera Blvd.
Miramar, FL 33023
954-862-2000
PD: Dion Summers
MD: Coka-Lani Kimbrough
www.thebeatmiami.com

WPOW - 96.5 FM
20295 N.W. 2nd Avenue,#300
Miami, FL 33169
305-653 – 6796 / Fax 305-770-1476
PD: Tony The Tiger
MD: Eddie Mix
www.power96.com

BALTIMORE

WERQ - 92.3 FM
100 St. Paul Street
Baltimore, MD 21202
410-332-8200
PD: Victor Starr
MD: Neke Howse
www.92qjams.com

CHARLOTTE

WPEG - 97.9 FM
1520 South Boulevard, Suite 300
Charlotte, NC 28203
704-342-2644
MD - Deon Cole
www.power98fm.com

WNKS - 95.1 FM
137 South Kings Drive
Charlotte, NC 28204
704-331-9510
MD - Keli Reynolds
www.kiss951.com

CINCINNATI

WIZF - 100.9 FM
705 Central Avenue, Suite 200
Cincinnati, OH 45202
513-679-6000
MD - Terri Thomas
www.wizfm.com

WKRQ - 101.9 FM
2060 Reading Road
Cincinnati, Ohio 45202
513-699-5102
www.q102online.com

CLEVELAND

WENZ - 107.9 FM
2510 St. Clair Avenue, N.E.
Cleveland, OH 44114
216-579-1111
MD - Eddie Bauer

DETROIT

WJLB - 97.9 FM
645 Griswold, Suite 633
Detroit, MI 48226
313-965-2000
MD: Kris Kelley
www.fm98wjlb.com

LAS VEGAS

KLUC - 98.5 FM
6655 W.Sahara Ave., # D110
Las Vegas, Nevada 89146
702-253-9800
MD - J.B. King
jb@kluc.com
www.kluc.com

RALEIGH

WQOK - 97.5 FM
8001-101 Creedmoor Road
Raleigh, NC 27613
919-848-9736
800-321.5975
MD - Shawn Alexander
www.k975.com

TAMPA

WBTP - 95.7 FM
4002 Gandy Blvd
Tampa, FL 33611
813-832-1000 / Fax 813-832-1090
MD - Jeff Kapugi
www.957thebeat.com

WLLD - 98.7 FM
9721 Executive Center Drive, # 200
St. Petersburg, FL 33702
727-579-1925
MD - Beata
www.wild987.com

MEMPHIS

WHRK - 97.1 FM
2650 Thousand Oaks Blvd, 4th Floor
901-259-1300 / Fax 901-529-9557
Memphis, TN 38118
www.k97fm.com
MD: Devin Steele
www.k97fm.com

KXHT - 107.1 FM
6080 Mount Moriah Rd
Memphis, TN 38115
901-375-9324
MD: Big Sue
bigsue@hot1071.com
www.hot1071.com

WMPW - 98.9 FM
5629 Murray Rd.
Memphis, TN 38119
901-682-1106
MD: Doughboy
www.power99memphis.com

KJMS - 101.1 FM
112 Union Ave
Memphis, TN 38103 -
Clear Channel Communications
MD: Eileen Nathaniel
www.smooth101.com

BOSTON

WBOT - 97.7 FM
500 Victory Road
Quincy, MA 02171
617-472-9447
MD: Lamar Robinson
www.wbothot977.com

WJMN - 94.5 FM
99 Revere Beach Pkwy.
Medford, MA 2451
781-290-0009 / Fax 781-290-0722
MD: Chris Tyler
www.jamn945.com

THE INDIE FORUM
FOR

INDEPENDENT
ARTISTS & LABELS

GETTING YOUR CD OUT

STARTING A LABEL

INDIE DEALS

INDIE TIPS

DISTRIBUTION

CD REFERENCE

CD MANUFACTURERS

GETTING YOUR CD OUT

Regardless of whether you are a legitimate indie label or a kid just making hot trax in the basement and then selling CDs in front of your local Wal-Mart, the bottom line is, you have to *"get your music out there!"* And in Urban music, especially in Hip Hop & Rap, artists, producers, djs and independent companies will more than likely have to take it to the street, or go "underground' in the early stages of releasing and promoting their music. So if you have put together your best material, and have it produced, mixed well, and hopefully made it presentable in the packaging, artwork, and even mastered, I say, "go for it!" Get it out there, and try to get that "buzz" every artist or company needs, to get to that *next* level of success... regardless of some of the specifics involved.

Specifics? The details of whether or not you are set up as an *official* label entity, barcodes, etc, etc. For the most part, you need to get your music on a CD and start to get it distributed out into the public to create a buzz. And for the record: I am by no means saying *not to do all the correct and legal,* as far as your business set-up procedures.   But, I am saying be proactive, and get your music on a CD, and then take it to the street! Do it either as a promotional and marketing tool, or even to sell "your *personal* copies", if someone wants to buy it. The bottom line is that you need to have something to hand someone; a copy of *what you do*; your music, that's in a "fixed" and *tangible* form... a CD.

There are countless number of guys putting out CDs; compilations, single releases, mixtapes, or just having their CD ready to sell at their live shows. And any of this can be done fairly simple, as long as you got product.   But I do suggest that if you are going to have something that is going to represent you or your company, then make sure that you at least have a few things *very tight* and put together with a *enough* effort to help give yourself the *opportunity* for a positive response and/or reward from your CD drop and presentation to the world.

IF YOU'RE GOING TO PUT IT OUT

1. Make sure that the songs are tight - and they *are* your best recorded performances

2. Get your songs mixed and mastered the best you can. **Do not compromise this step.**

3. Get professional Photos and have a CD cover made with the help of a graphic artist. Include your contact info.

STARTING A RECORD "COMPANY"
STANDARD STEPS FOR SETTING UP A RECORD LABEL

Step 1: NAME YOUR COMPANY

You will need to research the name you pick to make sure it does not already exist for another company filed in your local government databases. Also do a trademark search at the US Patent & Trademark Office - **www.uspto.gov.**

- A **trademark** is a word, phrase, symbol or design, or a combination of words, phrases, symbols, or designs, that identifies and distinguishes the source of the goods of one party from those of others. *(Courtesy of US Patent & Trademark Office – www.uspto.gov)*

Step 2: FILE FOR A FICTITIOUS NAME LICENSE (aka - D.B.A.) with the state. A search is performed to make sure that the name is not already in use.

- **Fictitious Business Name** - *Businesses that use a name other than the owner's must register the fictitious name with the county as required by the Trade Name Registration Act. This does not apply to corporations doing business under their corporate name or to those practicing any profession under a partnership name. (Courtesy of www.sba.gov)*

Step 3: GET A BUSINESS LICENSE. You will need to go to your county clerks office and file for a business license / permit to do business as a record company.

- **Business License** - *You will need a business license to operate your company "legally."* Also, if the business is located within an incorporated city limits, a license must be obtained from the city; if outside the city limits, then from the county. *(Courtesy of www.sba.gov)*

Step 4: BUSINESS SET-UP. You will need to decide in which business manner to file your company: Sole Proprietorship, Partnership, or Corporation.

- **Sole Proprietorship** - *an unincorporated business that is owned by one individual. It is the simplest form of business organization to start and maintain. The business has no existence apart from you, the owner. Its liabilities are your personal liabilities. You undertake the risks of the business for all assets owned, whether used in the business or personally owned. You include the income and expenses of the business on your own tax return. Your SSN is your Tax ID number.*

- A **partnership** is when two or more persons carry on a business. Each person contributes money, property, labor, or skill, and expects to share in the profits and losses of the business. A partnership must file an annual information return to report the income, deductions, gains, losses etc., from its operations, but it does not pay income tax. Instead, it "passes through" any profits or losses to its partners. Each partner includes his or her share of the partnership's income or loss on his or her tax return.

- A **Corporation** is a separate legal entity with its own identity separate and apart from its shareholders (owners). As a separate legal entity, a corporation is responsible for its own debts. Normally, shareholders, directors, and officers are not responsible for corporate liabilities. If the corporation suffers losses, the corporation itself must bear those losses to the extent of its own resources, and not the personal assets of the individual shareholders. Thus, the corporation protects the owner of a business against personal liability. A corporation generally takes the same deductions as a sole proprietorship to figure its taxable income. A corporation can also take special deductions. The profit of a corporation is taxed to the corporation when earned, and then is taxed to the shareholders when distributed as dividends. However, shareholders cannot deduct any loss of the corporation. (Incorporatetime.com)

Step 5: GET A FEDERAL TAX ID – EIN - If your company is a Partnership, LLC or Corporation, or if you have employees, you will also need a Federal Tax ID. A federal tax identification number, also known as an employer identification number or EIN is a number assigned to your business by the IRS. Any business offering products or services that are taxed in any way must get a federal tax ID number. To obtain an EIN you must complete IRS Form SS-4. It is a good idea to apply for an EIN before you open for business.

(More info at: **www.irs.gov,** or call the IRS Business and Specialty Tax Hotline: **800-829-4933**)

Step 6: OPEN UP A BUSINESS BANK ACCOUNT - Most banks will require your Fed. Tax ID - EIN to open a corporate or partnership bank account.

Step 7: GET A RETAIL LICENSE
If your company will be selling to the public, get a retail license or permit at some point. Most states have sales tax laws set up so that if you sell your CD to someone in your state, you are supposed to collect the sales tax.

THAT'S IT!

You are now officially legal and set to operate as a record company.

Of course, the administration, planning, organizing and actual functionality of a business set up to perform and make profit as a label, take much more than just being a legal or official company. The success of a record company will be determined by many other factors; the talent, money, experience, organization, personnel, marketing savvy, network affiliates, promotional budget, administrative and management skills of the labels core personnel, great accounting and creative people with the drive it takes to succeed. And a little luck is always welcome too.

INDEPENDENT CHECKLIST
IMPORTANT ADVICE, REMINDERS & TIPS FOR INDIE LABELS

One of the most challenging tasks for an independent artist or company is making the move to actually releasing a record to the public. And whether or not the release is intended as a promotion freebie or a "for profit" CD for sale, it is still a lot of work involved if you expect to win. This section of Music Powers is not intended to be a play-by-play course of actions to tell you "how" you can beat the challenges of launching a successful indie label. This section is just a simple reminder/checklists of important things that will help you get your music in position to make money from sales or to put yourself in position to get a major recording deal... *if you have a "hot" record.*

❑ **TEST YOUR MUSIC - DJs ARE KEY.** Before you go out and spend all of your money to release a record, make sure that you have tested your material everywhere you can get access and feedback of what the people like (or don't like). This means that you will need to get your songs to as many club DJs as you can... ones that will give you feedback of what people really like.

❑ **GET YOUR UPC BARCODE** - you will need to become a member of the Uniform Code Council (UCC). Contact: Uniform Code Council, Inc. - 7887 Washington Village Drive, Suite 300 - Dayton, OH 45459 - 937-435-3870 www.uc-council.org - The UPC Bar Code should be on the *back* cover of the CD.

❑ **Register your song with SOUNDSCAN** - www.soundscan.com
Mail: Nielsen SoundScan - ONE NORTH LEXINGTON AVENUE, 14TH FL. - WHITE PLAINS, NY 10601 - (914) 684-5500 - FAX (914) 684-5606
Client Services: (914) 684-5525 Ph. - (914) 684-5680 Fax
ClientServices@soundscan.com

❑ Submit your music to **Broadcast Data Systems (BDS)**, to **monitor airplay tracking.**

TO CONTACT BDS:

CONTACT: **KYLE BROWN** Rap, Hip-Hop, R&B Administrator brown@bdsonline.com	**Los Angeles** 6255 Sunset Blvd., 19th Fl Hollywood, CA 90028 (323) 817-1506 Ph. (323) 817-1511 Fax
New York 1 N. Lexington Ave., 14th Fl White Plains, NY 10601 (914) 684-5600 Ph. (914) 684-5680 Fax	**Miami** 550 11th St. Ste. 201 Miami Beach, FL 33139 (305) 777-2371 Ph. (305) 777-2372 Fax

Send all mixes of your single releases (preferably on CD) to:
BDS
8100 N.W. 101st Terrace
Kansas City, MO 64153
Attn: Encoding Department
When submitting your music to BDS please provide the following information:
Artist Name - Song titles with specific mix names, if applicable - Label - Radio Format(s) - Contact Information
You can submit your CD's and MP3's electronically through a secure Virtual Encode website. Call 1-800-688-4634

❑ Create a **Catalog Number** for your CD release.

❑ Before you start distributing your CD, **COPYRIGHT YOUR RELEASE**. You can register your sound recording by submitting **Form SR** to the Copyright Office for $30.

❑ Make sure your final music **mixes are pro quality** and mixed the best that you can afford.

❑ Have your **graphics and artwork** *professionally* done.

    CD Cover design
    CD disc art design – on the Disc
    CD Insert - CD liner notes / CD Tray card design

❑ Use a **professional mastering** lab and engineer.

❑ **Utilize Local and Regional Record Pools** as much as possible. This is another way to network with DJs who can help test your songs.

❑ Seek to get on the hottest **Mixtapes** that the DJs are releasing. This is a proven way for artists and songs to get great exposure to the public.

❑ Target a list of media outlets and **distribute your press kit** - Include a biography, cover letter, and CD

❑ Set up a **Website.** Make it informative – shows, audio snips, bio, press, etc

❑ Make the best of your **street campaigns and street team** promotions - posters, postcards, biz cards, stickers, etc.

❑ Distribution and **circulation to Radio stations** and dj mix shows
❑ **Hire a publicist** for press releases to get you more exposure.

❑ Set up an **Electronic Press Kit (EPK)** - market to various entertainment sites, music news sites, music forums, etc.

❑ **Gig as much as possible** - Plan a Promotional tour, and a budget to advertise it

❑ Be prepared to have a **follow up release** once you have built up a fan base

❑ **Video** – If your budget allows, shoot a low cost video

❑ Keep in mind - **A&R AT THE MAJOR LABELS ARE LOOKING** for acts with a regional "buzz"; artists that are selling out shows, getting radio airplay *on their own*, and also selling a few units on their own.

Note:
WHEN GOING THROUGH DISTRIBUTORS

❑ HAVE *PLENTY* OF FREE PROMOTIONAL CD COPIES FOR THE DISTRIBUTORS AND RETAILERS, ALONG WITH MUSIC FOR ALL OF THE IN-STORE LISTENING STATIONS. Get some good "stand-out" visual promotional items. A Promo One Sheet, Posters, Counter Displays & point-of-sale promotional items. Also make the most of the counterpace area that many stores allow artists & labels to leave their biz cards, flyers, stickers, and other promotional material. NOTE: Space for posters and counter promotions are many times only available as "purchased ad space"

❑ TAKE PART IN CO-OP ADVERTISING OPPORTUNITIES for radio and print ad campaigns. Co-op advertising is when a retailer will pay for some advertising of your CD being available or on sale (mentioning the store of course), and the retailer will deduct the cost of the ad campaign from the purchase he makes from the distribution company. Then the distributor will do the same deduction - to be charged back to the record label.

INDEPENDENT DEALS

By Ben McLane, Esq.

These labels tend to specialize in a particular style of music and obviously have smaller rosters. This can work to the artist's benefit because the act should receive more attention. Also, an independent will usually have some form of distribution in place, which is necessary to put records in stores. Many independents have become successful subsidiaries of major labels, which have provided them with major label distribution.

DISTRIBUTION DEALS

Here, the artist delivers to a record company an agreed amount of completed product (e.g., compact discs). Then, the label will distribute the product to stores. Sometimes, the label will also market and promote the product. Otherwise, this duty is left to the act. For its services, the label will collect a percentage of the selling price of the record.

PRODUCTION DEALS

In this type of deal, the artist signs on with a production company (usually headed by an established producer). These deals are normally structured like a regular recording agreement. In essence, the producer will record the act's music and then attempt to obtain a deal with a record label. If the production company is successful in procuring a deal, the royalty paid by the record company to the production company on records sold will be divided between the production company and the artist.

PRESSING AND DISTRIBUTION DEALS (P&D DEALS)

In this situation, the artist delivers a fully mixed master and finished artwork to the record labels, which in turn manufactures and distributes the records. One advantage of this kind of deal is that the artist should be able to obtain a higher royalty on sales because the act has already paid for the costs of recording the product. Since it seems that major labels prefer to see what the public responds to before making a large financial commitment, many artists are considering independent labels, distribution deals, production deals, and P&D deals in order to prove that they do appeal to a record buying audience. As a warning, some of the operations listed above can be suspect. Thus, an artist should make sure that any deal made is with a reputable entity/person.

Music Powers

INDEPENDENT DISTRIBUTION

INTRODUCTION

Record Distribution is the 'process' of getting records into retail stores. While most major labels use their own distribution, most "indie" labels usually use regional independent distributors and sometimes, national independent distributors - depending on the product's popularity and the label's promotional dollars. The following information is a basic summary of conventional independent record distribution.

THE 411

This is how it works: Distributors buy CDs from the labels and then sell the CDs to the retailers. This is done usually by PO (Purchase Order) or on a consignment basis. Then, the retailers then sell the CDs to the public. If you are running your own indie label, normally you will sell your CDs to a distributor for 50 percent of the retail list price. The distributor will then make the CDs available for purchase to retailers with a charge of around $2.00 or 25 percent of the wholesale price. Smaller retailers may also purchase through 'One-Stops' or have their stock supplied by 'Rack Jobbers.'

...One Stop?

- *Retailers can also buy through 'one-stops,' which is to some extent like a centralized store that sells product from different distributors to retailers. One-stops make a way for retailers to purchase all of the different CDs they want to order or stock... all through 'one' store & one account - as opposed to having many different accounts through many different distributors.*

... Rack Jobber?

- *Rack jobbers provide CDs to retailers whose main business may not be a record store. Rack Jobbers purchase CDs from labels and then stock them in the racks that they operate within retail stores. (Courtesy of Berklee.edu & Ben McLane, Esq.)*

... Consignment?

- *A condition that payment is expected only on completed sales and that unsold items may be returned to the one consigning Purchase Order? A commercial document used to request someone to supply something in return for payment. (Courtesy of dictionary.com)*

THE CHALLENGE

Now getting Distribution as an "indie" can be pretty difficult, but it's important. In the beginning, you can sell a lot of your product directly to the retailers in your own area, but when it comes to getting your record into the larger chains and to the masses, you will need distribution. One of the last things you want to happen is to have your song finally being played on the radio and/or getting lots of street attention from your promotional campaign, then having people *not* being able to find it! This means that the consumers don't know *where to buy it*, and the retailers won't know *how to buy it.* So getting a distributor at some point should be something every indie label should seriously consider.

MARKETING & PROMOTION

Now it may not be so easy to convince a distributor that your CD is going to sell, or that your company is the next *Def Jam*. Depending on your market and audience, one of major influences in getting distribution is having some radio play. It is radio that will normally make a demand at retailers and the retail orders for your CD.

You should also be aware that many distributors won't even touch your project unless you've been in business for a while or have made some impact on your own at first. This means that you've probably had success selling your CD at your live shows, on the Internet, and also selling direct to retailers on your own (probably by consignment). You will need to be out working your street team and doing live dates as much as possible. You will have to make certain you get the distributor a very clear picture of your promotional campaign, along with whatever positive reviews and "independent" success you've had. If you've got some "hustle in you," a *great* plan, $ and a little luck, you'll stand a shot of having the distributor take on your project. Oops, almost forgot... you may also be required to send the distributor any past *SoundScan and/or BDS information.*

... *SoundScan?*

- *Nielsen SoundScan is an information system that tracks the sales of music and music video products throughout the United States and Canada. Sales data from point-of-sale cash registers is collected weekly from over 14,000 retail, mass merchant, and non-traditional (on-line stores, venues, etc.) outlets. Weekly data is compiled and made available every Wednesday. Nielsen SoundScan is the sales source for the Billboard music charts. Nielsen SoundScan tracks your sales on CDs by the UPC bar code. Once you get your bar code, then you just register it with SoundScan so sales of your CD can be counted. (Courtesy of Soundscan.com)*

... BDS?

- **Broadcast Data Systems** - BDS uses computers to monitor radio broadcasts. These computers monitor radio stations - 24 hours a day - 7 days a week. Once a song has been recognized, BDS identifies the exact time, date, and station for that play. BDS listens to more than 1100 radio stations in more than 128 markets and detects over 1,000,000 songs a week.

Important! - Please make sure you contact someone at the distributor before sending anything. This will mean getting on the telephone and selling yourself! If the distributor is not looking for your package, then they will probably *not see it!* If you don't take this advice, you may be in for a very disappointing experience about the *laws of correspondence*. By the way: This is a rule for *any* company solicitation.

If you can get a distributor to take on the project, you can normally expect the distributor to want an exclusive contract, except in special arrangements. You will want to hire an attorney when negotiating the terms of your contract. To protect yourself, you *will want a way out* if the distributor goes under or files bankruptcy. It's actually going to be in your best interest to do whatever background research you can by simply checking out how long the company has been in business, and also finding out what other labels or what product they are distributing. Once you know this, just call up the other labels and find out if other companies have been satisfied with their ability to get records into the stores and if the distributor has made timely payments.

TIMELY PAYMENTS?

Don't Panic - You can probably expect a payment (depending on pay schedules) within 45 days to 3 months of your invoice to the distributor. A delay in total accounting paid is usually to be expected, due to returns and whether or not your CD sells. Sometimes, it can possibly take up to six months to receive payment for the records that were shipped. Your invoice should include the invoice date, shipping date, exactly what was shipped, the distributor's Purchase Order number, the invoice number and the total amount due.

HOW DISTRIBUTORS PAY
By Ben McLane, Esq.

Although it is a bit complicated, a distributor normally has an arrangement with a store, where the store can "return" any record it orders for a refund or credit from the distributor *if it cannot sell the record over a certain period of time*. Since there is no way for a distributor to know how many records sold to a store will ultimately be sold to customers (and hence not returned), the distributor will hold back a "reserve" of the sales monies it was paid by the store for a period of time to see if there are returns (which are common). This is how a distributor protects itself so it does not overpay the artist. To combat this, the artist needs to provide in the distribution agreement that there is a return limit. (The average is 25% for an album and 50% for a single.) Also, the artist needs to provide that the reserve can only be held back for a limited time (the shorter, the *better*).

Used by permission of By Ben Mclane, Esq. - © Ben McLane

"HI... I'M NEW HERE"

There is also another reality that you may have to deal with. And that is that many distributors may not want to deal with a new record label that only has one or two artist. So if this is you, when you do decide to step to them, *you better step correct!* Go to them with the your product on a silver platter. That means that you not only want distribution, but you are also in *need* of a distributor. Convince them (with possible *proof*) that you've sold so many records on your own, that you need to expand. This also means that your CD, your promo, your artwork & graphics, your sales at the live shows, reviews and local chart action & whatever possible radio play will all need to be laid out on the table if you expect them to jump at your *'first-time, one-artist' status.*

 **MONEY TALKS!**

If you're going for National distribution, then you better also make sure the distributor you've chosen can *deliver* nationally, and you can deliver the $. Some big retail chains will only deal with national distributors. So you may need to ask your distributor if he can deliver beyond a certain region, if that's what you desire. If the distributor can deliver, and you think you're ready to go for it... then be prepared to spend a lot of money marketing and promoting your product. Most distributors will want and need a lot of free promotional copies, posters, one-sheets and whatever else you have that will help promote your project... all at your expense! Most distributors will be expecting you to also participate in many of the co-op advertising opportunities they have going to help get buyers interested. So if you want to hang with the big-boys, you can. Just bring big-boy dollar$ to the party.

Note: It will be important that you get a distributor who has "direct accounts" with most of the major record store chains and national retailers like Best Buy, Tower, etc. If the distributor doesn't have direct accounts with the retail chain, then it may not be a good idea to be exclusive to that particular distributor.

 *... One-sheet?*

• *A one-sheet is an advertising review of the marketing and promotional plans your label has... to sell records. It will have information about the artist & his or her credentials, a photo of the CD cover, the list price, barcode information, the catalog number, etc. You will need to include any sales strategy and marketing plans that will help the distributor strongly convince retailers to stock your record.*

Make sure you put some serious effort ($) into the graphic layout of your one-sheet. It will need to be very professional and designed to be attractive to the eye. It will basically need to be 'eye-candy' to the potential retail buyer, and serious ammunition for the distributor's sales department to solicit to the stores.

Include the following information on your One Sheet:

Artist, Title, Category, Catalog Number, Barcode, List Price, Format, The Label, Brand Logos, Promo & Marketing Campaigns, Reviews, Featured Artist & Producers *(that are selling points)* Distribution Company & Contact Info

ONE SHEET SAMPLE

Artist

Format
Catalog
Genre
Prics

Bar Code

Release

General
Bio info

Promo &
Marketing

Single(s)

Video

Feature Artists
& Producers

Radio

Label &
Distribution
Contacts

KIEAUN THE GOLDN'CHILD

Format: **CD**
Catalog: **MP468 – 008**
Category: **Hip Hop / Rap**
List Price: **$18.98**

UPC Bar Code

8 08843 44333 8

Release Date: July 2006

As Midwest and Southern hip-hop settles into its place in history, a new voice roars from what many refer to as the "New Motown of the South." It's a voice that is piercing yet passionate, a voice of love, anger, fun, pain, struggle, and triumph! The voice of Kieaun

Media Coverage
❑ *"Voted Best New Rap Artist & Performer for 2004" - METRO URBAN NEWS – Charlotte*
TV Promotions: UPN, Comcast – TV-One, BET. Radio: Power106, V103, Hot107
Upcoming Reviews in VIBE, Source, XXL, Rolling Out

Featuring the hit singles

"Shake Dat" & "Where You At?"

• **Video to debut on BET's Rap City & 106 & Park – July 25**
• **Guest Video Appearance by "Mr. Ball"**
Album features: **Da Vin 007, Cat Atl, The Ruff Roll & More**

Producers: **Big Producer Mayne - DJ Miguel - Chase - Vince & SkyHi**

• **Hitting Urban / Hip Hop & CHR Radio in 22 cities.**
• Key Markets: So. Cal, Chicago, Miami, Atlanta, Memphis, DC, Detroit, Houston

Order Info:

Artist: **Kieaun The GoldnChild**
CD Title: **Where You At?**
Label: **DCE – DreamCatchers**

Executive Producer
Sabrina
Montgomery

www.dreamcatchersentertainment.com

Distributed by:
MUSICPOWERS
845-612 Roswell Rd. NE
Suite 200C – 866
Marietta, GA. 30062
Contact: 1- 800-574-7777

www.musicpowers.com

BE DETERMINED

Once you get distribution in place, you will now have to take your marketing and promotional hustle up a level or two. This means working your butt off. Distributors get the records in the stores ... but it's up to you to market yourself so that people come in the stores to *buy it!* So get prepared to "walk your talk." You will have to be able to compete with other indie labels just like yourself, who have dreams and aspirations of building a great company with a good distributor to get their records into stores. And every Indie label will want the same, if not more attention than the next. You will need money. You will need resources and very creative marketing and promotion to compete. You will also need a great product and a willing to work yourself and your whole crew, so you reach the desired goal... *profit* ($). One of the things that I have learned over the years is…"NOTHING'S TOO HARD ...IF WE DO IT WILLINGLY!"

INDEPENDENT RELEASE REQUIREMENTS
by Ben McLane, Esq.

❑ **First,** the artist should obtain a **UPC BARCODE** to put on the packaging so that sales can be tallied. There is a fee and the process is not immediate.

> To get information on obtaining *your own* UPC Bar Code, you will need to become a member of the Uniform Code Council (UCC). Uniform Code Council, Inc. - 7887 Washington Village Drive, Suite 300 - Dayton, OH 45459 - 937-435-3870
> **www.uc-council.org**

- *Note: There are also some companies that you may acquire a 'free' bar code for your CD by having your CDs duplicated by their company.*

❑ **Second,** the artist must file a fictitious name statement (aka DBA) in the county where the business will be operating. This allows the act to do business under an alias (e.g., Crazy Records). The forms can be obtained at the county clerk's office without charge. Within 30 days of filing, the statement must be published in a local newspaper once a week for four successive weeks. Then, an affidavit showing proof of publication must be filed.

❑ **Third,** the artist should obtain a local business license. This is required by the city and provides a source of income to the city. For the sale of CDs, a retail sales license will be needed. There is a fee. To obtain fee information, call the local government information number and ask for business licensing.

❑ **Fourth,** the artist should obtain a resale license (seller's permit). This allows the artist to buy and sell CDs without paying any sales tax until after it is collected from the consumer, or in the case of records sold through stores, the store will pay the sales tax. This will avoid having to pay a separate sales tax on the CDs ordered from the pressing plant, the CD artwork, the printing of the package, etc. This can be procured from the State Board of Equalization.

Music Powers DIGITAL DISTRIBUTION

Digital Music distribution has become a must focus for all indie labels and indie artist alike. Let's just be real, maybe you're still running to your local music store to buy CDs, which is great, but many of these kids with MP3 players really would rather download your song *instantly* to their iPod or whatever music player they have.

The Apple iPod

And just in case you've been snoozing the past few years... A digital download is simply an authorized legal digital single or album release by labels or indie artists that can be purchased by downloading it through one of the many on-line music services like iTunes, Napster, MSN Music, and many others.

As far as getting set up when you're first starting out - I highly suggest that most new labels and new indies seriously consider checking out CD Baby at www.cdbaby.net for one of the most current "no-headache" ways to get music digitally distributed to many of the main digital download services on the internet. And also Ingrooves at www.ingrooves.com There are other services, but I would say that these two services are places to start your search for a company who can set your music up to be downloaded everywhere, and you collect.

HFA

❏ **From the Harry Fox Agency:** For audio-only full permanent downloads, a mechanical license is required. If you expect to deliver less than 2,500 DPD's, you can obtain the license through HFA Songfile. If you have an established HFA Licensing Account, you can also obtain the licenses through eMechanical, or if you need to obtain licenses in bulk (over 100 titles) please submit HFA's DPD Application. Depending on your use, you may need to obtain other kinds of licenses that HFA does not provide. (Courtesy of HFA).

❏ I also highly suggest visiting HFA (Harry Fox) website - www.harryfox.com

THANK ME LATER

You may also be *very* interested in the idea of selling your *own* digital downloads by using a service called PayLoadz, which actually works with your on-line Paypal account. I use this service myself – and it's great! Go to www.payloadz.com for more information.

The following is a select list of digital music services that sell
Digital music downloads:

Apple iTunes
www.apple.com/itunes

AudioLunchbox
www.audiolunchbox.com

BuyMusic
www.buy.com

Chondo
www.chondo.net

DigiPie
www.digipie.com

Emusic
www.emusic.com

Liquid Digital Media
(Wal-Mart)
www.liquidaudio.com/services

LoudEye
www.musicstore.mymmode.com

MP3tunes
www.mp3tunes.com

MSN Music
www.music.msn.com

MusicNet
www.musicnet.com

MusicNow
www.aol.musicnow.com

Napster
www.napster.com

NetMusic
www.netmusic.com

OnlinePromo
www.opmusicshop.com

PlayIndies
www.playindies.com

Rhapsody
www.listen.com

Ruckus
www.ruckusnetwork.com

INDEPENDENT DISTRIBUTORS

101 DISTRIBUTION
101 Distribution/Mailroom
1928 East Highland, Suite F-104
Phoenix, AZ 85016

101 DISTRIBUTION/ Corporate
Offices
2375 East Camelback Road, 5th Floor
Phoenix, AZ 85016
Tel.: 602-357-3288
Toll-Free: 1-866-735-5101
Fax: 602-357-3288
www.101distribution.com
www.101d.com

ADA HEADQUARTERS
72 Spring Street - 12th Floor
New York, NY 10012
212-343-2485
www.ada-music.com

ADA WEST COAST
3300 Pacific Avenue
Burbank, CA 91505
818- 977-0552
www.ada-music.com

AEC ONE STOP GROUP
4250 Coral Ridge Drive
Coral Springs, FL 33065-7616
800-329-7664
www.aent.com

ALLIANCE ENTERTAINMENT
4250 Coral Ridge Drive
Coral Springs, Florida 33065
954-255-4429 - Fax 954-255-4990
www.aent.com

ARROW DISTRIBUTION
11012 Aurora Hudson Rd.
Streetsboro, OH 44241 U.S.A.
330-528-0410
www.arrdis.com

ATAK DISTRIBUTION
P.O. Box 1027
La Cañada, CA 91012-1027
415-775-2240
+

ATAK alternate address - 923 Post St
San Francisco, CA 94109
www.truehiphop.com

BIG DADDY
162 North 8th Street
Kenilworth, NJ 07033-1127   U.S.A.
908-653-9110 - Fax: 908-653-9114
www.bigdaddymusic.com

BROWN ENTERTAINMENT GROUP
160 Crystal Brook, Griffin, GA 30223
770-233-8946
www.begbiz.com

CD BABY
5925 NE 80th Ave
Portland, OR 97218-2891
503-595-3000 / 503-296-2370
www.cdbaby.com

CITY HALL RECORDS
101 Glacier Point, Suite C
San Rafael, CA 94901
415-457-9080
www.cityhallrecords.com

CROSSTALK DISTRIBUTION
1323 South Michigan
Chicago, IL 60605
312-786-1185 / 312-786-1186 fax
www.crosstalkchicago.com

CTD, LTD., DBA CARROT TOP DISTRIBUTION, LTD.
935 W. Chestnut - Suite LL15
Chicago, IL 60622
312-432 -1194 / 312 -432 -1351 fax
www.ctdltd.com

DANCEFLOOR DISTRIBUTION
95 Cedar Lane
Englewood, NJ 07631
201- 568-7066 / Fax 201- 568-8699

GALAXY MUSIC DISTRIBUTION

2400 Josephine St.
Pittsburgh, PA 15203
Phone: 800-542-5422   Fax: 800-542-8863
Galaxy One-Stop
215-426-3333 / Fax 215-426-2667
www.galaxymusic.com

KOCH ENTERTAINMENT DISTRIBUTION LLC

Attn: Marketing Dept.
22 Harbor Park Drive
Port Washington, NY 11050
516-484-1000 / Fax 516-484-4746
www.kochint.com

KSG DISTRIBUTING, INC.

1121 W. Flint Meadow Drive
Kaysville, UT 84037
800-225-1243
www.ksgdist.com

NAVARRE CORPORATION

7400 49th Ave. North
New Hope, MN 55428
800-728-4000, Fax 763-533-2156
www.navarre.com

NEMESIS MUSIC DISTRIBUTION

3520 Hargate Rd.
Oceanside, NY 11572
Tel 516-764-5180, Fax 516-764-5294
www.nemesis-music.com

NORWALK RECORD DISTRIBUTORS

1193 Knollwood Circle B
Anaheim, CA 92801 U.S.A.
714-995-8111, Fax: 714-995-0423
www.norwalkdist.com

NUENDO MUSIC GROUP

125 W 141st Street, Suite 24
New York, NY 10030
Tel 212-926-3587, Fax 509-696-2475
www.nuendomusic.com

RED DISTRIBUTION

2531 Briarcliff Rd NE Suite 215
Atlanta, GA 30329
404-679-6084
www.redmusic.com

RED MUSIC DISTRIBUTION

79 Fifth Avenue
New York, NY 10003
212-404-0600
www.redmusic.com

REDEYE DISTRIBUTION

1130 Cherry Lane
Graham, NC 27253
877 -REDEYE 1
336-578-7388 fax
www.redeyeusa.com

ROCK BOTTOM INC

6175 CROOKED CREEK RD NW
NORCROSS, GA
770-448-8439

RHYTHMIC INC.

40 Exchange Place - Suite 1718
New York, NY 10005
212-232-6067 - Fax 212-232-6068
www.rhythmicnyc.com

RYKO DISTRIBUTION PARTNERS

555 West 25th Street- 5th Floor
New York, NY 10001
Main Office:
30 Irving Place, 3rd Fl, New York, NY 10003
1-800-808-RYKO
www.rykogroup.com

SELECT-O-HITS

1981 Fletcher Creek Dr.
Memphis, TN 38133
901-388-1190, Fax 901-388-3002
www.selectohits.com

SOUTHERN MUSIC DISTRIBUTION

6900 PEACHTREE INDUSTRIAL BLVD NW
NORCROSS, GA
770-447-5159
www.southernmusicdigital.com

SOUTHWEST WHOLESALE

6775 Bingle Road
Houston, TX 77092-1102 U.S.A.
800-275-4799 Fax: 713-460-1480
www.southwestwholesale.com

SUPER D DISTRIBUTION

17822 A Gillette
Irvine, CA 92614 U.S.A.
866-778-7373   Fax: 530-668-3476
www.sdcd.com

TRC DISTRIBUTION

430 E. Grand Avenue, Suite "A"
South San Francisco, CA 94080
650-877-7330, Fax: 650- 877-7345
www.trcdistribution.com

UNIQUE DISTRIBUTORS

#110, Denton Avenue
New Hyde Park, NY 11040
800-992-9011 / 516-294-5900
516-294-1644 fax / 516-741-3584 fax
www.uniquedist.com

VIASTAR CORPORATION

2451 W. Birchwood Avenue, Suite 105
Mesa, Arizona, 85202
480-894-0311, Fax: 480-894-0074
www.electrickingdom.com

WATTS MUSIC DISTRIBUTION

C/O Watts Music
500 Ocean Avenue
East Rockaway, NY 11518
www.wattsmusic.com

Also see:
IODAlliance.com. | (415) 777-IODA
Amazon.com
Soundclick.com
Buyindiemusic.com
Rapstation.com

For more listings, please
visit
www.MusicPowers.com

Music Powers

CD TECHNICAL GLOSSARY

COMMONLY USED CD MANUFACTURING TERMS

❑ **CD MASTERING**

This is the process of creating a glass master CD from which compact discs will be reproduced in quantity.

❑ **REPLICATION**

Replication is basically the standard that is used to make mass amounts of CDs. This process uses a Glass Master process to make the duplicates by "stamping" your data into a CD.   This is the process that is usually used for runs of 1000 CDs or more. The process is cheaper than duplication because the data is actually made into the CD as opposed to being added to a CD.

❑ **DUPLICATION**

Duplication is the process of burning a CD-R the same as you do at home. Duplication is usually used when making smaller duplication runs to be manufactured. A CD-R is burned from the master CD-R and transferred to a blank disk, recorded using a CD recorder.   The speed of duplication is determined by the speed of the CD recorder and the amount of data to be recorded.

• *FYI – There is no "data" difference a glass mastered replication disc and the processed duplication method. The only real difference is the way the surface of the disc is marked. There is no quality difference between duplicated or replicated discs; both manufacturing methods are identical to the original master. The choice of replication or duplication is a matter of quantity and turn-around time.*

❑ **GLASS MASTER**

This is the only "true" Master and is created at the Factory. It's made of Glass coated by a chemical, which is burned off with a laser. The Glass Master is a "Negative." It's then metalized with a molten nickel compound and turned into a "Stamper." The stamper punches tiny pits in a CD much the same way a "Stamper" was used to press grooves in LPs back in the olden days of vinyl.
(Courtesy of greendotaudio.com)

❑ **RED BOOK STANDARD**

The International standard for CD audio. All audio CDs and CDRs (finalized) are "Red Book." Playback machines can vary greatly in their interpretation of E-32 errors, which when created cause a disk to be "out of spec" and rejected for Factory (Red Book compliant) replication. CD-DA (Redbook Digital Audio) is 16 bit. Newer equipment can "process" audio at 24 bit, but it's all dithered down to 16 bit eventually because all CD Players read only 16 bit data. *(Courtesy of greendotaudio.com)*

Music Powers

MASTERING

MASTERING 101

If you are planning to release your music commercially and be in any "real" competition with other commercial recordings coming out into the market, you will definitely need to have your music mastered. In the mastering procedure, final adjustments to volume level, equalization, compression, spatial enhancements, etc. can be made to your mix, to give it that "polished" sound you by and large hear on most major label recordings, and also put the overall tone of your music in good running with the other CDs being released commercially and played on radio.

Mastering your music is very important and should not be in the slightest way taken for granted. The mastering process is the last stage to "tweak" and technically improve the sound of the final mix before it is ready for release and CD manufacturing. In my opinion, I firmly believe that you should always get a professional mastering engineer and studio, or you may be asking for a lot of unneeded headache and grief. Also, take a look at the credits of virtually any successful CD release, and you will see that major labels and production companies normally use a very specialized professional for Mastering and not the same people doing the mix or the same guys who recorded the song. Why? Because pro mastering services make what was recorded and then finally mixed, *sound* better. So when you hire a great mastering engineer and facility to put that final "magic" into your record, it's normally worth whatever the cost is. Know this: when you hire a mastering professional, you are paying for not only a great room and gear, but you are also paying for intangible things like the experience and the ears of a mastering engineer; a guy that makes a living from "tweaking" records. Mastering is also as much an art as it is knowledge and technique.

Now because of today's world of home recording, desktop studio programs and software plug-ins, many new producers and artists are led to believe that they can simply take their mixes and run it through a few "pre-set" compressor and EQ plug-in settings in their computer software and get the results that they hear on their favorite CDs. The truth is that Mastering begins with an *experienced* Mastering ENGINEER, and then, the mastering suite or studio *control room* and then the equipment in the control room. In the *professional* mastering process, the engineer will optimize the level of your music, take out noise, clicks, etc. and clean up starts and fades of songs, do equalization and compression and de-ess parts as needed, arrange the order, and insert space between songs. He will also do other things like inserting PQ codes for CD replication.

When you have reached that point where you have worked *your best* to get the song and performance recorded and then mixed well, then please, *don't skip the Mastering phase of the project*. And even more important, don't leave the mastering "process" to the hands of someone without the *experience, knowledge and gear* to really get the job done correctly.   Just because your buddy bought the latest mastering software for your computer, doesn't mean he can actually do a good mastering job on your final mixes. Actually, you may end up doing more *harm* to your tracks than good. And also know this boys and girls: most real mastering engineers HATE the idea of someone bringing in a "half" mastered mess - to be fixed up by them, and then (re) "mastered" *correctly*. Listen up people; MASTERING IS A VERY SERIOUS PROCESS. If you are going to put a record out for "commercial" release, please seek a qualified Mastering Engineer & Studio. If you can't afford *professional* mastering, you probably *can't afford to put yourself into any real serious or competitive arena* – think about it. So I highly suggest taking the smartest road to sonic satisfaction; HAVE YOUR MUSIC MASTERED PROFESSIONALLY!

HOW MUCH?

Pro mastering will cost anywhere from $50 to $350 per hour (*or more*), depending on the mastering engineer and the mastering facility.

MIX DELIVERY

24 Bit DAT, 16 Bit DAT, CD-R, Data Files (WAV, AIFF, SDII, etc.), Analog Reel (1/4"). There is also another mastering technique called Separation Mastering, where multiple "sub-mixes" of sub-groups are used for the final stereo imaging of what is to be mastered. if you have questions, call the studio you plan on using and ask "anything" that you may be concerned about.

HOME TWEAKING - JUST FOR THE RECORD

If you are just trying to hump up OR "hype up" your tacks or songs a bit... just enough to test in clubs, demos or to get a little hype on the "sound" of things before pro mastering, etc., you can easily get a program like *Steinberg's Wavelab*, and also, I would suggest a few plugs like *Steinberg's FreeFilter, PeakMaster* & *Puncher, Timeworks Mastering Compressor & EQ, UltraFunkFX EQ & Compressor*, The *Waves* EQ and Compressor Packs, and also learn *how and when* to use them. Your monitors will also need to be good and accurate to "your" perspective of audible understanding. You will also need knowledge of understanding of the diverse ways to normalize and correct "DC Offsets" in your digital wave. Also, understanding both a frequency & phase analyzer will be helpful and pretty important for both mixing & mastering... especially when you get burnt out. OR, when you can't really be objective enough - because *you don't do mastering full time.* Think about this: you have probably made your mix sound the way you think is best, when you made the mix

In mixing and mastering, the most important tools will be your ears, experience, monitors and processing gear & technique. And of course, experience and technique means *knowing* which plugs (and what dedicated outboard gear) to use for the particular situation or job. Come on people, if you don't sing or play guitar, would you just go ahead and do the vocals yourself or fumble around on a guitar anyway, and then release it to the public and expect it to compete with the same CD out by Dr. Dre or Beyoncé.. If so, you are just setting yourself up for frustration and probable failure. But hey, you know there are some guys around that do some amazing things with just a few plug-ins. But if you have been through the Pro Mastering thing, you already know, most of the best mastering engineers like Herb Powers and Brian Gardner are still using some very specialized consoles for mastering and sometimes great vintage analog equipment too. But most of all, they have the *years and ears*.

So in closing out, like I said earlier, I "highly" suggest to everyone who is serious about their CD compete with other releases, go and hire a pro mastering service or find a great mix engineer that does *not* leave much room for the sometimes needed "fixes" done in Mastering. And even at that point, you may still need other subtle changes done with the over-all tone consistency of the music to be manufactured on a multiple-track CD release.

FINAL TIPS

Give the people who you hire to master your project an idea of what you are seeking. For example, you might let them know that you are competing in the West Coast Rap market that has acts like Dr. Dre and Snoop, etc., and you want the sound of things to be *"hot, and in your face."* I personally suggest that if you are not using one of the bigger, well-known mastering engineers and labs, that you actually give them a reference CD of music you like, that's in your competitive market or in your genre or musical vibe, and then let them take it from there. And last, clearly label everything you turn in, and you may want to give them the contact information of the engineer and studio that did your final mixes.

GOOD LUCK!

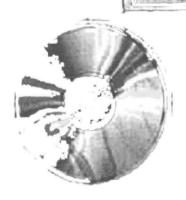

FOR MORE INFORMATION ON MASTERING
INCLUDING MORE LISTINGS OF THE BEST MASTERING FACILITIES IN OTHER CITIES
PLEASE VISIT US ON-LINE AT

MusicPowers.com

MASTERING DIRECTORY

ALLSTAR MASTERING
1400 NW 65th Avenue
Plantation, FL 33313
954-581-2226
www.allstarmastering.com

ART MASTERING
3200 N. San Fernando Blvd.
Burbank, CA 91504
818-843-1618 (x801)
www.artmastering.com

BLUEFIELD MASTERING
1408 Fairway Ridge Dr.
Raleigh, NC 27606
919-859-0102
www.bluefieldmastering.com

THE BOILER ROOM
3139 N. Lincoln Ave., # 214
Chicago, Il 60657
773-525-8551
www.brmastering.com

CAPITOL MASTERING
1750 North Vine Street
Los Angeles, CA 90028
323-871-5003
www.capitolmastering.com

CD MARKSMAN
2105 S. McClintock Dr.
Tempe, AZ 85282
480-377-9191
www.cdmarksman.com

CUPS N STRINGS
1542 15th Street
Santa Monica, CA 90404
310-656-9358
www.cupsnstrings.com

DISCMASTERS
2460 West Main Street, Suite D300
Saint Charles, IL 60175
888-430-DISC
www.discmasters.com

EASTGATE MASTERING
5054 Jay St., NE
Washington, DC 20019
202-396-7430
www.eastgatemastering.net

EARLE HOLDER
HDQTRZ Digital Studios
Atlanta, GA
404-643-8213
www.hdqtrz.com

EUROPADISK
24/02 Queens Plaza S.
Long Island City, NY 11101
718-407-7300
www.europadisk.com

FANTASY STUDIOS
2600 10th Street
Berkeley, CA 94710
510-4862038
www.fantasystudios.com

FINAL STAGE MASTERING
10 Music Circle S.
Nashville, TN 37203
615-256-2676
www.finalstage.com

FULLERSOUND
6157 NW 167th Street, F-6
Miami, Fl 33015
305-556-5537
www.fullersound.com

FUTURE DISC SYSTEMS
3475 Cahuenga Blvd.
Los Angeles, CA 90068
323-876-8733
www.futurediscsystems.com

GATEWAY MASTERING
428 Cumberland Ave.
Portland, ME 04101
207-828-9400
www.gatewaymastering.com

GEORGETOWN MASTERS
33 Music Square West, Suite 108B
Nashville, TN 37203
615-254-3233
www.georgetownmasters.com

BERNIE GRUNDMAN
1640 N. Gower St.
Los Angeles, CA 90028
323-465-6264

HIT FACTORY MASTERING
421 W. 54th Street, New York, NY 10019
212-245-0200

JEFF KING MASTERING
2260 Centinela Ave.
West Los Angeles, Ca 90064
323-646-7914 / 310-571-0500 (Studio)
www.thekinghimself.com

KITCHEN MASTERING
109 Brewer Lane
Carrboro, NC 27510
919-929-4494
www.kitchenmastering.com

THE LODGE
740 Broadway, Suite 605
New York, NY 10003
212-353-3895
www.thelodge.com

MARCUSSEN MASTERING
1545 North Wilcox Avenue
Hollywood, CA 90028
323-463-5300
www.marcussenmastering.com

MASTER CUTTING ROOM
250 W. 49th Street
New York, NY 10019
212-765-8496
www.mastercuttingroom.com

MASTERDISK
545 W. 45th Street
New York, NY 10036
212-541-5022
www.masterdisk.com

THE MASTERING LAB
6033 Hollywood Blvd
Hollywood, CA 90028 / 323-466-8589
www.themasteringlab.com

MASTERMIX
1921 Division Street
Nashville, TN 37203
615-321-5970

MAYFIELD MASTERING
2825 Erica Place
Nashville, TN 37204
615-383-3708
www.mayfieldmastering.com

MOONLIGHT MASTERING
2219 West Olive Ave., PMB 152
Burbank, CA 91506
818-841-2987
www.moonlightmastering.com

OASIS MASTERING
11335 Ventura Blvd.
Studio City, CA 91604
818-980-0411
www.oasismastering.com

PARAMOUNT RECORDING
6245 Santa Monica Blvd.
Hollywood, CA. 90038
323-465-4000
www.paramountrecording.com

PRECISION MASTERING
1008 N. Cole Ave.
Los Angeles, CA 90038
323-464-1008
www.precisionmastering.com

GLENN SCHICK (ATLANTA)
Crossover Entertainment Group (Temp location)
1310 Ellsworth Industrail Dr.
Atlanta, GA 30318 - 404-806-6920
For Billing or Mail send to:
1266 West Paces Ferry Rd. PMB 452
Atlanta, GA 30327
www.gsmastering.com

STERLING SOUND
88 10th Street, 6th Fl West
New York, NY 10011
212-604-9433
www.sterling-sound.com

UNIVERSAL MASTERING
10 Distribution Blvd.
Edison, NJ 08817
732-287-1222

CD MANUFACTURERS

CD Duplication / Replication Services

A BLACK CLAN, INC.
Atlanta, GA
877-706-7316
770-907-8665
www.ablackclan.com

ACDC-AUDIO CD & CASSETTE
12426 1/2 Ventura Blvd.
Studio City, CA 91604
818-762-ACDC (2232)
www.acdc-cdr.com

ADVANCED MEDIA
360 Glenwood Ave.
East Orange, NJ 07017
973 678 3700 Fax 973 678 1115
answers@amtone.com
www.amtone.com

AIX MEDIA GROUP INC.
8455 Beverly Blvd., Ste. 500
W. Hollywood, CA 90048
323-655-4116 Fax 323-655-8893
www.aixmediagroup.com

ALSHIRE
1015 ISABEL ST.
BURBANK, CA. 91506
818-843-6792
www.alshire.com

CAPITOL
1750 N. Vine St.
Hollywood, CA 90028
323-871-5003
www.capitolmastering.com

CD4 CD REPLICATION
4242 W SUNSET BOULEVARD SUITE 2
LOS ANGELES, CA 90029
323-663-7852

CD LABS
655 N. Central Ave., 17th Fl
Glendale, CA 91203
818-505-9581
www.cdlabs.com

UNIVERSAL MASTERING
STUDIOS WEST
5161 Lankershim Blvd, Ste. 201
N. Hollywood, CA 91601
818-777-9200 Fax 818-777-9235
www.universal-mastering.com

ANAPHORA MUSIC
1901 Enchanted Woods Pkwy,
Marietta, GA 30066
877-926-6224 / 770-926-6224
www.anaphoramusic.com

ATLANTA MANUFACTURING GROUP
158 Moreland Ave.
Atlanta, GA 30316
404-230-9559 / Fax 404-230-9558
1-866-230-9626
www.amgcds.com

CD FORGE
1420 NW Lovejoy #327
Portland, OR 97209
503-736-3261
www.cdforge.com

CD MARKSMAN
2105 S. McClintock Dr., Tempe, AZ 85282
480-377-9191
www.cdmarksman.com

CD ROLLOUT
4001 Pacific Coast Hwy, # 104
Torrance, CA 90505
310-791-7624
www.cdrollout.com

CHEAP CD DUPLICATION
2205 First St. #104
Simi Valley, CA 93065
800-836-7962 / 805-522-6556
www.cheapcdduplications.com

CRAVEDOG CD
3647 SE 21st Ave. Portland OR 97202
866-469-9820 / 503-233-7284
www.cravedog.com

CRYSTAL CLEAR
10486 Brockwood Rd
Dallas, TX 75238
800-880-0073
www.crystalclearcds.com

CTEX
7850 Bell Rd.
Windsor, CA 95492
707-838-4000
www.ctexinc.com

DIGITAL DISC
353 Hedge Row
Mountainside, NJ 07092
908-709-1243
www.digitaldisc.com

DISC MAKERS
7905 N. Route 130
Pennsauken, NJ 08110-1402
800-468-9353 / 856-663-9030
www.discmakers.com

DISK FAKTORY
17173-A Gillette Ave.
Irvine, CA 92614
1-949-477-1700
www.diskfaktory.com

DISC SERVICES
3102 Bernardo Lane, Suite 200
San Diego, CA 92029
760-432-8999
www.discservices.com

DUBS
29 W. 38TH St., 4th Fl.
NY, NY 10018
212-398-6400
www.dubs.com

DUNGEON REPLICATION
877-777-7276
www.dungeon-replication.com

DUPLIUM MEDIA
2029 Westgate Drive, Suite 120
Carrollton, Texas 75006

Tel: 972.512.0014
Fax: 972.512.0015
Toll Free: 800.928.2018
infousa@duplium.com

DYNAMIC SUN
900 Passaic Ave., E. Newark, NJ 07029
973-482-6749
www.dynamicsun.com

EUROPADISK
24-02 Queens Plaza South
Long Island City, NY 11101
800-455-8555 or 718-407-7300
www.europadisk.com

GLOBALDISC.COM
10 West 135th St., #14P
NY, NY 10037 USA
800-767-7664 or 212-234-8333
www.GlobalDisc.com

GREEN DOT AUDIO
Nashville, TN 37214
615-366-5964
www.greendotaudio.com

GROOVE HOUSE
5029 SERRANIA AVE.,
WOODLAND HILLS, CA 91364
888-476-6838
www.groovehouse.com

HELLMAN
10008 NATIONAL BLVD., # 280, LOS
ANGELES, CA 90034
310-204-3317
www.hellmanproduction.com

INDIE CD REPLICATION
1245 9th Ave Suite A
San Francisco CA 94122
888.430.7542
www.indie-cd-replication.org

JURGEN INDUSTRIES, INC.
17461 147th St. SE #13
Monroe, WA 98272
800.735.7248 / 360.794.7886
www.cdduplication-cdburning.com

MAGNETIC AIR
210 S. 8th St., Lewiston, NY 14092
866-424-4020
www.magneticair.com

MASTER MIND AUDIO
26 Route 13 - Brookline, NH 03033
603-249-9224 / 1-877-213-4512
www.mastermindaudio.com

MEDIA ONE
200 W. Pomona, Monrovia, CA 91016
800-586-9733
www.mediaonecompany.com

MIRUS SOLUTIONS
13777 Ballantyne Corporate Pl, # 450
Charlotte, NC 28277
704-752-3696
www.mirussolutions.com

MORPHIUS DISC
100 E. 23RD ST., BALTIMORE, MD 21218
410-662-0112
www.morphius.com

MUSIC MANUFACTURING SERVICES
25 Defries St., Toronto, Ontario, M5A 3R4
Canada
416-364-1943
www.mmsdirect.com

NATIONWIDE CD
103 Greenleaf St., Ft Worth, TX 76107
866-704-3579
www.nationwidecd.com

NERVE CENTER
808 West 28th Street
Minneapolis, MN 55408-2118
800-679-7787 / 612-870-4367
www.nervecenter.net

NOVA DISC
PO Box 20184
New York, NY 10014
212-691-8519 / 888-691-3150
www.novadisc.net

NYCD
350 7th AVENUE, 2nd Fl.
NEW YORK, NY 10001
212-502-0588
www.nycd.com

OASIS MANUFACTURING
12625 Lee Highway
Sperryville, VA 22740
540-987-8810
www.oasiscd.com

ON4 PRODUCTIONS
684 Antone St., NW, Suite 110
Atlanta, GA 30318
404-603-9900 / Fax 404-351-7775
1-888-710-5157
www.on4prod.com

PLAY-IT PRODUCTIONS, INC.
259 West 30th Street -3rd Floor -New York, NY 10001
212-695-6530 / 1-800-815-3444
www.play-itproductions.net

PROACTION MEDIA
301 E Bethany Home Rd, Suite A-135
Phoenix, Arizona 85012
877.593.4261 / 602.277.2011
www.proactionmedia.com

PRODUCTION PRO
780 BUSSE HIGHWAY, PARK RIDGE, IL 60068
847-696-1600
www.productionpro.com

PROJECT 70
433 Bishop St., NW, Suite CD
Atlanta, GA 30318
1-800-742-3108
404-875-7000 / Fax 404-875-7007
www.project70.com

RAINBO RECORDS
1738 Berkeley St..,
Sanata Monica, CA 90404
www.rainborecords.com

RAIN TREE
109 W. Main Street, Annville, PA 17003
717-867-5617
www.raintree.com

REX TRAX, INC.
1255 Buford Hwy., Suite 206
Suwanee, GA 30024
678-730-0008
www.climbonline.com

ROVIX
The Proscenium Tower
1170 Peachtree Street - Suite 1200
Atlanta, GA 30309
WWW.ROVIX.COM

S & J CD DUPLICATION
999 Blanding Blvd. Suite 10
Orange Park, FL 32065
888-269-7088 / 904-272-0580
www.snjcd.com

SNS DIGITAL INC
421 A-1 Pike Blvd.
Lawrenceville, GA 30045
877-442-0933 / 678-442-0933
www.yourmusiconcd.com

SUPER DIGITAL
1150 NW 17th Ave.
Portland, OR 97209
503-228-2222, Fax 503-228-6819
www.superdigital.com

STERLING DISK
15264 Herriman Blvd, Noblesville, IN 46060
317-773-3772
www.sterlingdisk.com

TAPE WAREHOUSE
2688 Peachtree Sq,
Atlanta, GA 30360
770-458-1679 / Fax: 770-458-0276

Toll Free: 1-800-659-TAPE (8273)
www.tapewarehouse.com

UNIVERSAL RECORDING
520 James Street, Lakewood, NJ 08701
732-367-3273
www.universaltapes.com

US DIGITAL MEDIA
21430 North 20th Avenue
Phoenix, Arizona 85027
877-99CDROM
623-587-4900
www.cdrom2go.com

WORLD MEDIA GROUP
6737 E. 30TH ST.
Indianapolis, IN 46219
317-549-8484
www.worldmediagroup.com

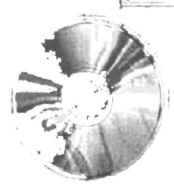

For more listings, please
visit
www.MusicPowers.com

Music Powers SPOTLIGHT BIG OOMP

Indie Label & Production Company – TV Show - Radio - Record Retailer

Biography

If you visit or live in Atlanta, GA., and you want to talk music *business* and the whole street grind, then one of the names that undeniably stands out over many is "Big Oomp" and his *entrepreneurial* expertise in the music game. Big Oomp, who is the CEO and founder of Big Oomp Records, also owns a chain of record stores, a UPN TV show; *Live with Big Oomp Camp*, a graphics company, a full-blown recording studio, and a management company.

Along with his TV show and retail business, Big Oomp also has a rock solid music publishing and production company that houses recording artist Baby D, as well as his production team: *Big Oomp Camp*; MC Assault, DJ Jelly, and of course, Big Oomp himself. Big Oomp Camp Productions are featured on hit selling CDs by YoungBloodz, Pastor Troy, Lil' Flip, Crime Mob, Rasheeda and more.

And if that wasn't enough, Big Oomp also has a radio show: *The Dirty South Showdown*, which is aired on 20 radio stations in the Southeast. Big Oomp Records has also been featured in numerous magazines like *Source, Murder Dog, Urban Network, Rolling Out* and *Creative Loafing*, to name a few.

www.BigOompRecords.com

Music Powers SPOTLIGHT
BIG OOMP

**Indie Label - Production Company – TV Show
Radio Show - Record Retailer**

Select Clientele & Production Credits

Eightball	Crime Mob
DJ Jelly	Lil' Flip
YoungBloodZ	Sammy Sam
Young Jeezy	Loko
A Dam-Shame	Intoxicated
Gangsta Boo	Baby D
Pastor Troy	Rasheeda

Music Powers

Exclusive Advice from Music Powers Advisor

BIG OOMP

Indie Label & Production Company – TV Show - Radio - Record Retailer

MAJOR VS. INDEPENDENT

1 There are a lot of new indie labels popping up, and some of these companies *believe* that they can make all of this money with their artist(s) on their own... *as an indie - without need of a major.* Given that you and your company has experience as an independent label, and also as a company that has major labels signing your talent, which is the better way *these days (2005)*?

Well, if you have a chance to get a major deal - *get the deal.* It's like this; if you were in high school, and you had a chance to go professional right out of high school, I would suggest you go "pro." This is because from the promotional end, the money end...the whole thing is like *90 times bigger* than being independent.

2 When you say "90 times bigger", do you mean as a label entity or as an artist?

➢ Right now, a major label is the way to go because the bootleggers have the independent game so squashed... to where you don't have much room to grow as a company. You will see yourself *spending a lot of money*, but not making a lot of money.

➢ For me, as a company going with a major label for my artist *and myself*, I just come out better getting a major deal because:

1. I get a *budget* **2.** I have my own production company, so I get a chance to do at least half the album or the whole album **3.** My artist gets *"major"* exposure **4.** If we get a hit record off of the album, it will blow my production company up also... for *more* money.

➢ Now if I decide to go independent, then I have a "LONG" ride, because with the bootleggers, they've got the game too chopped up right now. So if you're an independent label and you don't have major dough or money to spend, then you have to settle for working a city or area, and then go to the next area, and then to the next... unless you've got major dollars to just throw 60,000 or 70,000 units out there at one time, and also in 5 or 6 states at a time.

3 So if you are a new independent label, and you *don't have big money*, what can new entrepeneurs honestly expect?

If you don't have some big money to spend, you have to work from spot to spot. And as you work those spots, you aren't picking up any "real" money in return; you are just going to be dishing out money. And when you go into these little cities, there just aren't that many independent record stores anymore either; they've shut down now. So, there's nothing but the major retail chains there. And when you go into the "hoods," your CDs are being bootlegged... and you aren't getting *any of that money*; the bootleggers are getting your money. So I suggest that if you have a chance to go with a major label and get a deal... *get the deal*, and I don't care *what* kind of money or deal it is right now!

➢ Another thing to consider is that a lot of indie distributors have gone out of business too. Three years ago, there were many options to get Indie distribution, but now, between the Internet and the bootleggers, a lot of retail stores have closed. Wherehouse music closed, Music Network and their 100+ stores have basically closed...and left only a few stores open. So a whole lot of stores went out of business. And when that happened, that closed many of the One Stops. So a lot of people just ended up filing bankruptcy. Right now, basically the bootleggers got it on "lock"...*there may be more bootleggers than drug dealers!*

ARTISTS MUST WORK

4 So what is the best mind-set or approach to take if you are an artist that wants to be out *making money and getting his music some exposure*?

➢ If you are an artist and you're performing live, you *are* going to be able to eat and make some money, as long as you have a good show and a hot song. We have an artist, *Baby D that* works constantly, every single week, without having a *new* album out in 3 years. So an artist can eat, even when the label doesn't eat. I also have a group, *Intoxicated*, who has a song getting a little play on radio, and they have been eating pretty well too... and they don't have an album out right now either. They are just doing shows, and they *are getting paid.*

"...The label isn't making a dime yet, but the Artist is making thousands of dollars."

5 If an artist only has a little money to spend… to put out his record, should he spend his money into putting out a few singles or just work his one-best single?

➤ My comment on that is if you can get just one record that's "hot," go try and get yourself a major deal with it. If that one record is actually working, to me there's no need to keep putting out other records. If you've got that 1 record that's working, "run with it!" Because all a major label wants is 1 hit anyway. If you have some more hits… then great, but 1 hit will get you paid, and I hit will get you a major record deal. So if you've got a good single, and it's *"potent"*, and the people are loving it, and it's in demand, you run with that 1 single until it totally dies out, and *then you come with a 2nd single.*

➤ And as far as only having a little money to spend, really, you don't even have to have *any money* if you have a "hot" song, and you have a "way" to get it out to the *main* DJs or somebody who can get that record *heard; you don't even have to have a dollar!* A label or *somebody* is going to find you *anyway*. The majors are going to find you if you make some noise with the record. You're going to get a phone call *regardless*.

"…If the song is hitting radio, in-demand at retail, And especially if it's really selling … You 'are' going to get a call from the Major Labels!"

And just so I clarify, if you haven't gotten that call from the majors yet, you definitely put it out on your own… I do it!

THE MIXTAPE GAME

6 A lot of artist and indies seem to be focusing a lot of energy into being on a mixtape. What are your thoughts on the mixtape game… and is this something that an artist or label needs to be part of - to get *additional* support?

➤ Yes, Mixtapes are a big part of records *getting where they get!* Without being on a mixtape, you might have a long time trying to get your record hot. There's a lot of competition when marketing a record, so everybody who comes out with a record is trying to get on a mixtape. Even the major labels send songs out to the "main" DJs, who's tapes they *know* circulate. The labels know! The mixtape *thing*?…that's the way you go!

7 If you are a small label, should you even worry about the guy making money selling 20,000+ units of *his mixtape*, and *you not getting any of that money?*

➤ There's really nothing *you can do about it.* There's really nothing *I can do about it.* So when I drop stuff, I just try to make sure "I" can get on the *hottest* mixtapes. They are going to make their money, but at the same time, *it promotes my product and gets me out there too.* A lot of times, you can't even "get out there" *without* being on a mixtape. Like for instance, we hadn't even made any noise in Texas until we started getting on *"Swisha House"* Mixtapes. Texas, that's that *crazy* market, so we were not even tapped into that market really until we got on the Michael Watts Mixtapes. But now that we are on them, we're getting all kind of props out in Texas. And without his mixtapes, I don't know when it might have been time for us to even hit down in that region.

WORK AND NETWORK!

8 What's your best advice and wisdom to up-and-coming artist and entrepenuers who want to pursue the indie game?

1. You have to stay humble **2.** You have to network and meet people
3. You have to cut some deals sometimes, and even kiss a little butt.
4. You need to always stay working.   **5.** You have to stay focused!

For me, I'm always working; I don't have any set hours right now. I might stay in the office until 10PM at night sometimes. You have to keep your hustle going; that 24/7 drive... to make it. So you have to put in the hours and you definitely have to network. Basically, my whole thing is networking. If you stay in folks face, *with a good attitude*, something good will come up out of that.

"BEATS FOR SALE!"

9 What are your outlook on the Selling Beats game?

➤ I have a production company, so I love selling beats. We have a full production company, so when I wake up every day hoping to sell a beat for someone's album. Right now we are selling beats; placing productions on both major and independent projects.

10 And how do you contract with clients to sell beats and tracks as far as ownership goes?

➤ We sell beats as a production company to *get the production* on the song. There are a lot of people selling and making beats for $200 or whatever, and you don't ever have to talk to that dude again.. but that's not the way we do it. We "place" the beat, we get points and royalties. We produce the song basically, because we have a track record and the credibility to get the job done.

"...We have songs placed on major situations; Rasheeda, 112, Lil Flip, DSGB, Pastor Troy, YoungBloodZ, and a few more, so we "produce" the beat or track through Big Oomp Camp!"

SUBMITTING YOUR CD

11 ❑ *A letter was submitted.* "What's the best way to get my Underground CDs into local retail stores?"

This is how it goes...

❑ **1st way - Give the store your music for free, like a promotion**

❑ **2nd way - Put the record for sale in the store on consignment**

❑ **3rd way - The store *will* buy it, BUT ONLY IF IT'S "HOT!"** - If there isn't anyone coming in the store asking for your record, we're not buying it. My stores use to do that, but we don't buy like that anymore.

Here's the deal: First of all, a lot of the people who are selling independent albums now, are too stuck on the price from the "old days."  The prices are different now; it isn't like that anymore! Plus, you have bootleggers out there selling a CD that's on TV and Radio for $5... and then here you come as an Indie label wanting to sell your CDs *"wholesale"* to a store for $5 or more, *and your songs are not on TV ...or the radio!* So I tell people now, "If you bring your CD to us, and you can't give it to us for free, we can't pay anymore that $2 for it... and we can't buy any more than 5 or 10 of them. So from there, we'll stock it on the shelf, but 9 times out of 10, it doesn't get sold if you don't have anything going on or some promotions on it. There's too much other stuff in the store to compete with, and plus you are competing with the bootleggers on the street with the *"real" albums... selling for $5, or five for $20 (laughing)!* So if you don't have any Radio or TV, your butt is in trouble!

12 ❑ *A letter was submitted.* "For a new label or small company, what a fair price to do a consignment deal at smaller retail stores like yours?"

➤ If it's a record that has some good promotion, we will pay $5, but for a record with no promotion... $2.

13 ❑ *A letter was submitted.* "Do you have to be an certified company or record *label*, or can I use music that I made at home to sell in a record store?"

➢ Some stores. There are a lot of stores that you can get your stuff in without being a full-blown label. But the one thing you can bet on, you aren't going into any stores in a large city like Atlanta, asking them to *buy your CD*, and no one has been in there asking for the product, or if it's not on TV and Radio, or if no one has heard of it. Money is too scarce now. But you *don't* have to start a full label to get it into the store.

➢ Now, 9 times out of 10, you do need a bar code, it needs to be shrink-wrapped, and have a cover. But, with some independent retail stores, you *can* get in there without a barcode. Most stores will *only* take your product if you have a barcode because that's how they regulate inventory... by barcode. But now for my stores for instance, you don't have to have a barcode for us to take it.

14 What's the best advice you can give to aspiring artist and producers who are sending out demos, who really want to make sure their songs get listened to?

Well, I get a lot of demos. And there are at least 200 or more demos in my box every week, and it seems I never get a chance to listen to all of it. But as far as some advice, this is the way it works with our company: If a person *calls* my office saying, "This is such-n-so from such-n-so-place, did you get that demo?" I'm like, well let me look, and sometimes I'll find it and listen right then... and let them hear me listening to it. Or sometimes I'll ask them to call me back in an hour or by the end of the day, and then I get a chance to listen, and then let you know what's up. But now if a person doesn't call, or set up an appointment to come over and meet with me to have your stuff listened to, then I might not ever hear it.

See, by me talking to you, I try to show you some respect... and I *will* listen. But, if you're not calling or planning to *follow up*, it is just too many demos that come in for me to listen to everything...

Multi-Platinum Production Company – Indie Label – Record Retailer
TV Show - Radio Show – Music Publisher
Big Oomp's credits include
YoungBloodz, Pastor Troy, Rasheeda, DSGB, Baby - D, Crime Mob, Lil Flip, Eightball, Sammy Sam, 112, DJ Jelly ...and many others.
www.BigOompRecords.com

Music Powers

ADVERTISING & THE RULE OF SEVEN

ADVERTISING & MARKETING

OK crew, it's the way everything from Taco Bell's late-night commercials rotate on TV & radio, to those funny GEICO Insurance ads; "... *I just saved a bunch a* *money on my car insurance...*" It's called advertising, and it's very important! See, whether it's radio spinning that song you really didn't like "before", but now, after you've heard it 7 (or more) times... well, yeah, its kind of an ok song *now.*   And hopefully for the company spending money for those everywhere-you-look-and-listen ads, the public will believe the ad message and possibly make a purchase of that particular product. And what is that "magic" number that the marketing experts agree is "key" for most people to accept, and then "swallow" by reaching into their wallets?

 ...Seven

 *THE RULE OF...* 7

"THE RULE OF SEVEN?" *Hey, it's real folks.*
This means that you should be trying to get your
 project exposed with that concept or rule in mind. **FIRST:** Advertise your product in at least **7 *different* places**, allowing the potential consumer to be introduced to your music or merchandise. This means seeing your product or promos, reading or hearing (about) the product in those 7 different places you have chose to run ads in. Now, market your project by advertising over a reasonable length of time so that people will know about it, hear about it, and possibly think about your product *enough to acknowledge it* and then consider buying it. Seek out local, regional, and major national magazines and newspapers, TV, radio, Internet (banners ads, etc), promos in the street (posters, postcards, stickers, etc); basically everywhere you can afford to advertise your project. And don't forget about the "audible" drops in songs - advertising and marketing your project or company, "in the music". **Example**: Jermaine Dupri's voice, with shout-outs to "So So Def" in a record, or "This... is another Jazzy Pha Production", or just by using their unique trademark – vocally or musically in their records *("Whaaat!!!" ... "Okayeeee!" via Lil' Jon)*. All in all, just know that this all is part of the marketing, hype, promotion and "Rule of Seven' working and being effective. All of this normally helps to sell the record or product. I'm telling you this so that you and your team *know* that you will need to do the same when you have a plan and budget in place to make that "Rule of 7" happen for your own project. Advertising has always been key to getting a product out in the mass market. Let's face it, if

you have the best burger like Hardees… *what good is it, if no one knows that it's great?* And just think of other big companies. We all *already know* about Wendy's, Coca-Cola and McDonalds, but, all of these giant corporations *continuously* promote and advertise to *remind* your subconscious to consider and think of them, and hopefully accept the ad campaign enough to buy product. It's a fact, most people, if they see it enough in magazines, or *especially on TV*… people normally accept it, and eventually consider the product legitimate.

The Promoter

Creative Loafing Newspaper

Rolling Out Magazine

Access Atlanta AJC Newspaper

TO BE SUCCESSFUL IN YOUR MARKETING & ADVERTISING…

PERSISTENCE IS THE KEY!

According to business expert and author Jeff Williams (www.bizstarters.com), most sales experts claim that it can take up to **SEVEN SEPARATE** contacts of a sales prospect *before* he can actually be persuaded to finally buy your product. So, success in getting people to *learn enough about you* to be comfortable with you is vital… followed by *consistent* communications, along with a sufficient amount of watch-time of the public and media seeing you in print, radio, web, TV, etc. and what's been proven to be the best support of all; *word of mouth.*

Music Powers
SELLING & LEA$ING BEATS
"The Business of Selling Beats... To Slang or Not To Slang"
by Raaqim Knight, Esq. & Uleses C. Henderson, Jr., Esq.

INTRODUCTION

A rguably, there is nothing more important to a producer than the producer's reputation. Specifically, producers are valued by, among other things, their discography, the status of the artists they've produced, the number of Billboard hits they've produced, the SoundScan of albums containing masters (or "beats") produced by the producer, and their popularity (or "buzz") within the industry. With that said, *new* producers are eager to create a "buzz" for themselves within the industry, with hopes that their tracks will fall into the hands of an "industry exec" at a major record label, or an established artist looking to work with some "fresh" talent. Thus, a new producer may believe that leasing or selling (or what we will affectionately call "slangin") beats to various up-and-coming artists will accomplish this task by **(1)** providing the producer the best chance of getting his or her music heard as the artists seek record or production deals, and **(2)** allowing the producer to make some money along the way until a budgeted album project comes along. But let the producer beware! There are some important things that a producer must consider when slangin' beats, and we hope to touch on some of those issues in this segment.

While there are numerous issues to consider when slangin' beats to new artists, here we will concentrate on four general topics: **(1)** the producer-artist relationship; **(2)** the question of whether to lease or sell beats; **(3)** what a written agreement to sell or lease a beat should address; and **(4)** other considerations, including briefly, the pros and cons of slangin' beats via the Internet.

THE RELATIONSHIP: "PUT IT IN WRITING"

> "If you leave the studio with my music,
> ...You leave with a written agreement"
> NO EXCEPTIONS!

As a "no-name" or, to be politically correct, an "up-and-coming" producer, you will likely encounter a situation where an artist wants to "borrow" or "buy" a particular beat (or beats) from you, rather than enter into a full-blown production agreement. The artist may be a *new,* or up-and-coming talent, looking for beats to help her break into the industry, or he may be an established artist looking for a "new" sound at a premium (or "reduced") price.

Regardless of the status of the artist purchasing or "borrowing" ("leasing") a beat from you, the first thing to remember is *always* put the agreement in writing. This should be done before the artist even leaves the studio with a copy of the beat. The agreement does not have to be long or complex – it should merely set forth your agreement regarding the artist's use of the beat in language that both you and the artist understand.

Producers may be tempted to let an artist use their beats without going through the hassle of writing out an agreement. For example, the up-and-coming artist may be someone that the producer is on friendly terms with. The producer may think that their friendship will be ruined if the producer "gets formal" with him, or on the other hand, an established artist may be someone the producer views as a "pathway" into the biz.   Accordingly, the producer may fear ruining this relationship also by insisting on a written agreement.

Despite this apprehension, *you must put the agreement in writing*. Ironically, *not* getting the deal in writing poses a much greater risk of ruining a relationship than simply writing down your agreement.   In this business, countless friendships have gone down in flames – or up-in-flames, however you want to look at it – when the money started coming in and the division of that money had not been agreed upon beforehand. An established artist should be accustomed to using written agreements, and in most instances, will *respect* your professionalism in requesting an agreement in writing.   At the same time, the new artist will be forced to realize that you are running a business, and to take you and your music seriously.

Often, an up-and-coming producer will let an artist borrow a beat – figuring *"who cares, nobody's using it"* – without thinking about the financial aspects of letting him or her use the beat. For instance, if an artist using one of those beats gets signed and uses the beat on the resulting album, you will not have your points worked out.   Further, you won't know whether you are getting an advance, royalties, retaining your publishing, etc. Now you will have to go back and work out the deal in reverse. For an up-and-coming producer, working out a deal in reverse is not the best position to be in because the production company or record label will be applying pressure on the artist to get your beat for the *least amount of money possible*; either directly or by possibly giving the artist a bad deal which has the effect of squeezing you out.   That's just the reality of the business. Because the beat has already been created, the producer may not have much leverage in negotiating a desired production fee or advance.

At the same time, a producer may let an artist who is not likely to be signed, use a beat. But what if a second artist, who may have multiple offers for a record deal on the table, comes along and wants to buy that same beat? Will you have the right to sell him the beat? Or does the first artist get to use it forever in a *fruitless* search for a deal? If your agreement with the first artist were in writing you would know.

The last point is that you've got to strike while the iron's hot. A beat that an artist really likes now may be "dated" later. If the artist still wants to use it on an album, he will want to pay the later, devalued purchase price for the beat. Working out the purchase price and writing out the agreement before hand is a way to prevent that from happening. It also eliminates the artificial devaluation of the beat by the record/production company's deal with the artist.

Again, friendships are often ruined by the failure to put an agreement in writing. Avoid this unfortunate result and "put it in writing." You have to look at your beat-making endeavors as a business. And like they say – "business is business." The agreement does not have to be complex or use legal jargon, just agree on the terms and write them out. Your up-and-coming artist friends should recognize that you're doing this professionally and well-established artists will respect your initiative also.

SHOULD I SELL OR LEASE MY BEAT?

You should always consider your future objectives and goals as a producer before deciding to sell or lease your beats. You may produce tracks that you feel are "throw-away" beats and are probably more willing to sell these tracks to new artists. Naturally, you probably want to hold on to those beats that you feel are "hot" for an established artist or a more talented new artist. However, that "throw-away" beat may just fall into the right hands and become a hit, while your "hot" tracks might not make the album cut because the label decides to add some veteran producers to the roster to "beef-up" the album. For that reason, the decision of whether to sell or lease your beats requires you to consider several important issues – no matter how hot the beat is.

In general, when selling a beat to an artist or record label, a producer may seek to take advantage of the following income sources: **(1) Producer fees** – compensation for the value of your physical work and time spent creating the beat, **(2) Master purchase or "buy-out"** (for ownership of your portion of the master recording containing your beat) – compensation for the right to control the use of the master; **(3) Producer royalties** (paid in advance and on the back-end) – compensation for your services rendered in performing and/or creating the beat, in an amount determined by the number of copies of the beat (or records that contain songs that contain the beat) that the record label sells; and **(4) Publishing** – compensation for the use of your copyrighted material, including (a) the reproduction of your beat on individual records (mechanical royalties) and (b) the public performance of your beat (i.e., airplay/performance royalties).

Although we will discuss these income sources in further details, at this point it is only necessary to understand them as either up-front payments or back-end payments.

UP-FRONT PAYMENTS

The producer fee, amounts paid for the ownership or use of the masters, and advances against royalties are monies that a producer receives *before* the record label begins manufacturing and selling records/units. We call these amounts up-front payments.

BACK-END PAYMENTS

The balance of producer royalties (minus advances) and amounts representing publishing royalties are residual payments, which are made to the producer over time, following the manufacture, distribution and sale of units by a record label, on a per-unit and/or per-performance basis. In that regard, we consider royalty payments to be "back-end" compensation to the producer for his or her services in producing the beat.

LEASING A BEAT "ON SPEC"

With that said, when merely leasing a beat "on spec" – allowing the beat to be used by an artist *without a guarantee* that the beat will actually be used on an album manufactured, distributed and sold by a record company, a producer typically receives an up-front payment in the form of a production fee and/or an advance against producer royalties, but the producer still "owns" or retains his rights in the beat (the master).

In leasing a beat "on spec", the artist initially pays the producer only a fraction of the production fee or advance, and the balance of the agreed fee and/or advance is paid once the artist is signed to a record deal. In other words, when leasing or selling a beat on spec, a producer is paid a portion of his up-front money in exchange for the artist's *limited* use of the beat.

THE "QUASI-SALE"

When agreeing to what we call a "quasi-sale" of the beat, the producer is paid his or her entire production fee and/or other up-front monies. The producer also sells his interest in the master recording of the song containing the beat to the artist or record label, and his up-front payment should

> *...Quasi?*
> 1. *In some sense*
> 2. *Similar to*

include compensation for that sale. In exchange for these up-front monies, the producer will relinquish his or her right to collect back-end producer royalties, so the amount paid should reflect compensation for relinquishment of those rights as well. However, the producer will retain his or her publishing rights.

THE OUTRIGHT SALE

When a producer sells a beat "outright," the producer receives a purchase price consisting of **the producer fee**, the **value of the masters**, the **current value of the producer's back-end** producer royalties (including possible advances on that amount), and **an additional amount for his publishing rights** in the underlying composition – i.e., the producer sells his rights in the masters and the underlying composition. While this purchase price formula may *look* impressive, in actuality, beats are often sold "outright" for as little as $500. As you may have noticed, the difference between an "outright sale" and a "quasi-sale," as we have described them, concerns the sale of the producer's publishing rights.

KEEP IT REAL

When deciding on whether to lease or sell a beat, consider the foregoing scenarios and choose one that you feel will work best for *you*. But, you must remember the time-value of money. Even if everyone in the world agrees that your beat will be worth $1,000,000 next year, no one will pay you that entire amount today. In reality, it will be impossible to definitively predict what a beat will be worth in a year. Therefore, you must essentially estimate how much money the beat could make you in the long run.

If you are being offered an up-front amount that you believe is much less than the beat's long-term value, then leasing the beat or quasi-selling it may make sense. However, if you are being offered an up-front amount that is close to, equal to or larger than the beat's long-term value, then selling it outright may make sense. But let's keep it real. You may produce a beat that you feel "sucks," and some cat that you know couldn't sign a deal with the devil, loves it. It may be better to just take your money and run, rather than getting old and gray waiting for him to sign a record deal.

We know what you're thinking; that as attorneys, we should be telling you that all of your "intellectual property" is valuable. But in the real world, we've seen our share of producers who produce for every Tom, Dick, and Harry, and *never receive a nickel* from those artists. So just keep it real folks!

CONTENTS OF THE AGREEMENT

The parties involved in an agreement are ultimately the ones who set the terms of the agreement. But the services of an attorney can be invaluable in defining those terms. An attorney's understanding of the law and industry customs will help you write your agreement in a way that makes the parties' intentions clear and comprehensible. This is important, in the event that the contract is later read and interpreted by a judge and jury. The attorney can also help ensure that your agreement is not illegal based on some preexisting law or regulation *you may not be aware of*. Your music is your business and you obviously want your business to run correctly. So the best advice is to hire an attorney to guide you - especially in the early stages of your career.

As a "starving" producer, you may think that you cannot afford an attorney. But, there are attorneys who will do the work for you in exchange for payment on the "back-end." In essence, they will negotiate and write the contract for you and will include in the contract a provision that says that the beat's purchaser will pay the producer's attorney's fees directly to the attorney and subtract it from the amount the purchaser agreed to pay the producer. If you absolutely cannot or do not want to hire an attorney, as a last resort you can write the agreement yourself.

> ### THE FOLLOWING IS AN OVERSIMPLIFIED BUT USEFUL LIST OF WHAT THE WRITTEN AGREEMENT SHOULD DISCUSS:
>
> ⇒ Whether the beat is being sold/leased?
> ⇒ How long is the artist entitled to use the beat?
> ⇒ How much money do you get in exchange for the artist's use of the beat?
> ⇒ Who owns the masters?
> ⇒ Will you retain your publishing?
> ⇒ If leasing the beat, are you entitled to produce the artist on a later album?
> ⇒ If there are samples, who's responsible for clearing them?

THE TERM

The "term" is a fancy word used to describe the period of time during which a contract is in force. Thus, the term is important because it determines how long your contractual relationship with the artist will last.

With respect to "leasing", you should **never agree to a term that is longer than 18 months**. Limiting the term to no more than a year is ideal. A term of one year to 18 months gives the artist ample time to shop his or her song to a record label or production company. However, if the artist's songs are not strong enough to get him or her signed, you should not be forced to tie-up the beat with an artist that *cannot* get signed; possibly wasting an opportunity to sell or lease the beat to another up-and-coming artist who does have "signing potential." Who knows, good fortune may even lead to an established artist wanting to purchase that beat.

❑ **IMPORTANT:** Tracks typically have a short shelf life – meaning a track that might be hot *today*… may have "dated" sounds and a "dated" groove a year from now. You must view your beats not only as art, but also as a commodity. In view of that, a producer cannot afford to waste his or her beats on artists that can't commercially exploit them. After all, isn't fame and fortune at least one of the reasons you got into the game? Don't you dream of six-figure producer advances, and producing "platinum" artists? Well it won't happen if you waste your tracks on *three*-figure advances and "aluminum artists". All in all, limiting the term will force the artist to "use it, or lose it!"

THE PRODUCER FEE

As we briefly discussed above, a producer (or production) fee can be viewed as compensation for the physical labor, time and money you spent making a beat.

The producer fee can take the form of fees charged on an hourly rate or a lump sum charge. A producer should want most, if not all of the upfront money he receives for a beat, to be characterized as a *producer fee* rather than an *advance*. Producer fees are non-recoupable and paid to the producer without a "hitch," while an advance will be recoupable and will count against any producer royalties you may be entitled to. Always charge a producer fee, in *some* amount, for your beat, regardless of how the rest of the agreement is set up. Producer fees are especially appropriate when the producer does his production work and records an artist at his own studio.

When leasing a beat (selling the beat "on spec"), a producer may charge a fee ranging anywhere from $500 to $5,000 per track. Whether the production fee is closer to $500 or $5,000 should depend on how "hot" the beat is and how much the artist can *realistically* pay. If the artist has deals on the table, you should charge him more for the beat, because he has a greater chance of profiting off of your beat than does an artist with no deals on the table. Your notoriety as a producer will also influence what you can charge.

Once the artist to whom you have leased a beat is signed to a record deal, the artist will pay the remaining balance of the beat's full purchase price – i.e., the artist will buy out the producer's interest in the master. For example, a producer may want to negotiate a $10,000 advance for a beat from a record label; The producer may lease the beat on spec for $1,000, and the artist will pay, or cause the record label to pay the producer the remaining $9,000 when the artist gets signed to a deal. The $1,000 payment from the artist should be characterized as a producer fee. But, the producer will also want the payment of the remaining balance of the beat's purchase price to be characterized as a "production fee" as opposed to an "advance," to the extent possible.

If selling a beat – *either "quasi" or "outright"* – the production fee could range from $500 to $20,000 per beat. While the amount of work it took to make the beat might remain the same, the production fee should be higher because the production fee takes the place of the producer royalties you are giving up by selling your interest in the masters. The actual fee charged should be based on the same considerations discussed above – e.g., the quality of the beat, the artist's status, etc. The foregoing amounts represent typical ranges for an up-and-coming producer, but more established producers can charge production fees upwards of $200,000. Remember, your production fee *does not include your publishing*. That should be made clear in the written agreement as well.

ADVANCES

Advances are often paid "up front" with, or instead of, a producer fee, so they are often discussed together, but an advance actually represents a different income source than producer fees. In fact, the advance is really not even a stand-alone income source at all, but rather a portion of your back-end producer royalties.   The advance is, in effect, a portion of your back-end producer royalties, paid to you in *advance* of you actually earning those royalties through album sales.

The way it works is that once an artist using your beats signs a deal and sells some albums on which your beat is featured, you will be entitled to back-end producer royalties. When it is all said and done, the number of albums that are sold will determine the amount of producer royalties you are supposed to be paid. The advance is basically a down payment or deposit on those royalties that are paid to the producer by the artist, production company, or record label. The advance is credited (recoupable) against the amount of back-end producer royalties you are owed by the record label. In other words, the advance is subtracted from the producer royalties you actually earn. If your back-end producer royalties end up being less than your advance, you are "unrecouped" and won't get any back-end money for the use of the beat until your producer royalties exceed the amount of your advance.

Similar to producer fees, advances can range from $5,000 to $50,000 *or more* per song. But be careful, as record labels typically give artists album budgets on an "all-in" basis. This means that the "all-in" fee given to the producer to produce a song will include the advance, producer fee, studio costs, musician cost, etc. In addition, the record labels may even consider this amount as an "all-in" advance – meaning they will recoup (subtract) this amount from your producer royalties. In this instance, the label will recoup such costs from both you and the artist. Producers should make sure that the artist's "all-in" amount is clearly defined as an "all-in" fund, and that your recoupable advance is only a *small* portion of that fund. The contract should also make it clear that the artist is responsible for recouping that fund and that *you, as the producer*, will only be responsible for recouping your producer advance (or that portion of the "all-in" fund).

When you lease a beat, artists, production companies and record labels will want all of the money that they pay you up-front for the beat to be characterized as a recoupable advance.   That way, they can subtract the up-front money from amounts they will owe you later as producer royalties. You want the up-front money to be characterized as a *non-recoupable* producer fee.

In the end, if an up-and-coming artist can only agree to pay you a recoupable advance as opposed to a non-recoupable producer fee, you should take it if the actual check is big enough because, unless the artist's album becomes a major sales success, your advance will not likely be recouped, and you won't have any producer royalties coming to you anyway. Note: Keep in mind that it is not uncommon for an up-front payment to be split as part-producer-fee-part-advance.

❑ **IMPORTANT REMINDER:** Your advance only comes into play when leasing a beat. If you do a quasi-sale or outright-sale, you will be giving up your producer royalties. Also remember that your advance *does not* include money for the purchase of your publishing.

PRODUCER ROYALTIES

Similar to an artist royalty, a producer royalty is compensation for a producer's services in producing a record. This means that when a record containing your beat is sold, as a producer, you are entitled to a royalty payment from the sale of that record. In a record contract, the royalty is usually specified either in dollars-and-cents for each unit sold, or as a percentage of receipts. At specified intervals, or accounting periods, the record company will calculate your royalties, based on the number of records sold during that particular accounting period. The record company will then send you a royalty statement and check – to the extent that your royalties exceed the recoupable amounts that they have already paid to you. In most cases, a producer won't realize any royalties until an album has sold over 300,000 to 400,000 units. But this all depends on the artist's costs in making the album.

LEASING BEATS "ON SPEC"

With regards to leasing beats "on spec," if the beat is used on a master included on an album released by the artist, the producer should ask for an advance (in addition to the demo or spec fee), and a producer royalty. Most producer royalties range between 2% to 3% of the album sales. In most instances, the producer's royalty will be calculated on the same basis as the artist's royalty (*i.e.*, with respect to net album sales), on a *pro rata* basis – in proportion to the number of producer's tracks compared to the total number of tracks comprised on the album. On rare occasions, for superstar producers, a producer might be able to actually receive a flat royalty based on albums sold (*e.g.*, 1% of the album sales).

PAYMENT OF THE PRODUCER ROYALTY

With regards to payment of the producer royalty, a producer should ask that his or her royalties be paid retroactive to record one. This means that a producer will receive royalties retroactively based on all records sold, including those that were sold *before* the point when the recording costs were recouped. But the royalty payments will not begin until *after* the artist's recording costs are recouped (or paid back) at the artist's "all-in" royalty rate (*e.g.*, 8% to 15% of album sales). On a rare occasion, a producer may be able to receive his producer royalties as from record one, meaning that the producer would receive his producer royalties as soon as the first record is sold – which in most instances will account towards his recoupable advances before he is actually paid. However, on certain occasions, a label might only offer a producer to get paid proactively. In this instance, the producer would only get paid for records actually sold after the point that the recording costs of the album are recouped at the artist's "all-in" rate.

Producers must keep in mind their potential of receiving "back-end" royalties when negotiating how much of an advance they should receive "up front" from an artist, production company, and/or record company.   Remember that royalties will only be paid after the producer's advance has been recouped.   This makes it important for the producer – especially those producers who actually have a recording studio – to characterize at least half of the "up front" money that they receive as a non-recoupable production fee, instead of receiving the whole sum as a recoupable advance. In that regard, the larger the advance, the more units the artist will have to sell before the producer realizes any revenue from album sales.

Remember, however, if you have been offered an "up front" payment without any mention of an "advance," you want to characterize the entire amount as a production fee, not an advance. But to avoid a possible dispute later, you should clearly define within the agreement what portion of the "up front" payment will be considered an *advance against producer royalties*, and what portion is considered a *non-recoupable production fee*.

OWNERSHIP OF THE MASTERS

One of the trickiest issues you must deal with in a leasing situation is: "who will actually own the masters?" If you are leasing a beat, you should retain at least co-ownership of the masters with the artist. Our suggestion is, if at all possible, to retain all rights in and to the masters until the artist or record label "buys-out" your interest in the masters once the artist is signed by the record label. If you co-own the masters, the artist will still need to buy-out your co-ownership interest in the masters before the artist can deliver the masters to the record label pursuant to a recording agreement. In the situation of leasing beats (or selling them "on spec") the additional advance money paid to you by the record label would be considered as the "buy-out" of your co-ownership, or total ownership interest in and to the masters.

When agreeing to a "quasi-sale" of a beat, you are effectively "selling" your right to receive producer royalties. Thus, the amount of money that you agree to accept from the company or the artist (the "buy-out") should include an amount that represents the level of retail success you expect the record to achieve. In practice, the "buy-out" amount for the producer royalties is usually added to the amount being charged by the producer for the physical work and time spent making the beat. The resulting combined amount is then characterized as one lump sum producer fee. In such an instance, the up-and-coming producer must be cautious of losing sight of the fact that he is selling his right to a potentially lucrative, and potentially long-lasting, series of future royalty payments.

Producer charges for physical work to make the track		Producer charge for time to make the track in lab		Producer also adds a charge for the "Buy-out"
	+		+	

LUMP SUM PRODUCER FEE

While determining ownership of the master is a very tricky issue, it is one that needs to be addressed and not overlooked. Ownership of the master is critical from the artist's perspective because the artist wants to have the ability to shop the tracks and eventually sell and assign his or her interest in the tracks to the record label. However, as a producer, you want to retain your rights in the tracks until the artist actually finds "a buyer." Thus, any type of agreement, whether it is a lease agreement or an outright sale agreement, should specifically state who owns the masters.

Note: Even in a quasi-sale situation, while the artist would own the masters, the producer would still retain its copyright interest (publishing) in and to the underlying composition (the beat itself).

PUBLISHING

The final income source to discuss concerns the value of the producer's publishing interest in the beat. Publishing refers to the rights that you, as the creator (or author) of a musical work (your beat/the music recorded on the master), have with respect to controlling the reproduction and public performance of your musical work. These rights are called copyrights. The producer owns half of the copyrights in a song – the music, sometimes referred to as the "underlying composition," as opposed to the lyrics, which makes up the other half of the song.

The interesting thing about copyrights is that they last virtually forever – 75 years after the life of the author, which is long after any production or recording contract, would have expired. Therefore, a song written and recorded twenty years ago can be played on the radio today, and the owner of the copyrights would be entitled to a payment.

Often, a production company or record label will offer a producer a sum of money in exchange for this potentially never-ending income stream. But a producer should think long and hard before selling his or her publishing rights, because a hit song or just a song on a hit album may generate several tens of thousands of dollars.

MECHANICALS

To simplify things, publishing has two major income streams. The first are "mechanical royalties." Mechanical royalties are monies paid by a record company for the right to use a song on records. The publisher, which in most cases is you, issues a license to the record company that says, for each record manufactured and distributed, the record company will pay a royalty equal to a specified rate. This rate is often tied to a "statutory rate", set by the government, which often increases over time. (See Songwriting & Publishing Chapter)

PERFORMANCE ROYALTIES

The second major income stream is "public performance royalties." Public performance royalties are monies paid by various entities to you, for the right to play your song on the radio, on television, in nightclubs, amusement parks, live concerts, etc. Performing rights societies, such as ASCAP, BMI, and SESAC, issue licenses to these entities, keep track of their public performances, collect the monies, and pay you as the publisher.

In addition to these public performance payments, your publishing rights may provide additional income-generating opportunity, which include printed music, synchronization licenses, and foreign sub-publishing. Consequently, a producer stands to lose a substantial amount of revenue by selling away his publishing rights.

With all of this in mind, a producer should not be eager to sell his beats "outright." If you sell or lease a beat, you should retain your copyright (or publishing) interest in the beat. Many up-and-coming producers don't value their publishing rights and end up giving up all, or at least half of these rights as part of their producer agreements. Hold on to these rights because if you end up producing a hit record, a major publisher may come along later and give you a six-figure advance to enter into a co-publishing agreement with them. Signing a co-publishing deal with a major publisher is advantageous for a producer in the long run anyway because the publisher will do all the administrative grunt work to secure and exploit your publishing interest in your songs (in exchange, of course, for a 50% share in your publishing interest), while you concentrate on making hits.

Accordingly, the proper way to view your decision to sell your publishing or not is to consider whether the song using your beat will be a long term success, with lots of airplay. If so, then you should hold on to your publishing rights. There are countless examples of artists whose recording careers have ended, and who couldn't sell a new album to save their life, but who still receive a nice size check for the continued airplay of an old hit they recorded years ago. They help on to their publishing. The case may be, however, that you really need the money now and feel compelled to sell your publishing rights. If so, make sure that you charge an amount that is worth the future income stream that you will be giving up.

In the end, the decision to sell your publishing is a gamble and depends entirely on the potential success of the song utilizing your beat. But when in doubt, the producer should lean towards retaining his or her publishing rights.

PRODUCTION OF SUBSEQUENT LP(s)

Particularly with "on spec" agreements, a producer should insist on a provision that requires the artist to use his or her best efforts to cause the record label to retain the producer to produce one or more masters on a subsequent LP. This provision is important because often times once an artist is actually signed to a record label, the record label will insist on using different producers – either its in-house producers or producers with whom the record label is more familiar – to produce the record.

The following scenario illustrates the importance of this issue. You might produce all five or six of an artist's demo tracks, which end up being very influential in the artist getting a record deal. After the recording artist signs the deal, both you and the artist will probably begin working on new tracks for the recording artist's first LP. But after reviewing the LP, the A&R from the record label might insist that a hot track from the Neptunes or from Lil' John be added onto the album. You could very well find yourself not making the cut on the album. This is very unfair to you, especially if your tracks were the reason, or one of the main reasons, why the artist got signed to the record label in the first place.

To prevent this scenario from occurring, you should include in your producer agreement a provision similar to the one we just discussed. Since you leased the beat to the artist, and your beat will help get the artist a deal, the artist should agree to use his or her best efforts to, at least, have the song(s) that you leased to them placed on the record. Furthermore, your agreement with the artist should also require that the artist use his or her best efforts to allow you to produce other tracks on that album, or more tracks on subsequent LPs.

SAMPLING

Sampling, as you are probably aware, is the process of digitally isolating and recording a sound or sounds from previously recorded material for the purposes of incorporating the sampled sound (or sampled passage) with another recording. Sampling has become a very important tool in modern hip-hop and R&B music.

While sampling a "classic" hit can provide a unique twist to a beat, sampling also brings with it important and often difficult legal and economic issues. As a producer, you will probably want to use the most unique and distinct sample that you can find. Whether it be a song by the O'Jays, Aretha Franklin, Barry White, or even Kanye West's proverbial sample of Luther Vandross's "Still In Love," the cost for clearing these samples are often too high for many artists and producers to afford. In addition, many of the publishers of these sampled masters require that the artist give up a *substantial portion, if not all, of his or her publishing rights in the composition – arguing that the underlying composition being played for the public is really their sampled song.* As a result, this creates an often-troublesome problem for the producer. While he may have a great sounding beat, he may not be able to use it because he cannot afford to get the sample cleared.

CLEARANCE - WHO'S RESPONSIBILITY IS IT?

So who will be responsible for clearing samples that might comprise a recording? Well, in the scenario where a beat is leased, the artist will want to require the producer to have the responsibility of clearing the sample. The artist will argue that the production fees should cover the recording cost, and that the producer should be responsible for any cost in the production of the beat (including payment to any type of session musicians, union payments and any sample clearance fees).

As a producer, however, you will argue that the artist, or preferably the record label, should be responsible for clearing the sample.   If the record label really values the beat, the label should be willing to pay the fees in order to get the song cleared. The producer's point of view may carry more weight if the beat is considered to be a lead or a follow-up single to the record. This would cause the song to have a strong influence on marketing the artist's LP. However, the artist and producer should address the issue of sampling *as early as possible*.

OUTRIGHT SALE

In the scenario where a beat is sold outright, it is the artist's responsibility to get samples cleared, because the producer has signed over all of his or her rights in the beat. The artist might try to come back to the producer and argue that they paid for a beat that was "free and clear" of any further obligations. The parties' bargaining position will determine whether the producer can stand strong and avoid responsibility for the samples on the beat. To avoid any dispute, the producer should make it clear to the artist that he or she is responsible for clearing samples on a sold track, *before* the artist begins using it to shop for deals. This should be clearly stated within the agreement. After all, once the beat is sold, it isn't the producer's problem anymore.

CREDIT

Another important, yet often overlooked, provision that should be included within the producer agreement is providing for proper producer credit. This provision should be included whether leasing or selling the beat. Since a producer will lease or sell the track, not only for money, but also to get his or her name "out there" in the industry, a producer should always make sure that the artist agrees to give him proper producer credit on the LP. The producer credit is simply a statement that says, "Produced by Mr. Producer for Got More Beats Music," for example.

A producer credit is something that you definitely want to have incorporated within your agreement because as an artist and a song become more recognized, people will often look to see who the producer is. Since your reputation is a critical component of your success as a producer, you want to make sure that you are given proper producer credit for any tracks that you produce. Furthermore, the agreement should reflect that producer credits should be given to you on all advertisements that are larger than a half page, all billboards, all singles, etc.

Other Considerations
CATALOGING/TRACKING YOUR BEATS

A producer should *always* catalog and keep track of his or her beats. This practical point is oftentimes overlooked. Producers should catalogue and track their beats because producers who lease their beats to artists can: **(1)** forget that they leased the beat (and whom they leased the beat to); and/or **(2)** forget how long they promised the artist that they could use or lease the track for. This can become particularly cumbersome when a producer makes a CD containing 20 or more beats, and then gives that same CD to about three or four different artists. Chances are that two or more of those artists will want the same beat, or beats, for themselves. If a producer does not keep track of the beats that he promised a particular artist, the producer can run into a situation where a track might end up on three or four *different* artists' demos. It might seem like a trivial point, but if those artists get record deals, the producer will be in a tough position of determining which artist will be able to actually release that track on their album. That could be a very difficult position to be in as a producer – even though one might resort to the practice of giving the beat to the highest bidder. (Also see the section *"The Making Of Yeah!" How A Hit Song Almost Never Got Made")*

Even if a beat is sold to an artist, it is always good practice to catalog your beats so you'll know where your beats are being sold, to whom, and to which labels those artists are signed to. This is important in forming your discography and biography. Furthermore, it is important to have such information handy when it is time to issue mechanical licenses. All businesses should maintain accurate and detailed records and, again, your music is your business.

A simple cataloging system can entail **(1)** categorizing your beats by number or name, and **(2)** creating a track log. Make sure that you always give your beats either a reference name or number so they may be easily tracked. It might be difficult to name every track that you produce, that's why a numbering system might be a better convention. Any naming convention will do, for example, it could be as simple as naming your tracks starting from 0001, 0002, etc.

After naming your tracks, it is best to input those reference numbers into a track log. A simple track log can include the following: The beat reference number, the artist, the designation of whether the beat was either sold or leased, the date the track was provided to the artist, the label the artist is signed to, the writer's split for the song (e.g., 50%), and a column to provide any types of comments or notes. With modern technology, you can easily create a nice track log on an Excel spreadsheet or a tabled Word document. However you choose to catalog and track your beats, one thing that you definitely do not want to do is sell your beat twice.

BEAT NAME	BEAT REF NO.	ARTIST	SELL OR LEASE	DATE	WRITER SPLIT	LABEL	COMMENTS

PROTECT YOUR BEATS

Everyone has heard of (or should have heard of) the "poor-man's copyright" – you know, placing a copy of your music in a sealed envelope, and mailing it to yourself. While it may be a cost effective method of creating proof of the date by which your music was created, the "poor-man's copyright" is *not* an effective tool in securing your copyrights in your music.

Copyright literally means "the right to copy." The term "copyright," which refers to a group of legal rights held by authors of artistic works for the protection of their works, includes the exclusive right to reproduce, publish, sell copies of the copyrighted work, to make other versions of the work, and, with certain limitations, to make recordings of and to perform the work in public.

While copyright protection is granted to an author at the very moment the author's work is "fixed in any tangible medium of expression," one should formally register their music with the U.S. Copyright Office. In fact, before you can even sue someone for copyright infringement, which is a fancy term for "stealing your music," you must first register the work (beat/song) with the Copyright Office. To that end, you never know whose hands your beats may fall into, and while a poor-man's copyright can prove that you didn't steal a beat from someone, it cannot prove that someone stole your beat from you.

For example, imagine receiving a phone call one day from a friend who wants you to come by the studio later to help him "lace" a beat, and he says he'll give you a few bucks for your trouble. So you drop by the studio and, pretty much, produce the whole track. He gives you about $200 for "lookin' out," and you *never hear anything else about the beat*. Then one day, you hear the track on the radio, and you *freak!* There was no agreement, you received no production fee, you didn't copyright the beat, and most important, your *"boy"* gets credit for *your* production.

Imagine if one day some of your homies "come thru" the studio with someone looking for production. So you let them hear some of your tracks, and they dig 'em. You burn them a CD of some of your beats, and then you never hear from them again. Next, *without you knowing about it*, these folks turn around and *sell the beats* to another artist. After that, one day, to your surprise, you hear *your* beat on a single that has charted on Billboard. But you didn't think of copyrighting your music (registering it with the Copyright Office) *before* circulating it to some people you didn't know.

These may sound like rare and unfortunate scenarios, but, strangely enough, they really do happen. Most producers in these situations, while they are able to show proof of when they created *their* beat with a poor man's copyright, are discouraged from pursuing the costly litigation needed to prove their ownership of the beat that wound up on the radio. However, if a producer registers his or her beat with the Copyright Office, that registration provides the producer with a presumption of ownership of the music and, in addition, enables the producer to recover attorney's fees, and damages – which is the legal term for money – from people wrongfully using his or her music (without having to prove actual record sales). You can go to the U.S. Patent & Trademark Office website – www.uspto.gov – for information on how to register your beats with the Copyright Office. (The direct web address of the Copyright office is www.copyright.gov).

Also, if you are working on a beat with another producer, you should enter a co-writer agreement, stating both of your ownership interests in the beat (50/50, 60/40, etc.). You should then get the beat registered in *both* of your names as co-authors.

HIRE AN ATTORNEY

Despite all of this great information that we've attempted to give you in this segment, again, the best advice that we can give you is to hire a lawyer. No matter how much they think they know, producers writing their own contract runs the risk of overlooking an issue that might hurt them financially in the long run. An attorney can help a producer write an agreement that is clear and legally enforceable – preventing problems down the road.

We know what you are thinking – lawyers are expensive. This is true – relatively speaking. Lawyers' fees can range from $100 to $400 per hour, and sometimes as much as $700 per hour, depending on the experience and skills of the attorney (and his firm). But despite what you may think about them, attorneys are professionals who have gone to law school to prepare themselves to handle the complexities of written agreements such as these, and are usually worth the money spent. In fact, some attorneys might even handle matters on a contingency basis (they'll get paid on the back-end), especially for "working" producers. Such back-end payment percentages typically range from 5% to 7% of the deal. (Also see Entertainment Attorneys Chapter)

FINDING A *GOOD* ENTERTAINMENT ATTORNEY

❑ **First**: Talk to friends. Other producers in the industry use attorneys, especially established producers (most artists and producers use more than one attorney throughout their career), and they would be able to give you some insight on good attorneys.

❑ **Second**: You can look in the trade magazines. Oftentimes in the trade magazines, right next to an artist getting that six or seven-figure recording or publishing deal, will be his attorney. Granted, those attorneys might be on the more expensive side, but at least you will have a perspective and be able to identify potential lawyers once you have reached an established level.

❑ **Third**: Read your local industry journals. You will often times see articles written by entertainment attorneys. Specifically, in the case of articles, you can determine by reading an article whether that attorney can explain complex issues in a way that's easy for you to understand. This is often a good indication of a skilled attorney.

Regardless of which attorney you decide to use, make sure that your attorney has time to represent you. The "good" entertainment attorneys will often be booked solid with talent and work. If you are not a hot, and/or well-known producer or artist, you will typically be the last phone call that the attorney returns.

In the end, find an attorney that you *trust* and you *feel comfortable with* because he or she will have a hand in making the deals that will determine your success or failures in this industry.

SLANGIN' BEATS VIA THE WORLD WIDE WEB

Many "new" producers view the Internet as a new and promising way of marketing their productions skills and connecting with aspiring artists all over the world. However, there may be more cons than pros to shopping beats over the Internet. In this segment, we'll look at one "Internet producer's" approach to slangin' beats over the web, and talk about the pros and cons of this producer's approach.

LEASING RIGHTS

In one scenario, beats may be leased from a website, and the "Internet producer" allows one to use the beat for only one profitable commercial recording or broadcast purpose. The leased beat is essentially licensed to the customer on a non-exclusive basis. The Internet producer believes that this is a perfect solution for working on a low budget album.

In that regard, the leasing rights, or the license to the beat may be sold multiple times by the producer, and the beat remains on the website. Once and customer purchases the rights to use the beat, the producer sends the artist a CD in the mail. The CD contains the full beat in .wav format, and each track that comprises the beat, broken into separate individual .wav files. To document the deal, the producer sends the customer a signed contract granting a non-exclusive right, or license to use the beat.

Pros

This approach can be advantageous in that it gives the producer the ability to generate revenue by selling, and reselling beats over the Internet. In granting a non-exclusive right to use the beat, the producer can sell the beat to multiple artists at a flat rate. As a result, the more users who pay to lease the beat(s), the more income that is generated. Most importantly, the producer's beats won't be tied up to only *one* artist.

Cons

❑ **FIRST**: The biggest con to this scenario is that it is an administrative nightmare.   Under this approach, even though the agreement states that the artist can only use the beat for one profitable commercial recording or broadcast purpose, realistically, the producer won't be aware of most uses that exceed the rights awarded through their license.   In fact, the producer probably would not know that a customer is exceeding their license until a given track is a commercial success.   This is not necessarily bad *per se*, but just illustrates how impractical it is to "police" these licenses.

❑ **SECOND**: Sending "standard" contracts are not the best way to go in formulating producer-artist relationships.   In most instances, each agreement needs to be custom-drafted to fit the particular relationship and related circumstances.

❑ **THIRD**: By providing individually separated .wav files, the producer is simply providing its potential customers the means to sample the producer's production, chop it up, and reformulate it into another completely different beat.

EXCLUSIVE RIGHTS

Under another scenario, the "Internet producer" provides the customer with an exclusive right to use a beat for all profitable commercial or broadcasting purposes.   Once the exclusive rights are sold to the artist, the beat is no longer available on the website and will not be resold or transferred to another party. Once the customer purchases the exclusive rights to use the beat, the customer receives a CD in the mail.   The CD contains the full beat as an audio file, the full beat in .wav format, and the separate parts of the beat as individual .wav files.   In addition, the customer receives a signed contract granting them the exclusive right to use the beat.

Pros

Once again, providing beats over the Internet will enable the producer to sell beats to a wide variety of artist.

Cons

❑ **FIRST:** In this scenario, the producer grants the exclusive right to use a beat to an artist that he or she does not know.   Therefore, a "good" beat may get tied up by an artist that has no commercial potential.   This could potentially stop the producer from selling the same beat to an established artist, or an artist with some commercial potential.

❑ **SECOND**: This arrangement is again, an administrative nightmare. The producer will have to send contracts to potentially dozens of customers, and have to negotiate each contract individually. This arrangement requires very accurate and detailed cataloging and tracking of the "sold" beats, so the producer will know where beats are being licensed for publishing purposes.

❑ **THIRD**: The producer won't know whether the artist is working with a recording budget, and could potentially provide exclusive rights to a beat without negotiating a "suitable" advance or producer fee. The bottom line is that you could potentially shortchange yourself because you won't have an opportunity to assess the commercial potential of the artist and their project.

CUSTOM BEATS

In another scenario, the "Internet producer" makes a beat to the customer's specifications. The producer contacts the customer to discuss exactly how they want the beat to be custom tailored, and e-mail the customer an mp3 file sample of the beat as it is made. Once the customer has reviewed the sample, the customer may request changes, omissions, or additions to the beat. The producer will then edit the beat per the artist's request. Thus, the customer gets what they want and are not required to pay for the beat until they have heard the final version and agreed on it.

The end result is a beat that is made specifically for the customer, and the beat will not be shared with anyone until the customer releases the song himself or herself. Under this scenario, prices for the beats will vary and the producer can offer "package" deals.

Pros

Again, this scenario provides the producer greater exposure to sell beats, and will potentially enable the producer to work "personally" with artists all over the country (and the world). This may be fruitful in sharpening a producer's skills and tailoring them to different types of artists. The producer can also get an idea from the geographic demographics of customers to determine what types of beats or music are popular in certain regions of the country (e.g. *Go-Go* music in D.C., or *Crunk* music in the South). This is important when shopping beats to well known artists in certain areas because the producer will have insight into the types of beats and music that are popular in those particular areas. In addition, the producer can customize its deal packages according to the level of detail or the requested complexity of the beats.

Cons

This scenario has several disadvantages.

❑ **FIRST:** It is very difficult to customize a beat for an artist that you have little to no personal contact with. Most producers will agree that spending time "vibin'" with an artist is very important to the synergy of the artist-producer relationship.

❑ **SECOND:** This scenario can potentially be very time consuming for a producer, as the producer may be required to continually make additions, or continually tweak tracks for an artist. In many cases, the artist will be located in a different state or geographic region than the producer. The continuous back and forth of sending CD's or e-mailing .wav files can become inefficient. The "digital age" enables us to deliver .wav files fairly easily via email, and this type of creation process might not seem so bad for working with one artist. But multiply this process by tens or hundreds of clients, and a producer will see that they'll be spending most of their time tweaking tracks, rather than producing tracks.

❑ **THIRD:** This scenario is again, an administrative nightmare. The producer will have to send contracts to potentially dozens of customers, and have to negotiate each contract individually. And, similar to the foregoing arrangement, the producer will need to keep accurate and detailed records of these "custom made" beats for publishing purposes.

❑ **FOURTH:** The producer will not know whether the artist has some money behind their project or not. Here, a producer could spend a lot of time and effort customizing a beat without being knowledgeable as to the leverage the producer has in negotiating a "suitable" advance or fee. Similar to the foregoing scenario, you could potentially shortchange yourself because you won't have an opportunity to assess the commercial potential of the artist and their project.

PURCHASING BEATS

In the final scenario, a customer is not only able to purchase a beat from the website, but the "Internet producer" also transfers all of his or her copyrights and interests in the beat to the customer. Once the customer has decided on which beat it wants, the customer and producer will then negotiate a price and payment terms. After the producer receives payment, per their agreement, the producer will then deliver the beat to the customer as a full-length audio file for stereo use, and a full length .wav file, with separated tracks. To document the sale, the producer will provide a contract transferring all of the producer's rights and interest in the beat to the customer.

Pros

This scenario has some advantages.

❏ **FIRST:** The producer can make some quick cash and is provided with a means to market his production talents and sell beats to artists all over the country. The producer's beats may appeal to a wide variety of artists, and the producer may be able to sell a beat that the producer wasn't particularly "married to."

❏ **SECOND:** This arrangement is, administratively, fairly simple. In this instance, the producer only need to keep track of the "sold" beats, and may use a "standard" contract, changing only the name and contact information of the artist and the price of the beat.

Cons

Of course, this scenario has its disadvantages.

❏ **FIRST:** You could, again, potentially shortchange yourself because you won't have an opportunity to assess the true impact of the transaction – remember, potential publishing income should be considered when negotiating a purchase price.

The overriding disadvantage to this type of "sale" is that the producer will be giving up his copyright interest in the beat. We do not favor such forfeiture.

SUMMARY

Whether you are a seasoned veteran, or an up-and-coming producer, you should keep the foregoing points in mind when slangin' your beats. We wish you all the best in your pursuit of fame and fortune, and remember us when you get your first platinum plaque.

GOOD LUCK!

WE HAVE PROVIDED THE FOLLOWING TABLE AS A QUICK REFERENCE OF POINTS TO CONSIDER WHEN DECIDING HOW TO "SELL" OR "LEASE" YOUR BEATS:

Deal Point:	LEASE ("On Spec")	QUASI-SALE	SALE (Outright)
Rights Retained:	Copyright interest in beat	Copyright interest in beat	None
Term:	12 to 18 months	5 years	Forever
Producer Fee:	To be negotiated	To be negotiated	Included in purchase price
Advance:	To be negotiated	To be negotiated	Included in purchase price
Producer Royalty:	2% to 3%	None	None
Ownership of Master:	Producer and/or Artist	Artist	Artist
Publishing:	Producer retains	Producer retains	Artist acquires
Sample Clearance:	Producer or Artist	Producer or Artist	Artist
Credits:	Producer should be given credit	Producer should be given credit	Artist may or may not give credit

The comments expressed in this segment reflect the views of the writers and should not be regarded as legal advice.

Raaqim Knight, Esq. *is an associate at Manatt, Phelps & Phillips LLP in Los Angeles, and specializes in Entertainment and Corporate litigation*
Contact: 310-312-4323 *- rknight@manatt.com - www.manatt.com*

Uleses Henderson, Jr., Esq. *is an associate at Foley & Lardner LLP in Los Angeles, and specializes in Entertainment, Trademarks, Copyrights, Patents, and Intellectual Property litigation.*
Contact: 310-975-7961 *- uhenderson@foley.com - www.foley.com*

$10,000 SINGLE-SONG

EXAMPLE PRODUCTION BUDGET

- ARTIST: *THE REGIONAL "BUZZ" ARTIST*
- COMPANY / CONTACT: **THE REGIONAL RECORD LABEL / MR. A&R CONTACT**
- PRODUCER: **BIG-PRODUCER-MAYNE FOR KRUNKEST PRODUCTIONS, LLC**
- DATES: **FEBRUARY 26**
- STUDIOS: **MY-HOUSE LAB**
- MIXING: **DA-LOCAL-TOP-DOGG**

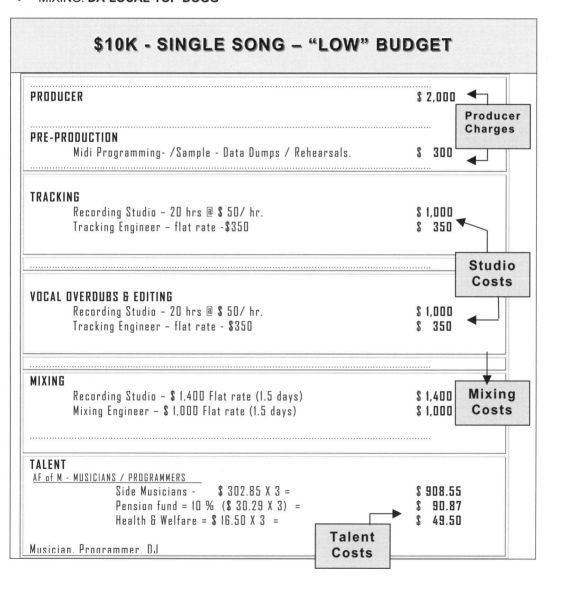

$10K - SINGLE SONG – "LOW" BUDGET

PRODUCER — $ 2,000

Producer Charges

PRE-PRODUCTION
Midi Programming- /Sample - Data Dumps / Rehearsals. — $ 300

TRACKING
Recording Studio – 20 hrs @ $ 50/ hr. — $ 1,000
Tracking Engineer – flat rate -$350 — $ 350

Studio Costs

VOCAL OVERDUBS & EDITING
Recording Studio – 20 hrs @ $ 50/ hr. — $ 1,000
Tracking Engineer – flat rate - $350 — $ 350

MIXING
Recording Studio – $ 1,400 Flat rate (1.5 days) — $ 1,400
Mixing Engineer – $ 1,000 Flat rate (1.5 days) — $ 1,000

Mixing Costs

TALENT
AF of M - MUSICIANS / PROGRAMMERS
Side Musicians - $ 302.85 X 3 = — $ 908.55
Pension fund = 10 % ($ 30.29 X 3) = — $ 90.87
Health & Welfare = $ 16.50 X 3 = — $ 49.50

Talent Costs

Musician. Programmer. DJ

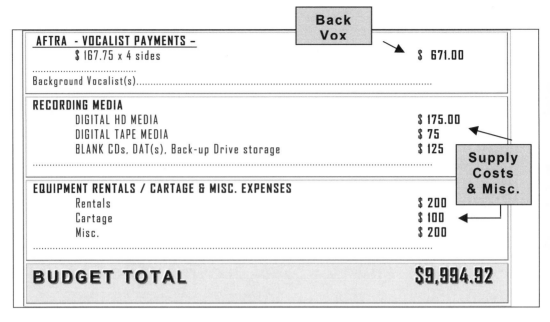

AFTRA - VOCALIST PAYMENTS -		
$ 167.75 x 4 sides		$ 671.00
Background Vocalist(s)..		

RECORDING MEDIA	
DIGITAL HD MEDIA	$ 175.00
DIGITAL TAPE MEDIA	$ 75
BLANK CDs, DAT(s), Back-up Drive storage	$ 125

Back Vox

Supply Costs & Misc.

EQUIPMENT RENTALS / CARTAGE & MISC. EXPENSES	
Rentals	$ 200
Cartage	$ 100
Misc.	$ 200

BUDGET TOTAL	**$9,994.92**

⇒ *Because of the low total, the sample budget above does not include any Mastering or Sample Clearance cost.*

Note: The above Production budget is *only a sample*. Every budget will most likely be different, so please consult your manager, attorney or music business advisor to structure your production budget so that it will reflect the particular needs for the particular project you are submitting to

GOOD LUCK!

**FOR MORE TEMPLATES AND SAMPLES OF BUDGETS, FORMS, ETC,
PLEASE VISIT US ONLINE AT**

MUSICPOWERS.COM/24

THE ARTIST 'ALL-IN' DEAL
"PAYING THE PRODUCER RECORD ONE ROYALTIES"

Most recently (Spring 2005), I've notice different postings on various websites, and also in print media with articles about Producer's Record One Royalties. And personally, I think these articles are great... me being a Producer. But, after sending a few of my clients and friends to go and learn a little more, everyone still seemed to be a bit confused. So I decided to write this segment of Music Powers, in hopes of it being a *small* bridge that might make clear, the fundamentals of artists "All-In" deals, as it relates and *affects* a producer's royalty payment(s), especially regarding the *waiting...* for the Producer's "Record One Royalties"

INTRODUCTION

O nce upon a time, back in the day, record companies on the whole handled most producer contracts. But finally, somebody at the label decided that the record company was spending way too much money (and time) negotiating their producer contracts for their artists. So currently, in this present day and time, the tendency at many of the labels, has been to make their artist deal with this accountability through what is commonly called an "all-in" deal.

"All-in" is short for all-inclusive. This means that the artist will have to pay the producer his royalties due, *from his or her own artist's royalties*. It works like this: The label will advance the producer money; pay the producer his royalties, but all by taking it out of the artist's royalties. And eventually, the producer will have to be paid *whatever* royalties is due, starting from "record one."

RECORD ONE?

"Record one" royalties are the way most producers get paid royalties. "Record one," means just what it sounds like; Producers get paid from the *first record* sold. And just so you know, there are different types of Record one royalties. The concern is not so much the idea of paying the producer from the first record sold, that's actually normal. The real issue to be concerned with is the "*when,* or at *what point*" do producers get paid their record one royalties. And the calculation to determine this *when* is many times based around the level of the producer that is hired. The level of the producer will have an influence over the way many labels approach the repayment (recoupment) in the artist's "all-in" deal.

LEVEL 1:
NEW TO AVERAGE LEVEL PRODUCERS
"He collects dough, when the artist's *net* royalty rate gets to "GO"

Most producers will start receiving royalties ONLY after the record company has recovered all artist expenses. But for the average producer the calculation of the "when do Producers get royalties" or what I call the "GO" point for paying the producer his royalties, is based on the artist "all-in" royalty rate percentage (%), *minus (-)* the producer's royalty rate percentage (%) or the net rate. In other words, as the record sells with new and average level producers, the record label will credit the recovery (recoupment) of expenses by using the net rate (Artist % *minus* Producer % = NET %). The label will NOT use the gross percentage rate (the complete Artist royalty %). The "GO" point here is: Once all the expenses are out of the red for the artist, using the *net* percentage rate, the label will then go back and pay the producer his royalty percentage from the very first record that was sold...minus of course, whatever advances the producer got up front. But because the royalty rate is not based on the artist total (gross) royalty rate, it will take a l o n g e r period of time for the producer to receive any royalty money... if ever!

For example:

Let's look at a *very imaginary* g r o s s all-in artist royalty rate of 8%. And let's say the producer's royalty is 3%, leaving the artist with 5% as the *net* percentage rate. The record company will recoup (recover) the cost of the expenses on the project based on the 5% *net* rate, instead of the *gross* 8% rate. This means it will take *longer* for the project to get out of debt. Why? Because the payback steps are smaller, so it simply takes a whole lot longer to actually get to the "GO" point (royalty payday), and getting the producer any royalty money he's due. And of course, the label is completely aware of this; *it was their clever idea to begin with.*

Once the project *is* out of the red, the label will ultimately go back and pay the producer his 3% from the 1st record sold, minus whatever advance money the producer originally got paid up front.

STILL CONFUSED...? VISUALIZE THIS:

We've all played the game *Monopoly®*. And we all love to pass "GO" and collect money. Now lets say that the dice are "loaded," and they come up 5 + 3, or a total of 8 every time...(the artist *gross* rate). Lets also say that every roll of the dice will represent the artist paying back his expenses to the record label. So, to get to the "GO" point, it would take *5 rolls of the dice* (5x8), and then the "GO" point (payday) would be reached (getting around the board). Once the "GO" point is reached, the producer can start to get royalties... payday baby...YEAH!!! *BUT* (uh-oh), since a level 1 producer is being used, and possibly on top of that, the artist is also a new or not a superstar, the label has only agreed to the recoupment (recovery) of the artist expenses to be paid back by using ONLY ONE DICE, *fixed on the number 5* (the net rate).   Now, it will take *8 rolls of the dice* to pay back expenses. So it will take a longer period of time before the "GO" point (payday) is reached. By the way, if you really want to visualize this, your imaginary game piece is *The Snail.*

It's like this: Instead of the record company permitting the artist to roll both dice (5+3), the agreement is set up so that the label controls how many dice our artist *The Snail* can use to get around the Monopoly board. In other words, the artist (in this scenario) only gets to use one dice, fixed on the number 5 (the net royalty rate). This means it will take longer to get to the "GO" point. This is because the record company has Mr. Snail's recoupment account paying the label back for expenditures at the smaller re-payment of one (1) dice or 5%...(the net rate), as opposed to the larger payment of TWO (2) Dice or 8%...(the gross rate). So it not only becomes harder to repay expense money for the artist, but it also takes l o n g e r to collect royalties for Level 1 – New to Average Producer.

LEVEL 2:
THE HOT – EXPERIENCED PRODUCER

"TWO DICE ARE BETTER THAN ONE"

OK, now that you know what "record one" means, and how Level 1 Producer royalties are calculated, let's look at Level 2 – Hot - Experienced Producers.

Level 2 - HOT Producers are the guys that have proven themselves, not only from great work in the past, but these guys are usually having current success too. With all of this said, now the artist gets to use both dice (5 + 3) to roll around the Monopoly board. For the artist, this means "Hot Producers" will no doubt want a bigger ($) advance, but, still may not get the artist and/or label to agree to *any* higher points or percentage (%) towards the producers royalties (3%). The one thing that does normally change with Hot Producers is a different way "record one" royalties and recoupment issues are negotiated. The label is usually willing to change the way expense payback or recoupment is calculated for the artist "all-in" deal. In this scenario, recoupment is at a "combined rate" of 5% +

3%, or the *gross* royalty rate of 8%. This means that the producer will get to the "Go" point much sooner than when recoupment was only at 5% (the net rate) because the combined royalty rate is being used. The artist game piece would now transform into *Mr. Turtle*...still slow, but faster than *The Snail*.

IMPORTANT: I guess now I should clarify that *I know* of NO artist that actually gets to actually *collect the FULL unaffected* gross royalty. Most majors labels will apply a deduction for packaging, which is about 25%, and a "CD reduction cost" (?) of about 10%. I am only using the terms net and gross, to make it easier for you to recognize the different calculating factors used in determining the producer's "Record-One" royalties." Plus, if the artist *is only* getting 8% (or points) as their "all-in" artist's royalty rate…

…Oh well ?

LEVEL 3:
THE SIX-FIGURE "SUPER-PRODUCER"

Columbus, GA, to Virginia Beach
Dre, Kanye, and Tuff Jew Beatz
Pha and Pharrell …and So So too
Producing hits, that's "…Whaaat!" they do!

Ok crew, there's really not a whole lot to say here, except that these are the Super-Producers of today's Hip Hop, Rap and R&B/Pop music scene. These are the "hit-makers" of modern-day urban music …and maybe beyond. As far as the dice illustration in the previous section…well, the dice may or *may not* apply to the deals these producers are sometimes able to get. There have been times when a producer of this status has been able to get their "Record-One" royalties *without* the repayment of *anything* other than their original advance, which I might add, might be as large as some new artist's *complete* recording budget. I'll never kiss and tell, but let's just say that "Kirk" and "Spock" are livin' very *large and in charge!*

Here's the deal: When an artist has his or her "all-in" budget, and then has decided to use a producer of this stature, the producer may not beat-down the artist's budget with a "wounding" up-front dollar advance (...I think the first African Slaves heard this too), but the artist should know, if the producer is *not* charging "crazy-big" up-front, then in most cases, a Super-Producer *will* seek to get paid from the very 1st record sold, *without* recoupment concerns for anything other than the original advance (if he took one) that he got up front. And the producer may challenge that the front money he got was for production *fees* (labor and time making the production), as opposed to "advances" against future royalties. And yes, this kind of deal is extremely hard to come by, but it does exist for Producers who have consistently sold millions and millions of records, along with staying at the top of the Billboard charts, and also the way the producer has marketed "himself" to the public. So the Super-Producer and his popularity and image *also* become great selling points to market a release. (For reference: Jermaine Dupri, Lil Jon, and P. Diddy, among others).

For the most part, I believe an artist would have in his own best interest to actually pay a bigger advance, and deal with the recoupment issues like the Level 1 or 2 calculations. This way, the artist might avoid having to pay a Super-Producer his record-one royalty due, from outside sources of income like performance and touring money.   This can happen if the Level 3 (Super-Producer) is getting an extremely high percentage or points. In high-percentage cases, the producer might get paid royalties before the artist has actually recovered all the expenses from the project. And the artist would be accountable. And not to sound repetitive, but you can bet that the Level 3; Super-Producer, will want, and normally get more than a 2 or 3% royalty rate; more like 4 or 5%, and with bigger escalations; like 1 point (%) or higher at Gold (500,000 units sold), and then an additional ½ to 1% at Platinum (1,000,000 units sold). So is it worth it? Well, sometimes yes, and then sometimes absolutely not. There are some very good arguments out there that make sense, both good and bad, especially when it concerns a new artist's budget and his recoupment. But, if the artist is prepared to tour and perform, many cases, the "new" or established artist might not see too much money from record royalties, but the artist might make many millions of dollars from touring off of a few "mega-hits" that one of these Level 3, Super-Producers has made for them. And let's not forget about the songwriting & publishing royalties that an artist will many times make from collaborating with the Super-Producer. So I guess it really depends on the particular artist, and of course the ability & willingness of the record label to *exploit and promote* the given situation of using the Level 3 - "Six-figure Super-Producer" on their album project.

Note: All of these examples of paying the Producer are basically based around an artist "all-in" budget. There will be many cases in which the Producer himself has his own "all-in" budget, to produce one or multiple "cuts" for the artist that still fall under the umbrella of the Artist all-budget. If that is the case (which is actually normal these days), All producer "all-in" budgets will have to deal with recoupment issues on some level or another… whether as an advance or as a production *fee*, or both. Oh, and by the way, there *are* some Super-Producers getting well over $125,000 per song for an "all-in" production payment to produce artists. And recently, I was told that one of the more popular, Level 3 Super-Producer teams *are* getting an impressive $300,000 per song as their "all-in" production fee… whoa, now that's a production team definitely on the right "trek"… ☺!

GOOD LUCK!

❏   *For more research on Producer's "Record One" royalties and Artist "All-In" Deals, I highly suggest the books: All You Need To Know About The Music Business and This Business Of Music.*

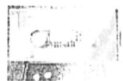

Music Powers
LOST IN TRANSLATION
"POINTS TO $ENSE"

Converting Points (%) to dollar amounts for Artists & Producers

In the following example, let's assume that…

The **Artist** is getting	15 points (15 %)
The **Producer** is getting	3 points (3 %)

Ok - Here is the Breakdown:

Most major labels base these points or percentages (%) on the "Suggested Retail List Price" or 'SRLP" of current CDs - $18.99. Now, from first glance it *appears* as if the artist will collect a cool 15-point royalty…this translates to around $2.85 per CD.

The SRLP ($18.99) multiplied by the gross artist royalty (15%) = $2.85

The formula would read like this:

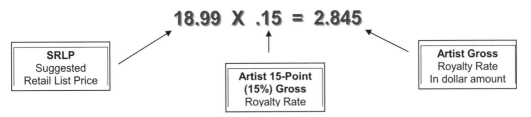

BUT HOLD UP! – We must first subtract the 3-point (3%) royalty for the producer's points, which equals around $ .57, leaving the artist with 12 points (12%), which translates to $2.28 per CD.

The SRLP ($18.99), multiplied by gross artist's points (15%), minus the producer's points (3%) = the artist's net royalty points (12%)
…Which breaks down to $2.28 per CD for the artist

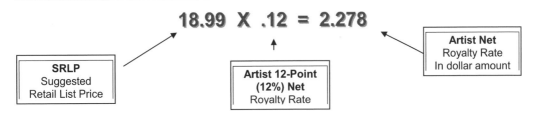

THE PRODUCER'S POINTS BREAKDOWN:

> **The SRLP ($18.99), multiplied by 3% (producer's points) = 57 cents**

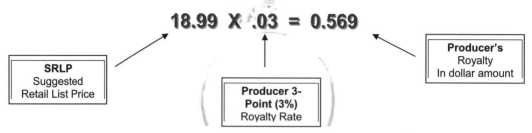

The formula would read like this:

$$18.99 \times .03 = 0.569$$

SRLP Suggested Retail List Price	**Producer 3-Point (3%)** Royalty Rate	**Producer's** Royalty In dollar amount

□ IMPORTANT NOTE:

If you are a Producer, this DOES NOT mean that you as the producer will get the complete 57 cents, *unless* you produced every song on the CD. To calculate the producer's *actual* amount due per song, you must divide the 57 cents by the number of songs *on the CD*. That is the amount the producer would actually get per song.

For example:
Let's say a Producer produces *one song* on a CD-Album project that contained **15 songs**. To calculate the producer's royalties, the formula would work like this:

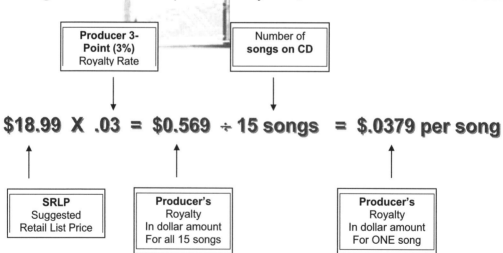

Producer 3-Point (3%) Royalty Rate	**Number of songs on CD**

$$\$18.99 \times .03 = \$0.569 \div 15 \text{ songs} = \$.0379 \text{ per song}$$

SRLP Suggested Retail List Price	**Producer's** Royalty In dollar amount For all 15 songs	**Producer's** Royalty In dollar amount For ONE song

- *Ok – now that we've got the Producer's Breakdown clear let's continue*

For the Artist – now there's now going to be a deduction for packaging: 25%. So take off *another* $0 .57 for that. Now the artist is getting $1.71 per CD.

> **The SRLP ($18.99), multiplied by net artist's points (12%), minus 25%**
> **= 1.709**

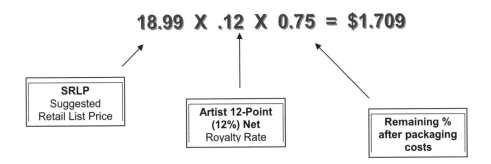

The formula would read like this:

$$18.99 \times .12 \times 0.75 = \$1.709$$

| SRLP Suggested Retail List Price | Artist 12-Point (12%) Net Royalty Rate | Remaining % after packaging costs |

And now last, there's this 'new' technology of having your music on a CD… "What's that about?" ☹...*Hmm, it's about 10 more percent Mr. Baller... ouch!!!* Now, the artist will get $ 1.54 a CD. Meaning, the artist started out getting $2.85 per CD, but ended up getting just a little more than $1.50 per CD… *for our 15-point royalty artist.*

> **The SRLP ($18.99), multiplied by net artist points (12%), minus 25% for**
> **packaging, minus another 10% for being on CD = 1.538**

The formula would read like this:

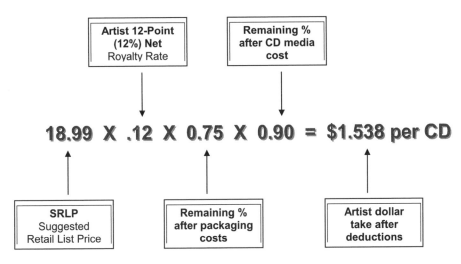

| Artist 12-Point (12%) Net Royalty Rate | Remaining % after CD media cost |

$$18.99 \times .12 \times 0.75 \times 0.90 = \$1.538 \text{ per CD}$$

| SRLP Suggested Retail List Price | Remaining % after packaging costs | Artist dollar take after deductions |

This breaks down to meaning that 1 point or 1 percent… after all is "said, and 'over-done" would be equal to about $ 0.10 (ten cents) for several artists. And if you factor in a few other shocking things, like a 15% allowance for returns and *whatever*, it gets even further downhill, to 1 point being equal to around 8 cents for the recording artist, or a 15-point royalty artist getting around $1.20 to $130 a CD.

This information is primarily being given so that artists & producers recognize what to expect when the music industry, particularly labels and production companies want to talk and negotiate the terms of royalty disbursement in points instead of dollar amounts.

Also, if you're still in school, and you want to *count* your money, ...then don't skip your math class!

GOOD LUCK!

Music Powers
RECORD DEALS
Basics of an artist's recording deal

First of all, to tell you any *specific* 'how-to technique' that would promise you a recording contract would be telling you a lie... it can't be done, unless of course the deal is with your own label. In truth, there is no exact way to get a deal...period. But, if you've been paying attention and read the earlier sections of advice in this book, then you should be well aware of what it will probably take for you to attract a major label or production company to get them interested in signing you.

We've suggested that you create a "buzz", get a team, make a plan, and keep a positive mindset and attitude all with the hopeful surroundings of positive energy and people. We have also stressed getting good production help and developing your skills. As already mentioned, being ready means having your act tight *before* showcasing what you have to offer; giving yourself the best chance to capitalize on whatever opportunity that is eventually presented. **But also know this:** Getting a deal can happen by just being in the *right place at the right time*, or through a favored relationship, or just being very lucky. But primarily, outside of all of the "buzz" and hype you create, and whatever "noise" you can make on your own; selling a few records on your own, having a great live show, and getting a little radio support, it basically is going to boil down to you having some hot music. And it's usually better if you have an identifiable unique sound that the people like... and A&R believes in enough to possibly risk giving you a shot. And if you have more to offer, like a network of *reachable* DJs, MDs at radio, a great street team, and some great promotions that have you known throughout the region (or beyond), then that's even better.

To get label execs excited and hyped about you, your song(s) really need to speak for themselves... along with the right image that works for whatever "sound" you have. And most times, you'll still need someone on your team with some hustle in him or her to sell you. This is why the book starts out with you being told that you should find management, and/or an attorney first... or *someone* as a spokesman/salesman to help make your music career move to that next level. All of this is to put you in a position that will give you the best chance of obtaining your recording contract objective.

TODAY'S REALITY

Now in reality, today more than ever, the Hip-Hop and Rap music game is (over) saturated with new acts popping up everywhere, and all over the country trying to get a record deal. So, just know that it is very, very competitive, so you *will* need to have some real "fire" and potent music that people like, so that you stand out from the rest of the crowd. So let's repeat this once again crew; I highly suggest that you have some very tight music… maybe even a regional hit, a "buzz" in the streets" an image that works with your sound or vibe, decent representation, some luck, and also good timing. Know that timing is very, very important. There are times when you may actually be ready, but the label or A&R interested needs to wait until the next quarter's budget to sign you. Or, the A&R guy at the label is possibly in a position to sign you, but he just has too much on his plate at the time he checks out your project.

CASH WON'T ALWAYS GET YOU "ON"

There are countless stories about people who *had* money, who went broke *trying* to make an artist's project take off. Now, to some degree money can buy you "in" …in a sense. But I'm here to tell you, sometimes money is spent all over the place by these indie labels and independent artists… money that is sometimes bankrolled by all kinds of ill-gotten cash, or even legit money… and I've seen guys lose their butts, and then some.

Note: There are a few side-door or back-door ways to get a production company or label's attention… sometimes other than pushing the 'artist thing'; like pushing yourself as a songwriter, background vocalist, or the producer thing first, and then *moving* into the whole artist thing later. For reference, research the early careers of Babyface, Pharrell (Neptunes), Kanye West, Timbaland, Ashanti, Debra Killings, and others. **IMPORTANT:** In today's urban music industry, it will be of tremendous significance to most labels, for you to also be a "solid" songwriter. This will definitely raise your appeal to prospective record labels.

Now, getting back to the business of record deals, as the book description says, I can certainly point out some of the things you must be aware of to at least increase your knowledge on some of the issues to be concerned with when you are looking for, or finally get that big record deal offer.

WHAT IS A RECORD DEAL?

A record deal is a written agreement between a record company and an artist that states that the company will distribute and market the performances of the artist's music project. The artist will deliver his exclusive services as a performer to make sound recordings for the record company. The record company will then sell (or lease) these performances for hopeful profit, over a specific amount of albums and/or time. The record company usually puts up the cost in making, promoting, and manufacturing the artist's project, but only as a *loan* against whatever future royalties the artists will be entitled to. The money that the label spends in the artist's behalf will be recouped (recovered) from the sales of each

CD that is sold. The artist will then be entitled to (according to what's agreed upon in the contract) payments from the sales of these recordings, once all expenses from the cost of making the project is out of the red or clear. And it's best you know now, out of the red …and/or clear means, 100% recovery, and many times, *more than 100%* …if the record company is given the right to hold money towards the next or *future* recording projects.

Now that you know fundamentally what a record deal is, you also need to be aware that there are different types of deals, with different situations. So whatever you do, as I have said over, and over… many times, do it with the help of an entertainment attorney and personal manager when negotiating any of the following areas regarding a record deal.

ADVANCES
By Ben McLane, Esq.

An advance is a payment made ahead of royalty payments, to be earned in the future. Advances are recouped by offsetting your future royalties against the money that's been given and/or allocated to you.

Upon being offered a record deal, most artists are very interested in the amount of money they will be paid to record the album. The money, which a label pays to an artist to sign and record an album, is called an "advance." However, as this section will point out, an advance is similar to a loan and thus it has to be paid back, or recouped, from the artist's royalties. In other words, the advance has to be paid back in full before the artist sees any money.

There are essentially two kinds of advances. First, there is what is known as a signing advance. A signing advance is a sum of money paid to an artist to induce the artist to sign the deal. Generally, this money will be used by the artist to live on while the he is making and promoting the record. The other type of advance, which is more widely used today, is called the "recording fund". A recording fund is a set amount of money, which is utilized to record the album. Whatever the artist does not spend on recording costs, the artist gets to keep. The label normally prefers to offer a recording fund because it is tied to a recording budget, which the label has pre-approved. As a result, this tends to keep the artist from recording a terrible album in order to pocket the majority of the money.

The amount of the advance is based upon a number of factors. These factors include, but are not limited to, the style of music the artist creates, how badly the label wants the artist, whether the artist has had any success in the past, the projected sales of the album, and how strong the negotiators are for both sides.

In reality, it is more than possible for an artist to never even see a royalty. Remember, the advance is paid back from royalties. For example, if the artist got a $100,000.00 advance but only earned $60,000.00 in royalties, the artist is still unrecouped by $40,000.00 and would not see a dime until the label was paid back in full. Also, even if the artist may have sold enough records to be fully recouped, by the time the label has made an official accounting of the sales in order to pay a royalty, it will already be time for the artist to go back to the studio and borrow another budget from the label. For this reason, there would not be a royalty until the artist has paid back *both* advances. The key is to use the advance monies effectively and economically. Depending on the circumstances, it may be best to negotiate a smaller advance and a higher royalty rate. Furthermore, it might be smart to negotiate a smaller advance and have the label increase the amount of money used to promote the record. Finally, since advances are recoupable only from royalties, even if the record flops and the label drops the artist, the artist does not owe the label personally.

ROYALTIE$

Royalties are monies that are payable to a recording artist, producer, songwriter or publisher from the sale of phonorecords or CDs - after deducting expenses. In the article below, we will address royalties, as it applies to the recording artist contract.

HOW CAN A LABEL TURN YOUR 16% ROYALTY INTO A 6% ROYALTY?
Returns, reserves, and other standard deductions

WHAT THE RECORD COMPANY *SAYS* vs **WHAT THE RECORD COMPANY *MEANS***
(BASED ON A CD THAT HAS A VALUE OF $10)

...Definition of "Net Sales":

THE RECORD COMPANY SAYS:
"...Eighty five percent (85%) of gross sales, less returns, credits, and reserves against anticipated returns and credits."

➤ **THE RECORD COMPANY MEANS:**
This clause indicates that the label is going to reduce your royalty based on records that might get returned because you only get paid on royalty bearing units.

- As an example, let's think about a CD that has a value of $10. The "net sales" definition means you're only going to get paid on 85 of every 100 units shipped.

THE RECORD COMPANY SAYS:
2. Container Charge:
"...The applicable percentage, specified below of the Gross Royalty Base applicable to the Records concerned: ...Compact discs, New Technology Configurations...25%"

> **➤ THE RECORD COMPANY MEANS:**
> **2.** This clause indicates that $2.50 cents comes off that $10 before you apply the royalty percentage.

THE RECORD COMPANY SAYS:
3. In the royalty paragraphs:
"... Not withstanding anything to the contrary herein, the royalty rate for any Record in the audio only compact disc configuration shall be eighty percent (80%) of the otherwise applicable royalty rate set forth in this agreement." (New Tech is 75%)

> **➤ THE RECORD COMPANY MEANS:**
> **3.** This clause means that your royalty percentage (the one you apply to the dollar figure after figuring in the 85% rule and the 25% container charge) is further reduced by 20%. Have I mentioned the absurdity of a container charge for "New Tech" In other words, digital distribution where there are no manufacturing costs? (And don't forget that the reduction there is 25%, not 20% as with CDs).

THE RECORD COMPANY SAYS
4. From the same royalty section above:
"... No royalties shall be payable to you in respect of Records sold or distributed.... as "free", "no charge", or "bonus" Records (whether or not intended for resale; whether billed or invoiced as a discount in the price to [Record Label's] customers or as a Record shipped at no charge)."
This paragraph will contain a host of other carve-outs for such things as promos, etc.

> **➤ THE RECORD COMPANY MEANS:**
> **4.** This clause means that if you don't negotiate to have a cap or ceiling on the free & promotional goods the record company will give away ... you're going to be in trouble.

It is important to remember that artists' contract royalty rate is *not* statutory, transparent, nor is it public. Traditional contract royalties begin at a much smaller "11 to 13 percent" (not 16), and allow for that royalty amount to be further diminished through a process of *unfair* deductions that are standardized within the industry.

To understand this royalty reduction, multiply an 11 percent royalty rate by 85 percent for a "free goods" deduction. Then multiply it by 75 percent for a packaging deduction. Then multiply it again by 75 percent for a "new media" deduction. After this process of deduction, an 11 percent royalty is effectively reduced to less than 6 percent.

So take care of your advance money…
It may be all you'll see for awhile!

• *In publishing this document we are not attempting to say that these clauses are illegal, nor are we suggesting that artists who sign these contracts do so without excellent representation.*

Used by permission of Future of Music Coalition, Inc.
©Future of Music Coalition, Inc. - All rights reserved.
www.futureofmusic.org

ARTIST ROYALTY RATE REFERENCE

Please use the following rates as only a reference of what record labels pay to the recording artist. These numbers are not law... but they are a good reflection of what the industry trends have been. Artist royalty rates will be based on either the Suggested Retail List Price (SRLP) or the Wholesale Price of their CD. The numbers below are referenced to the SRLP. If your contract is based on the Wholesale Price, you can multiply these numbers by two (2)... i.e., just double everything.

ARTIST / LEVEL	% - POINTS (SRLP)
"NEW" - (level 1)	9 % - 13%
"ESTABLISHED" – (level 2)	14% - 17%
❑ "SUPERSTARS" - (level 3)	18% - 20%

❑   *any times, artist of this magnitude are only signed to the label as a trophy and marketing statement to attract and/or influence other opportunities. The label may actually profit less money than usual... but the company becomes more   "visible."   (Research Janet Jackson, Michael Jackson, Whitney Houston & Master P.)*

HOW MUCH MONEY CAN I EXPECT?

If you are a new artist signing to a major record label you can expect to get anywhere from $35,000 to $100,000 (or more) as a signing advance. When I was in LA, working with a few labels, we normally told new artists that they could expect to have an advance that was probably equal to 10% (or a little more), of whatever their over-all budget would be. Of course this really depends on too many things to get into any specific details, and every single deal is different. That's why you get a good attorney and manager to help. But, like anything else when there is a demand, know that it eventually boils down to how much the company really wants to sign you.

If you are an established act, with some pretty good sales from past recordings, you may get an advance of $250,000 or more. And once again, these signing advances are not to be confused with budget or artist "all-in" advances to make the music project. These examples are monetary advances for you to live on... not for *recording* your project. But now with an all-in deal, the artist would get to keep whatever money is left from the budget.

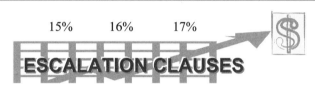

15%   16%   17%

ESCALATION CLAUSES

Sales: 250,000 | 500,000 | 750,000 units

You will absolutely want to have escalations (or increases) added to your royalty rate when you're negotiating your contract. Basically what this means is that along with whatever royalty rate was negotiated for you... once your sales reach a certain level, you will be entitled to a bigger royalty percentage. For example - say you are getting a 14% royalty to start. But in your contract you've got an escalation clause that says you will get an extra 1% for every 250,000 units sold. This would bring your royalty rate up to 15% at 250,000 units and 16% at 500,000 units... and so on. (This is only an example)

RECOUPMENT

• *Recoupment is the reimbursement of all advances, recording costs, and other expenses by an artist to a record company... from the artist's royalties.*

For example, if you are given a $50,000 advance and you have recording, promotional and video costs that total $450,000, then $500,000 (the total) will be recouped or taken from your royalties.

In most cases you will not collect any royalties from the sale of your CD until the record company has recouped (recovered) all of the money that they have spent on you... and possibly a little extra for the next project. And you might as well know now, unlike the movie biz, or any other entertainment business, in the music business... the record company makes the artist pay for everything. Let's look into this further. Read on...

THE SNAIL'$ PACE

By Chris Standring / www.aandronline.com

Every single promotional penny spent on promoting your record, be it video costs, indie radio promotion or retail programs etc, is recoupable from your royalty points in some way, depending on how your contract is set up. Some things are charged to the artist at 100%, some 50%. What this means is that in order for you to recoup let's say $100,000 in promotion, the record company will have to receive income almost 10 times that amount before you clear that recoupment. (Don't forget, you the artist don't see a penny until your recoupment is clear). How is this so? When $100,000 of income goes to the record label, only 15% of that goes towards your recoupment. You are recouping at a snail's pace because you are recouping at 15% of the pie! That means that realistically, you can never really make money because if records are selling well, the label will continue to spend X amount of promotional dollars which in turn gets recouped at the 15% snail's pace.

Used by permission of Chris Stranding
© Chris Standring / www.aandronline.com

CROSS-COLLATERALIZATION

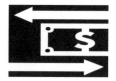

Cross-Collateralization, in layman's terms is a clause or section made within a recording contract, which permits the record company to deduct money that you owe from advances, promotions and recording costs on one project... to be recovered from your future earnings on other projects.

For example: Let's say you are given an advance of $150,000 to do your 1st CD project. But the CD didn't do that great and you only recouped $75,000 from total sales. Under cross-collateralization, the $75,000 that you owe the record company from the 1st CD - will be paid back from the sales created on the next CD. Now the snail only has one leg! (And for anyone who just had the thought, snails don't have legs ...*exactly*)

MUSIC VIDEOS

I'd like to let all up-and-coming new artist know - Please try to have a little creative and business approval over the making and cost of your music video. Try to be involved, and aware of the expenses as much as you can, because the cost of making a music video isn't cheap! A good quality music video budget is easily $50,000 to $150,000+.

One way many artist are getting around the idea of paying out so much money for videos is getting companies like Hummer, Verizon, etc. to pay for the video by way of product placement in the music video itself. (The motion picture industry has done this for years) This can be a great thing, but at the same time... you better know that video broadcasters like MTV do not approve. So whatever way you figure out - as far as *how* to pay for your video... just make sure you're very much involved with the detail$.

- **Note**: Music videos are under the jurisdiction of SAG contracts. Performers should contact the Guild or visit the SAG website at www.sag.org for further information. The direct line to SAG Music Contracts is 323/549-6864

AUDITS
By www.futureofmusic.com

An audit clause is an important section in the agreement between an artist and a record company that will allow the artist the right to have access to the record company's books and records (usually once a year). You want this as an artist so that you can determine the accuracy of the label's bookkeeping.

Note: If you're signed to the label through a production company, you may not be able to audit the record company directly. But you should be able to work out a clause that states you will receive a copy of all accounting statements that are related to you. *You can audit the production company.*

AUDITING THE LABEL -This means just what it sounds like. When artists don't believe the numbers they are being told (how many records they have sold, etc.) they have to pay for a lawyer to file for an audit and they have to pay their accountant to go to the label and try to make sense of the numbers.

Even if an accountant finds that the label has been grossly negligent in its payments to the artist, in most major label contracts the only penalty imposed on the label is to pay the amount that it owes to the artist.

MERCHANDISING

Merchandising is basically the way a company can sell different
items that have your photo or likeness on them. You need to know
that merchandising can bring in a lot of money. It's important to
Have the last word and approval on everything that's made with your photo or
name on it. This means t-shirts, hats, posters... everything. And be sure not to
give the record label 100% of your merchandising rights. You should fight for as
much of this piece of the pie as possible (60% is a good starting place).

PRODUCTION DEALS? ... WELL, JUST BE CAREFUL

..."Production Deal?"

- **A Production Deal** is when an artist signs with a production company (usually headed by an established producer). The producer will record the artist's music and then attempt to obtain a deal with a record label. If the production company is successful in getting the deal, the royalty paid by the record company to the production company will be divided between the production company and the artist.

If you are an artist that is signed to a production deal, this means that you are
actually signed straight to the production company, not the record label. The
production company is the one who has the contract with the label... ok.

Now I am not trying to make this out to be a bad thing... or a negative thing for
artists. Actually, there are deals that artists make with production companies that
actually were their way "in" the game. But, I can tell you from my own
experience, and also what I've seen many times over, there are a lot of
production companies making some pretty ugly deals for artists to "get on" the
scene. Most of the production companies want some of the publishing rights to
the artist's songs, and the advance money is usually very little too. But the real
thing is that the deal is just "jacked" from the get go for the artists, because he is
signed to a production company who is getting a big chunk of what the main
record label is paying out.

For example: Lets say you had 2 different artists that got deals. Artist #1 has
signed a deal directly to a major label and will get his advance from the label, a
recording budget, and also a net 9 or 10% royalty (after the 3% producer payout)
And if the major is interested in owning some of the publishing, then normally the
artists will be offered a publishing deal, complete with it's own set of advances
and so forth. But, now let say that Artist #2 is signed to Big-Producer-Mayne
Productions, that has a deal with that same major label – but to distribute their
artist #2. Well the production company will be getting usually 40% to half of the
advances along with the artist, and also the production company will get half of
the points too. So Artist #2 gets about a 5% royalty rate. And on top of that, the

production company will want a piece of the publishing pie… and for probably NO advance money, just as *part of the deal*. Now this is not a rule… but I have seen it over and over and over again. And if the artist was dumb enough to not get an entertainment attorney (his own), he might also find himself paying for everything attached to the project, and it being recouped ONLY from *his own share* of the split. …*Ouch!* So if you are an artist, just be careful about what kind of production deal you sign into. I've watched guys I know with hit records who couldn't even keep their regular bills paid, but the owner of the production company was living large. One thing that you should consider is getting some type of clause that states that you have to sign off and agree to whatever deal is made in your behalf with the main label the production company is dealing with.

In closing out about the production deals situation, sometimes you will pay some "new-guy-blues" dues, especially in the beginning… one way or another. But never think that you are *supposed* to be cheated…and it's ok. And on the other hand, you could do everything right or make what seems to be the best decisions to "get in" with all the right people around you, and you still not get a great deal. Let's just look at some of the artists that have sold millions of CDs, but still had to file bankruptcy. And of course there is much debate that the real reason for these bankruptcy fillings were to take advantage of the Bankruptcy Laws, which allow an artists to break a recording agreement, but some artists are just really "broke". **Note**: Many times, once you prove yourself, the game can change in your favor. Many artists (and producers) that I know, do make the labels pay 'big-time' later on… for all the years of getting less-than respectable contracts in the beginning years. So, I guess what I'm saying is, if you have the talent, skills, music, and drive it takes to "get on" or get signed, it still won't hurt if you are somewhere praying that it all just *somehow* works out so you can also get paid once you "get on".

FLOW THROUGH
by Ben McLane, Esq.

In the music industry today, producers and production companies are signing a large number of artists to production deals, which are essentially record contracts. Then, the production company will enter into a recording agreement with a record company in order to obtain distribution and marketing for the production company's releases. Hence, the artist is actually released by a label with which it has no direct contact or contract. This situation presents a unique problem both to the artist and the production company with respect to royalty computations in particular. I will explain.

The artist fears that the production company will receive a higher royalty percentage from the record company than the artist receives from the production company. Oppositely, the production company fears that it has given the artist a higher royalty percentage than it will receive from the record company.

For example, the artist's agreement with the production company reduces royalties paid on foreign sales by 50%. Yet, the production company's contract with the record company only provides for a 25% reduction in royalties on foreign sales. In this instance, the production company gets a windfall because it gets seventy-five cents on the dollar, while the artist only gets fifty cents. In another example, the artist's agreement with the production company caps free goods at 20%. Yet, the production company's contract with the record company limits free goods at 30%. Here, the artist receives the windfall because the production company must pay the artist on the basis of one extra record for every ten records sold.

There are various ways to handle this inconsistency so that the playing field is level.

First, and most popular, is what is known as the "flow through" provision. This means that no matter what the agreement between the artist and production company, the artist will receive the benefit of any more favorable royalty computation in the production company's contract with the record company.

Second, the production company and artist agree that the artist's royalties will be a set percentage of what the production company receives from its agreement with the record company.

For example, 50% of the money received by the production company from the record company will belong to the artist. **Third**, and least definite, is for the artist to attempt to negotiate the highest royalty percentage it can get from the production company.

The "flow through" model can be applied to other main provision of the artist's contract with the production company (e.g. term). The key is to make sure that the provision offered by the production company will match the provision the production company receives from the record company.

THE REAL NUMBER$

In a recent article written by John Leland in the New York Times - He broke the economics of the rap record deal brilliantly. Leland spoke to a music industry accountant who had this to say.

Let's say you're a successful artist? Your last album sold, say, 1.5 million copies; a performer with such a track record might negotiate an advance against royalties of around $1 million. This sounds like a lot of money. But out of their advances, performers pay for all recording costs, including studio time and personnel.

As hip-hop has become more successful, album sales and radio airplay increasingly depend on big-name producers like the Neptunes, Timbaland, and Jermaine Dupri, who charge anywhere from $35,000 to $100,000+ per song. Many rappers also call in other artists for duets or cameo appearances at $10,000 to $50,000 a song. The performer also pays for the rights to any digital samples, which vary widely in cost.

RECORDING COSTS = $700,000
LEAVING +$300,000
PERSONAL MANAGER GETS 20 PERCENT
-$60,000
BUSINESS MANAGER OR ACCOUNTANT TAKES 5 PERCENT
-$15,000
THE ATTORNEY MIGHT GET 5 PERCENT OF THE ENTIRE ADVANCE
-$50,000
AFTER THESE FEES THE ARTIST HAS
+$175,000
TAXES: - $70,000
LEFT FOR THE ARTIST: + $105,000

⇒ *Now, many performers also get money for concert appearances or publishing fees. But in turn, Mr. Padell said, his Hip-Hop clients often support a network of parents, siblings and friends, and many of them tithe to their churches. Leland ends, Mr. Padell said that performers who make a 500,000-copy gold album, might end up with more money working for UPS. (Used by permission of bet.com / The Blackspot)*

DEMO SUBMISSION

When you're going to submit your demo to anyone in the music industry who can really help you, please keep in mind that these professionals receive hundreds of demos every week. So make sure that the music you send is your very best effort. Like the old saying goes... *you never get a second chance to make a first impression.* If your demo is not ready, then don't send anything!

I would also highly suggest that you make contact with the person or department you are soliciting to first. I can remember being at Motown, and actually coming across a few demos that were in the "throw-out" pale that were actually pretty good. Why were they being thrown out? Because since so many tapes and CDs come in, that unless someone was actually expecting a package from an artist or his manager, demos would basically end up in the hands of the interns or worse, in "the box" (a throw-away collection of unsolicited music packages). So please, I can't emphasize enough the importance of *making contact first.* If you wanna play the odds with the chance of being heard by just sending in your demo without making a contact first, you would be better off going to Las Vegas and playin' the slot machines... serious.

A GOOD DEMO PACKAGE

> ➤ 3 to 4 Songs – Studio Quality (preferably mixed) –Best song(s) 1st
>> ➤ A Professional Photo
> ➤ A Short professional Bio - (newspaper / magazine review is cool too)
>> ➤ A brief list of credits from the CD (who's doing what)
> ➤ If you have a good video – include it! (Even a great live performance)
>> ➤ Detailed Contact information
> ➤ If you have had some impressive sales and radio-play on your own – then you should also send your SoundScan and BDS information too.

For more information on
Record Deals & Contracts
Including Major Record Labels A&R Contacts

Please visit:

www.MusicPowers.com/24

www.MusicPowers.com

Music Powers

COPYRIGHTS

The most important step to protect your music and intellectual property rights, will be making sure that you have registered your music with the Copyright Office

INTRODUCTION

T he Copyright section of Music Powers has been put together to give you a basic understanding, along with the steps you should take to protect your music creations. Not having suitable registered proof that you are the owner of your creation may cause you to lose certain rights that come with registering your works with the Copyright Office. Copyright Office Registration, and getting the rights that come with it is not to be done with the "poor-man's copyright; *mailing a copy back to yourself*, or any other *nonsense,* if you plan on having the backing of the US Congress set of laws and regulations regarding infringement and legislative pay support for music you own the rights to for licensing, etc. So read this segment of Music Powers, and follow the simple steps to protect yourself. Also, I have decided to provide a little bit of information for those of you who may be interested in knowing *when* to use certain Copyright Forms.

BY DEFINITION, WHAT IS A COPYRIGHT?

A Copyright is the exclusive right, granted by law for a stated period, usually until 70 years after the death of the surviving author of the work, to make, dispose of, and otherwise control *copies* of literary, musical, dramatic, pictorial and other copyrightable works. The exclusive right is set forth in the 1976 Copyright Act Section 106.

Now, the law says that Copyright is secured *automatically* when the work is created, and a work is "created" when it is fixed in a copy, and that your music actually has a legitimate copyright as soon as you can get your song or music "fixed" into a *tangible* format of expression. This just means that you either need to get your song recorded into some type of recorder, or get it written down or logged into some type of records file. But to truly protect yourself, along with some very great advantages and benefits that are backed by the US Government, it's best to register your music with the Copyright Office.

By registering your music with the Copyright Office, you will not only have a better record of proof that you are the owner of the music, but you will also get certain rights when it comes to lawsuits, and benefits for you if you must make a claim for copyright infringement… just incase someone uses your music *without* your permission or the right to do so.

HOW TO REGISTER YOUR SONG

TO REGISTER YOUR SONG WITH THE COPYRIGHT OFFICE, DO THE FOLLOWING:

1. Send a request for a form SR or PA application to the Copyright Office, Library of Congress, 101 Independence Avenue, S E., Washington, D.C. 20559-6000 or download the application from the website: **www.copyright.gov**

 Note: To order an application by telephone, call (202) 707-9100.

2. When the application is completed (properly), send it back to the Copyright Office with:

(a) If *unpublished* - **One copy** of manuscript, lead sheet OR sound recording of the best edition...*or*

(b) If *published* - **Two copies** of manuscript (sheet music) OR a sound recording of the best edition...***and***

(c) The appropriate *non-refundable* registration fee, which is presently $30, by money order, bank draft or check, made payable to ***Register of Copyrights***.

MAIL EVERYTHING BACK IN ONE PACKAGE TO:
Library of Congress Copyright Office 101 Independence Avenue, S.E. Washington, D.C. 20559-6000

Note: Make payment to: Register of Copyrights

Now, the wait time for application processing, and getting you your certificate back in the mail is kind of long (about 5 to 6 months), but your song is actually registered as soon as the Copyright Office gets your package (if everything is correct in the package; the application, and the fee).

FORM PA, FORM SR... SO, WHICH ONE?

FORM PA: For published and unpublished works of the performing arts (musical works and dramatic works, pantomimes and choreographic works, motion pictures and other audiovisual works), use Form PA (Performing Arts). **Musical compositions that are recorded on disc or cassettes are works of the performing arts**, and should be registered with Form PA.

The top of Form PA says:

> **When to Use This Form:** Use Form PA for registration of published or unpublished works of the performing arts. This class includes works prepared for the purpose of being "performed" directly before an audience or indirectly "by means of any device or process." Works of the performing arts include: (1) musical works, including any accompanying words; (2) dramatic works, including any accompanying music; (3) pantomimes and choreographic works; and (4) motion pictures and other audiovisual works.

- The bottom line is that Copyrights in songs are usually filed on Copyright Form PA.

For Example: Let's say a writer, "Big-Producer-Mayne" writes a song (words and music) called *"Bounce it Baby Girl."* Although he may have recorded it, if he is only interested in registering the song work (the underlying or musical composition), but **not** the actual *recording*, Form PA should be used.

FORM SR: For published or unpublished *sound recordings*, use form SR (Sound Recordings). **But please sticky this:** Registration for a sound recording alone is NOT the same as registration for musical, dramatic, or a literary work that has been recorded. Form SR is used for registration of the particular sounds or a particular recorded performance.

The top of Form SR says:

> **When to Use This Form:** Use Form SR for registration of published or unpublished sound recordings. It should be used when the copyright claim is limited to the sound recording itself, and it may also be used where the same copyright claimant is seeking simultaneous registration of the underlying musical, dramatic, or literary work embodied in the phonorecord.
>
> With one exception, "sound recordings" are works that result from the fixation of a series of musical, spoken, or other sounds. The exception is for the audio portions of audiovisual works, such as a motion picture soundtrack or an audio cassette accompanying a filmstrip. These are considered a part of the audiovisual work as a whole.

Form SR should also be used if you wish to make one registration for both the *sound recording* and the original work (musical composition). You may make a single registration using form SR *only* if the copyright claimant is the *same for both the sound recording and the musical composition.*

- The bottom line is that Copyrights in sound recordings are to be registered on Copyright Form SR.

For Example: Let's say an artist, "The Regional Buzz" performs and then records *"Bounce it Baby Girl"* which was written by "Big-Producer-Mayne." After the artist "Regional Buzz" gets permission, clearance, and a license from "Big-Producer-Mayne," if "Regional Buzz" wants to submit the recording for copyright registration, Form SR should be used.

VERY IMPORTANT NOTES:

> ❑ **If you are the owner of both the song composition, and the sound recording of the particular song, you can just use Copyright Form SR to register both of these separate elements as one registration. This is sometimes normal when it comes to producers who write their own music and then record it as a production.**
>
> ❑ **Sounds accompanying a motion picture or other audiovisual work should *not* be registered on Form SR.**
>
> ❑ **You may also file *multiple* songs as a collection of songs.**

MORE ON COPYRIGHTS

By Ben McLane, Esq. – © 1998 Ben McLane – Used by permission

If you are a musician or songwriter, the copyright law affects your craft, so it is important to have a basic understanding of it.

The term "copyright" really means that the creator has the right to copy. If an artist writes an original song, that artist is the owner of the copyright. As it pertains to artists in general, the copyright law basically grants the creator the right to (1) reproduce (e.g., make copies), (2) distribute (e.g., sell copies) and (3) perform (e.g., play the song live). Once the song is in a tangible form (i.e., written), the artist should take steps to protect the work. In essence, an artist needs to prove the date of creation. Actually, under the present copyright law, a work is copyrighted once it is written or recorded. However, it is best to have proof of creation by getting your music securely copyrighted by the Copyright office. It is also important to put the proper copyright notice on songs and recordings that are presented to the public, such as a demo. The copyright notice for songs and sound recordings must include three elements: the symbol © (for lyric sheet or sheet music) or _ (for tapes, records, CDs), the year of publication and the name of the copyright owner.

SONGWRITING & PUBLISHING

INTRODUCTION

In the music industry, both songwriting and publishing can be very rewarding ways to generate income from the songs you craft and/or own the rights to. As the songwriter, your job is to create, conceive, and construct lyrics and/or music to form songs. As the publisher, you (or another publisher or administrating company) will exploit the songs in your catalog to the public by way of licenses issued in your behalf through performance rights organizations such as BMI, ASCAP, or SESAC, and mechanical licenses either through The Harry Fox Agency or through direct licensing. There are also Digital Licenses.

In order to protect your interest, when it comes to having your songs in a position to earn you income - if the song is ready to be released to the public, take the following steps:

Step One

If you have not written the song completely by yourself, or if there are other parties involved who have ownership rights such as a publisher, you should have all of the owners; authors and publishers involved sign into a summary agreement of the musical work(s, which is commonly referred to as a "Split-Sheet".

Split Sheet?

- A "Split-Sheet" is a basic overview contract between all the collaborators and publishers involved - outlining the various percentages of authorship and ownership to a song. (See Split-Sheet Template)

Step Two

Get a Copyright on the song(s). A Copyright is the exclusive right, granted to the owner, by law, for a period of time to control and make copies of their intellectual property. So, one of the most important administrative duties you MUST do to protect your rights to your song or intellectual property is registering your works with The Library of Congress - Copyright Office. If you do not register your material, you may lose certain rights that are granted to you by law - when it comes to licensing and infringement.

Complete the appropriate Copyright form application (Form PA or Form SR), along with a payment of $30 to: Register of Copyrights. Don't forget to add (2) two copies of the finished song, and prep to mail it to: The Library of Congress - Copyright Office, 101 Independence Ave, SE - Washington, DC 20559-6000 (This is not an option... protect yourself!) - (Also, see Copyrights Section)

Step Three

Complete the appropriate Registration and Song Clearance Form from whatever performance rights organization that you are with (BMI, ASCAP, SESAC).

Step Four

Fill out the needed form(s) with The Harry Fox Agency (If HFA is your publishing company's agent). This is so money can be collected *in your behalf* from any sales of records by a record label.

Step Five

Make sure you check over everything above; the paperwork, and possibly even have it reviewed by your manager or whomever that you use on your team to get counsel from or do administrative duties. After everything looks in order... and your team says it's a go... mail everything out, and also keep a record of what you have sent.

Beyond the possible complex issues of any split agreement negotiations, or for certain digital & foreign licenses ...

That's It!

NOW - LET'S GET INTO SOME DETAILS...

READ ON

Ok, let's just start off in this section by saying that for the longest time now, Rap, Hip Hop and R&B music *is* the "Pop" or popular music of these days. And I don't really think that there's anyone out there who can *convincingly* debate this. Just look at whatever songs are listed in the top 20 of the *Billboard Hot 100* charts.

The concern though, is not so much with most of the "Superstar" or major label artists that are co-writing most of the songs they are performing. At *that* level of success, you're presumed to have enough sense to have a great team of *professionals* around you to help guide you along - *to get you paid* for your songs. But, what I'm really talking about is the *non-payout* that sometimes takes place with the "new-to-mid-size" level artist/songwriter, or *especially* the ones signed to a regional independent label or production company… it's sometimes a little alarming. It's kind of crazy to me when new songwriter-artists repeatedly, over and over…*and over again*, keep signing into agreements; split-sheets and/or songwriting/publishing contracts that *take away so much*. And what's even worse, many of these companies are not even paying these kids on *what they are due…legally.*

I have personally watched talent just sit and either not know what to do or either too scared to do anything or to "make waves" that might cause a problem with their so-called "hook-up" with the industry or company. And most of this sad reality is mainly due to a lack of *knowledge & understanding* on some of the most fundamental music business practices; hiring your *own* attorney…*NOT the attorney of the producer or company you are signing with.* And also getting a little *educated* about this whole business of songwriting and publishing. See, one of the biggest incomes for you if you're an artist -songwriter is through the licensing and publishing of your songs …*especially* with Mechanical License royalties.

Have you or your crew sold 50,000 units or more, on your 15-song, *22-cities-and-still-marching-strong* CD, through an Independent label that *you don't own*? If the answer is yes, how much money did *you* get in mechanicals? If you wrote all of the songs, I hope you got at least $40,000 or more. *It can actually be a whole lot more!* But hold up, let's just say you only *co-wrote* all of the songs on your 15-song CD, and you just hit the 20,000 units sold status. Did you know that you as "*your own publisher*" could be due over $12,000 in mechanicals?

…Do I have your attention now?

Check this: A few years ago, I had the incredible opportunity to work with one of the most prolific songwriter/artists of modern-day R&B/Pop music. I won't disclose *his* name, but after the 3rd day in the Studio, in the middle of re-working a song that R&B recording artist/songwriter Joe had written for him, I asked our un-named artist to just try something like what was written for one of his earlier big hits. And then this *un-named* artist told me, "You know, I've never received a royalty on that." (Huh? …what!) So I asked, "What do you mean… what are you talking about?" He then politely told me again… and *this time*, with looks of support from his wife, "I have *never* received a royalty check in my life!" Wow, I was totally blown away! If I disclosed all of the many "Mega-Hits" that he had co-written, you would be messed up just like I was. And just so you know, I checked the RIAA status of about 4 or 5 records: Gold and Platinum albums he wrote on, so we are probably talking about *at least* $750,000 - as his co-collaborator "take", in just the mechanical royalties alone. And for all you know-it-alls, no, he had not gotten some big publishing advance that left his royalties-due in recoupment. But somebody was, and definitely *still is*, getting "Big-Bank" dollar$. So who's getting his money? The publisher. And this *particular* publisher probably had him sign over all of the rights to the songs he wrote, and tied it in his recording artist contract or production agreement. This sometimes happens when dealing through production companies (and labels too). Is it wrong? I don't know, is it? Actually, it's not illegal. Is it unethical? Probably. Could it have been avoided?

...Yes

MECHANICAL LICENSES 101

One of the first things a new artist that writes his own material will need to do is set up his or her *own* publishing company, and then get a grip on the basics (at least) of Mechanical Licensing and royalty pay.

A Mechanical License is an authorization that is issued by a publisher (or an agent of the publisher like Harry Fox) to a record label. This license will give the record company the right to record and make public a specific composition at an agreed-upon fee for each record that is made and sold. The agreed-upon fee *does not* have a ceiling price, and can vary. Also, because of the Mechanical Licensing laws, *if the song has been copyrighted and ready for distribution*, the writer is entitled to (as a minimum) what is called a Compulsory Statutory Mechanical Royalty Rate.

...Harry Fox?

• **Harry Fox Agency** *(HFA) is the foremost mechanical licensing, collections, and distribution agency for U.S. music publishers.*

...Mechanical Licensing Laws?

• *Under the United States Copyright Act, the right to use copyrighted, non-dramatic musical works in the making of phonorecords for distribution to the public for private use is the exclusive right of the copyright owner. However, the Act provides that once a copyright owner has recorded and distributed such a work to the U.S. public or permitted another to do so, a compulsory mechanical license is available to anyone else who wants to record and distribute the work in the U.S. upon the payment of license fees at the statutory "compulsory" rate as set forth in Section 115 of the Act. (Courtesy of HarryFox.com)*

STATUTORY ROYALTY RATES

❑ For the period January 1, 2004 to December 31, 2005 the statutory mechanical royalty rate is as follows:

8.5 Cents for songs 5 minutes and less
OR
1.65 Cents per minute - over 5 minutes*

*For example:
5:01 to 6:00 = $.099 (6 x $.0165 = $.099) 6:01 to 7:00 = $.1155 (7 x $.0165 = $.1155) 7:01 to 8:00 = $.132 (8 x $.0165 = $.132)

⇒ *On January 1, 2006, the rate will be raised to 9.1 cents for songs 5 minutes or less and 1.75 cents per minute or fraction thereof over 5 minutes. (Courtesy of Harryfox.com)*

For example: At the latest statutory mechanical royalty rate (Summer 2005), on a Platinum (one million in sales) selling CD-Album, you would be entitled to $85,000 per song on the CD. And if you wrote all the songs on a 15-song CD *(with no controlled composition clause)*, this would mean the total money due would be: $1,275,000.00, and that's in just Mechanical Royalties alone. Now that's a lot of money. And imagine if you had a "single release" *along with the CD album, remixes, bonuses, and import releases.* You could be paid "per-side" as it appears on each of these and the CD single too!

...Controlled Composition Clause?

• A **controlled composition** *is when a composition written or co-written by the recording artist (and sometimes the producer per the artist contract) under an exclusive recording agreement that typically states - the record company will only pay 75 percent of the minimum statutory rate - on many times, only 10 cuts per CD and two cuts per single, regardless of the actual number of sides or length of the composition(s)....*☹

Now, one of the things songwriters and publishers also need to take in mind, is that many songs, especially if they are successful, are sometimes re-released. And since the Statutory Mechanical rate changes, publishers should always seek a pay rate in the license, at least equal to or "keyed" to whatever the rate is *at the actual time of manufacturing.* This way, if the record is released or reissued many years later, the songwriter and publisher would get the rate that is up to date, as opposed to the older rate when the song first came out. My songwriter/producer friend, Sigidi (*"Take Your Time, Do It Right"* by The SOS Band), schooled me about this, and he would know. He still, to this day makes income from re-issues of that "monster-hit" record he co-wrote and produced on the SOS Band.

PERFORMANCE LICENSES

The Spence Law firm

One of the exclusive rights a copyright holder enjoys is the right to perform the copyrighted songs publicly. The copyright holder may also authorize others to perform the musical composition publicly. Such authorizations are accomplished through the use of performance licenses. This type of license is important for music copyright holders, because it can generate substantial income through radio play, television broadcasts, movie soundtrack exhibitions both in the US and abroad, as well as live public performances.

Performing rights societies, such as ASCAP, BMI and SESAC assist music publishers and composers by issuing licenses to companies and establishments which publicly perform, or allow others to publicly perform, music as part of their business operation. These performing rights societies also monitor and audit their licensees to make sure their music usage correctly reflects the performance royalties paid to the composers and publishers. Blanket licenses are usually issued to music users and the income derived from those and other licenses are then divided up through complicated formulas and paid to the copyright owners.

PERFORMANCE ROYALTY
By Ben McLane, Esq.

There are several ways that songwriters can make money in the music business. One of the most significant is from royalties generated by the public performance of their songs. These royalties result from what are called "performance rights."

In the United States, "performance royalties" are paid out mainly by two performance rights societies, BMI and ASCAP. (Most foreign countries also have their own societies.) Under the copyright law, a songwriter controls the public performance of that songwriter's songs. In essence, a songwriter designates either BMI or ASCAP as his or her agent for the public performance rights of that songwriter's songs. A songwriter can only affiliate with one society at a time. BMI or ASCAP have arrangements with the parties - such as radio, television, concert venues, restaurants, etc. (essentially any user who performs music publicly) - who want to use the songs in the societies respective catalogs. For a licensing fee, BMI or ASCAP will grant to that user what is called a "blanket license", which means that the user can play any song, by any songwriter or publisher affiliated with that society, any number of times. It must be stressed that fees are collected from the entity or venue user, not from any actual performer.

The money earned by a songwriter from the societies (i.e., the performance royalty) is proportionate to the volume of airplay of the songwriter's songs. Performance royalties are based on extremely complicated formulas. Basically, however, the societies monitor radio and television airplay to determine how often a song is heard and by how many people. The larger the audience and the more times a song is played, the more the income. Since it is impossible to cover all media outlets, BMI and ASCAP rely on estimates based upon samples. BMI obtains its samples from radio station logs and television cue sheets (lists of compositions used on television). ASCAP gets its samples from taping radio stations and from television cue sheets. After deducting operating expenses, the societies divide the fees up and pay it to their affiliated writers and publishers. Both societies pay quarterly.

BMI and ASCAP represent both songwriters and publishers. It should be noted that even where a songwriter is represented by a third party publisher, that songwriter needs to also join a society because songwriters and publishers are paid separately by the societies. To join ASCAP, a songwriter must have at least one song either published, recorded, or publicly performed. To join BMI is a bit easier. The writer must have a song either published, recorded, or likely to be performed publicly. As for which organization is best, each songwriter will have to decide that for themselves because it is difficult to say with certainty which society pays more. Both BMI and ASCAP will be happy to send out information brochures to interested applicants.

Choosing a performing rights society is an important decision for a songwriter to make because if a song ever becomes a hit, the performance royalties can be substantial. Thus, any serious writer should find out about affiliating with either BMI or ASCAP

Used by permission of Ben McLane, Esq. – ©1998, Ben McLane - www.benmclane.com

SYNCHRONIZATION LICENSES
The Spence Law firm

Synchronization licensing addresses the act of combining, or synchronizing, audio works to video works. A "sync" license is necessary whenever a visual image is accompanied by sound. This most often involves television programs, commercials, videos, or motion pictures, but can also involve computer games, Internet sites, and other media not yet developed.

Synchronization licensing is another part of the right of reproduction granted exclusively to copyright owners under the Copyright Act. Although "synchronization" is not mentioned specifically, publishers are given the exclusive right to authorize the reproduction of their music in copies, such as television programs, motion pictures, and home videos. In other words, publishers can grant the right for producers to synchronize their music with a visual image, either on video or film. This grant is usually non-exclusive and is entirely at the songwriter or publisher's discretion.

Generally "sync" licenses do not include the right to use the title of the song as the title of the production, or to incorporate the story of the song into the production, although those rights can also be negotiated, for an additional fee, of course.
Sync licenses should not be confused with performance licenses in movies or television broadcasts as indicated above. A producer will need both a sync

license and a performance license of some type to use a song in a broadcast or publicly performed movie. Because many programs into which music can be licensed also generate performance revenue, the publisher of the licensed music must take actions to obtain music "cue sheet" for the production. Failure to review or file the cue sheet with the performing rights societies can cost both the composer and publisher a substantial amount of money, which cannot be recovered later.

PRINT LICENSES

Licensing printed copies of music (sheet music) is how the derivation of the term "music publishing" originated. Until the early 1900's, this was the only method music could be reproduced and distributed to the public. A print license allows for the reproduction of printed copies of music such as sheet music, folios, concert arrangements and the printing of lyrics in magazines, advertising, and books.

Although not the income producer it once was, print licenses, especially for well-known songs or well-known songwriters, can still generate substantial income. The print music publishers have become very creative in marketing their material, sometimes printing folios containing all the songs from a hit movie or album.

MORE ON FILM & TV
By Ben McLane, Esq.

There is a major source of income that many songwriters overlook: the use of music in television or film. Television and film producers need material for their projects. Not only is there money involved in licensing music for television and film, the use of a song in either of these mediums can mean widespread exposure. However, a producer will require the songwriter to sign a contract so that the producer can "license the rights." This allows the producer to utilize the material in whatever way the producer wishes.

In the world of film and television, decisions are made quickly and the producer will generally license the song, which is the *easiest* to obtain - at the cheapest price. The producer will not use a song until there is satisfaction that all of the rights are "cleared" (i.e., the copyright owner has granted the producer the right to use the song). If there are several songwriters, clearance must be obtained from each. Thus, songwriters need to make sure that the rights are easily obtainable.

The earnings generated from the use of a song in television or film normally come from performing and synchronization rights. A significant portion of ASCAP and BMI (performance rights societies) revenues are collected from television broadcasters (in the United States, motion pictures do not generate performance royalties payable by ASCAP or BMI). These monies are divided up amongst ASCAP and BMI writers and publishers. Therefore, songwriters are advised to become members of one of these societies, and register with them all songs written. A producer will not usually take a chance on using unregistered material because of the likelihood that the rights may not be available. Further, in the television and film business, music is reproduced when it is recorded on the soundtrack for the production. The right for the producer to make such a reproduction is called a synchronization right and the producer must negotiate a synchronization ("sync") license for each composition to be used.

If the song is used in a television program, the amount of money made depends upon the way in which the song is used and when it is aired. If a song is performed in prime time, ASCAP and BMI will pay more money because supposedly more people are watching. Synchronization fees for television are modest compared to film for mainly two reasons: (1) the synch fee takes away from the producer's bottom line profit; and (2) the songwriter and publisher stand to make money from the exposure.

If the song is used in a film, the fees paid for the synch license can be much higher than television for mainly two reasons: (1) films are generally produced on a much higher budget than television programs; and (2) the rights to exhibit the song in all media (i.e., film, television, video) for the duration of the copyright are usually obtained by the producer.

Now, more than ever, there is an abundant need for songs in major and independent films, network and cable television, and other media. Hence, there are chances out there for songwriters to generate revenues and gain exposure for their music; these opportunities should not be overlooked or scoffed at.

DIGITAL LICENSING BASICS – RIGHTS & DEFINITIONS

Digital licensing is the licensing of copyrighted musical compositions in digital configurations, including but not limited to, full downloads, limited-use downloads, on-demand streaming and CD burning (Courtesy of Harryfox.com)

❑ **DIGITAL MILLENNIUM COPYRIGHT ACT (DMCA):** This newly enacted law implements two global treaties designed to protect creative works in the digital era. It prohibits the manufacture and distribution of devices the primary purpose of which is to "pick" the electronic "locks" protecting copyrighted material online. This prohibition enables effective enforcement against those seeking to pirate copyrighted music online. The greatest gains from passage of this legislation will be realized internationally. This bill will serve as a model for ratification and implementation of the World Intellectual Property Organization (WIPO) treaties in other countries, where protection of sound recordings online is not sufficient. Formal U.S. ratification of the treaty package helps move the worldwide ratification effort closer to the 30 countries that must ratify the treaties for them to take legal effect. The law also includes important provisions that clarify the rights of copyright owners and the responsibilities of online service providers to guard against piracy online. In addition, the DMCA also contains critical provisions relating to the licensing of music on the Internet and amending the Digital Performance Right in Sound Recordings Act of 1995. (Courtesy of RIAA)

DOWNLOADS (FULL, PERMANENT)/DIGITAL PHONORECORD DELIVERIES

❑ A full, permanent download (DPD) is each individual delivery of a phonorecord by digital transmission of a sound recording (embodying a musical composition) resulting in a reproduction made by or for the recipient. DPDs reside on a recipient's computer indefinitely. DPDs may be transferred to portable devices or burned onto CDs (in accordance with the rules set by the digital distributor of a specific DPD). DPDs fall under Section 115 of the Copyright Act and are currently licensed at the statutory rate for physical phonorecords. (Courtesy of Harryfox.com)

DOWNLOADS (LIMITED, TETHERED)

❑ A limited download is a digital file that is delivered electronically to a computer to reside there for a limited period of time. There are two types of limited downloads: limited-time download (i.e. the song resides on the computer for 30 days) and limited-use download (i.e. the song is can be heard 10 times before it can no longer be played). Limited downloads are also referred to as *tethered* downloads. (Courtesy of Harryfox.com)

❑ There are many types of digital rights for licensing: **CD Burn, Interactive Radio, Non-Interactive Radio, On-demand Interactive Streaming, Restricted & Unrestricted Downloads**

FOREIGN PERFORMANCE
By Ben McLane, Esq.

If a songwriter composes a hit song, it is quite possible that the song will receive airplay in foreign countries. If so, there will be what is called "performance money" due that songwriter from the foreign countries playing the song. This article will explain the process of distributing "foreign performance" monies to the songwriter.

Any serious songwriter should first become a member of one of the United States performance rights societies: BMI, ASCAP or SESAC ("societies"). The songwriter will enter into a contract with the society chosen, giving that society the right to license the public performance of that songwriter's songs. The societies have arrangements with the parties (radio, television, concert venues, restaurants, etc.) who want to use the songs in the societies' respective catalogs. For a licensing fee, the societies will grant to that user what is called a "blanket license," which means that the user can play any song, by any songwriter or publisher affiliated with that society, any number of times. Publishing companies enter into a similar agreement with the societies.

The money earned by a songwriter from the societies (the "performance royalty") is proportionate to the volume of airplay of the songwriter's songs. Performance royalties are based on complicated formulas. Basically, however, the societies monitor radio and television airplay to determine how often a song is heard and by how many people. The larger the audience and the more times a song is played, the more the income. Since it is impossible to cover all media outlets, the societies rely on estimates based upon samples. After deducting operating expenses, the societies divide the fees up and pay it to their affiliated writers and publishers. Societies pay quarterly. All major foreign countries also have a performance rights society. All of the U.S. societies have "reciprocal agreements" with the major performance rights societies throughout the world. Based upon their own individual rules and procedures, these foreign societies log and (after deducting an operating fee) pay the U.S. societies for performances in the foreign territories of the works that are in the U.S. societies' catalog. The U.S. societies (after deducting their own processing fee to analyze the foreign performance monies) in turn pay the songwriter the foreign performance money earned. If there is a separate publisher of the song, societies pay 50% to the writer and 50% to the publisher.

Now, and in the future, there is great potential for money to be earned outside the U.S. For this reason; songwriters must position themselves to be able to collect all that is owed them. Joining a performance rights society is the key.

FOR MORE INFORMATION ON SONGWRITING & PUBLISHING - PLEASE VISIT:

www.copyright.gov
www.bmi.com
www.ascap.com
www.sesac.com
www.nmpa.org
www.harryfox.com
www.riaa.com

Music Powers
SONG SPLIT SHEET
Split-Sheet Example

Song Title:	
Date:	
Project:	

PERCENTAGE (%) SPLITS REGARDING:
Check all that apply

❑ Copyright Ownership _____	❑ Publishing % _____
❑ Songwriter % _____	⇒ Other % (see bottom of page) _____

OWNERSHIP (%) PERCENTAGES

SONGWRITER(S) (%)	Affiliation BMI, ASCAP SESAC	PUBLISHER(S) (%)	Affiliation BMI, ASCAP SESAC
Name & contact info		Name & contact info	

Agreed to by:

_____   Date :_____

_____   Date :_____

_____   Date :_____

_____   Date :_____

⇒   ADDITIONAL INFORMATION & NOTES:

Music Powers

SONGWRITERS & PUBLISHERS BEWARE OF

THE

"CONTROLLED COMPOSITION"

CLAUSE

By Wallace Collins, Esq.

"Mechanical" royalties, so called from the days when the only recordings sold were piano rolls, which mechanically triggered a player piano, now represent royalties due to songwriters and their publishers for each copy of a record sold. Effective January 1, 2004, the statutory mechanical royalty rate in the United States was increased to $.085 per song. Pursuant to the U.S. Copyright law, this higher mechanical rate is applicable to all recordings made and distributed on or after 2004. However, due to certain ambiguities (vagueness) in the Copyright law, almost all record companies use their substantial leverage over new recording artists to cause them to enter into record contracts which substantially reduce this statutory mechanical rate pursuant to a controlled composition clause, often referred to as the "3/4 rate" since it typically reduces the amount to 75% of the statutory rate.

Under U.S. Copyright law, Congress established a statutory mechanical royalty rate for songwriters and their publishers based on an upward-sliding scale tied to a cost-of-living index on a per song per record basis. However, the controlled composition clause, one of the many royalty-reducing provisions in any record contract, contractually reduces the mechanical rate for a songwriter/ recording artist and its publisher on songs written or otherwise "controlled" by the artist. Most such clauses not only reduce the payment per song, but may also put a limit on the total number of songs on which payment will be made and may fix the point in time at which the calculation will be made (thereby circumventing the cost of living index increase).

A detailed analysis of a controlled composition clause is beyond the scope of this article. However, for a simplified example of how it works, lets assume a typical clause, which might say that the songwriter/artist will receive 3/4 of the minimum statutory mechanical rate payable on a maximum of 10 songs per LP.

The mechanical royalty on the artist's entire LP has a cap of 60 cents (3/4 rate x 10 songs) so that, even if the songwriter/artist writes 12 songs for its own album, the artist's publishing, which should be worth about 96 cents an album at the full rate, is only allocated 60 cents under this clause.

To further illustrate, assume the 12-song album has 6 songs written by the artist and 6 songs from outside publishers. The outside publishers are not subject to the artist's 3/4 rate so the 6 outside songs get the full rate and are entitled to a total of about 48 cents. Since the mechanical royalty on the entire LP has a contractual cap of 60 cents, the recording artist's publisher is limited to applying the remaining 12 cents to the artist's 6 songs, so that the artist's publishing is worth 2 cents per song.

To take it another step further, imagine a case where 8 of the 12 songs on the LP were from outside publishers. The outside publishers would be entitled to about 64 cents in mechanical royalties. Since the artist's contractual cap is 60 cents, then for each LP sold the songwriter/record artist would actually owe its record company 4 cents which would be deducted out of its recording royalties. In addition, the artist's own 4 songs receive no mechanical royalties at all.

Some controlled composition clauses also contain language, which further reduces the mechanical rate on mid-priced and budget sales, etc., providing for a 3/4 rate on the 3/4 rate. In addition, record contracts often contain several subparagraphs that eliminate royalty payments for free goods and records sold below wholesale price, etc. Several of these categories would ordinarily be subject to mechanical royalties absent the controlled composition clause and, although this provision reduces mechanical royalties on the artist's publishing, it does not reduce payments to outside publishers and writers since they are not subject to the terms of the artist's contract.

The most treacherous dilemma for the songwriter/artist is that, even if the record company does not expressly acquire the artist's publishing rights in its contract, the value of the artist's publishing may so greatly be reduced by the controlled composition clause that the artist may find it difficult to get a publishing deal elsewhere. This is particularly true if the mechanical royalties are cross-collateralized with the artist royalties which means that, until the artist is recouped, no mechanical royalties are payable on the recording artist's publishing.

The foregoing scenarios raise numerous legal concerns for the record labels. The presence of antitrust and restraint of trade claims arises since virtually all labels have the three-quarter rate in their contracts giving the artist little, if any, choice. Since the controlled composition language is almost identical in each label's contract, it might not be all that difficult for a plaintiff to establish circumstantially that the labels conspire to fix the rate. A claim of interference with prospective financial advantage could be raised since the controlled composition clause devalues an artist's publishing rights. Another pertinent (related) issue to be considered is whether, under partnership law (where one partner can bind the partnership), an artist's co-writer who is not actually a signatory to the record contract is subject to the 3/4 rate by virtue of being a "partner" in the song's creation.

Although a controlled composition clause can be made somewhat less onerous (difficult) through some firm negotiating, record companies are generally inflexible on this provision and their stubbornness can only be lessened if they have an ardent desire to sign a particular artist.

In fairness to record companies, with the very high cost and high risk of the record business, the companies need to cut costs where they can to try to make a profit on the few artists who do succeed. However, the question is one of whether devaluing the artist's publishing is a fair way of doing it. Record companies contend that, since they are financing the production and marketing of the artist's recordings, the artist should give them a break on the publishing royalties they would otherwise have to pay. However, whether the contractual reduction by a record company of the Congressionally legislated mechanical royalty rate would hold up if challenged in a court of law has yet to be tested.

Moreover, in the wake of Congress amending the Copyright law last session to allow for performance rights for digital transmissions, the time is right when Congress reconvenes for lobbying efforts by songwriter organizations and publisher groups to bring attention to the 3/4 rate issue and the need to clarify certain ambiguities in the copyright law so as to better protect songwriters and their publishing rights.

Wallace Collins is an entertainment lawyer with the New York law firm of Serling Rooks & Ferrara, LLP. He was a recording artist for Epic Records before attending Fordham Law School.

Wallace Collins, Esq.
254 WEST 54TH ST. - 14TH FLOOR
NEW YORK, N.Y. 10019
212-245-7300
www.wallacecollins.com

THE CONTROLLED COMPOSITION PIE

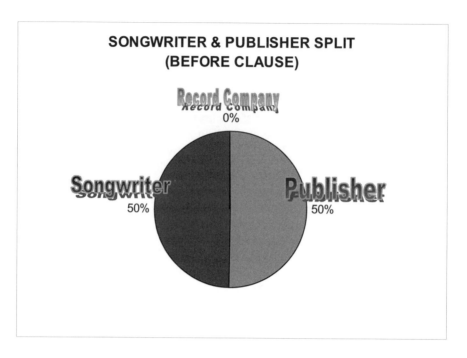

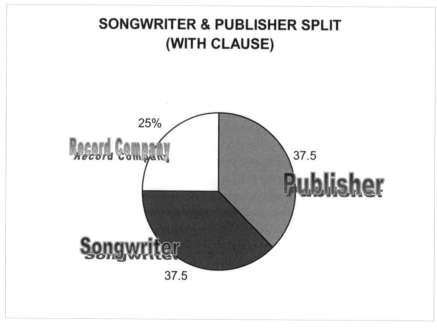

Music Powers

STARTING A PUBLISHING COMPANY

Starting your own publishing company is actually not that hard. You as a songwriter may truly benefit from setting up your *own* publishing company, because not only will you be able show off your own catalog of songs you've written, but also, you may exploit songs of other writers that you acquire material from. You will also be able to collect your money from mechanical, performance and digital licenses *direct*, as opposed to getting your money through another publisher, especially if the publisher is controlled by only one person paying or writing checks. *(Also see Advice from Collipark Record's Michael Crooms; Beat-n-Azz, formerly DJ Smurf)*.

Step 1 - First of all, you will need to think up a few really 'you-neek' names for your company. I suggest trying as many combinations of words and "new" words as you can possibly think of (that you like). BMI and ASCAP, including local government business databanks already have many of the most common names taken. So like I said, be unique. Many big-name artists sometimes can't use their *established* artist names because they are too close to other names that already exist. So with this being a reality, many recording artist spell their known names *backwards*. For example: ECAF Music for Babyface, or ECNIRP Music for Prince.

Step 2 - You will need to join a Performance Rights Organization such as BMI, ASCAP, or SESAC. Decide on what affiliation you want to be with and request the necessary information and application to join as a writer and publisher affiliate. You can only be an active member of one organization.

BMI - www.bmi.com	**ASCAP** - www.ascap.com	**SESAC** - www.sesac.com
ATLANTA P.O. Box 19199 Atlanta, GA 31126 404-261-5151	**ATLANTA** 541 Tenth Street NW - PMB 400 Atlanta, GA 30318 404-351-1224	**NASHVILLE** 55 Music Square East Nashville, TN 37203 615-320-0055
LOS ANGELES 8730 Sunset Blvd. 3rd Floor West West Hollywood, CA 90069-2211 310-659-9109	**NASHVILLE** Two Music Square West Nashville, TN 37203 615-742-5000	**NEW YORK** 152 West 57th ST - 57th Floor New York, NY 10019 212-586-3450
NASHVILLE 10 Music Square East Nashville, TN 37203 615-401-2000	**NEW YORK** One Lincoln Plaza New York, NY 10023 212-621-6000	**LOS ANGELES** 501 Santa Monica Blvd - Suite 450 Santa Monica, CA 90401-2430 310-393-9671
NEW YORK 320 West 57th Street New York, NY 10019-3790 212-586-2000	**LOS ANGELES** 7920 W. Sunset Boulevard, 3rd Fl. Los Angeles, CA 90046 323-883-1000	

Step 3

Now you must get your company set up with the local city / county / state government to get a business license / permit to do business as a music publisher. You will need to decide in which business manner to file your company -Sole Proprietor, General Partnership, Corporation, D.B.A. (Doing Business As), etc. You will also need a Federal Tax ID to complete your applications to BMI, ASCAP, or SESAC.

More resources for business license & tax id info:
www.allbusiness.com
www.sbaonline.sba.gov
www.irs.gov

Step 4

Open up a Business Banking Account. If you've followed the steps above, and your credit is not *totally* ruined... bad checks, etc. - you should have no problem opening an account. And even if your credit is bad, there are still ways to do this. But it will require some extra effort on your own.

Step 5

Once you get your affiliation, and have some music on CD that is getting ready for distribution to the public, contact The Harry Fox Agency (HFA) to request information and an application to join. This is so they can issue mechanical & digital licenses to collect money in your behalf - from the sales of CDs, etc with songs that you own the rights to. They also can perform audits when considered necessary.

THE HARRY FOX AGENCY, INC
711 THIRD AVENUE
NEW YORK, NY 10017
212-370-5330
www.harryfox.com

That's all there is to it...

Good Luck!

Music Powers

PUBLISHING DEALS

For the most part, publishing agreements can vary from writer to writer and publisher to publisher, but there are a few concerns that all songwriters need to take in mind when considering a publishing deal. And for the most part, if you are expecting to sign into a publishing situation I highly advise that you seek and find an experienced entertainment attorney to guide and counsel you *before* signing into any publishing agreement with anyone.

OK - basically, the way a song is split up, is into 2 different halves - the writers share, and then the publishing half or share. So for 100% of any revenues that a particular song generates, it will be 50% for the songwriter(s), and 50% for the publisher(s).

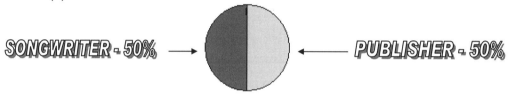

Now, there *are* different types of publishing deals. There are single-song deals, as well as year-to-year deals with options, etc. Also, there is the standard exclusive songwriter publishing deal, where the publisher will advance the songwriter money and basically own the copyright of the song(s).

An example of what a standard songwriting contract might say:

The Songwriter hereby sells, assigns, transfers and delivers to the Publisher, its successors and assigns, a certain heretofore unpublished original musical composition, written and/or composed by the named Songwriter now entitled _____including title, words and music, and the right to secure copyright throughout the entire world, and to have and to hold the said copyright and all rights of whatsoever nature thereunder existing, subject to the terms of this agreement.

This **"standard" publishing deal** is a many times a complete "split" of all the income the song(s) generate; 50% for the songwriter, and 50% for the publisher, but, the publisher will normally have given the writer an advance of some kind, so the publisher will not pay the writer any money collected for any songwriter royalties *until* the advance has been recouped.

In consideration of this agreement, the Publisher agrees to pay the Songwriter an advance of $_____in hand paid, receipt of which is hereby acknowledged, which sum shall be deductible from any payments hereafter becoming due the Writer(s) under this agreement.

Then there are **co-publishing deals**, where the songwriter has his own publishing company, and makes a deal with a second publisher, and both publishers many times may *co-own* the copyright and publisher's share of income. In this situation, most times an advance in also given that has to be recouped.

An example of a co-publishing agreement's copyright language:

c. The composition is to be copyrighted in the joint names of the parties hereto, and the composition's joint ownership, under the terms of this agreement, shall be for the life of the copyright and of any renewal of the copyright and of any renewal terms anywhere in the world.

The basic split of income from a song in this type of deal will be 50% for the songwriter, 25% for the songwriter's publishing company that he or she *owns*, and the remaining 25% for the publishing company he or she does the co-publishing deal with; over-all it will be a 75%-25% split (if no administration fees, etc are calculated in). Or maybe an easier way of thinking of it will just be that the writer keeps his or her "writer's" share, and then the *publishing share* will be split 50/50 or whatever the agreed upon deal is.

An example of a co-publishing agreement's percentage language:

a. _____ and _____ agree to CO-PUBLISH the composition on a fifty fifty (50-50) basis: First Party to receive fifty (50%) percent, and Second Party to receive fifty (50%) percent of any and all of the publishing receipts of said composition.

b. Public Performance Rights in and to the composition will be assigned to and licensed by (The Performance Rights Organizations – ASCAP, BMI or SESAC) and is here authorized to pay directly to each of the publishers the following: (a) First Party, 50%; (b) Second Party, 50%.

AN EXAMPLE
In a very imaginary situation, where NO advances had been issued...

Let's say, we have two different songwriters - Mr. Adam and Ms. Eve, who write a song called *"He Tricked You, Then I Got Tricked"*. Mr. Adam has his *own* publishing company called **Bad-rib Music,** *which* made a *"co-publishing deal"* with **3n1 Music Publishing**. And let's say that Ms. Eve has a *"standard songwriting publishing deal"* with **Live D Music Publishing**. *If NO advance had been paid to each of these writers,* the **1 song disbursement from Mechanical royalties (in 2005), on 12,000 records, which would be about $1,000 collected, would breakdown to looking something like this:**

| SONGWRITING % SHARE = **$500** | PUBLISHING % SHARE = **$500** |

Mr. Adam's songwriter's take **$250**

Ms. Eve's songwriter's take **$250**

Mr. Adam's own publishing company – **Bad-rib Music** gets **$125**

3n1 Music Publishing will get **$125**, *...because of the co-publishing deal with* **Bad-rib Music** *– Mr. Adam's company*

LIVE D Music Publishing will get **$250** *...because Eve made a standard songwriter's deal...*

Now, more often than not, most publishing deals that are offered to songwriters, especially in Hip-Hop and R&B music... the *better* deals come about because a song or songs have been placed on a project that will be getting ready for release, or has already been placed on a project that is already been released and probably doing well.   Most publishers will only offer a contract with *big* money on the table, if the song(s) are in a position or going to *be in a position* to make money. This is why it's so important, if you are a stand-alone songwriter, to be collaborating with producers and also artists that have projects being released. And the major publishers like BMG or EMI will usually consider approaching   songwriters,   or   especially   songwriter/producers   and artist/songwriters when they *know* that there are songs placed on a CD project and are going to be promoted, especially if the song or songs are going to be on a major label release. ˙And then there are major corporations like Sony or Warner that have music divisions that routinely offer publishing deals to strengthen their overall catalog's worth. When one of these music giants knows the project is coming out, especially when the project is on one of their affiliate companies, and they *believe* the project is going to be successful and promoted well, they believe that they will probably make "x" amount of dollars. With this being the case, they may start seeking out the songwriters who are involved on the project, and offer them a publishing deal. Also, if a songwriter has multiple song projects being placed on major labels, especially if the writer has collaborated with successful major artist(s) or major producers, what ends up happening is that publishers will many times offer incredible amounts of money up front on the deal. And this is a pretty good position to be in if you want a publishing deal because the attorney you hire can negotiate the best situation for you, not only in the advance money, but also a better overall deal through a co-publishing contract or **administration deal**, as opposed to a *standard* songwriter deal. But **Note**: Commit this to memory: If you are considering a publishing deal, *in most cases*, there needs to be advance funds offered; m o n e y … *laid out* on the table.

..Administration Deal?

• *An **administration deal** is when a songwriter signs a deal, usually with a bigger company to collect money from the publishing of his or her songs. The administrator may get anywhere from 10% to 20% of all that they collect, and then the songwriter (and his company) will get the balance. The administration deal may last anywhere from 1 year to 3 years to several years, just depending on the deal. In an administration deal, the songwriter and his or her company own the copyright.*

Before I finish this section of *this* segment, I do want to let you know that publishing deals are different in almost every case. I think the main thing any writer with a publishing company should be concerned with if they are approached with a deal, is taking a hard look at just who is offering the deal. And songwriters can't get too caught up on owning all of there publishing either if there is a great situation being presented; in reality, you should not always think that owning most of or all of your song – having your own company is the best way to go, particularly if a great publishing deal is being presented… you might just *miss out* on opportunity, and end up owning the majority or 100% of *nothing*. I have personally signed into a publishing agreement that got me about $40,000 in advance, and I had no control or ownership of anything… but in reality, most times many songwriters end up giving up part or all of the copyright, but in exchange for keeping the bills paid through payments from the publisher and the publisher's ability to get potential work and songs placed. I have watched one of my best friends sign into a publishing deal with one of the biggest major publishers that was *crazy* lucrative; like $250,000 up front for the 1st year, with escalations every year the publisher picked up the option top renew his contract – based on a song he *co-wrote* that topped the Billboard charts at No. 1 for about 8+ weeks. Not only did he get the major publishing deal, but also because he was a producer, the publisher got him on about 30 productions as a producer, and they were all major projects. But, to go to the *other* end of the scale, I've watched one of my other friends sign over his copyright and publishing on a song and take a single-song deal with a small company for only $3,000… and the song was being placed on a *major*…major project, that *everyone* (except him apparently) *knew* would be a success. And to top it off, *his song* ended up being the "BIG-HIT" …*ouch!*

So, just know that all deals *are* different, and that's why you should always have an attorney to counsel you. Also, in today's "new" music industry, better deals are being made all of the time, especially since artists and producers are becoming more educated, and publishers are finding new ways to find revenue for publishing; video games, ringtones, on-line music services, digital jukeboxes and digital background music services. And the best way a songwriter, artist, or producer can stay on top of his or her game is to simply have great representation to make the best deal for them. In addition, it's not uncommon these days for artists/songwriters or producer/songwriters to get co-publishing deals with advances that *start* in the six-figure category, and then have the rights to the song revert *back* to the writer at some point. See, the advance money is just one part of having a good publishing deal. There are also other issues like reversions, audits, the term of the contract, the territory and sub-publishing, the cost of litigation if the song you *say you wrote* turned out to *not* be so – with an infringement lawsuit on the table. So, as I've already said, just have an attorney on your team, to make the best deal possible.

Ok… now, read on…

WHAT IS A PUBLISHING DEAL?
…and do I really need one?
By Wallace Collins, Esq.

The term "publishing," most simply, means the business of copyrights. As a songwriter you own 100% of your song copyright and all the related publishing rights until you sign those rights away. Under the law, copyright (literally, the right to make and sell copies) automatically vests in the creator the moment the expression of an idea is "fixed in a tangible medium." (In other words, the moment you write it down or record it on tape.) With respect to music, there are really two copyrights: a copyright in the musical composition owned by the songwriter and a sound recording copyright in the sound of the recording owned by the recording artist (but usually transferred to the record company when a record deal is signed).

You own the copyright in your work the moment you write it down or record it, and you can only transfer those rights by signing a written agreement to transfer them. Therefore, you must be wary of any agreement you are asked to sign. Although it is not necessary, it is advisable to place a notice of your copyright on all copies of the work. This consists of the symbol "c" or the word "copyright", the author's name, and the year in which the work was created, for example: " (c) John Doe 1993."

The filing of a copyright registration form in Washington D.C. gives you additional protection in so far is it establishes a record of the existence of such copyright and gives you the presumption of validity in the event of a lawsuit. Registration also allows for lawsuits to be commenced in Federal court and, under Federal law, allows an award of attorney's fees to the prevailing party. Currently, the filing fee is only $30.

As defined by the copyright law, the word "publish" most simply means "distribution of copies of a work to the public by sale or other transfer of ownership, or by rental lease, or lending." As a practical matter, music publishing consists primarily of all administrative duties, exploitation of copyrights, and collection of monies generated from the exploitation of those copyrights. If you make a publishing deal and a publisher takes on these responsibilities then it "administers" the compositions. Administrative duties range from filing all the necessary registrations (i.e., copyright forms) to answering inquiries regarding the musical compositions.

One of the most important functions of music publishers is exploitation of a composition or "plugging" a song. Exploitation simply means seeking out different uses for musical compositions. Music publishers have professional quality demos prepared and send them to artists and producers to try to secure recordings. They also use these tapes to secure usage in the television, film, and advertising industries.

Equally important as exploitation is the collection of monies earned by these musical usages. There are two primary sources of income for a music publisher: earnings that come from record sales (i.e., mechanical royalties) and revenues that come from broadcast performances (i.e., performance royalties). Mechanical royalties are collected directly from the record companies and paid to the publisher. Performance royalties are collected by performing rights organizations - ASCAP, BMI, and SESAC - and then distributed proportionally to the publisher and to the songwriter. In addition to plugging and administrative functions, it is also important to know that there is a creative side to music publishing. Since producing hit songs is in the best interest of both the writer and the publisher, good music publishers have whole departments devoted to helping writers growing and develop. The creative staff finds and signs new writers, works with them to improve their songs, connects them with co-writers, and hopes the outcome will be hit records.

If you decide to do a publishing deal then the main issue for negotiation is going to be the language pertaining to the calculation and division of the monies. In the old days, most deals were 50/50 because there was a concept that the "writer's share" was 50% and the "publisher's share" was 50%. This, of course, was an invention of the publishers. Legally, these terms have no such inherent meaning but their calculation is defined in each individual agreement. Most modern publishing deals, however, are referred to as "co-publishing" deals and the monies are usually calculated at around 75/25 meaning the writer gets 100% of the 50% writer's share and 50% of the publisher's 50% share for a total of 75%. It is best for the writer to insist that all calculations be made "at source" so that there are not too many charges and fees deducted off the top before the 75% calculation is made… fees additional. Keep in mind, however, that the advance paid to the writer by the publisher is later recouped by the publisher out of the writer's share of income from the song. So, the net business effect is that the publisher pays the writer with the writer's own money to buy a share of the copyright (and the right to future income) from the writer.

Although a writer can be his own publisher and retain 100% of the money, the larger publishers in the music business usually pay substantial advance payments to writers in order to induce them to sign a portion of their publishing rights to the publisher - and this can be a good thing for the writer. Although a deal for a single song may be done with little or no advance payment (provided there is a reversion of the song to the writer if no recording is released within a year or two), there should be a substantial advance paid ($5,000-$25,000+) to a writer for any publishing deal with a longer term (e.g., 3-5 years).

Publishing deals have to do with *more than just the money*… and since every music publisher is different, it is important for the songwriter to assess both the *business and the creative* sides of a music publisher *before* signing a deal.

Music Powers

MAJOR PUBLISHING COMPANIES

ALMO / IRVING MUSIC - LA
360 North La Cienega Boulevard
Los Angeles, CA 90048
310- 289-3500

BMG MUSIC - LA
8750 Wilshire Blvd.
Beverly Hills, CA 90211
310-358-4700 / Fax 310-358-4727
www.bmgsong.com

BMG MUSIC - NY
1540 Broadway, 39th Floor
New York, NY 10036
212-930-4000 / Fax 212-930-4263

CHERRY LANE - NY
6 East 32nd Street - 11th Floor
New York, NY 10016
212-561-3000 / Fax 212-683-2040
www.cherrylane.com

CHERRY LANE - LA
5757 Wilshire Blvd., Suite 401
Los Angeles, CA 90036
323-904-4510 / Fax 323-904-4520
www.cherrylane.com

CHRYSALIS MUSIC - LA
8500 Melrose Avenue - Suite 207
Los Angeles, CA 90069
310-652-0066 / Fax 310-652-2024
www.chrysalis.com

CHRYSALIS MUSIC - NASH
1204 16th Ave. South
Nashville, TN 37212
615-327-4797
www.chrysalis.com

DREAMWORKS MUSIC
331 North Maple Drive - Suite 300
Beverly Hills, CA 90210
310-288-7722
www.dreamworkspublishing.com

EMI MUSIC – LA
CONTACT: BIG JON PLATT
2700 Colorado Ave., Suite 100
Santa Monica, CA 90404
310-586-2700 / Fax 310-586-2758
www.emimusicpub.com

EMI MUSIC - NY
1290 Avenue Of The Americas
42nd Floor
New York, NY, 10104
212-830-2000

FAMOUS MUSIC - LA
10635 Santa Monica Blvd. - Suite 300
Los Angeles, CA 90025
310-441-1300, 310-441-1317
Fax 310-441-4722

FAMOUS MUSIC - NY
1633 Broadway, 11th Floor
New York, NY 10019
212-654-7418 / Fax 212-654-4748

HITCO MUSIC
500 Bishop Street NW, Suite A-5
Atlanta, GA, 30318
404-352-5911 / Fax 404-352-4033

PEERMUSIC - NY
810 Seventh Avenue, 10th Floor
New York, NY 10019
212-265-3910 / Fax 212-489-2465
newyork@peermusic.com

PEERMUSIC - LA
5358 Melrose, Suite 400
Hollywood, CA 90038
323-960-3400 / Fax 323-960-3410

QUINCY JONES MUSIC
3800 Barham Blvd., Suite 503
Los Angeles, CA 90068
323-882-1340 / Fax 323-874-0143
www.quincyjonesmusic.com

ROSEN MUSIC
Los Angeles, CA 90025
310-230-6040 / Fax 310-230-4074
www.rosenmusiccorp.com
steven@rosenmusiccorp.com

SONY/ATV MUSIC - LA
2100 Colorado Ave.
Santa Monica, CA 90404
310-449-2100 / Fax 310-449-2518
www.sonyatv.com
info@sonyatv.com

SONY/ATV MUSIC - NY
550 Madison Ave., 18th Floor
New York, NY 10022
212-833-4729 / Fax 212-833-5552
www.sonyatv.com

SPIRIT MUSIC GROUP
137 Fifth Ave, 8th Floor
New York, NY 10010
212-533-7672 / Fax 212-979-8566

TVT PUBLISHING
23 East 4TH Street - 3rd Floor
New York, NY 10003
212-979-0842

UNIVERSAL MUSIC - LA
CONTACT: DONNA CASEINE
2440 S. Sepulveda - Suite 100
Los Angeles, CA 90064
310-235-4700 / Fax 310-235-4904
www.umusicpub.com
www.universalmusicpublishing.com
www.umpg.com

www.umusic.com
UNIVERSAL MUSIC - NY
1755 Broadway, 8th Floor
New York, NY, 10019
212-841-8000

UNIVERSAL MUSIC - NASH
12 Music Circle South
Nashville, TN 37203
615-313-7676

WARNER CHAPPELL
57th Broadway
New York, NY 10019
212-419-2600
www.warnerchappell.com

WARNER-CHAPPELL MUSIC - NY
1775 Broadway, 23rd Floor
New York, NY 10019
212-419-2600
www.warnerchappell.com

WARNER-CHAPPELL MUSIC
10585 Santa Monica Blvd. – 3rd Fl
Los Angeles, CA 90025
310-441-8600 / Fax 310-470-8780
www.warnerchappell.com

WINDSWEPT PACIFIC
9320 Wilshire Blvd., Suite 200
Beverly Hills, CA 90212
310-550-1500 / Fax 310-247-0195

ZOMBA MUSIC - NY
137-139 W. 25th St.
New York, NY 10001
212-824-1744 / Fax 212-242-7462
www.zomba.com

ZOMBA MUSIC - LA
9000 Sunset Blvd., Suite 300
W. Hollywood, CA 90069
310-247-4300 / Fax 310-247-8366

Music Powers

THE MAKING OF YEAH!

How a hit song almost never got made

Lil Jon comes up with the music track.

WHHAAAATT!!! OKAYEEEEEEEE!!!

Sean Garrett and J. Que Smith write lyrics.

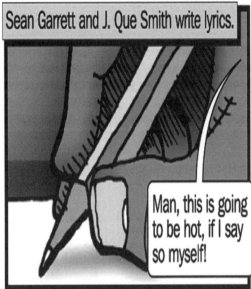

Man, this is going to be hot, if I say so myself!

Garrett plays the song for record exec L.A. Reid, who doesn't think it's up to Usher's standards.

Reid, just listen to it. It's the next big thing!

Garrett and Smith rewrite the chorus to give it a little story. Reid likes it.

Let me make the changes and then just maybe he'll let it be recorded.

THE MAKING OF YEAH!

How a hit song almost never got made

It sounds like Michael Jackson should be doing this.

Man, I am so not feeling this joint.

Usher isn't sure it's an "Usher song," but records it anyway (with help from Ludacris).

Over Thanksgiving in Miami, Reid hears the same Lil Jon track on Petey Pablo's "Freek-A-Leek."

WHAT!

♫ Shameka. Keisha. Tara. Shawna. Sabrina. Crystal. Daronda. ♫

Reid flips, calls Garrett's boss, Shakir Stewart, and cusses him out.

What the #@*% is going on? Get this thing straightened out NOW!

Stewart sends Lil Jon back into the studio, where he and his collaborators come up with new keyboard chords.

Yo man, Reid is upset! Let's just make some changes to smooth things over.

It shouldn't be a problem. Let's get LRoc down here.

THE MAKING OF YEAH!
How a hit song almost never got made

THE MAKING OF YEAH!

How a hit song almost never got made

"Yeah!" helps Usher's "Confessions" rack up history-making first-week sales.

Reporting by SONIA MURRAY / AJC   Illustration by JEROME THOMPSON / Staff
©2005 The Atlanta Journal-Constitution – Reprinted with permission by The Atlanta Journal-Constitution

SAMPLING CLEARANCE

Sampling is when sound bytes are removed electronically from a master recording and through technological imitation placed within the context of another composition. The length of the bytes can be limitless and can contain lyric and music in combination or in part from any segment of the score. Depending upon the length of the bytes and how they are used, unauthorized sampling could be held to be a copyright infringement of the sound recording from which they were taken and from the musical work they first appeared in.

So, if you *are* planning on using samples in your music from other previously recorded songs, especially for distribution, then you must... I said must... one more time gang, *"YOU MUST GET CLEARANCE!!!"* Please don't wait until the last minute to contact the publisher who owns the rights to the song. Also, you will need to negotiate with whoever (like the label) actually *owns* the masters from which you have borrowed the sample. If you don't get early clearance from these two, the difference in their cooperation or their willingness to work with you, i.e. the cost - it might be overwhelming.

I decided to reach out to one of the entertainment attorneys, Ben McLane that advised me on the Music Powers project, and I asked his *best* advice concerning Sample Clearance, and he simply told *me, "Use a professional Sample Clearance company or consultant!"*

OK- so basically it's like this, a sample clearance pro can take you through the whole process and advise you, and they know *exactly* what to do and *how* to get it done. They already have relationships with the labels and publishers most times, and overall, they will probably save you a whole lot of time and aggravation as opposed to if you are trying to get a sample cleared on your own. Researching who owns the copyright and masters alone is enough stress and time, and for the most part, hiring a sample clearance company to handle the negotiations and possible research it takes to get a sample cleared is just worth it. But, you should go ahead now and put this to memory; most publishers and owners of the masters *will* want some type of advance payment up front… and there is no set price for this. Also, publishers may also want a percentage of whatever revenue the song generates. So be smart; get clearance, and also hire a sample clearance professional to help you

.

Places to do your research to find the copyright owner(s):

| www.bmi.com | www.ascap.com | www.harryfox.com | www.copyright.gov |

The information you will need for Sample Clearance:

THE ORIGINAL SONG YOU SAMPLED FROM	THE NEW SONG
Song Title:	New Song Title:
Copyright Owner:	Songwriter:
Publisher:	Publisher:
Songwriter:	Artist:
Artist:	Label:
Record Label:	Distributor:
Describe the original song, within the new song:	Distribution Amount:
	Release Date:

❑ **Note**: So not to confuse anyone, if you are borrowing from a song by actually replaying the part in the song, then you will only need clearance from the publisher.

GOOD LUCK

Music Powers
LEGAL MIXTAPES?

Recently, a rap group's manager out of Atlanta asked me, *"How do you put out a legal Promotional Mixtape?"*

So, I reached out to entertainment attorney Ben Mclane, and here was his response:

> The formal way to do it would be to contact the different labels that the artists are signed to and *get permission* to release the material on the Mixtape.

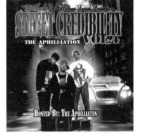

> You should also contact the music publishers that represent the songs, so you can get mechanical licenses to release the Mixtape. *See bmi.com and ascap.com to see who controls the songs*

> Also, if the artists are "indie" (not on a label), you just have to contact the artists and deal with them directly.

THE REALITY

⇒ *"Of course, most Mixtapes never bother with these proper steps above since they are usually "under the radar" and also because this process can take some time, but that is the proper way to do it"*

Ben McLane, Esq. of McLane & Wong, is a full service global entertainment law firm
Specializing in music law www.benmclane.com

Mclane & Wong

Music Powers

SAMPLING - COPYRIGHT - MUSIC CLEARANCE & LICENSING SERVICE DIRECTORY

COPYRIGHT CLEARINGHOUSE, INC.

405 Riverside Dr.
Burbank, CA 91506
818-558-3480
Fax 818-558-3474

DMG CLEARANCES

13 Robin Drive
Hockessin, DE 19707
302-239-6337
Fax 302-239-6875
Info@dmgclearances.com
www.dmgclearances.com

MUSIC REPORTS, INC.

405 Riverside Dr.
Burbank, CA 91506
818-558-1400
Fax 818-558-3484
www.musicreports.com

MUSIC RESOURCES, INC.

6671 Sunset Blvd., Suite 1574-A
Los Angeles, CA 90028
323-993-9915
Fax 323-993-9921
mr@musicresources.com
www.musicresources.com

PARKER MUSIC GROUP

2934 1/2 Beverly Glen Circle
Suite 220
Bel Air, CA 90077
818-905-9552
Fax 818-905-7807
www.musicclearance.com
randy@musicclearance.com

SAMPLE CLEARANCE LIMITED

162 W. 56th Street, #306
New York, NY 10019
212-707-8804
Fax 212-707-8952
dwiesses@sampleclearanceltd.com

Music Powers

TALENT & BOOKING AGENTS

Talent and booking agencies are in the business of booking artists for work. Agents are important because they help to keep you working by soliciting your live show to different club and concert promoters, nightclub owners and managers, college events, city and county music events, regional live performance venues, etc. to get gigs for you or your group. The different unions – AFM, AFTRA, and SAG, govern licensed booking agents, so the majority of talent agencies *do* have to follow certain regulations.

AFM - AMERICAN FEDERATION OF MUSICIANS
AFTRA - AMERICAN FEDERATION OF TELEVISION & RADIO ARTIST
SAG - SCREEN ACTOR'S GUILD

CHECK THE AGENTS REP

Make sure when choosing a booking agent, you do similar background checks as mentioned in the previous chapters – Check for their clients. Also, find out if there have been any complaints or lawsuits, *and what the outcome was.*   **Note:** Make sure the agency has the connections with the *right* promoters and clubs to keep your money coming in from live performances.

HOW LONG DO I CONTRACT WITH THEM?

Seek only to sign with a talent and booking agency for at most, one year. This way, you will be covered if things don't go well between your agent and yourself. There are actually many, many booking agents out there, so finding another agent to represent you should not be too difficult. If you really want to feel secure with this decision, when you're seeking out the right agent, you should have enough confidence in your personal manager to assist in handling this responsibility (see Personal Management).   Now, maybe you're beginning to understand the importance of getting good management.

COMMISSIONS - HOW MUCH?

Expect to pay nearly all talent and booking agents a commission of 10% of the income that's generated by their bookings. And although it's not always possible, seek to pay on your "net" take. Of course, whatever the commission is, if the agent is *keeping* you paid, and the gigs are good, don't stress. The bottom line is, *"If you're planning on performing... so that money is always being generated night-to-night, you will need a good talent agent!"*

GOOD LUCK!

TALENT & BOOKING AGENTS

Select Talent & Booking Agents in the USA

THE AGENCY GROUP- W
9348 Civic Center Dr - 2nd Fl
Beverly Hills, CA 90210
310-385-2800
www.theagencygroup.com

THE AGENCY GROUP – E
1775 Broadway - Suite 515
New York, NY 10019
212-581-3100
www.theagencygroup.com

**AGENCY FOR THE
PERFORMING ARTS**
9000 Sunset Blvd. – 12th Fl
Los Angeles, CA 90069
213-582-1500

AMERICAN TALENT
173 Main Street
Ossining, NY 10562
914-944-9500
www.americantalentagency.net

ARTIST GROUP
150 East 58th St. – 19th Fl
New York, NY 10155
212-813-9292

CENTRAL ENT. GROUP
166 5th Ave - 4th Floor
New York, NY 10010
212-921-2190
www.cegtalent.com

CHAMPION SOUND
3609 Boren Street
San Diego, CA 92115
619-287-1729
www.championsound.com

**CLEAR CHANNEL
TOURING**
200 Basse Rd.
San Antonio, TX 78209
210-822-2828

COAST II COAST
3350 Wilshire Blvd. - # 1200
Los Angeles, CA 90010
213-471-1100
www.artistbookings.com

CONTAGIOUS MUSIQ – E
1000 West Ave. - Suite 925
Miami Beach, FL 33139
305-534-9358
www.contagiousmusiq.com

CONTAGIOUS MUSIQ - W
P.O. Box 20624
Seattle, WA 98102
206-322-0593
info@contagiousmusiq.com
www.contagiousmusiq.com

**CREATIVE ARTIST
AGENCY**
9830 Wilshire Blvd.
Beverly Hills, CA 90212
310-288-4545
www.caa.com

ENTOURAGE TALENT
133 West 25th Street
New York, NY 10001
212-633-2600
www.entouragetalent.com

EVOLUTION TALENT
1776 Broadway – 15th Fl
New York, NY 10019
212-554-0300

HIGH ROAD TOURING
751 Bridgeway – 3rd Floor
Sausalito, CA 9 4965
415-332-9292
www.highroadtoruing.com

ICM - BEVERLY HILLS
8942 Wilshire Boulevard
Beverly Hills, CA 90211
310-550-4000
rb_hiphop@icmtalent.com
www.icmtalent.com

ICM - NY
40 West 57th Street
New York, NY 10019
212-556-5600
rb_hiphop@icmtalent.com
www.icmtalent.com

MONTEREY PENINSULA
509 Hartnell Street
Monterey, CA 93940
831-375-4889
www.mpanewyork.com

**VARIETY ARTIST
INTERNATIONAL**
1924 Spring St.
Paso Robles, CA 93452
805-237-4275

**WILLIAM MORRIS AGENCY
- NY**
1325 Avenue of the Americas
New York, NY 10019
212-586-5100
www.wma.com

**WILLIAM MORRIS AGENCY
- LA**
One William Morris Place
Beverly Hills, CA 90212
310-859-4000
www.wma.com

**WILLIAM MORRIS AGENCY
- MIAMI**
119 Washington Ave - # 400
Miami Beach, FL 33139
305-938-2000
www.wma.com

Management – Talent Consultant – Entertainment Co.

"Helping Others Reach their D.R.E.A.M.S."

D.ream, R.appers, E.ntertainers, A.ctors, M.odels

Founded by Sabrina Montgomery, DreamCatchers Entertainment (DCE) is one of Atlanta's most recognized companies that was built and established to help others nurture their God-given talents, and show that dreams *can* become a reality. The company's mission: Helping talented individuals - singers, rappers, dancers, actors, comedians, models, and other entertainers achieve their goals and dreams of having a successful career in the entertainment industry.

Through years of networking, DreamCatchers has become an extremely resourceful engine. These resources are utilized to aid talent and driven individuals along the sometimes-challenging road to success. DreamCatchers resources also help talent to establish relationships through networking, and more importantly, provide opportunities.

DreamCatchers Entertainment is becoming not only one of Atlanta's fastest growing entertainment companies, but also, due to the company's focus, continuous hard work and tremendous growth, the company now handles everything from organizing fashion shows, parties, charity events, talent bookings, photo shoots, model management & promotions, street and club promotions throughout the Southeast. Our list of duties is ongoing and never-ending as are our obligations to make sure entertainers are given the opportunity to "Catch their Dream"!

Management – Talent Consultant – Entertainment Co.

www.DreamCatchersEntertainment.com

404-454-4200

SPOTLIGHT
DreamCatchers Entertainment
Sabrina Montgomery

Some of DCE's current and past clients include

BME Recordings
Arista
Billboard Music Conference
Music Powers
Atlantis Music Conference
VIBE
1st Annual Hip-Hop Conference in Atlanta
Crunk Energy Drink
The Underground Talent Mart on UPN
SUMC
Phenomenon TV on PAX
Kieaun the GoldnChild
Ill-Noise Entertainment
GSU Spotlight
Georgia State University Concerts & Events
GSU's Infinite Appeal Modeling Organization
Fashion Show Coordinator & Creative Consultant
Iceberg Magazine, Street Masters Magazine
...and more

Music Powers

Exclusive Advice from Music Powers Advisor:

DreamCatchers Entertainment
Sabrina Montgomery

Management – Talent Consultant – Entertainment Company

FINDING GIGS

1   What's the first thing an artist needs to do to find live gigs?

One of the first things an artist needs to do is to create a strong team to help get the project off the ground. This team needs to *consistently* keep their ears and eyes on whatever is going on in the streets for new gigs. Starting off, your team may only consist of supportive family members and/or friends, if you don't have an established managerial team to help push, promote, and sell your show, music, and project to different promoters. As you continue to build, some people will go and new ones will come… until you find who and what you need to get the job done, or… until a *seasoned* manager comes along to take the project to the next level.

➢ Once you have a strong team established, I encourage all artists to promote to a point to which they can start putting their own shows together for more exposure and also for more profit. This requires getting your *own* venue, handling your own street promotions, and any and all expenses. Many times, no one can promote "you" better than *you*… If done right.

➢ Resourceful guides for upcoming events and gigs are your local newspapers, entertainment guides, and magazines

⇒   *for Atlanta:*
      …Creative Loafing, Access Atlanta, and Rolling Out

Also, check flyers, radio, and Internet searches for various events such as open mics, showcases, conferences, auditions, or submissions for opening acts. All of these elements are critical to your search in finding live gigs.

2   When an artist is first starting out, how long of a show or set is needed?

➢   Most promoters only allow one song, or maybe a 3 to 5 minute show upfront, so it's good to start with a show-cd around that length. As promoters get to know you and acknowledge your talent, they will start asking you to do a longer show, usually from 7 to 10 minutes, depending on the event. As your song(s) begins to pick up, and starts getting you more attention, you'll definitely start to get paid (at some point), and when that time comes, the length of your performance will be written into your booking contract.

ORIGINAL TRACKS VS. COVER SONGS

3   Should an artist do all original material, or cover songs, or a mixture… what?

➢   It's good for new artists to do a mixture of material; perhaps a few bars with a familiar beat to allow people to vibe with you, and then once you do the beat and gain their attention, transition into your own material. Be sure that if you pick a classic beat, you represent that producer or artist to the *fullest* because you will be tuned out if you murder a classic, or a hit.

4   Do artists *absolutely* have to hire a professional talent agent to book them, or can they get their package to club owners & promoters themselves?

➢   Once an artist has his or her show and package together and if they're *ready*, they can definitely get it to club owners and promoters themselves. But, this is *only* effective if they are out in the streets grinding and networking. If artists find that they *don't* have the connections, then it's usually only a matter time and working harder; making a "buzz," all until their presence is felt and they are well respected. Now if you know you're not a great speaker or not business savvy, be sure to have someone on your team that is. *But know this…*

"…You, your label name, and everyone around you, represents your business!"

The last thing you want to do is to upset a club owner or a promoter that you'll need to do business with in the hopefully very near future. This applies when speaking with labels and the djs too.

➢ Another thing, artists that are consistently performing and hitting the streets are generally very well known for their *work* ethics and are usually gaining a name for themselves and their music.   Promoters, potential managers, club owners, and others in the entertainment industry who may be able to assist, usually *notice these work ethics,* which sometimes opens *more* doors, or at least more opportunities to be heard.

COLLEGE & HIGH SCHOOL GIGS

5 How can an artist get gigs at the Black Colleges and also High Schools?

An artist can get gigs at black colleges and high schools faster by getting

involved in the community and many of their events. Getting involved with community events may help to open doors for those events that are regular for Black Colleges such as homecomings and spring concerts. You can sometimes submit your package for possible admission as an opening act, but that depends on the *need* of an opening act, and also the relationship you, your manager, or someone on your team has with the concert committee, student activities group, extracurricular activities, or other school committees that are in charge of these types of events. It will differ from school to school.

➢ High Schools aren't going to be for everyone because of the content of the music. So it's good to revise the music if you're submitting to a high school, in particular, so everything they hear is *clean* and positive. Some events within these systems are sponsored by record labels, which sometimes (for a fee), will then allow artists to perform, while others may be headed or contracted out to a particular promoter. Listen for the promoter's name, or check out the flyer and reach out to that company. If they are doing that gig, chances are they have a few other school related events on the way. You'll at least have a "bug" in that promoter's ear, in hopes of participation on the next event. And if you are seeking out gigs in the school systems, by all means, *never* get rude, and always remain humble.

GETTING PAID

6 What's a good price to charge for a new act, a mid-experience act, and also, an artist with 2 years experience or more as a *seasoned working* performer?

➢ A good price for a new act to charge, if they have a strong street "buzz" in their area, or a song on the radio in their area, can be anywhere from $2,000 to $5,000, depending on their popularity or the song's popularity. The price will continue to rise as the song gets more popular or continues to spread throughout the region, or as it climbs the charts.

➤   A mid-experience artist is going to cost more, depending on previous success and current status. They will probably average around $5,000 to $15,000. An experienced seasoned performer, and a hot record will probably average from $15,000 and up. All of these prices of course are rough figures, but it gives a general idea of what beginning, average, and seasoned artists tend to make with the support of the streets and/or radio, and so on. *As an artist hits a crossover audience, the numbers tend to get higher and higher* - $50,000 to $100,000 easily (*Usher, B2K, Lil Jon, Outkast,* & other high profile artists).

OPENING SHOWS FOR CONCERTS

7   How do artists get booked to open up on shows for established acts and on the big regional shows?

➤   Artists get booked to open shows and on big regional shows in just about the same manner as high schools and colleges. If you don't have a hot single working that has already gained dj and/or radio recognition, or the promoter himself isn't "putting you on," then you will probably be asked to submit a package for consideration (which is sometimes followed by a fee). Sometimes, you have promoters that allow you to "hop on" the show as a *paid* sponsor of the event or tour. The key to a lot of these gigs, until your music speaks for itself, is to continue to grind, and more importantly to network as you grind. And remember that your image, your character, and your work ethics will speak for you, when your song hasn't (...yet!) Again, "Stay humble!"

8   Should an artist have a DJ & Road Manager, or is it ok to mainly do track dates by yourself?

➤   A new act should at least have a road manager on the road to speak for them, and also handling the in-and-outs such as keeping up with itineraries, show CDs, promotional items, etc., and any other necessary elements that the artist shouldn't have to worry about. Plus, it adds a bit of professionalism to the package, as long as the artist is well represented. As long as the artist doesn't forget that he is still representing himself even when he isn't even saying anything. FYI: Keep the fellows that just want to cause problems (in the beginning for sure) at home. This is your job, and it should be run as your business. Think about it; you can't take your friends to work with you anywhere else. Personally, I know of artists who have *never been asked back,* and some that rubbed djs the wrong way; to where they *stopped* playing their music and/or had it pulled from radio because of the artist attitudes, or because of their entourage. You don't want that; work hard for 10 years to make it happen, cut up for 30 minutes to demeanor it, and in less than that, you've completed destroyed it. In closing out, if you have a good dj that is *down for the grind*, then I say, *"go for it... as long as it adds to your show!"* But, if your funds *aren't* right, and you are creating an extra expense, then hold off for now. All of that will fall into place in time, when it comes to "all that."

ACCOUNTANT / BUSINESS MANAGERS

Your business manager / accountant's primary job is to keep your money and investments in good standing, which by and large means you'll have a more comfortable life *with* money, than without; struggling to pay your bills, even though you're "making it" on paper. See, eventually, if you are making any money from this business, you *will* need a good business manager / accountant to help with your bank balances, investments, financial planning and one of the biggest issues in this industry; your federal and state taxes. Oh, and by the way, for those of you who *don't know* this, most artists, producers and songwriters are basically paid as self-employed vendors or independent business owners from the labels, publishers, agents, promoters, royalty collection services, and licensing agents, etc.... and there *are no taxes taken out* when they pay you. Consequently, this means you *will have to plan ahead*, and have a good accountant / business manager on your team, so you *don't* end up like so many other *creative* people in this industry (including myself), who have had some very serious tax troubles.

There are producers and artists that I occasionally hear from or hear about, and many of these great creative people have been hit pretty hard with some of the business and tax realities, and financial *challenges* that come with success in the music industry. So, If you are making money in the music business, whether it be from grinding up and down the road, to finally getting those great "all-in" advances for your productions, you will need an accountant on your team or crew to help save you the grief that comes with poor financial planning.

A great business manager will also know how to help you set up your budgets and advances when they come in, so that you or your company actually makes the best of the money through different types of accounts - like money markets, etc. Roger Neal Smith, a Los Angeles financial expert once told me, *"Artists and producers, who regularly get budgets, need to learn to make their money work better for them."* And I firmly agree. I have too many friends that are actually making big big money, but are struggling money-wise...and it is mainly because of poor accounting (or NO accounting) and careless business management of their money. By the way, if you're single, and *have no dependents*, if or when you *do* get your first million-dollar payday, you better know this; in 2005, the Federal Income tax due is *over* $ 331,000.00. So, seek out a good business manager / accountant to help keep you on top of your finances.

...Money Market Account?

• *A money market account is a type of savings account offered by banks and credit unions just like regular savings accounts. The difference is that they usually pay higher interest, have higher minimum balance requirements (sometimes $1000-$2500), and only allow three to six withdrawals per month. Another difference is that, similar to a checking account, many money market accounts will let you write up to three checks each month. (Courtesy of www.money.howstuffworks.com)*

CHECKS & BALANCES

Because your business manager / accountant will be responsible for paying out commissions and making deposits into your account from performances, royalties and advances, etc., make sure you have knowledge of *all your expenditures*. No checks should be sent out without your approval... and at times, no checks should go out without your *own* signature! Also, ask your business manager for monthly tax reports and certainly, your financial balances. In addition, get a statement of any outstanding receivables due from monies payable from all music-generated income.

MONEY GOALS

In truth, money is a very necessary part of our lives, so it's important to set money goals when planning out your future. You will have to stay focused and determined about following your business manager / accountant's advice about your money and whatever plans they set up for you. And just like following the advice of your attorney or personal manager, your accountant's guidance can keep you from *over*-doing it ("*Mr. Baller*") when the money comes rolling in. Your business manager can help you to possibly keep more coming in, than what's going out. Also, a good business manager can help you map out a financial *plan* that will help get you on the best path for your personal and business money goals. If they're your financial advisor, they will provide you with their experience and expert advice, so you not only know what you have, but you'll also know what you can achieve with proper money management, planning and investing.

 **INVESTIGATE**

When researching the background of a specific business manager, if you have some type of reservations about them, make the time to do some type of background check for complaints from past clients and lawsuits. You can always check with the Better Business Bureau, or just ask others on your team; your attorney, personal manager, etc., or others you know in the entertainment industry. By doing this, It will help you make the *best* decision... if this potential team member is right for you, when it comes down to handling *your* money!

SOME LAST MINUTE MONEY TIPS

• *Most people, who know where their cash goes, and how they spend it, end up spending less and saving a whole lot more. So, keep up with cash purchases!*

• *Keep up with your credit situation for both your personal and business financial wellness - Equifax (800-685-1111), Trans Union (800-916-8800), Experian (888-397-3742).*

• *You may really want to consider incorporating your company, to if nothing else - save money on your taxes. The personal liability apprehension is just one of the advantages to incorporating.*

GOOD LUCK!

TAX TIPS

By Ben McLane, Esq.

If a person is actively pursuing a career as a musical artist, and not just playing/writing as a hobby, that person is engaged in a trade or business (i.e., the music business). Hence, an artist can use the Internal Revenue Laws of the United States to his or her advantage. This article will discuss the main deductions that an artist can utilize for the purposes of paying taxes.

So long as an artist incurs expenses that are "ordinary and necessary" in pursuit of that artist's career, the expense should be deductible. However, any expense deducted from a tax return must be backed up by documentation. Therefore, it is imperative that an artist keep complete records of any and all expenses paid in pursuit of the artist's career. Usually, the record will be a receipt.

Note: The IRS does not consider a cancelled check, by itself, adequate to verify a deduction; a receipt is more official and credible. An account book is also recommended to keep track of expenses. The main deductions to be aware of are as follows:

TRAVEL

❑ This would include air, bus, taxi or train fares, and any related transportation.

MEALS AND LODGING

❑ These are deductible if related *primarily* to business.

CAR

❑ Gas, repairs, parking, and depreciation are deductible in total. As an option, in lieu of deducting all the car expenses added together, an artist can simply keep track of the mileage and just take the standard deduction of $0.36 per mile.

ENTERTAINMENT

❑ Meals, drinks, etc. are 50% deductible so long as *primarily* business related.

EQUIPMENT

❑ For an artist, many tools of the trade are deductible. These would include such things as musical equipment, instruments, computer, etc. Moreover, if an artist uses a portion of their home or apartment on a regular basis for business (e.g., practicing, recording, booking, etc.), that portion is deductible as a home office. This means that a percentage of the rent/mortgage and utilities are deductible. For instance, if an apartment has 4 rooms and 1 is used for business, 25% of the rent and utilities are deductible expenses.

The foregoing is to give an artist an overview of potential business deductions. It is advisable to contact an accountant before filing a tax return to confirm that the artist's particular situation allows for these, and/or other tax deductions.

MCLANE & WONG
20501 Ventura Blvd., Suite. 217
Woodland Hills, California 91364
818-587-6801

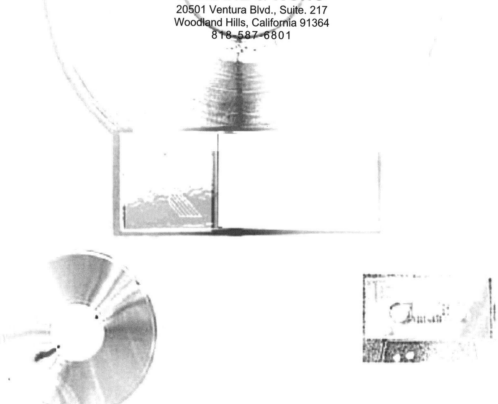

Music Powers
ACCOUNTING – BIZ MANAGEMENT

Select Accountants in Atlanta, New York & Los Angeles. For more listings, including other cities - Please go to www.MusicPowers.com/24

ATLANTA

A-1 TAX ACCOUNTING & FINANCIAL SERVICE
10902 Crabapple Rd.
Atlanta, GA 30303
770-664-4044
www.horrigancpa.com

ACCOUNTANT'S TAX CONSULTANTS & LAWYERS
3551 North Cooper Lake Rd, SE
Atlanta, GA 30303
770-431-1978

BANKS, FINLEY, WHITE & CO, CPA
3504 Main Street
Atlanta, GA 30337
404-763-1002

MELVYN R. BURROW, JD, CPA
131 Ponce De Leon, Suite 230
Atlanta, GA 30308
404-875-5626 / Fax 404-875-1344

DELOITTE TOUCHE TOHMATSU
191 Peachtree St., Suite 1500
Atlanta, Georgia 30303
404-220-1500 / Fax 404-220-1583
www.deloitte.com

FRAZIER & DEETER, LLC
600 Peachtree Street, NE
Suite 1900
Atlanta, Georgia 30308
404-253-7500 / Fax 404-253-7501

CARINA M. GIBBS, PC
Clairmont Center
290 Hwy. 314, Suite A
Fayetteville, GA 30214
770-460-1411, 770-716-4066
Fax 770-460-1611

ROBERT E. KITTRELL, C.P.A., P.C.
1841 Peeler Road, Suite A
Dunwoody, Georgia 30338
770-396-4222 / 877-452-5713
Fax 770-396-4225
info@kittrellcpa.com
www.kittrellcpa.com

KPMG LLP
303 Peachtree Street, NE, Suite 2000
Atlanta GA 30308-3210
404-222-3000 / Fax 404-222-3050
www.kpmg.com

LEGACY PLANNING SERVICES, LLC
1500 Klondike Road, Suite A 107
Conyers, Georgia 30094
770-761-7178 / Fax 770-761-7177
bob@legacyplanningservices.com

JOHN MASTERS, CPA, P.C.
10 Lenox Point
Atlanta, Georgia 30324-3168
404-240-0048 / Fax 404-240-0446
jmasters@jmasters.com

MOORE COLSON
1640 Powers Ferry Rd.
Building 11 , Suite 300
Marietta, GA 30067
770-989-0028 / Fax 770-989-0201
www.moorecolson.com

SHIRLEY OSBORNE
Osborne & Associates, PC
2470 Windy Hill Rd., Suite 138
Marietta, GA 30067
770-955-5441 / Fax 404-955-2159

PRICEWATERHOUSECOOPERS LLP
10 Tenth Street, Suite 1400
Atlanta, GA 30309
678-419-1000 / Fax 419-1239
www.pwc.com

SMITH & HOWARD, CPA
1795 Peachtree Street, NE, Suite 300
Atlanta,, Georgia 30309
404-874-6244, 888-881-4300
Fax 404-874-1658
www.smith-howard.com

SUBDRA VANN, CPA
74 Moore Ave.
Marietta, GA 30080
770-424-4635 / Fax 770-424-4860
svanncpa@yahoo.com

JONES & KOLB
Certified Public Accountants
Ten Piedmont Center - Suite 100
Atlanta, GA 30305
404-262-7920 / Fax 404-237-4034
info@joneskolb.com

MJ PHILLIPS COMPANY
5540 Old National Hwy Suite 8
College Park, GA 30349
404-763-3131 / Fax 404-763-3545
mjp@mjphillipscpa.com

NEW YORK

BDO SEIDMAN, LLP
330 Madison Ave
New York, NY 10017-5001
212 885-8000
Fax 212-697-1299
www.bdo.com

BRUCE BALSAM, CPA
675 3rd Ave
New York, NY 10017
212-972-7500 / Fax 212-972-7050

DELOITTE TOUCHE TOHMATSU
Two World Financial Center
New York, NY 10281
212-436-2000
www.deloitte.com

ERNST & YOUNG LLP
5 Times Square
New York, NY10036
212-773-3000
www.ey.com

KPMG LLP
345 Park Avenue
New York NY 10154
212-758-9700
www.kpmg.com

PRICEWATERHOUSECOOPERS LLP
1177 Avenue of the Americas
New York, NY 10036
646-471-4000
www.pwc.com

PROTAX ACCOUNTANTS
14 Penn Plaza, Suite 1513
New York, NY 10122
212-714-9070 / Fax 212-279-6250

ROTENBERG MERIL SOLOMON BERTIGER & GUTTILLA, P.C
Park 80 West, Plaza One
Saddle Brook, NJ 07663
201-487-8383 / Fax 201-490-2080
www.rmsbg.com

WLODINGUER, ERK & CHANZIS
15 East 26TH ST. – SUITE 1803
New York, NY 10010
212-683-4200 / Fax 212-683-4329
www.wecnyc.com

JEFFREY WOLF, CPA PC
230 W.41 Street 15th Floor
New York, NY 10036
212-382-2451 / Fax 212-382-2452

LOS ANGELES

BOLDEN GRANT & ASSOCIATES
3856 W Martin Luther King Jr.
Los Angeles, CA 90008-1757
323-291-6513

DELOITTE TOUCHE TOHMATSU
Two California Plaza
350 S. Grand Ave. - Suite 200
Los Angeles, CA 90071
213-688-0800
www.deloitte.com

GREER LAURIE MANAGEMENT
824 Moraga Drive
Los Angeles, CA 90049
310-440-4466

KAUFMAN, BERNSTEIN, OBERMAN, TIVOLI & MILLER, LLC.
2049 Century Park East
Suite 2500
Los Angeles, CA 90067
310-277-1900 / Fax 310-277-2049

KPMG
KPMG Tower - Suite 2000
355 S. Grand Avenue
Los Angeles, CA 90071-1568
213-972-4000
www.kpmg.com

MOULTRIE ACCOUNTANCY GROUP
100 Corporate Pointe - Suite 300
Culver City, California 90230-8764
310-568-1250 / Fax 310-568-1253
www.moultriecpa.com

PRICEWATERHOUSECOOPE RS LLP
350 South Grand Avenue - 49th Floor
Los Angeles, CA 90071
212-356-6000
www.pwc.com

PRICEWATERHOUSECOOPE RS LLP
400 South Hope Street - 22nd Floor
Los Angeles, CA 90071-2889
212-236-3000
www.pwc.com

SIMMONS & ASSOCIATES
25031 W. Avenue Stanford - #100
Valencia, CA, CA   91355
661-295-5282 / Fax 661-295-6982

DANIEL L. SMITH, CPA
139 S Beverly Dr Suite 315
Beverly Hills, CA 90212
310-556-8920

Music Powers

PRICELESS ADVICE
TO HELP *YOUR* CAREER

Here's some advice that can help take your game up a level or two. These are very important guidelines that should help keep you moving forward towards success!

1. Ultimately you must be conscious that you are seeking to do something that is much greater than yourself...*by yourself*. With this in mind, please surround yourself with the best energy and then the best people you can find - to help you reach your goals and dreams of *being* successful. My advice is to begin with God – *ALWAYS keeping Him first!* Then, get a great team of people around you to help you out. For the most part, "You" must have enough faith *to "march"* what you believe you can accomplish. You should never *leisurely* walk towards a goal. You must also realize that *believing in yourself*, without *doing for yourself*...is lifeless!"

I highly suggest the following reading:
Chapter 4 – Faith: The Prerequisite to Power
*From **"THINK AND GROW RICH"** by Dennis Kimbro & Napoleon Hill*

2. Learn as much as you can about the music industry. Seek out the help of insiders and key players to help you along. Market 'what' you *know...* and '*know*' your market. This means that you should *never advertise that you're an idiot!* Always be aware that knowledge *is* POWER! If you fail to prepare, you may be preparing to fail! Learn that *being successful* is about **a.** *what* you know, **b.** *who* you know, and **c.** *Understanding how & when to apply it all.*

3. Make sure that every single one of your presentations is as tight as possible. This means that you should get a professional package made up for yourself. Bad presentations hurt more than most artists, producers, songwriters, managers, and Indie labels realize... and the 2nd time around *may* never come. *Remember the rule about 1st impressions.*

4. Always have an Entertainment Attorney check over any contract(s) ...*before* signing. Don't let *anyone* rush you into committing to *anything* before seeking out wise counsel... especially when making crucial decisions.

5. Seek to build a very, very strong fan base doing live shows. And you should be performing as much as possible. Definitely do not limit yourself to just the clubs. Do High Schools, Colleges, City & County Events, and Private Parties too. Believe it or not, The Indie Label BME Recordings (Lil' Jon & The Eastside Boys, Lil Scrappy, etc.) got jump-started by doing House Party Promotions and Events.

All of these performing opportunities will help to get your name and company out to the community. And if your show is tight… you never know who might be there …*and listening.*

6. Once you get your live show happening, then it's time to take your CD production and marketing "quality" up a notch. So when you get an established and solid work schedule… spend the time, effort and *extra* money to invest in making your CD and promotional materials the absolute best they can be.

7. Seriously consider hiring a Professional Media Consultant, a Marketing Team, and/or Publicist. These professionals will help get you the exposure you want *and need.* You must also make the most of the Internet *as much as possible* to expose and create a sense of legitimacy "online." People these days want to look on the web for information about any and everything. So make sure you have a good and *positive* Web presence. This is very important!

8. Always have your CD ready for sale (or as a promo giveaway) at all of your live performances or any music networking events - like artist showcases or any Music Community or Industry Trade shows.

9. For the Indie artists and labels - If you live in one of the Major Cities, don't limit your marketing to that one city. Get out to all of the smaller markets (cities & states) around that region. Many, many new (and established) artists and companies build a very strong fan base in the smaller markets… with *more* support and luv than in *their own* hometowns. So make sure you do live performances and "big-time" promote your music, products, etc. to the smaller markets around the major areas.

10. Never send *unsolicited* packages or music to industry people, companies, or radio stations…period! Always contact them (call …*or write*) for approval and *someone to be on the look out for your hard work and efforts* you have put into your package. If you are a new artist - this *also* means that you should not just 'show up' at a company or radio station… and then think they will be open to greeting you with open arms. If you don't have a big name or some type of relationship with the place you are visiting, don't just pop up without any warning. Most Industry people, labels, and radio stations are busy.

11. Go to as many of the Music Seminars, trade shows, networking events, DJ Pool meetings and Music Industry conferences, as your time (*and sometimes your budget*) will allow. You will often meet many of the people who can very much help you, along with gaining more knowledge about how the music *business* side works.

12. Even if you've got talent and skills, you better know that "The Powers That Be"… able to help you - have to *want to help you.* This probably means that you have the energy, heart, know-how, and sense of focus (…and business) that will *allow them* to risk giving you a shot. You really will need them to like you, and like working *with* and *for you* too. I know of many artists, producers and managers that have played *themselves, and dealt themselves "out" of the music game...* simply because no one wants to deal with their attitudes or the way they handle their opportunities. *Attitude & Altitude go hand in hand.*

13. Once you get a grip on the music business basics, some promotion, a little marketing, and the team of players you *will* need (via industry networking and making friends), don't forget that ultimately - it is your music and yourself that will need to represent you the most (to the fans and public).

14. Whenever *possible*, get your money, or at least *some of it* - up front! ...and *still seek a residual or back-end payment!*

15. When it's time to pay your bills, *sign your own checks!*

...And if you ever find yourself getting confused, stumbling or frustrated, *please*... see rule # 1

GOOD LUCK!

THE FINALE

Well crew, that's it! I hope you've really been able to absorb the information that I have provided. I realize that some of the ways that I've presented the material may seem a little simple and straightforward, and all I can say to that is... Thanks. I've truly made a very conscious effort to do *just that!* (Make it easy) Would you rather I take up your time feeding you a bunch of... "Immense terminology that departs significantly above your cranium, hitherto *nonetheless*, I might *articulate* the p r e c i s e and *accurate* fixation?"

...Hmmm? I'm waiting.

Please... just try to *e m b r a c e* the information. This is pretty much my way of giving something back, and also *"Paying It Forward"* (great movie!) ...in hopes *you don't* have to go through some of the bad experiences I've had over the years in this crazy music game. Overall, the music industry has been great for me, but there *have been* some really bad choices I've made – just from being unaware of some of the most *fundamental* music business issues. And even though I (and most of my industry friends too) have had and *tried* to read the *other* more popular music business guides out... most of these books always seemed to be *too much* for creative people. Even the look and feel of these books when reading them, give off an unapproachable vibe. They seem to have been written for lawyers... *by lawyers.* So *hopefully,* this book can be your "bridge" between your hunger to discover more, and the many other *convoluted* ways of learning the music business. (*See... now go look it up* ☺)

You know, recently I got a compliment from another music producer who I very much respect, and *personally, I think* he is very talented and knowledgeable about the biz too. Anyway, after reading a few of the Music Powers book sections, He said, *"I've always believed if someone is able to break down some of the more complex and difficult issues in anything... in a way that even the simplest mind can understand... there lies the brilliance of the teacher."*

Thank You!

...to every single person who tolerated me, helped me, and most of all, showed me some luv while I was making...

"The Music Powers That Be..."

THE SUMMARY

By Willie Hunter
Entertainment Reporter - Publisher

Now that you've reached the end of *The Music Powers That Be*... it's time to go out with new excitement to make your mark in music. You've been well informed through the author's personal experiences, his knowledge, his listings of valuable industry resources, and access to his colleagues; many of the world's top music industry people, who have given advice to assist you in your music career.

After going through these pages, now you should be well prepared to go out and make the most of your career in the industry. With formal educational institutions such as colleges and universities charging upwards of $12,000 per year to study the various fields encompassing the music industry, one can really learn many of the music business essentials for a small fraction of the cost in 'The Music Powers That Be'.

I have personally witnessed Cirocco as a writer and producer create powerful musical masterpieces. But now, He's created a masterwork that will impact the public on a whole new level.

Willie Hunter

Music Powers
...About The Author

CIROCCO

Producer/Engineer – Consultant – Composer/Arranger - Songwriter

Biography

Listening to a broad range of artists provided fuel for his creative drive, and by the time Cirocco was finishing High School, he was playing guitar professionally with national groups. Before he knew it, he was part of two different recording acts: Pure Gold (Rowe Productions/Capital Records), and Family Plann (Bill Lowery Music Group/T.K. Records). "We toured with some big acts, Including Cameo, The O'Jays, and Millie Jackson... that experience was priceless to me," Cirocco adds.

Once off the road, Cirocco's concentration was original music. Soon he teamed up with producer Jeff Glixman *(Kansas, the Georgia Satellites, Black Sabbath and Yngwie Malmsteen).* Through Glixman, and bassist, Jerry 'Wizard' Seay, Cirocco began tour rehearsals as a 'fill-in' guitarist for the Funk – Rock – R&B band Mother's Finest ("Love Changes" CBS / ATCO). Cirocco soon signed an artist/producer development deal with Glixman's Axis Recording Studios to enhance his own studio skills.

Within three years, his demos attracted the interest of six major record labels, when Orpheus / Hush Productions *(Freddie Jackson, Mellissa Morgan, Najee)* heard Cirocco's well-crafted songs, and invited him to New York. "I was on the next plane," he smiles. Eventually, Geffen Records was selected as Cirocco's recording home. But even though an entire album was completed, the project was never released, as a result of major changes at Geffen's fledging Black Music Division. Down, but never out, Cirocco was asked to go to Los Angeles by Motown & MCA Records. "It was time to move on and grow... so again, I was on the next plane."

Cirocco soon found himself busy in the studio producing and writing for The Boys (MCA), Johnny Gill (Motown), Shanice Wilson (MCA), The Good Girls (Motown), Howard Hewett (Elektra), Georgio (RCA), Leon Sylvers (Motown), Smokey

(Motown) ... etc., etc...*the list goes on.*   Later that year, Cirocco signed to Motown Records as a Staff Producer and A&R Production Consultant.

Cirocco's projects include collaborating with "The King of Pop", Michael Jackson, for the Sega Video Game "Sonic The Hedge Hog"; theme music for BET's "Comic View"; additional production & remix chores for Quincy Jones featuring Tamia; and also additional production work for Alvin Speights and Dallas Austin for the Grammy winning release - Fanmail by TLC.

Some of Cirocco's latest music concentrations have been both creative and professional music business consulting for various music productions and special projects for Manuel Seal Jr., Alvin Speights, Mac Ten Publishing, John Crossland, Rika Muranaka, Charlie Wilson, Oliver Stone Productions, Pilot Music/ESPN Sports Center, PepsiCo, GM-Lincoln Mercury, Brad Buxer, WRM Inc., DreamCatchers Entertainment, Kass Publishing, Sigidi Abdallah, Jacopo TV Productions, Allenhouse Films, ABlackClan Records, Emperor Records, Titanium Recording and many up-and-coming indie producers, artists, songwriters, and managers. Cirocco was equally proud of his participation with the release: "Heaven" (by Ebony Croom & 2Mac) in which he produced and co-wrote for the Special 9-1-1 / September 11 relief fund - sponsored by Kass, The United Way & New Life Outreach.

Currently, Cirocco is writing, producing, and mixing new material for "Mr. Ball" featuring The Ying-Yang Twins, along with doing original music for the new Coolio movie "Tapped Out" from Artisan Pictures Entertainment. And if that was

Cirocco at Titanium Studio

not enough, he's also the author of *"The Music Powers That Be..."* a new music industry book that will truly E M P O W E R the next generation of artists & record producers to make better choices for success by

attaining the knowledge & *real* contacts they will need in order to win... and *not* get cheated playing the music game! Cirocco says, *"I think it's the best help available for new artists & producers with more talent than money!"*

Music Powers
SPOTLIGHT
CIROCCO

Producer/Engineer – Consultant – Composer/Arranger - Songwriter

∞ SELECT CLIENTELE / SELECT DISCOGRAPHY

MICHAEL JACKSON * MOTOWN RECORDS * STEVIE WONDER * GEFFEN
RECORDS * SONY MUSIC * MCA * VIRGIN * CHARLIE WILSON * TLC
DALLAS AUSTIN * PEPSI COLA * ARISTA RECORDS * SEGA * QUINCY
JONES * THE TEMPTATIONS * RCA * ELEKTRA * BET * VIACOM * PRIORITY
BMG * ARTISAN PICTURES * THE UNITED WAY * WARLOCK
MANUEL SEAL JR * ALVIN SPEIGHTS * MAVERICK ENTERTAINMENT GROUP

TAPPED OUT – ARTISAN PICTURES
JOHNNY GILL
HOWARD HEWETT
THE TEMPTATIONS
THE GOOD GIRLS
DYMOND
QUINCY JONES (FEATURING TAMIA)
THEME MUSIC -BET - COMIC VIEW
ANDREW LOGAN
THE BOYS
TLC
MICHAEL JACKSON
GEORGIO
LA LA
SMOKEY ROBINSON
FREDA PAYNE
GARY ADKINS
PEPSICO
GM
VIACOM

Done

~~Em~~ for Record Pool   cam Record Pool
D J Bull MP3 @ yahoo . com

ILRECPOOl@ ~ya~ AOl . com
→ Sent message I would like To service The Pool
Can you Please sent me The Requirements

NWW.ATL web Radio. com   Jumpin Jack

Done   MILDO148@ yahoo. com

Sam @ soundworks-sf.com

DC
Disconnected

MISCELLANEOUS RESOURCES

SELECT DIRECTORY OF INDUSTRY RESOUCES
DJ/RECORD POOLS - GRAPHICS - WEB DESIGN & HOSTING - MUSIC SITES
RECOMMENDED RESOURCES & READING

Record Pools

AMERICAN RECORD POOL DC
310-659-7852
www.americanrecordpool.com

**BAY AREA HIP HOP
COALITION** MESSAGE
510- 419-0396

BIGCITYDJ'S MESSAGE
404-501-0220
www.bigcitydjs.com

CMBE MUSIC POOL DC
619- 470-3111

OK **C & M RECORD POOL** Email
251-438-1599

CONNECTICUT MUSIC POOL
203-789-0038 DC
www.ctbeats.com

FLAVOR POOL
www.flavorpool.com

HEAVYWEIGHTS DC
1-888-998-2041
www.heavyweights.org

HOLLA AT YA BOY To Web
513-851-8260
www.orbitalhiphop.com

ILLINOIS RECORD POOL
708-732-6731 Email
www.recordpoolcharts.com

ILL TRENDZ DC
510 435-2198

INLAND EMPIRE DC
909-657-3277

INTERNATIONAL RECORD
619-476-1288 DC
www.irspool.com

JUMPIN JACK
404-663-1130

LEGION OF DOOM DC
404-684-5898
www.lodrecordpool.com

MIAMI RECORD POOL OK
954- 563-3888

MILLION DOLLAR POOL
404-766-1275
1-877-659-3057 Email
www.mildol.com

904 TAMPA OK
813-977-6909
www.904tampa.com

NORTHWEST DANCE NO
206-440-9780
www.nwdma.org

THE PROS MESSAGE
510-839-3000
www.theprosrecordpool.com

RADIO BUMS DC
303-412-9909
www.radiobums.com

RESOURCE RECORD POOL
323- 651-2085 DC

SOBAD DC
408 277-0111
www.sobad-djs.com

SOUL DISCO
415-776-2462

SOUNDWORKS Email
415-487-3980
www.soundworks-sf.com

SOUL CHOICE MESSAGE
416-439-5959
www.soulchoice.ca

S.U.R.E. DC
718-904-0500
www.surerecordpool.com

TEXAS STAR DC
817-652-9400

THE RECORD POOL
www.therecordpool.com

TJS DJS RECORD POOL
850-878-3634 DC
www.tjsdjs.com

URBAN FORCE POOL Lookup
312-226-URBA
www.urbanforcedjpool.com

UPSTART RECORD POOL
904-448-9211 MESSAGE
www.upstart-
entertainment.com

Great Graphics & Printing

A BLACK CLAN
1-877-706-7316 (Toll Free)
www.ablackclan.com

BLAZE 1 GRAPHIXS
678-508-3027
www.blaze1graphixs.com

SANDY DE LA BRETONIERE
www.rebelvision.net

CLUBFLYERS.COM
1-800-433-9298
www.clubflyers.com

DESIGNSNPRINT
678-886-8792
www.designsnprint.com

GLOVER GRAPHICS
586-354-0111
www.glovergraphics.biz

HIPHOPFLYERS.COM
1-866-400-6870
www.hiphopflyers.com

MARKSTARRGRAPHX
1-888-339-7892
www.Msgraphx.com

PHATEFX
323-276-5060
www.phatefx.com

SIGNATURE DESIGNS
1-866-525-0550 (Toll Free)
www.sigdesigns.com

ZACK VAZ - CD GRAPHICS
718-781-7119

YOUNG GUESS GRAPHX
905-384-0814

EB HOSTING DEALS

IX WEB HOSTING
1-800-385-0450
www.ixwebhosting.com

BLUEHOST
1-888-401-4678
www.bluehost.com

EASY CGI
1-866-327-9244
845-920-0100
www.easycgi.com

HOST EXCELLENCE
1-800-792-1197
www.hostexcellence.com

INTERLAND
1-800-392-2032
www.interland.com

IPOWERWEB
1-888-511-HOST
www.ipowerweb.com

YAHOO WEB HOSTING
1-866-781-9246
www.smallbusiness.yahoo.com

Web Design / Flash

www.rebelvision.net

www.10e20webdesign.com

www.andrewpaulhelms.com

www.finerdesign.com

www.gyanart.com

www.in8design.com

www.interland.com

www.leveltendesign.com

www.nrjdesign.com

www.reignmedia.com

Add-ons for websites

www.killersites.com

www.java-scripts.net

www.dynamicdrive.com

webmastertoolscentral.com

SITES TO PROMOTE MUSIC

ALLHIPHOP.COM
www.allhiphop.com

ATL URBAN MIX
www.atlantaurbanmix.com

BAMA HIP HOP
bamahiphop.homestead.com

BET - www.bet.com

CD BABY
www.cdbaby.com

CONTRABANDIT.COM
contrabandit.com

CT BEATS - www.ctbeats.com

DA COME UP
www.dacomeup.com

DIRTY SOUTH RADIO
dirtysouthradio.com

DIRTY SOUTH RAP
www.dirtysouthrap.com

DOWN SOUTH.COM
www.down-south.com

DOWN SOUTH RAP
www.downsouthrap.com

HIPHOP CANADA
www.hiphopcanada.com

HIPHOP-DIRECTORY
hiphop-directory.com

HIPHOPDX www.hiphopdx.com

HIPHOPSITE
www.hiphopsite.com

IAPRADIO - www.iapradio.com

ILL MUSIK
www.illmuzik.com

MEMPHIS RAP
www.memphisrap.com

SOUND CIRCUIT
www.soundcircuit.com

SW CONNECTION
southwest-connection.com

WWW.WORDOFSOUTH.COM

RAP INDUSTRY
www.rapindustry.com

RAPTALK - www.raptalk.net

REBELVISION - www.rebelvision.net

SOUNDCLICK .COM
www.soundclick.com

SICCNESS.NET www.siccness.net

HIGHLY RECOMMENDED

www.RapCoalition.org
www.FutureProducers.com
www.DynamicProducer.com

RECOMMENDED READING

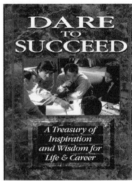

Music Powers
INDUSTRY GLOSSARY & INDEX
LEARNING THE LANGUAGE

A

ADMINISTRATION – *306, 308*
The supervising for a fee (generally a percentage of income), usually by a major music publisher, of a smaller music publisher's financial and copyright matters regarding one or more songs or an entire catalog. The administrator does not necessarily own a share of the copyright, although one co-publisher could administer another co-publisher's share.

ADVANCE – *85, 239, 271, 275*
The payment in advance of royalties to be earned in the future, and recouped by offsetting that future earned royalties against the money advanced. Advances are usually non-refundable.

A LA CARTE SERVICE
A service that allows a consumer to either stream, download or burn music on a fee per transaction basis. Examples include the Apple iTunes and Buymusic.com (Courtesy of Harryfox.com)

A&R (ARTISTS AND REPERTORY) – *29, 51, 52, 57,111, 120, 199*
The department in a record company that selects and deals with new artists, songs, and records.

AUDIO/VISUAL WORK
An industry term for film, television, or any other visual production.

ASSIGNMENT OF COPYRIGHT
The transfer of ownership of a copyright from one party to another, which must be in writing to be effective.

AUDIO HOME RECORDING ACT
That portion of the Copyright Act (§1001-1010) that provides for royalties to be paid to songwriters, music publishers, recording companies and recording artists for the importation or manufacture of digital audio recording devices (e.g., digital tape players) or media (e.g., CDs and tapes).

AUDIT – *277, 292*
Conducted by an independent accounting firm, an audit verifies shipment and sales levels for each audio and music video format after returns. In addition, the audit calculates what product has been shipped for sale, net after returns, versus product used for promotional purposes. A formal certification report is issued and sent to the record company.

AUDIT CLAUSE – *277*
An important clause in any agreement between a songwriter and a publisher, or any business agent, that allows the songwriter the right to have access to the publisher's books and records (usually once a year), so that the songwriter can determine the accuracy of the publisher's accounting practices.

AUTHOR
The creator of "Intellectual Property" such as literary, musical, and dramatic works; choreography; pictorial, graphic, and sculptural works; audio/visual works and sound recordings. Therefore, the word author can denote composer, lyricist, record producer, choreographer, artist, photographer, writer, or other creator (see "Work for Hire").

AUTOMATIC RENEWAL

Works originally copyrighted between 1964 and 1977 are granted an automatic renewal term (See **EXTENDED RENEWAL TERM**) by the Copyright Act, without the necessity of the writer having to file a renewal registration form in order to preserve copyright protection, as was the case for earlier copyrights. However, filing a Form RE (along with payment of the appropriate fee) for automatically renewed works is recommended in order to obtain certain statutory benefits

AUDIO VISUAL INDEX (AVI)

A database containing title and production information for cue sheets which are available from a performing rights organization. Currently, BMI, ASCAP, SOCAN, PRS, APRA and SACEM contribute their cue sheet listings to the AVI.

B

BACKGROUND MUSIC

Music used (other than as feature or theme music) that creates mood and supports the spoken dialogue of a radio program or visual action of an audio/visual work.

BERNE CONVENTION

Preeminent international copyright treaty to which the U.S. is a signatory. Notable for prohibiting administrative formalities in order to acquire copyright protection, Berne grants a higher level of protection in foreign countries than does the UCC, the other international copyright treaty, to which the U.S. adheres.

BLANKET LICENSE – 292, 297

For an annual fee, radio and television stations, public broadcasters, cable stations, universities, restaurants, programmed music services, etc. can acquire a "blanket license" from a performing rights organization. This license gives them the right to perform every piece of music contained in the respective repertoire as often as they wish during the term of the license.

BOOTLEGGING – 225, 226, 229

Unauthorized recording and selling of a song.

BURNING

Recording music to a CD or portable device. A blank CD is placed into a CD Re-Writable drive that is connected to a PC. When each song is transferred, it is automatically "burned" into the blank CD. (Courtesy of Harryfox.com)

BUSINESS MANAGER – 281, 331

A hired representative who helps you with your financial planning, investments, taxes, collecting revenue from contracts, and other financial matters.

C

CATALOG (UE)

The most commonly used word in reference to the collection of songs owned by a publisher/songwriter

CISAC

The International Confederation of Societies of Authors and Composers, which represents 161 musical creators' and copyright owners' organizations in 87 countries

COMMON INFORMATION SYSTEM (CIS)

A collection of global databases which are used as sources of documentation for royalty distributions by CISAC members.

COMPOSERS

The men and women who create musical compositions for motion pictures and other audio/visual works, or the creators of classical music compositions.

COMPULSORY MECHANICAL LICENSE – 290

A license provided by the Copyright Law allowing anyone to record a song that has previously been commercially recorded with authorization, as long as they pay at least the royalties set by a Copyright Arbitration Royalty Panel. For the period January 1, 2004 to December 31, 2005 the statutory mechanical royalty rate is as follows: 8.5 Cents for songs 5 minutes and less or 1.65 Cents per minute - over 5 minutes

CONTROLLED COMPOSITION – 291, 299

A composition written or co-written by the recording artist (and sometimes the producer per the artist contract) under an exclusive recording agreement. *Typically*, the recording company will pay only 75 percent of the minimum statutory rate on only 10 cuts per CD and two cuts per single, *regardless* of the actual number of sides or length of the composition(s).

COPYRIGHT – 243, 248, 249, 283

The exclusive right, granted by law for a stated period, usually until 70 years after the death of the surviving author of the work, to make, dispose of, and otherwise control copies of literary, musical, dramatic, pictorial and other copyrightable works. The exclusive right is set forth in the 1976 Copyright Act Section 106.

COPYRIGHT DEPOSIT REGISTRATION – 249, 283, 285, 310

To register a musical work under the 1976 Copyright Act:
Send a request for an application to the Copyright Office, Library of Congress, *101 Independence Avenue, S E., Washington, D.C. 20559-6000 or download the application from the Copyright Office website at* http://lcweb.loc.gov/copyright/forms/ or from the BMI website's Songwriters' Toolbox at **http://bmi.com**

To order an application by telephone, call (202) 707-9100.
2. When an application is completed, send it back to the Copyright Office with:
a) one copy of manuscript, lead sheet or tape if unpublished or
b) two copies of manuscript (sheet music) or tape if published and
c) the appropriate registration fee, by money order, bank draft or check, made payable to Register of Copyrights.

COPYRIGHT ARBITRATION ROYALTY PANELS (CARPs)

As successors to the Copyright Royalty Tribunal, CARPs consist of private citizens appointed by the Register of Copyrights to act as arbitrators in matters of setting periodic changes in the royalty rate for the compulsory mechanical license, as well as for compulsory licenses for distant signal cable television transmissions and public broadcasting. CARPs also determine entitlements to the royalties received by the Copyright Office for the latter two licenses and under the Audio Home Recording Act.

CROSS-COLLATERALIZATION – 276

Provisions made within a record contract or publishing contract which allows the moneys that are owed from advances, recording costs, etc. to be recouped by the company from your future earnings.
When collateral for one loan is also serving as collateral for other loans

CUE SHEET

A listing of the music used in a television program or motion picture by title, composer, publisher, timing and type of usage (e.g., background, feature, theme) usually prepared by the producer of the program or film

D

DERIVATIVE WORK
A work derived from another work, such as a translation, musical arrangement, sound recording, or motion picture version.

DIGITAL MILLENNIUM COPYRIGHT ACT (DMCA)
That portion of the Copyright Act which implements two international treaties, the WIPO Copyright Treaty and the WIPO Performances and Phonograms Treaty. The DMCA also creates limits of the liability for copyright infringement of Internet service providers under certain conditions, as well as addresses other matters.

DIGITAL PERFORMANCE RIGHT IN SOUND RECORDINGS ACT OF 1995
For more than 20 years, the RIAA has been fighting to give copyright owners of sound recordings the right to authorize digital transmissions of their work. Before the passage of the Digital Performance Right in Sound Recordings Act of 1995, sound recordings were the only U.S. copyrighted work denied the right of public performance. (Courtesy of RIAA.com)

DIRECT LICENSE
In reference to performing rights, a license obtained by a music user directly from the copyright owner allowing the user to publicly perform the licensed work.

DISTRIBUTOR – *201, 209, 226*
A business operation that provides music product from record manufacturers to one stops, rack jobbers, retail and other outlets for ultimate sale to consumers. Distributors often provide marketing and promotion support to record labels and retailers. (riaa.com)

DOWNLOADS (FULL, PERMANENT)/DIGITAL PHONORECORD DELIVERIES – *295*
A full, permanent download **(DPD)** is each individual delivery of a phonorecord by digital transmission of a sound recording (embodying a musical composition) resulting in a reproduction made by or for the recipient. **DPDs reside on a recipient's computer indefinitely**. DPDs may be transferred to portable devices or burned onto CDs (in accordance with the rules set by the digital distributor of a specific DPD). **DPDs fall under Section 115 of the Copyright Act and are currently licensed at the statutory rate for physical phonorecords.** (Courtesy of Harryfox.com)

DOWNLOADS (LIMITED, TETHERED) – *207, 295*
A limited download is a digital file that is delivered electronically to a computer to reside there for a limited period of time. **There are two types of limited downloads: limited-time download** (i.e. the song resides on the computer for 30 days) **and limited-use download** (i.e. the song is can be heard 10 times before it can no longer be played). **Limited downloads are also referred to as *tethered* downloads.** (Courtesy of Harryfox.com)

E

ENCODING
The conversion of a sound recording into a digital file format. (Courtesy of Harryfox.com)

EXCLUSIVE RIGHTS
The right of a copyright owner to exclusively authorize recording, performance, dramatization or other uses of his works, as set forth in the Copyright Act.

EXCLUSIVE SONGWRITER AGREEMENT – *305*
A contract between a publisher and a songwriter in which the songwriter assigns all songs written during the term of the contract to the publisher in return for a percentage of royalty income. Such an agreement usually involves advances paid by the publisher to the songwriter.

EXPLOIT

When used in relation to publishing, "exploit" refers to encouraging the licensing and commercial use of a particular copyright.

EXTENDED RENEWAL TERM

The term of copyright for works registered under the 1909 Copyright Act was extended, under the 1976 Copyright Act and subsequent amendments, so that copyrights, if renewed, will be protected for 95 years — an additional 39 years from the time of the original copyright. Under the prior copyright law of 1909, the term of copyright was two 28-year terms, or a total of 56 years.

F

FAVORED NATIONS CLAUSE

A term commonly used in the entertainment/music industry to protect one's established salary or royalty rate. A favored nations clause may provide, for example, that no one can be paid more than the contracting party for talent or material similarly used, and if someone is, the contracting party will receive the same treatment.

FEATURE WORK

On television, a performance that constitutes the main focus of audience attention at the time of the performance. The vocalists and/or instrumentalists, respectively, must be on camera except where the music is used as part of a choreographic routine that constitutes the main focus of attention. On radio, a performance that is the sole sound broadcast at the time of the performance.

G

GRAND RIGHTS

"Grand rights" is the term used to describe "dramatic" performing rights. This would cover performances of musical comedies (Broadway and off-Broadway), operas, operettas, ballets, as well as renditions of independent musical compositions in a dramatic setting where there is narration, a plot and/or costumes and scenery. The copyright owner has the exclusive right to issue licenses and collect fees for grand rights. The use of a musical work in a non-dramatic public performance is not a grand right: it is a "small" performing right licensed through a performing rights organization.

H

HARRY FOX AGENCY (HFA) – *207, 287, 290, 304*

Harry Fox is an agency that represents music publishers to negotiate and collect royalties from mechanical, digital, and foreign licenses. **Harry Fox Agency** (HFA) is the primary mechanical licensing, collections, and distribution agency for U.S. music publishers.

I

INFRINGEMENT – *249, 283, 287, 309, 319*

A violation of the exclusive rights granted by the copyright law to a copyright owner.

INTERNATIONAL STANDARD RECORDING CODE (ISRC)

A unique number which will be assigned to a specific recording of a musical work.

INTERNATIONAL STANDARD WORK CODE (ISWC)

A unique number that which will be assigned to a musical composition to assist in electronic identification of performances.

J

JUKEBOX LICENSING OFFICE (JLO)

A Nashville-based organization representing ASCAP, BMI and SESAC in the licensing of coin-operated phonorecord players.

K

KEY PERSON CLAUSE – *19, 20*

A "key person clause" provision in your contract basically means if a manager leaves a company, you can also leave the company with no monetary or lawful obligations.

L

LEAD SHEET

A hand-made (usually) reproduction on paper of a newly-written song.

LIBRARY

A collection of musical compositions that are licensed by the publisher or administrator for use as background, theme, or score music, on radio, broadcast and cable television, films, or video productions.

LICENSE – *80, 207, 244, 251, 287, 290, 292*

A license is a grant to a "user" permitting use of a copyright for any of the following:

1. **Mechanical** (records, tapes, CDs).
2. **Non-dramatic performance** (public performance of a song over radio/TV/club/hotel/concerts).
3. **Grand Rights** (dramatic performance of a musical work, musical comedy, play, opera, operetta, or ballet).
4. **Synchronization** (the use of a musical composition on the soundtrack of an audio/visual work for theatrical exhibition or television).
5. **Print** (sheet music, folios, songbooks or other printed editions. The grant is usually made for a specified period of time and for a designated territory).
6. **Commercial** (the use of a musical composition as part of an advertisement).

LOGS

Schedules prepared by radio and television stations for BMI indicating by title, writer and artist all music performed on the station during a particular time period. Used as a basis for payment by BMI to writers and publishers.

M

MASTER – *80, 84, 200, 235, 239, 242, 243*

A completed recording of a song from which multiple copies are manufactured.

MECHANICAL LICENSE – *290, 321*

The license issued by a publisher or his agent, usually to a record company, granting the record company the right to record and release a specific composition at an agreed-upon fee per unit manufactured and sold.

MP3 – *207, 253*

MPEG Audio Layer-3, or MP3, is the compression technology commonly used to make digital audio computer files relatively small while maintaining high audio quality. It is one of many formats used for uploading and downloading on the Internet. (courtesy of RIAA.com)

N

NON-EXCLUSIVE RIGHTS
The performing rights held by United States performing rights organizations are non-exclusive, because at the same time that the organizations have the right to license performances of works, the writers and publishers have the right to license them directly to music users. Other rights may also be granted on a non-exclusive basis.

NOTICE OF COPYRIGHT
When a work is published (publicly distributed), a notice of copyright should be placed on all copies. Its use is optional, however, and a work that does not carry a copyright notice does not lose any protection. If a notice is used, it should contain three elements:

    1. ©, or the word "Copyright," or the abbreviation "Copr."
    2. The year of first publication.
    3. The name of the copyright owner.

O

ONE STOP – *201, 226*
A wholesale source for music product, primarily used by independent record stores which purchase product from there for retail sale. (Courtesy of RIAA.com)

ONLINE MUSIC SUBSCRIPTION SERVICE
This is a service that allows a consumer to either stream, download or burn music for a set fee for a set period of time. Examples of subscription services include, but are not limited to, Listen.com's Rhapsody, eMusic and Napster. (Courtesy of Harryfox.com)

P

PA FORM – *284, 285*
The form used to register a copyright with the Copyright Office. PA stands for "Performing Arts."

PARODY
A satirical imitation of a literary or musical work. Permission from the owner of the copyright is generally required before commercial exploitation of a parody.

PEER TO PEER (P2P)
Also referred to as file sharing, peer-to-peer is a newly popular type of application in which, rather than accessing files from a central server, users access a common network hub and open up portions of their own computer's hard drive to the public for downloading. However, any unlicensed P2P activity is illegal and can result in criminal prosecution and/or fines. (Courtesy of Harryfox.com)

PERFORMING RIGHTS ORGANIZATION – *288, 295, 303, 310*
An association or corporation that licenses the public performance of non-dramatic musical works on behalf of the copyright owners, such as the American Society of Composers, Authors, and Publishers (ASCAP), Broadcast Music Incorporated (BMI), and SESAC, Inc. These performing rights organizations issue licenses to users of publicly performed, non-dramatic music for a fee, and then pay performing rights royalties to the publishers and songwriters of the performed works. Performing rights and copyright organizations throughout the world include:

PER-PROGRAM LICENSE
A license agreement available for broadcasters from a performing rights organization in lieu of a blanket license. A per-program license bases its fee upon revenues from only those programs using music licensed by that organization.

PERSONAL MANAGER – 15
A person who helps the artist, producer or songwriter in the growth and supervision of hie or her music career.

PHONORECORD
A term used in the Copyright Act to describe the material object in which sounds, other than those on a soundtrack of an audio-visual work, are fixed and from which they can be reproduced. A CD and a cassette tape are both phonorecords.

PIRACY
Unauthorized copying of a record or tape.

PRINT MUSIC – 244, 294
Music used in the following printed editions:

> **1. Sheet Music** — Musical compositions printed on unbound sheets of paper containing the music and lyrics for both popular and classical music.
> **2. Folio** — A collection of songs written by various artists, having a common link or theme (love songs, top hits of an era, selections from a Broadway show, etc.).
> **3. Arrangement**s for a particular musical instrument (i.e., accordion, banjo, guitar, drums, piano, etc.).
> **4. Concert Edition** — A collection of songs arranged for performance for a group of voices or instruments, commonly available in choral, orchestra, and/or band arrangements.
> **5. Method Book** — An educational or method book containing instructions and exercises for developing and improving techniques categorized to their level of difficulty.

PRINT RIGHTS – 244, 294
The exclusive right conferred by the Copyright Act to print sheet music, folios, band parts and instrumental arrangements.

PUBLICATION
Defined by the Copyright Act as "the distribution of copies or phonorecords of a work to the public by sale or other transfer of ownership, or by rental lease or lending. The offering to distribute phonorecords to a group of persons for purposes of further distribution, public performance, or public display, constitutes publication." However, merely performing a new song in public doesn't "publish" it.

PUBLIC DOMAIN
Refers to the status of a work having no copyright protection and, therefore, belonging to the world. When a work is "in" or has "fallen into" public domain it means it is available for unrestricted use by anyone. Permission and/or payment are not required for use. Except with respect to certain foreign-originated works eligible for restoration of copyright, once a work falls into the public domain ("PD"), it can never be recaptured by the owner.

PUBLISHER – 22, 101, 244, 287, 303, 305, 310
A person or company that publishes and exploits songs, scores, or compositions, usually acquired from the author via an assignment of copyright.

R

RECAPTURE OF RIGHTS
The right granted to an author and certain of his/her successors under the Copyright Act (but excluding works made for hire), under certain conditions and certain limitations, to recapture rights to a copyright previously granted to a publisher or other grantee. Because this is a detailed and complex procedure, you should consult your attorney on recapturing rights to your works.

RECOUPMENT – *259, 261, 275-276, 289*
The repayment of advances, recording costs, and other expenses by an artist to a record company from the artist's royalties. *Example - if the artist is given a $50,000 advance and has recording & video costs totaling $200,000, then $250,000 can be recouped (taken from) the artist's royalties. The artist in general **will not** accumulate any royalties from the sale of his or her CD until the record company has recouped all of its expenses.*

RENEWAL OF COPYRIGHT
A registration by the author or his heirs (or their authorized agent) in the U.S. Copyright Office that renews for a second term of 67 years a copyright originally registered prior to January 1, 1978. Works originally copyrighted prior to 1964 that were not renewed in their 28th year of copyright have fallen into the public domain. Works originally copyrighted between 1964 and 1977 are automatically renewed by statute, regardless of whether a renewal registration is made for them. See **AUTOMATIC RENEWAL**. There is only one term of copyright for works written on or after January 1, 1978, generally the life of the author plus 70 years.

RESTORATION OF COPYRIGHT
The procedure by which the owner of a copyright in a work that originated in a foreign country that is a member of the Berne Convention or World Trade Organization, that is still protected there, and that fell into the public domain in the U.S. because, among other reasons, it failed to comply with certain formalities that had been a part of U.S. law can have U.S. copyright protection retroactively revived. Restoration is accomplished by filing a form GATT with the U.S. Copyright Office.

RINGTONE
A ringtone is an excerpt of a musical composition embodied in a digital file and rendered into audio. Ringtones are stored in an end-user's mobile telephone, pager or other portable communications device and played whenever the device activates its ring or alert function (upon the arrival of a call, message or other notification). **There are two basic types of ringtones: Phonic Ringtones and Pre-Recorded Ringtones.** Phonic Ringtones are, most commonly, standard MIDI sound files that are either monophonic, where the ringtones are recreated using standard single notes, or polyphonic, where notes can be played simultaneously creating harmony and/or counterpoint. Pre-Recorded ringtones play actual clips from sound recordings (Courtesy of Harryfox.com)

RIPPING
Unlike burning where music is transferred onto a CD, ripping is the process of copying sound recordings from a compact disc and placing that copy onto a computer's hard drive. (Courtesy of Harryfox.com)

ROYALTIES – *21, 31, 52, 81, 84, 240-242, 259, 266, 272, 275, 292, 310*
Monies that are payable to a recording artist, producer, songwriter or publisher from the sale of *phonorecords* or CDs - *after deductions of expenses. (A percentage of the income from a piece of music, or invention that is paid to the author, composer, producer, or artist).*

S

SACD
The SACD is similar in concept to the standard CD with an additional high-density layer. It debuted in 1999 in a format that uses the digital audio format DSD (Direct Stream Digital) and a 4.7GB disc with 2.8 MHz to provide the consumer with a realistic audio experience. One of the most noted features of the SACD is its very high audio quality. The SACD currently can be found in three disc configurations. The first two types contain only the DSD data. The Single-Layer SACD, containing one DSD layer, holds 4.7 GB of data. The

Dual-Layer SACD has two DSD layers, allowing it to contain twice as much data. The single and dual-layer discs can only be played on a special SACD player. The Hybrid SACD contains one DSD layer (4.7 GB) and a conventional CD layer. This allows the disc to be played on both a standard CD Player and the SACD player. (Courtesy of Harryfox.com)

SAMPLING – *76, 101, 149, 245, 319*
When sound bytes are removed electronically from a master recording and through technological imitation placed within the context of another composition. The length of the bytes can be limitless and can contain lyric and music in combination or in part from any segment of the score. Depending upon the length of the bytes and how they are used, unauthorized sampling could be held to be a copyright infringement of the sound recording from which they were taken and from the musical work they first appeared in.

SCORE
The music that is used in synchronization to an audio/visual work, or the body of music composed for a dramatic-musical work

SINGLE SONG AGREEMENT – *305, 308, 311*
A contract between a publisher and songwriter(s) where the songwriter assigns to the publisher the copyright in one particular song in return for a percentage of royalty income. Sometimes referred to as a "one-off" contract.

SMALL PERFORMING RIGHTS
This term is used to describe the non-dramatic public performing rights that are represented by and licensed through the performing rights organizations. In the United States these are BMI, ASCAP and SESAC. Performances of individual musical works on radio and TV and at hotels, restaurants, on programmed music services, and in concerts are "small" performances. These performing rights cover individual musical works used in non-dramatic renditions and are to be distinguished from "grand rights." Note that when individual musical compositions are used in a dramatic setting, with action, scenery and dialogue, as may be the case in a "revue," it could be considered a "dramatic" performance and not be covered under a performing rights organization license (see **GRAND RIGHTS**).

SONG SHARK
A purported music publisher who charges a fee for exploitation services to songwriters that a legitimate music publisher would bear himself. Songsharking is not illegal, but is considered highly unethical in the music business.

SONGWRITERS
The men and women who conceive and construct the lyrics and music to create songs.

SONGWRITER/PUBLISHER CONTRACT
An agreement entered into between the two parties that set, among other things, the terms under which the composition(s) is transferred (assigned) and income is earned and divided.

SOUND RECORDING – *284, 285*
The copyrighted musical work that results from the fixation of sounds onto a phonorecord.

SOUNDSCAN – *197, 202, 233*
The **tracking and reporting of retail sales** of audio, video, and book products.

SOURCE LICENSE
In performing rights, a license granted by the copyright owner to the person, producer, or organization being licensed to record or distributes the work, (e.g., in a taped program) so that the performance of the recorded work needs no further license.

SPLIT PUBLISHING – *305, 306*
When more than one publisher holds the publishing rights in a song. Each of the several publishers is called a "co-publisher."

SR FORM – *284, 285*

Copyright registration form for a sound recording, usually obtained by the record company to protect the fixation of sounds on the recording. An SR form can be used to register the song (the © copyright) as well as the sound recording (the (P) copyright), if the copyright claimants of both are the same.

STAFF SONGWRITER

A songwriter who has an exclusive agreement with a publisher.

STATUTORY COPYRIGHT

Copyright protection acquired by virtue of the provisions of the U.S. Copyright Act.

STATUTORY DAMAGES

Monetary damages obtainable by a copyright owner of a work for its infringement. The amount is at the discretion of the court, but ranges from $500 up to $20,000 for each infringement, and up to $100,000 if the infringement was willful. If actual damages and profits attributable to the infringement would be greater than statutory damages, the copyright owner can choose to seek those instead.

STATUTORY (COMPULSORY) MECHANICAL LICENSE RATE

The compulsory mechanical license rate has been in existence since the 1909 Copyright Act. The statute places a ceiling — per record, per song — on the royalty a copyright owner can obtain (the royalty rate of 2 cents remained the same from 1909 to 1978). Provision was made, under the 1976 Copyright Act, for a periodic review of the rate. Such a review took place in 1980, whereby the royalty rate was increased in yearly increments. The statutory rate for 2005 is 8.50¢ per song - for each copy of the CD or tape distributed or 1.65¢ per minute of playing time, whichever is greater. For subsequent years, the mechanical rates will be as follows:

- **2005: 8.5¢ per song or 1.65¢ per minute**
- **2006: 9.1¢ per song or 1.75¢ per minute**

STREAMING/ON-DEMAND STREAMING

Streaming is when a digital file is delivered electronically to a computer, read in real time by the computer and is stored temporarily on the computer for the purpose of a one-time use. It is analogous to a radio transmission. On demand streaming is the term given to streams that have been prepared and are available for users who wish to play a specific song at a specific time. (Courtesy of Harryfox.com)

SUB-PUBLISHING

A contractual arrangement between an original publisher of a song and a foreign publisher to handle the exploitation, licensing, and collection for the song in the foreign publisher's territory.

SYNCHRONIZATION RIGHT – *244, 293, 295*

The exclusive right of a copyright owner, granted by the Copyright Act, to authorize the recording of a musical work onto the soundtrack of an audio/visual work. The song is synchronized with images on the screen, hence the name.

SYNCHRONIZATION ROYALTIES – *244, 293, 295*

The amount of money earned by the publisher (and, consequently, divided with the songwriter) for the use of a song for which a synchronization license has been issued.

T -thru- Z

TALENT AGENT – *18, 323, 328*

A person who arranges live shows & performances or any other paying opportunities for an artist or musician. Also known as a booking agent.

VIDEO BUYOUT

An agreement by which the buyer (user) agrees to pay the licensor a flat fee for the use of a song, with no increase based on sales of videocassettes/discs.

VIDEO ROLLOVER

An agreement by which the buyer (user) agrees to pay the licensor a continuing fee (either in advance or based on sales as per agreement). Every time a specific sales point has been reached, the fee is "rolled over," i.e. paid again.

WEBCASTING

Webcasting generally refers to the streaming of audio on the Internet, and is sometimes called Internet radio. Webcasters may be Internet-only services that transmit several different genre-based channels, re-transmitters of traditional AM/FM broadcasts, or services that syndicate music programming as background music on Web sites. HFA does NOT handle webcasting licensing. (Courtesy of Harryfox.com)

WORK MADE FOR HIRE

As defined in Section 101 of the 1976 Copyright Act, this is a work prepared by an employee within the scope of his/her employment, or a work specially ordered or commissioned for use by another person in accordance with a written document as a contribution to a collective work, motion picture, audio/visual and other certain types of works, the nature of which is specifically defined in Section 101 of the Copyright Act. In the case of a work made for hire the employer is considered the author of the work under the Copyright Act (and unless the parties agree, otherwise owns all the rights in the work).

WORKSNET

A new global system for managing information about musical works, their creators and owners.

Glossary compilation - Used by permission from:

Broadcast Music, Inc. – www.bmi.com
The Harry Fox Agency, Inc - www.Harryfox.com
Recording Industry Association of America – www.riaa.com